Israel and the Occupied Territories

A Study of the Educational Systems of Israel and the Occupied Territories and a Guide to the Academic Placement of Students in Educational Institutions of the United States

Lynne Rosengrant Franks
Director, Office of International Student Services
Queens College
City University of New York

1987

A Service of the International Education Activities Group of the
American Association of Collegiate Registrars and Admissions Officers

Washington, D.C.

Placement Recommendations Approved by the National Council on the
Evaluation of Foreign Educational Credentials

Library of Congress Cataloging-in-Publication Data

Franks, Lynne Rosengrant.
Israel and the Occupied Territories.

(World education series)
"A service of the International Education Activities Group of the American Association of Collegiate Registrars and Admissions Officers."
"Placement recommendations approved by the National Council on the Evaluation of Foreign Educational Credentials."
Bibliography: p.
Includes index.

1. Education—Israel. 2. School credits—Israel—Evaluation.
3. Education—West Bank. 4. School Credits—West Bank—Evaluation.
5. Education—Gaza Strip. 6. School credits—Gaza Strip—Evaluation.
I. American Association of Collegiate Registrars and Admissions Officers. International Education Activities Group. II. Title. III. Series.
LA1441.F7 1987 370'.95694 87-18817
ISBN 0-910054-87-8

Publication of the World Education Series is funded by grants from the Bureau of Educational and Cultural Affairs of the United States Information Agency.

Contents

Tables and Charts

Sample Documents

Preface

This project would not have been accomplished without the excellent advice, boundless energy and good humor of my monitor, Caroline Aldrich. The encouragement, editorial expertise and special personal qualities of Henrianne K. Wakefield and Miranda B. Knowles, Managing Editor and Assistant Editor, respectively, have made this experience all the more personally rewarding. James S. Frey was an excellent reviewer and editorial contributor. AACRAO's Executive Director J. Douglas Conner, the WES Committee chaired by Kitty Villa, the National Council, and USIA each represent a unique commitment to international education through their support of the World Education Series.

I feel fortunate to have had the opportunity to meet many school, university and government officials who made my work both personally and professionally rewarding. Dov Keren-Ya'ar of the Israeli Council for Higher Education has been a dedicated educator and a delightful person to know. Dr. Jacob Rootenberg, Rashid and Mohammed Hamid, Riad Malki, Alon Maoz, Neil Saad, Shalan Alayan and Naheda Al-Husseini answered endless questions, translated numerous documents and brought life to the complexities that fade in translation. Also in New York, individuals in the Israeli Consulate, Jordanian Consulate, the Palestine Liberation Organization and the U.N. Division for Palestinian Rights were most helpful and generous.

I spent several months weaving in and out of the worlds of Israeli and Palestinian society as I traveled throughout Gaza, Israel, the West Bank and Jerusalem. Few have had the rare opportunity to see it through the eyes of both worlds as did I. I am grateful to Musa Bikerat whose trilingual talents and native familiarity provided me with experiences I would not have otherwise known. I would like to thank some of the many people who assisted me while I was there—David Good, Daniel Krauskopf, Robert Peterson, John Viste and Ahed Bseiso of the U.S. Consulate; the U.S./Israel Foundation; the U.S. Embassy; AMIDEAST/East Jerusalem and Gaza; Arie Shoval, the Ministry of Education (Israel); David Dickman, NITT; William Lee, Ahmed Moussa, Said Filfil, and Ms. Lamis Alami, UNRWA; Dido Alon, ORT; Techia Karcz and Prof. N. Levtzion, Israeli Council for Higher Education; and the Ministry of Education, Amman. I met many people at numerous institutions and educational offices whom I remember well and regret I cannot acknowledge individually; to each of you, my sincerest appreciation. I would like to give special thanks to President Khanfer, Dr. Nabir Al-Jabari, Mukhlis Hammouri and the faculty of The Hebron University for their gracious hospitality.

From professional services to personal support, several individuals at Queens College have guided me through this project. I would like to thank Pearl Sigberman, Muriel Devack, Marjorie Mahon, Richard White, Tadesse Araya for their attention to my needs and help. Betty Mason, Director of Admissions, and Alan Margolis, Senior Registrar, have been major contributors through their generous, unquestioning support.

To my family and extended family, I must express my gratitude for their patience throughout these past two years. To those special people who have unwittingly influenced my intrigue with the Middle East, I dedicate this book.

ISRAEL AND THE OCCUPIED TERRITORIES

Historical Chronology

The following chronology is included only to provide a broad framework of chronological reference points. Since contemporary affairs of the Middle East remain volatile and strained, even historical events, their sequence, and significance are open to differences of interpretation. Hence, this chronology makes no attempt to be definitive or exhaustive and should not be interpreted as such.

1897 First World Zionist Congress meets in Basle, Switzerland.

1917 The Balfour Declaration states Great Britain's position favoring the establishment of a national home for the Jewish people in Palestine that recognizes the civil/religious rights of non-Jewish communities in Palestine.

1922 British census of Palestine lists population as 590,890 (78%) Muslim; 73,024 (9.6%) Christian, mostly Arab; 83,794 (11%) Jewish; 1% Other. (Said, 17)

1922-1948 Mandate Period. British Mandate places Palestine and Transjordan (today, Israel, the West Bank, Gaza Strip, and Jordan) under its administration. French Mandate places Syria, Lebanon, Iraq under France. Independence gained by Egypt in 1936, by Syria in 1943, by Lebanon in 1945. Transjordan becomes independent in 1946, subsequently renamed the Hashemite Kingdom of Jordan.

1936-1939 Palestinian uprising and rebellion against the British. McDonald White Paper (London, 1936) promises Palestinian Arabs independence within 10 years; restriction on Jewish immigration for next 5 years to 75,000.

1942 Zionist conference rejects McDonald White Paper and calls for Jewish army.

1946 *Anglo-Palestinian Yearbook* (1947-48) estimates population of Palestine in 1946 as 1,303,887 Palestinian Arabs (68%), and 608,225 Jews (32%). (Said, 11)

1947 Worldwide pressure to provide home for displaced Jews. Civil war breaks out. British turn dilemma over to newly established United Nations. U.N. votes to partition Palestine into a Jewish State and an Arab State and designates Jerusalem international territory.

1948 British Mandate over Palestine ends; State of Israel proclaimed; 96,000 Palestinian Arabs left homeless. War between Arabs and Jews continues.

1949 Under armistice agreements, Jews gain about 70% of Palestine; Palestinians retain Old City of Jerusalem, the West Bank and Gaza Strip. Jordan annexes West Bank; Gaza Strip placed under Egyptian administration.

1956 Nasir of Egypt nationalizes the Suez Canal. Israel briefly invades and occupies the Sinai and Gaza until March 1957.

1964 Palestine Liberation Organization (PLO) is founded in Jerusalem.

1967 Six Day War. Israel occupies Golan Heights (of Syria), Gaza Strip and Sinai (of Egypt) and Jordanian West Bank including E. Jerusalem. U.N. Resolution 242 calls for withdrawal of Israel from territories occupied in 1967 War; acknowledgement of sovereignity, territorial integrity, political independence of each state; settlement of refugee problem.

1973 Yom Kippur War. European Economic Council Foreign Ministers call for Israeli withdrawal from territories occupied since 1967.

1976 Civil war erupts in Lebanon.

1978 Camp David Agreements between Egypt, Israel, and the U.S. lead to Peace Treaty between Egypt and Israel in 1979, return of Sinai to Egypt, normalization of diplomatic relations between Egypt and Israel.

1980 Iran-Iraq War begins.

1981 Israel annexes Golan Heights, bringing Syrian territority under Israeli law.

1982-1985 Israel invades Lebanon in operation "Peace for Galilee" and remains in active state of war with Lebanon into 1985.

1987 Iran/Iraq, Israel/Lebanon and Lebanese civil conflicts continue.

Section I. Israel

Chapter 1

Introduction

Basic Facts: A Country Profile

Israel was proclaimed a state by Zionist leaders in Palestine on May 14, 1948, the last effective day of the British Mandate. It was not until 1949 that an undeclared state of war between contiguous Arab states and Israel technically ended with armistice agreements establishing ceasefire boundaries. It is Israel within these borders that is the exclusive focus of Section I, Chapters 1-8. The occupied territories of the West Bank, Gaza Strip, and Golan Heights are discussed separately in Section II, Chapters 9-14. For an explanation of historical events which preceded and followed the June 1967 War, see the "Historical Chronology" located in the front of this volume.

THE LAND—DESCRIPTIVE AREA AND LOCATION. Israel is situated in the Near East, also described as the Middle East, along the eastern coastline of the Mediterranean Sea. It is bordered by Lebanon to the north, Syria and the Golan Heights to the northeast, Jordan and the West Bank on the east, Egypt and the Gaza Strip to the southwest, and the Gulf of Aqaba at its southern tip.

With a total area of 7,993 square miles (approximately the size of New Jersey), Israel stretches 260 miles from north to south and has a varying width of from 10 to 65 miles. Israel, excluding the Occupied Territories, represents approximately 77% of pre-1948 Palestine.

THE JEWISH CALENDAR. The Jewish calendar is based upon a 354-day lunar cycle adapted by leap years to the solar cycle; dates based upon this calendar appear on all official documents, including educational records. The Jewish New Year 5748 begins September 24, 1987. Approximate conversions from the Jewish calendar to the Gregorian calendar can be made by adding or subtracting year for year, or by determining the numeric difference between the two systems (5748—1987 = 3761 years) and adjusting accordingly. For example, the Jewish year 5740 is eight years before the point of reference year 5748 and eight years before the corresponding year 1987; therefore, the Jewish year 5740 corresponds to 1979 (1987—8 = 1979, or 5740—3761 = 1979. For Israeli Arab documents, see "The Islamic Calendar" in Chapter 9.

DEMOGRAPHY. Israeli sources report a total population of slightly over 4.2 million (1984), of which 83% (3.5 million) are Jewish and 17% (750,000) are "non-Jewish," i.e., mostly indigenous Palestinian Arabs who comprise approximately 13% Muslim, 2.4% Christian, and 1.6% Druze and other. (For clarification see "Population" and "Ethnicity, Nationalities and Religious Constituencies" in Chapter 9.)

Population, immigration/emigration, and a Jewish majority are considered by Israel of primary importance to the maintenance of a Jewish state. Of concern is the fact that according to government reports immigration was down to 11,298 in 1985, representing a 41% decline over 1984 and reaching the lowest point since 1948. Emigration, on the other hand, increased to 17,882 in 1984, compared with 2,500 in 1983, and 8,100 in 1982. At the same time, independent Israeli demographic studies indicate that if Palestinian residents of the West Bank and Gaza Strip are taken into account, the current Jewish population constitutes but 64% of the total and that, if birth rates continue as in the past, near parity will be reached between the Jewish and Arab population within 25 years. As one of many approaches addressing this concern, educational exchange, particularly studying abroad in Israel, is encouraged and supported by Israel.

OFFICIAL LANGUAGES. Hebrew (Irit, a modern version of the language of the Old Testament) and Arabic are the official languages.

JERUSALEM. On the basis of armistice agreements signed in 1949, Jerusalem was divided by the so-called "Green Line" into East and West Jerusalem. West Jerusalem was claimed and inhabited by Israeli Jews; East Jerusalem was claimed by Jordan and inhabited by Palestinians later granted Jordanian citizenship. As a result of the June 1967 War, East Jerusalem was occupied, then annexed, by Israel. Today, Palestinians live in East Jerusalem while Israelis live in both East and West Jerusalem.

In 1950, Israel proclaimed West Jerusalem its capital. The United States, along with most other countries, does not recognize this action and maintains its Embassy in Tel-Aviv. The policy of the United States—reflective of the 1947 United Nations' proposal that Jerusalem be accorded international status—is based upon the city's historical and religious significance as the sacred shrine to the world's three major monotheistic religions (Judaism, Christianity, and Islam) and the belief that, as such, the status of Jerusalem should be determined by international agreement. On July 29, 1980, the U.N. General Assembly called upon Israel to withdraw from all occupied territories including East Jerusalem. On July 30, 1980, the Israeli Knesset declared both East and West Jerusalem to be the capital of Israel.

The occupation and annexation of East Jerusalem present certain technical and legal ramifications which tend to complicate and distort reporting of population and educational statistics, particularly in terms of the Arab constituency. For details, see "East Jerusalem" in Chapter 9.

GOVERNMENT. Israel is a parliamentary republic consisting of executive, legislative, and judicial branches. Due to the lack of consensus over the scope of religious law in government, there is no formal constitution. Instead, the government operates on the basis of several constitutional laws enacted by the Knesset, and others inherited from the period of the British Mandate that—it is anticipated—will become part of an eventual written constitution.

The President of Israel, a representative head whose functions are primarily symbolic or ceremonial, is elected by the Knesset for no more than two five-year terms. The Prime Minister, the Chief Executive, is nominated by the President traditionally from the party receiving the highest number of votes and able to form a coalition government with various minority parties. The Prime Minister appoints and heads the Cabinet, Israel's executive body, which is composed of Ministers responsible for various Ministries (Defense, Foreign Affairs, Education and Culture, etc.). The Prime Minister and the Cabinet are collectively responsible to the Knesset.

The Knesset is Israel's highest legislative body. It is a single-chamber parliament consisting of 120 members (presently 113 Jews and seven Arabs) who are elected at-large from a party list for a term of four years.

The Supreme Court oversees the judicial branch which is composed of secular and religious courts independent of the executive and legislative branches and of one another. Judges are appointed by the President at the recommendation of a public nominations commission. Each major religious group has its own courts and full jurisdiction in matters of personal status and canon law.

THE MILITARY AND EDUCATION. The Israeli military, known as the Israeli Defense Forces (IDF), has an impact on education primarily resulting from compulsory military service and subsequent reserve duty. Beyond that, its influence on education is felt in para-military programs in schools, and through public entitlements, educational deferments, and alternative arrangements for orthodox students. In addition, the IDF administers all affairs in the unannexed Occupied Territories, including education, which are discussed in Section II.

Israelis serve in the military at an age traditionally associated with higher education in the United States. Those enrolled in postsecondary and higher education usually have completed active military duty, are two or more years older than their U.S. counterparts, frequently married, and employed. Compulsory military service is in effect for all qualifying Jewish women, aged 18-25, and Jewish and Druze men, aged 18-29, for two and three years, respectively. Married Jewish women are exempt, Arab Muslims and Christians may not serve, and orthodox Jewish men and women may request an exemption. For orthodox service-age men enrolled in *talmudic* academies *(yeshivot)*, an alternative arrangement called *Yeshivat Hesder* combines induction into the IDF and military training with *Torah* Studies in a program lasting four to five years. After active service, reserve duty obligates men up to the age of 55 and single women up to the age of 34 at least 30 days annually. Whether faculty or administrator, student or staff, reservists are called up at any time with disrupting effects on education.

Students who have been accepted by postsecondary or higher educational institutions in disciplines deemed necessary by the military, such as medicine, engineering, technological fields, and nursing, may request a deferment. If granted, a deferment assumes basic training before study and active duty upon graduation. Beyond the normal requirement of two to three years, any deferment carries with it an extended military obligation of one year for every year deferred.

The Ministry of Education and Culture supports the Ministry of Defense by incorporating IDF needs into programs initiated through the schools. Gadna, an acronym for the para-military training program for youth, is one such school program. Currently, incentives for studying literary Arabic and Arab culture have been instituted in response to military priorities.

Many public entitlements are contingent upon military service. Educational entitlements include eligibility for pre-academic preparatory programs *(mechinot),* financial aid, dormitory priority, etc. *Yeshivah* students who request waivers from active military service routinely receive them, but still receive benefits. Israeli Arabs are ineligible for both enlistment in the military and entitlements to social and educational benefits which are contingent upon military service.

The Impact of Cultural Origin, Political Persuasion, and Religious Belief

The Jewish population, primarily comprised of immigrants and their children, represents a multitude of diverse cultural and ethnic origins, political persuasions, and religious beliefs. These factors contribute to a social and political climate that has influenced, among other things, educational developments throughout the history of Israel.

The two main Jewish ethnic groups are referred to as Ashkenazim and Sephardim. Ashkenazim, the "Western" element from northern and eastern Europe, were instrumental in establishing the State of Israel and continue to be dominant in spheres of political, economic, and educational influence. In the area of education, which has a direct impact on social and economic status, Western educational models, espoused by the Ashkenazim and implemented in the early years of the state, were found to be ineffectual in the assimilation of the non-Western population and unsuccessful in achieving desired educational and social goals.

The Sephardim, representing a slight majority, are referred to as non-Western, "Eastern," Oriental and North African Jews. (Technically, the Sephardim originated from Spain and Portugal, but the loose social reference includes those from Islamic countries in the Middle East, Near East, and Africa.) Claiming measurable discrepancies in economic, social, and educational opportunities, they have exerted their influence in recent years, affecting the adoption of extensive social programs and the expansion of educational opportunities. In education, their influence has resulted in the restructuring of classes into heterogenous groups, the discontinuation of mandatory psychometric tests in the school system, the relaxation of criteria used to determine educational streams, the restructuring of the Matriculation Certificate *(Teudat Bagrut)* examinations, and the development of *mechinot* (pre-academic preparatory programs).

Jewish groups representing different socio-political ideologies mainly originating in Eastern Europe have influenced Israeli education as well. The Histadrut (the General Federation of Labor), AMAL (the Vocational Education section of the Histadrut), and the Organization for Rehabilitation Through Training (ORT) have had a substantial impact on the development of technological/vocational education. The labor movement, represented in the educational system before 1948, introduced socialism and pioneering as a modern alternative to religion. Labor settlements called *kibbutzim* (collective settlements) and *moshavim* (cooperative villages) have provided another social and educational option that exists to this day. Modern *kibbutzim* and *moshavim* provide schools which incorporate the general, agricultural, and technological/vocational education of the state-prescribed curriculum; some assist in the assimilation of new immigrants *(olim)* through *ulpanim* (language and culture programs), while still others coordinate programs with the universities for overseas students.

The diversity of religious belief and practice within Jewish society spans the spectrum from "secular" to "ultra-orthodox" and is an accepted reality affecting compromises in educational, cultural, and political decision-making. The differences of opinion concerning the degree to which religion should be incorporated with secular study has resulted in various educational options. Regardless of the type of school or the parents' religious philosophy, however, the official (state) educational system incorporates religion, Judaica, and Israeli studies in a substantial proportion of the curriculum. The teaching of Bible, *Talmud* (Jewish law), and Jewish/Israeli consciousness is an integral part of the prescribed curriculum from kindergarten through grade 12, although the approach and subject content vary considerably. Outside the official system, the ultra-orthodox Agudat Israel schools, *talmud torah*, *yeshivot*, and *"yeshivah high schools"* provide other educational alternatives to strictly observant parents (see "Schools, Schools, Schools" later in this chapter).

The Israeli Arab population is represented by those indigenous Palestinians and their descendants—primarily Sunni Muslim, but also Christian and Druze—who remained within the boundaries of Israel established in 1948-49. Characterized initially as " . . . emotionally wounded, socially rural, politically lost, economically poverty-stricken and nationally hurt . . ." Palestinians were left without political leadership and an educational elite. (Mar'i 18) Physically located in enclaves or villages, they numbered 150,000 then and approximately 620,000 today. While technically Israeli citizens, their integration and participation in Israeli society is negligible. Instead, Palestinians circulate within an isolated subculture, unable to identify with or operate through the Jewish-Zionist political framework and precluded from affecting policy in areas of direct concern, such as labor unions and their educational institutions. Palestinian interaction with Israeli society has occurred mainly out of economic necessity through employment in menial occupations as a result of the loss of their agrarian means of livelihood. In short, Israeli Arabs have little influence on their Jewish compatriots and are dissuaded by design from affecting their own institutions and destiny.

The Druze are a close-knit Arab community of somewhat-isolated mountain dwellers who follow a secret religion originating in, but since separated from, Islam. The Israeli Druze hold a different position in Israeli society than their fellow Palestinians. Characteristically cooperative with the government of the country in which they reside, the Druze leadership declared their allegiance to the state once it was proclaimed and volunteered to participate in the responsibilities of citizenship including military service. Seen by some as a reward for Druze cooperation with the authorities (Mar'i 66) and by others as a political move to divide the Palestinian community (Graham-Brown 42), the Druze Education Committee, an administratively distinct unit for Druze education, was created by the Israelis in 1977-78.

The Committee was given responsiblity for setting the curriculums for Druze schools in Israel proper and the occupied Golan Heights. Curriculum changes have been instituted, particularly in Arab culture and history, to the extent that the Druze now are portrayed as having a heritage distinguishable from that of Arabs or Palestinians. "Arab" has now been dropped as a class modifier for the Druze (be the reference a type of school, official statistics, or casual conversation). The younger generation and Druze academics, however, aspire to express their Arab identity and have voiced objection to the substance and motives behind these changes. Directing a letter to the Minister of Education and Culture in March 1986, the Druze students at The Hebrew University of Jerusalem requested that the Druze Education Committee be abolished stating that there is no special Druze heritage, that the books issued by the Committee contradict the roots of Arab Druze heritage, and that the curriculum lowers the level of education among the Druze. Official Israeli response said that the demand was political. (*Al Fajr*, Vol. VII, No. 306, p. 14)

Christian schools were introduced in the Middle East over a century ago by western European religious groups and have continued to serve over 10% of the Christian and Muslim population up through today. Their private, apolitical nature provided a modern European education to an elite segment of the society that frequently benefitted economically and socially at a time when it was acceptable to identify with the European establishment. The departure of the Turks and British, however, followed by almost two decades of military administration over the Arab communities in Israel, affected local Arab involvement with these foreign schools. On the one hand, those Arabs who could afford it and those teachers who were nonconformists sought refuge in these Christian schools rather than in the Israeli government schools. On the other hand, the independence of surrounding Arab nations and the aftermath of the 1948 war inspired an awakening of Arab nationalism which often found its adversary in the association with or adulation of western cultures.

A reduction in political and financial support from abroad, coupled with local Arab demands for cultural, educational, and national relevance, encouraged Christian schools to relinquish their autonomy for the sake of survival. In order to receive funding from the Israeli government, they were required to adopt the Israeli Arab curriculum and examination system. While the schools benefited financially, the students, who were now studying under a curriculum geared towards the Israeli Matriculation Certificate, found an increased opportunity for Israeli higher education. Most schools are now staffed by local Palestinian teachers and administrators, rather than foreigners. As a result of these changes, Christian schools have survived the transition and have regained some of their status by synchronizing their schools with the political, economic, and socio-cultural realities that surround them. As noted by Kleinberger (Mar'i 61-64), however, the sacrifice in autonomy required of Christian schools is paradoxical to the full autonomy and financial support granted state religious and independent (orthodox) schools in the Hebrew sector. Thus the Christians as a minority within a minority have no more political influence over their institutions than do the Muslims to which they are culturally and ethnically identified.

Arab Sector Education

While Arab sector education is officially incorporated into the state educational system, it functions administratively, linguistically, pedagogically and economically as a separate entity through the Arab Education Department. This department within the Ministry of Education and Culture is headed by a Jewish Israeli. One of the two deputies is an Arab while the other is Jewish. All but a handful of supervisors are Arab. School teachers and administrators are mostly Arab while a few Arabic-speaking Sephardim appointed during the fifties still teach. As in the Hebrew sector, budgets, goals, policies, teachers' appointments, curriculums, and textbooks are dictated through the government down the chain of command. The Arab Education Department is by its nature and function political.

Pedagogic control is maintained through these same governmental measures. Curriculums are of particular concern since they are cited as the major reason that Palestinian academic achievements are below those of Israelis and Palestinians in other educational systems. In general, concern is expressed over the emphasis of culturally contradictory and irrelevant course requirements in Jewish and Hebrew studies (civics, geography, history, history of the Jewish people, language and literature, etc.) presented from a Jewish-Zionist perspective at the expense of an already-diluted Arabic studies syllabi. This concern becomes all the more significant due to the importance placed on this information in the Matriculation *(Bagrut)* examinations. (See Arab curriculum schedules in Chapter 3 and Censorship under "Education under Occupation" in Chapter 9.)

Arab academic criticism of their educational system focuses also on a lack of contemporary teaching attitudes, methodology, and goals as a hindrance to the overall advancement of their society. Teaching methodology, while taught according to current educational philosophy, has a tendency in practice to revert to outmoded group-directed learning, rote memorization, and traditional means of discipline.

With a population growth of 4% and a larger percentage of children attending and continuing in school, the number of teachers, classrooms, and physical facilities in the Arab sector have never kept pace with needs. A current shortage of 5,000 classrooms and 2,000 qualified teachers has been met by renting space in inadequate community facilities and decreasing intake at Arab Teacher Training "Seminars" by just under 50% over the past decade. (Mar'i 55) This state of education reflects an inadequate level of funding, for reasons discussed below, and is exacerbated by the disallowance of contributions from outside sources.

Defining the Scope of Education Through Legislation

Education legislation, some of which is summarized below, provides a chronology of the development of education before and since the establishment of the state and also defines the scope and jurisdiction of government in the administration and implementation of state educational policy.

Although instituted by the British in Palestine during the period of the Mandate, certain aspects of the 1933 Educational Ordinance are still operating in Israel today. For example, a school is defined in terms of the systematic teaching of more than 10 individuals and and is required to be registered with the government within one month of its establishment. Registration is also required of all persons wishing to teach in any school so defined. Other provisions of the Ordinance stipulate government authority over schools maintained by public funds and the state right of overall supervision in order to maintain public order and good government. Local authorities, on the other hand, are granted the authority and responsibility for the maintenance and provision of public school facilities.

The Ordinance established a "Hebrew public system" in Palestine to parallel the then-existing government Arab school system. In actuality, a private system of education for the Jewish community was functioning, first under the Jewish Agency (1920-32), and then under the Va'ad Leumi, the Department of Education of the National Committee of the Jewish Community (1932-48). (Note: The Jewish Agency of today was established under the British Mandate in 1929 as an agency for all Jewry, Zionist and non-Zionist, while the Jewish Agency referred to above was only Zionist.) The significance of the British approval for a Hebrew public system had little to do with British administrative or pedagogic influence but rather provided public funding for the maintenance of its schools and teachers.

During the period of educational administration by the Va'ad Leumi, a "Trends" system was in operation. Essentially the Trends system consisted of semi-autonomous groups of schools operated by competing interest groups representing various philosophical or religious tendencies, each responsible for their own schools, curriculums, and student enrollment. The trends were named General, Labor, and Mizrahi and were characterized as follows:

1. General—Secular, apolitical schools tolerant to religion but promoting nationalism and Zionism.
2. Labor—Schools promoting socialism and the virtues of labor rather than religion, and adhering to nationalism and Zionism.
3. Mizrahi—Schools sponsored by Mizrahi, a religious, political party formed in 1904 within the Zionist movement and, today, the nucleus of the National Religious Party. They promote nationalism, Zionism, and religious observance by teacher and student.

Agudat Israel, a fourth trend (not operational as such until after 1948), served followers of Agudat Israel, a world organization of non-Zionist orthodox Jews with schools stressing religion and religious observance rather than contemporary, secular education.

Operation of Jewish schools under the various trends continued after the establishment of the state until 1953 when the State Education Law was enacted. Government Arab schools established during the British Mandate continued to operate as a separate entity for those Palestinians who remained within the 1948 borders of Israel; however, education was administered by Israelis under a Department for Arab Education within the Israeli Ministry of Education and Culture.

The Compulsory Education Law, enacted by the Knesset in September 1949, provided for free and compulsory education from kindergarten through grade 8 for children aged 5-14, and for those 14-17 years of age who had not completed grade 8 (working youth). While the Trends system continued to operate, the new law vested governmental authority and responsibility for the comprehensive system of compulsory and teacher education in the Ministry of Education and Culture. The Ministry's responsibilities were designated as the preparation of curriculums, the appointment and employment of teachers, teacher training, supervision, and inspection. The local authorities (municipalities and regional committees) were assigned responsibilities for the provision and maintenance of school buildings and equipment as well as implementation of compulsory education through the registration and transfer of students. Local government also had the legal authority to assess parents according to their means for "special services" such as textbooks and materials, school meals, insurance, and extracurricular activities.

As the years of compulsory and free education were gradually extended beyond primary education through legislative amendment, the government and local authorities extended their areas of responsibility to the secondary level. Amendments to the Compulsory Education Law enacted in 1978 and 1979 extended free and mandatory education first to grade 9, then to grade 10. In 1978, effective 1979, free but not compulsory education was extended to grade 12. In 1984, effective 1985, legislation to be phased in over a six-year period was enacted which provided for free nursery school beginning at age three. In the Arab sector, however, implementation of these amendments remains inoperable due to the lack of facilities and funding to support it.

The competitive and political nature of the Trends system became a source of disunity and debate among organizations, parents, and educators. Following years of discussion over the Trends system, the enactment of the State Education Law of 1953 abolished the Trends system and established in its place the official state education system. The state system classified schools into one of two categories (State or State Religious), established a Department of Religious Education to ensure religious standards in State Religious schools, defined the aim of state education common to all schools (except Arab), and specified goals of education in Israel.

The primary aim of the State Education Law was to remove the political nature of the Trends system and to replace it with a common, uniform, and unifying objective. The aim of state elementary education ". . . is founded upon the values of the culture of Israel and scientific achievement, upon love of the homeland and allegiance to the State and the People of Israel, upon a conscious perception of the memory of the holocaust and heroism, upon training in agricultural labor and trade skills, upon pioneering and the endeavor to establish a society founded on freedom, equality, tolerance, mutual assistance and love of one's fellow man." (*Ministry of Education and Culture Report*, 1981, 4) The goals of Israeli education were instituted by and for the Jewish sector. In spite of attempts to formulate policy for the Arab sector, however, Arab education has functioned for nearly four decades without defined direction.

The official state education system established new categories of schools within the system and classified those that fell outside it.

1. State Schools *(Mamlakhti)*—Jewish and Arab secular schools encompassing the former General Trend, Labor Trend, and Arab schools.
2. State Religious Schools *(Mamlakhti Dati)*—Religious schools encompassing the former Mizrahi Trend and some Agudat Israel schools.
3. Independent Schools *(Hinuch Atzma'i)*—"Nonofficial recognized" orthodox schools run by Agudat Israel; outside the administrative and pedagogic control of the state educational system but, nevertheless, funded for the most part by the state (the government pays 85% of the educational budget, including teachers' salaries, while the local authorities provide similar pecuniary aid and services).
4. Exempt—Unofficial, unrecognized schools that are subject to essentially no governmental control and receive no state funding. They include international and mission schools as well as orthodox *hadarim* (singular, *heder), talmud torahs, yeshivot,* and *kollelim,* all of which teach only religious subjects. While technically required to register according to the Educational Ordinance and to comply with health and sanitary codes, in actuality most ultra-orthodox schools are not registered as "exempt" and have no contact with the Ministry of Education and Culture.

See "Schools, Schools, Schools" for more information.

In 1958, the Council for Higher Education Law established the Council as the sovereign body for higher educational affairs of the state with the authority to recognize or withhold recognition of institutions of higher education, to authorize recognized institutions to award academic degrees and titles, and to tend to other higher educational concerns as described in Chapter 8, "Higher Education."

The most dramatic change in education occurred as a result of the enactment of the 1968 Reform Education Act. This legislation reorganized the structure of education from a primary-postprimary (i.e., secondary) system represented by grades 1-8 and 9-12, respectively, to a primary-intermediate-secondary structure for grades 1-6, 7-9, and 10-12. Implementation has been in progress for almost two decades and still just over half the system has been transformed. This massive undertaking has involved not only the building of new facilities, but the revision of all curriculums for grades 7-12.

An Overview of Education in Israel

The Ministry of Education and Culture functions as the embodiment of the government for the official state educational system in Israel. (For background, see "Defining the Scope of Education Through Legislation" above.) Education is compulsory from nursery school and kindergarten through grade 10, and free from nursery school and kindergarten through grade 12. The structure of the official state educational system, excluding nursery schools and kindergartens, follows one of two concurrently operating patterns represented today in almost equal number:

Pre-Reform—Effective from 1948 to the present according to the following 8-4 pattern of education:
Primary—Eight years, grades 1-8, ages 6-14;
Secondary—Four years, grades 9-12, ages 14-18.

Reform—Effective from 1969 to the present according to the following 6-3-3 pattern of education:
Primary—Six years, grades 1-6, ages 6-12;
Intermediate (Junior High)—Three years, grades 7-9, ages 12-15;
Secondary (Senior High)—Three years, grades 10-12, ages 15-18.

The official state educational system categorizes schools as either State *(Mamlakhti)* (Hebrew or Arab) or State Religious *(Mamlakhti Dati)* (Hebrew only). The State schools (75%) are classified according to the language of instruction and are identified as either "Hebrew" sector schools or "Arab" sector schools. The State Arab sector schools are either Arab Muslim, Arab Christian or Arab Druze, officially classified as Arab (including Muslim and Christian) or Druze. All State schools along with State Religious schools (20%) comprise 95% of all formal education.

Outside the official state system, two groups of schools exist. The "nonofficial recognized" group, referred to as Independent *(Hinuch Atzma'i)*, consists of ultra-orthodox schools run by members of Agudat Israel and represents approximately 5% of the total. In addition, a group of "exempt," "unofficial and unrecognized" schools not accounted for statistically operate and include ultra-orthodox, traditional religious schools *(hadarim, talmud torahs, yeshivot* and *kollelim)*, as well as foreign and missionary schools.

Secondary schools, while continuing to function within the categories described above, are further identified according to the type of "orientation," i.e., curriculum—general (academic), technical, or agricultural. Schools which offer one of these three programs are called one-track schools; schools offering more than one of these programs are called multi-track schools, comprehensive schools, or *makif*.

Tertiary level education is classified as either postsecondary education or higher education. Postsecondary institutions are under the jurisdiction of the Ministry of Education and Culture and/or the Ministry of Labor and Social Welfare, and include Teacher Training "Seminars" and Technological Colleges offering programs varying in length from one to three years. These institutions are not authorized to award degrees. Institutions of higher education are under the jurisdiction of the Council for Higher Education and include the universities, the Technion-Israel Institute of Technology, and other, nonuniversity institutions of higher education. Certain two-year regional college programs, which are under the supervision of one of the universities, are also under the academic jurisdiction of the Council. Undergraduate nonuniversity degree programs are four years in length, while university first degree programs are three or four years in length. With the exception of the regional colleges (technically not institutions of higher education), all institutions of higher education award degrees and are granted other privileges designated only to institutions under the Council for Higher Education (see Chart 1.1).

The financing of education in those areas which fall under the jurisdiction of the Ministry of Education and Culture (MOEC) is dictated by the national budget for education. Monies are allocated through regional districts which in turn distribute funds to the municipalities or local authorities. Funding also comes from other ministries such as Defense, Health, Labor and Social Welfare, and Religious Affairs, as well as from many individual contributions, local voluntary groups, and Jewish international charitable organizations, e.g., Hadassa, the Histadrut (General Federation of Labor), the Organization for Rehabilitation Through Training (ORT), and the Women's International Zionist Organization (WIZO). Most school buildings are owned by local authorities or private or public bodies. In addition, settlement and development towns are given priority access to educational loans or subsidies. Thus, since educational resources partially depend upon the economic level and political influence of the local community, the quality of education and programs varies accordingly. While priority funding considerations are given to socially and economically disadvantaged Jews, Arab education suffers most for obvious political and financial reasons. The financing of postsecondary education comes primarily from the MOEC for teacher training and through the MOEC and the Ministry of Labor and Social Welfare for technological training. The financing of higher education is discussed in Chapter 8.

The Academic Calendar

The academic year for kindergarten through intermediate (K-9) extends from September through June; for secondary school and postsecondary Technical Colleges, Teacher Training "Seminars" and Colleges, from September 1 through June 20; and for institutions of higher education, from late October or early November through June. The school year is divided into semesters or trimesters lasting a total of 220 days. The school week in the Hebrew sector is five and one-half to six days (Sunday through Friday) with the amount of time in class on Fridays determined by the extent of religious observance. In the Arab sector (public and private), the school week is five days in Christian schools (Saturday and Monday through Thursday) and six days in Muslim and Druze schools (Saturday through Thursday).

School vacations and holidays include the standard two-month summer vacation in July and August, and, in the Hebrew sector, one week during both *Sukkot* and *Chanukah;* two to three weeks before and during *Pesach* (Passover); one- and two-day vacations for all other Jewish holidays and Israeli national holidays (see below). The dates of religious observances are based on the 354-day lunar calendar. Their incidence on the solar calendar moves the date of observance forward 11 or 12 days each year which is then adjusted by leap years to the solar cycle. Institutions of higher education set their own holiday calendar. For the Arab sector, see "Holidays" in Chapter 9.

Rosh Hashanah (Jewish New Year 5747)	10-04-86
Rosh Hashanah (Second Day)	10-05-86
Yom Kippur (Day of Atonement)	10-13-86
Sukkot (Days of Tabernacles)	10-18-86
Sukkot (Second Day)	10-19-86
Shemini Atzeret (8th Day Assembly)	10-25-86
Simchat Torah (Rejoicing the Law)	10-26-86
Chanukah (Feast of Lights)	12-26-86
Chanukah (First Day of 8 Days)	12-27-86
Tu B'Shevat (Tree Planting Festival)	2-14-87
Purim (Feast of Lots)	3-15-87
Pesach (Passover, 8 Days)	4-15-87
Yom Hashoa (Memorial to the Holocaust)	4-26-87
Israel Memorial Day	5-03-87
Israel Independence Day	5-14-87
Yom Yerushalayim (Jerusalem Day)	5-27-87
Shavuot (Feast of Weeks)	6-03-87
Shavuot (Second Day)	6-04-87
Tisha B'av (Memorial to the Destruction of the Temple)	8-04-87
Rosh Hashanah (New Year 5748)	9-24-87

Schools, Schools, Schools

Schools in Israel are identified according to various classifications as well as described in terms of sponsorship by various movements, organizations or religious groups, according to the nature of the curriculum, or on the basis of other distinguishing characteristics. The following section briefly defines these schools and exemplifies the diversity of education in Israel.

Agudat Israel. A network of Independent ultra-orthodox *yeshivot* sponsored by Agudat Israel, a religious and political party.

AMAL Schools. A network of schools sponsored by AMAL, the Vocational Education section of the Histadrut (General Federation of Labor).

Boarding Schools (Pnimya). As in the United States, schools which serve also as the home of residence. *Yeshivot, kibbutz,* and agricultural schools are often boarding schools. Approximately 30% of all high schools in Israel board.

Chaklai. Agricultural secondary schools.

Community Schools (Beit Sefer Kehilati). Schools serving as a center for social, cultural, and athletic activities for the whole community; the "old-fashioned village school" concept.

Chart 1.1. Structure of the Education System of Israel

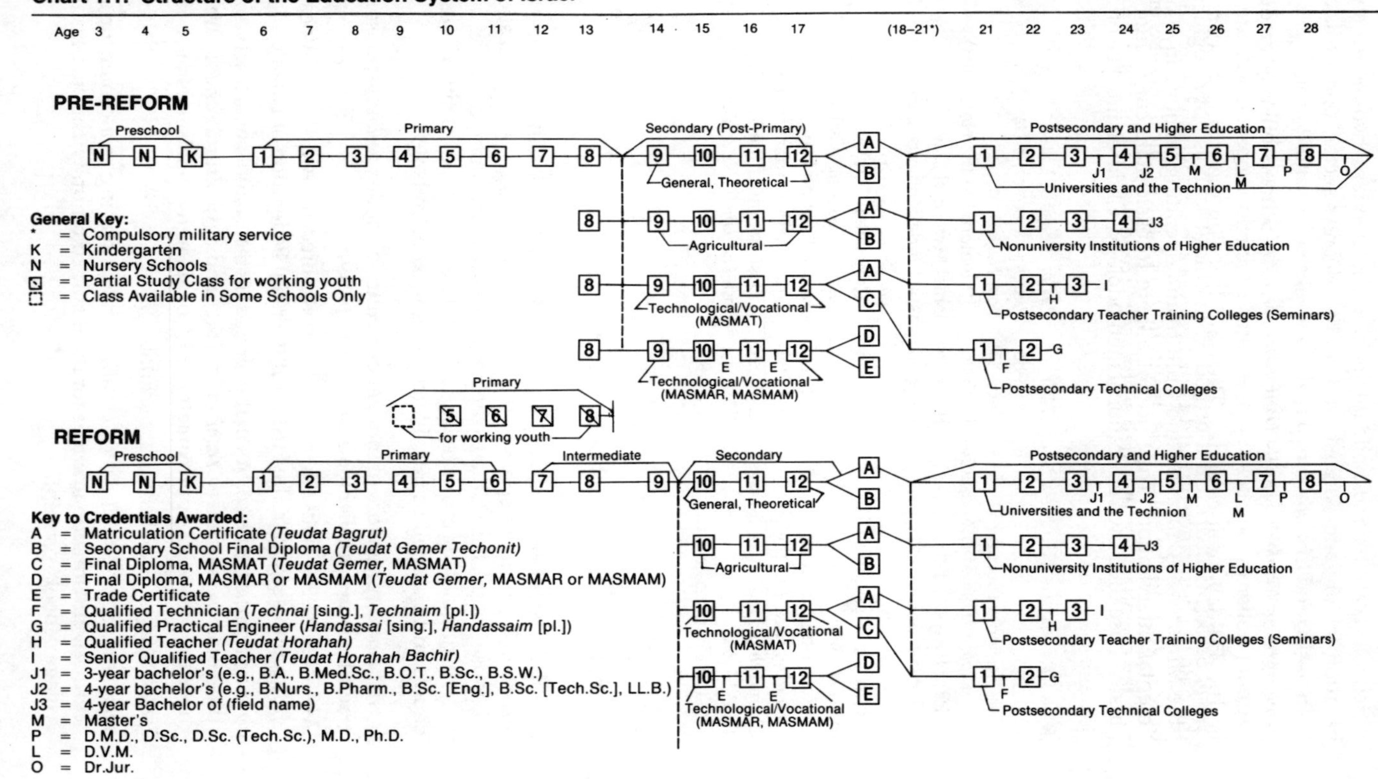

Comprehensive Schools (Makif). Schools offering more than one track (general, technical or agricultural) and permitting change of track according to aptitude and skills.

Elementary or Primary Schools (Beit Sefer Yesodi). Schools offering grades 1-8 (Pre-Reform) and grades 1-6 (Reform).

Exempt Schools (Patour). Ultra-orthodox, unofficial schools not recognized by the Ministry of Education and Culture and operating without any governmental intervention. They do not adhere to basic state curriculums, but instead use their own educational methodology. Children must be officially exempted from compulsory education under the Compulsory Education Law in order to attend these schools, hence the basis for the name.

Experimental Schools (Nisyoni). Independent and recognized schools, not under the auspices of the Ministry of Education and Culture. Teaching is more individualized and classes are smaller.

Hadarim (Heder, singular). Traditional ultra-orthodox one-room, one-teacher primary schools for boys 4-13, offering strictly religious instruction—Bible, *talmud* and commentaries; exempt and unofficial; most replaced by *talmud torahs.*

Hinuch Atzma'i. Independent schools; a classification of schools which are "nonofficial recognized." Mostly orthodox religious schools which, following the spirit of Agudat Israel's Council of Sages, usually place greater emphasis on religious education and observance than State-Religious schools and select students and teachers accordingly.

Iyuni. General (academic) secondary schools.

Intermediate or Junior High Schools (Chativat Beinayim). Schools offering grades 7-9 under the Reform system.

Kollelim. Advanced *yeshivot* for men who are normally married and funded by the *yeshivah* or other religious sources.

MASMAM. Acronym for *Maslul Miktzoi Ma'asi.* The practical vocational school track leading to a Diploma and/or professional (trade) classification; the lowest level of the three technological/vocational tracks.

MASMAR. Acronym for *Maslul Miktzoi Ragil.* The regular vocational school track leading to a Diploma and/or professional (trade) classification; the middle level of the three technological/vocational tracks.

MASMAT. Acronym for *Maslul Miktzoi Ragil Marchav.* The secondary (academic) technological/vocational school track leading to a Matriculation Certificate *(Teudat Bagrut)* or Final Diploma, MASMAT; the highest level of the three technological/vocational tracks.

Mizrahi Schools. A network of religious schools, sponsored by Mizrahi, first operational during the British Mandate and one of the Trends.

Miktzoi. Technological/vocational secondary schools, also called technical, vocational, or professional schools.

Na'amat Schools. A network of schools and day-care centers sponsored by Na'amat, an affiliated women's organization connected with the Histadrut.

ORT *Schools.* A network of technological-vocational schools sponsored primarily by the Organization for Rehabilitation Through Training (ORT).

Recognized Schools (Beit Sefer Mukarim). Schools acknowledged but neither maintained nor supervised by the Ministry of Education and Culture.

Secondary or Postprimary Schools (Beit Sefer Tichon or Chativat Elyona). Either a general reference, including intermediate (grades 7-9) schools, secondary (grades 10-12), or both (grades 7-12) under the Reform system, or grades 9-12 in the Pre-Reform system.

Senior High School. Reform secondary schools offering grades 10-12.

State Schools (Mamlakhti). Official government secular schools comprised of separate Hebrew and Arab sectors under the Ministry of Education and Culture.

State Religious Schools (Mamlakhti Dati). Official government religious schools under the Department of Religious Education within the Ministry of Education and Culture.

Tali Schools. Jewish state schools, affiliated with no particular movemement, which devote more time to Jewish sources and traditions than required in State (secular) schools; often incorrectly identified as *Mesorati* (Conservative).

Talmud Torahs. Ultra-orthodox, traditional Jewish primary-level schools maintained by the community, gradually replacing *hadarim.*

WIZO *Schools.* A network of schools sponsored by the Women's International Zionist Organization (WIZO).

Yami. The Nautical Academy secondary school where academic studies are integrated with lessons on the sea and sailing.

Yeshivah High Schools. Advanced religious secondary-level academies (for boys) offering traditional Jewish studies in the morning and secular studies in the afternoon, resulting in a longer school day; orthodox and ultra-orthodox; may follow a state-prescribed curriculum.

Yeshivot (yeshivah, singular). Advanced religious secondary-level academies (for boys) teaching traditional Jewish studies; orthodox and ultra-orthodox, exempt and unofficial. Differs from *yeshivah* high schools in that secular subjects are not normally taught.

Zionist Labor School. A state school in Jerusalem with curriculum enhancement promoting the principles of the early Zionist Labor movement.

Chapter 2

Preschool, Primary and Intermediate Education

Preschool Education: Nursery Centers and Kindergartens

The Compulsory Education Law of 1949 mandated compulsory kindergarten education for all children 5 years of age. In June 1984, legislation amended the Compulsory Education Law to include free and compulsory preschool education beginning at age 3, effective Fall 1985, to be phased in over a period of six years.

The Ministry of Education and Culture strongly encourages the development of early childhood centers for children in the Hebrew sector below the compulsory kindergarten level. In 1983-84, the *Statistical Abstract of Israel*, No. 35 (1984) reported that 64% of all 2-year-olds, 90% of all 3-year-olds, and 98% of all 4-year-olds were enrolled in nursery centers and kindergartens. For the same year, it reported preschool enrollment in the Arab sector to be about 20% of all 3-year-olds and about 30% of all 4-year-olds. Nurseries are administered by local authorities or by voluntary organizations and usually employ an early childhood teacher and an assistant; fees are assessed according to family income. Tuition-free attendance is offered to all children in the Hebrew sector from development towns and low socio-economic conditions.

Kindergarten education is statistically classified as either Hebrew or Arab. Most Hebrew sector kindergartens are public rather than private and enroll 100% of all 5-year-old children. The lower school—an institution housing several kindergarten classes together with several first and second grade classes in the Hebrew sector—is a recent development that is expected to ease the transition between kindergarten and primary school. Arab kindergartens are usually attached to the primary school and enroll about 95% of all 5-year-olds.

Primary and Intermediate Education

The Pre-Reform and Reform Systems

Beginning with the Compulsory Education Law of 1949 until the Knesset Education Reform legislation of 1968, the primary cycle of compulsory and free education existed within a framework of eight years (grades 1-8). The 1968 Reform introduced in 1969 a six-year primary cycle (grades 1-6), followed by a three-year intermediate (grades 7-9) and three-year secondary cycle (grades

10-12). Implementation of the Reform system has been gradual. As of 1980, approximately half of all children in grades 7 and 8 were in intermediate schools operating under the Reform framework, while the rest remained in Pre-Reform primary schools offering grades 1-8.

Classifications of Schools and Enrollment

Primary and intermediate schools are classified according to sector as either Hebrew or Arab. The Hebrew sector is further identified as State secular *(Mamlakhti)*; State Religious *(Mamlakhti Dati)*; Independent, Recognized *(Hinuch Atzma'i)*; and unofficial/unrecognized or exempt (see Chapter 1, "Introduction," for details). The Arab sector is comprised of schools for Muslims and Christians or Druze. In 1977-78, when the Ministry of Education and Culture placed the Druze sector under the supervision of a separate administrative unit, a separate statistical category was created. See "The Impact of Cultural Differences, Political Persuasion and Religious Belief" and "Arab Education" in Chapter 1 for details.

THE HEBREW SECTOR. A profile of Hebrew primary education as documented by the *Statistical Abstract of Israel*, No. 35 (1984) indicates 545,667 pupils enrolled in grades 1-8, but does not identify the figures as either Pre-Reform or Reform. Of those in grades 7 and 8, 35,244 (53%) and 32,376 (51%), respectively, were studying in intermediate schools. According to school classifications, 74.7% were studying in State secular schools, 19.5% in State Religious schools and 5.8% in Independent schools (orthodox, mainly Agudat Israel). There were 478,047 students in 1,501 primary schools (grades 1-8) of which 11,632 students were in 209 special schools for handicapped children. Of the 95,476 students enrolled in 263 intermediate schools (grades 7-9), 81.2% were in State secular schools, 18.1% in State Religious schools, and 0.7% in Independent schools.

THE ARAB SECTOR. A profile of Arab primary education *(Statistical Abstract)* shows 150,447 pupils enrolled in grades 1-8, undesignated as either Pre-Reform or Reform. Of those in grades 7 and 8, 7,240 (42.7%) and 6,596 (43.3%), respectively, were studying in intermediate schools. There were 136,611 students in 330 primary schools (grades 1-8) of which 962 were in 15 special schools for handicapped children. Of the total 136,611 students enrolled in Arab primary schools, 15,440 (11.3%) were Druze. There were 19,207 students enrolled in 51 intermediate schools (grades 7-9, including preparatory schools in East Jerusalem) of which 77% were Muslim and Christian and 23% were Druze. Druze statistics in both primary and intermediate schools include Druze from the Syrian Golan Heights since its annexation in 1982.

THE COMPOSITE. The combined Hebrew and Arab sector data indicates a total enrollment of 614,658 students in primary schools (78% Hebrew, 22% Arab). In intermediate schools, the combined enrollment was reported as 114,683 (83% Hebrew, 17% Arab). Total population is reported as 83% Jewish, 17% Arab.

The Primary Curriculum

The Educational Reform Act of 1968, which introduced a six-year primary, three-year intermediate, and three-year secondary scheme, established a priority to modernize the curriculums for the entire educational system. Curriculum revisions were undertaken not only to update knowledge in various disciplines, but to provide adaptations and considerations for the lower socioeconomic elements of the Jewish population. By 1978, all curriculum revisions for grades 7-9 of the State and State Religious schools in the Hebrew sector were completed. Between 1978-80, all curriculum revisions for the primary schools in the Hebrew sector were completed, including revisions of syllabi for various disciplines and the development of complementary learning materials. All curricula for the Hebrew sector found applicable in whole or in part (with certain modifications) are or will be translated into Arabic for the Arab sector. Changes in the Hebrew sector schools usually take effect in the Arab sector about 10 years later.

The principal goals of the curriculum in the Hebrew sector are the development of acceptable social behavior, development of language skills, health and safety education, and deepening awareness of Jewish cultural values and traditions in all sectors of Israel's population. The curriculum of both State and State Religious schools is rooted in Jewish culture and history, Jewish literature and philosophy, the Bible, and the *Talmud* (Jewish law). Jewish holidays and special national events (listed in Chapter 1) are incorporated into the curriculum. State Religious schools stress a religious way of life, follow a more extensive formal religious curriculum, and are staffed by observant teachers.

In the Hebrew sector, the Bible (Old Testament) is the primary source of values education and one of the sources in the study of geography, history, language, literature, science, etc. The Bible is taught in the State and State Religious schools as a subject in the curriculum of all grades from 1-12. Portions of the *Talmud* are taught in grades 7-12 of State schools and in grades 5-12 in State Religious schools, wherein formal religious education is more extensive, intensive and central to the academic program. The teaching approach varies from religious to cultural, ethical, or secular, depending upon the school.

In the Arab sector, study of the Islamic, Christian, or Druze religion is prescribed and taught according to criteria different from that of religion taught in the Hebrew sector. The applicable religious texts—the *Koran*, the Bible, *Hadith* (sayings of the Prophet Mohammed), and *Fiqh* (Islamic law)—are not identifiable subjects or specified units within a subject such as literature. (In the Hebrew sector, the Bible, *Talmud*, *Mishna*, *Aggadah* and *Talmud* are studied independently from Hebrew Literature.) The Arab curriculum designates twice as much time to the study of Judaism and its related texts as to study of the Koran or Bible. The intent of religious studies (Koran or Bible) is language acquisition or literary appreciation rather than religious, cultural, or historical knowledge. (Mar'i 85-87) This is explained further in "Education under Occupation/Censorship" in Chapter 9.

Other subjects taught at the primary level in both sectors are Agriculture, Arabic, Arts and Crafts, English or French, Geography, Hebrew, History, Mathematics, Music, Physical Education, Natural Sciences, and Social Studies. In 1978, Arabic was introduced in the fourth grade of some Hebrew sector schools with the intention of making Arabic a required subject throughout Hebrew primary schools; Arabic is not required, however, in the Hebrew sector and the study of it is not widespread. In the Arab sector, Hebrew is mandatory beginning in the third grade. In both sectors, all classes and grades have a weekly "guidance hour" for social interaction and discussion under the direction of the homeroom teacher.

The Intermediate School and Curriculum

Intermediate or junior high schools are regional schools and usually comprehensive. Classes are grouped into heterogeneous homerooms that combine students of all achievement levels within each grade. Class size runs up to 41 students. The atmosphere, dress code, and discipline generally appear relaxed. In comparison to U.S. education, Israeli education at this level exhibits greater breadth and less depth. Many subjects are studied at the same time, the "load" in each subject is lighter, individual subject classes meet less frequently, and the six-day week is broken up by field trips and other activities outside the classroom. The homeroom teacher *(mechanekh/et)* is the main teacher for evaluation, administrative procedures, disciplinary problems, and parent interaction.

The curriculum includes Arabic (Arab sector), Arts and Crafts, Bible, Civics, English, Geography, Hebrew (in the Hebrew and Arab sectors), History, Mathematics, Natural Sciences, Physical Education and, sometimes, Art and Music. Elective subjects are determined by the school and may include a second Foreign Language (Arabic or French), additional Art or Music, Computer Studies, and individualized subjects. English, Mathematics, and Science (beginning in grade 8) are taught according to achievement level. See also "The Primary Curriculum" above.

Two other programs are introduced in grade 9: SHELAH (the Hebrew acronym for Field, Nation, Society) and vocational training. SHELAH consists of weekly lessons given by a special counselor and a monthly day-long field trip. The lessons cover knowledge of the country; its history and landscape; the Zionist settlement and the establishment of the state; basic problems of the state—society, development, settlement, and security; and Jewish identity. SHELAH also involves fieldcraft, campcraft, first-aid, interschool competitions and conferences, and preparation for army service. Vocational subjects are sometimes offered to promote technical secondary education.

Examinations and Promotion

There are no Ministry of Education and Culture (MOEC) leaving examinations in any of the State or State Religious primary or intermediate schools. Up until 1972-73, a State scholastic test *(seker)* was held upon completion of grade 8. The results were used to determine those most suitable for postprimary education and those eligible for graduated tuition awards. Since 1973, tests and examinations have been administered through the schools and symbolic certificates have been issued by the principals. Promotion has not been restricted on the basis of performance on state examinations since 1973.

Compulsory aptitude and psychometric tests were used for kindergarten children entering primary school, for primary school pupils entering intermediate schools, and for intermediate pupils seeking entry to a secondary school of their choice. In November 1985, however, the Director-General of the MOEC approved the recommendation made by a special committee that the tests be abolished through grade 12. The committee concluded the tests could be stressful or otherwise detrimental to the child and promoted "undesirable homogeneity" in the structuring of classes.

Tests and examinations are conducted in the schools on a regular basis throughout the year. A common grading system is in effect throughout primary, intermediate, and secondary education and is illustrated in Chapter 3 under "Grading." Grade reports usually are issued each semester or trimester; transcripts are available yearly. Promotion to each successive grade is without restriction. No external leaving examination or certificate marks the end of the primary or intermediate cycle. Parents, in consultation with the school, decide the type of education and secondary school the child will attend.

Academic Calendar

The academic calendar in official schools begins September 1 and ends June 30, and represents a total of 220 school days. Kindergarten classes are from 8 a.m. to 12 or 1 p.m. Hebrew sector schools operate only in the mornings, while Arab sector schools are double-shifted with a two-session day for separate groups of children. The school week in the Hebrew sector is six days (Sunday through Friday) and five days or six days in the Arab sector. There are 30 hours each week in kindergartens, 24 periods in grades 1-3, 26 periods in grade 4, 30 periods in grade 5, 33 periods in grade 6, and 36 periods in grades 7 and 8 (where a period represents 45-50 minutes). Schools are not in session on religious or national holidays. Jewish holidays are discussed in Chapter 1, Muslim and Christian holidays in Chapter 9. See also "Academic Calendar" in Chapter 1.

Chapter 3
Secondary Education

Background

Secondary education for the Jewish population in Palestine prior to 1948 originated under the influence of East European Jewish immigrants. The schools they established resembled the Eastern European *gymnasium* with which they were familiar and were characterized as elitist, serving a particular socio-economic sector of the population destined to higher university education and positions of influence within society.

The challenges of social and economic development inherent in the establishment of a new state have throughout the past 39 years been encumbered by the need to implement extensive socialization and educational programs designed to promote assimilation of new immigrants in order to bridge the gap between various Jewish ethnic groups. The cultural, social, economic and educational differences that have made assimilation difficult have been hampered, too, by the numerous native languages spoken. "Absorption," assimilation, and educational goals could not be met within an elitist educational framework as originally envisioned. Thus, the characteristics of Israeli education which resembled European education of yesteryear have been transformed gradually, intentionally, and regularly through legislation and educational revision into an educational system uniquely suited to the social and economic needs of Israel.

The Structure of Secondary Education

The Educational Reform Act of July 1968 introduced a restructuring of the Israeli educational system which is discussed in the preceding chapters. Until that time, the system included one year of kindergarten, eight years of primary, and four years of secondary education. The Reform Act reorganized the structure by reducing the primary cycle from eight to six years and by splitting the secondary cycle into two three-year cycles: intermediate (junior high) and secondary (senior high). Implementation of the Reform began in 1969 but has taken effect gradually; 50%-60% of the schools are now operating under the Reform system. The two simultaneously operational systems at the secondary level are summarized as follows:

Pre-Reform: A 4-year secondary cycle, grades 9-12, for children 14-18 years of age.

Reform: A 6-year secondary cycle, grades 7-12, subdivided into intermediate, junior high, grades 7-9, for children 12-15; secondary, senior high, grades 10-12, for children 15-18.

These systems work within the Free Compulsory Education Law of 1979 which provides compulsory education through grade 10 and tuition-free education through grade 12.

This chapter focuses on senior secondary education, grades 10-12. Intermediate, lower secondary education, is discussed in Chapter 2. The information within this chapter is equally applicable to those studying in Pre-Reform schools, grades 9-12.

Classifications of Schools with Statistical Profiles

Since the State Education Law (1953), secondary schools have been categorized in line with the system initially established for state primary education. Accordingly, there exist Hebrew schools—State (secular), State Religious, Independent, and Exempt—as well as Arab schools, Muslim, Christian, and Druze. The following profiles are based upon information from the *Statistical Abstract of Israel*, No. 35, (1984) according to these categories.

THE HEBREW SECTOR. Of the 166,097 students enrolled in senior high schools, 75.5% were in State (secular) schools, 20.1% were in State Religious schools, and 4.4% were in Independent (mostly Agudat Israel) schools. There is no reporting for schools in the Exempt category.

THE ARAB SECTOR. Of the 29,462 students enrolled in senior high schools, 92.3% were Muslim or Christian and 7.7% were Druze. Druze statistics include those from the Syrian Golan Heights since its annexation in 1982.

THE COMPOSITE. When both Hebrew and Arab sectors are compared, secondary enrollment is represented by 85% Hebrew and 15% Arab. The total population figures are reported as 83% Jewish and 17% Arab (see Table 3.1).

Senior Secondary Education

General Characteristics

Secondary education was once characterized as following a trend or track such as Agriculture, Humanities, Mathematics and Physics, Social Science, Technology, etc. This system was abolished and replaced with a more flexible framework that allows students to choose the breadth and depth of each subject according to ability or inclination. This is not to say that a student may not follow a school-prescribed program emphasizing one major subject. Students do frequently choose a major subject and follow a prescribed program for that major. Examples of these prescribed school programs are given in Table 3.6. At the same time, a student may choose a "combination of subjects," a phrase used on the Matriculation Certificate in place of a specific major. As in the past, schools remain classified according to one of three "orientational" tracks which essentially reflects a curriculum framework prescribed by the Ministry of Education and Culture to insure minimum and consistent standards.

Table 3.1. Secondary Enrollment and Schools by "Orientational" Track and Sector

	Hebrew Sector			Arab Sector		
	Pupils		Schools*	Pupils		Schools*
Secondary Schools	166,097		499	29,462		75
One-Track	(96,266)		334	(18,071)		(53)
Comprehensive	(69,831)		165	(11,391)		(22)
"Orientational" Tracks						
General	74,413	(44.8%)	278	24,227	(82.2%)	59
Vocational	79,713	(48.0%)	305	4,651	(15.8%)	36
Agricultural	4,698	(2.8%)	26	584	(2.0%)	2
(Continuation)	7,273	(4.4%)	55	–	–	–
Total	166,097	(85.0%)	499	29,462	(15.0%)	75

SOURCE: Adaptation from *Statistical Abstract of Israel*, No. 35 (1984).
*Total schools by track exceeds total schools indicating tracks within comprehensive schools were counted each as a school by track.

These "orientational" tracks, or types of education, include general (academic, theoretical), technological/vocational, and agricultural and rural education. Within these tracks, schools remain operational according to the Israeli classifications described above. Schools may offer one "orientational" track (one-track schools) or they may offer two or more "orientational" tracks (multitrack or comprehensive schools, i.e., *Makif)*. For more common terminology of various types of schools, their descriptive definitions, and special characteristics see "Schools, Schools, Schools" in Chapter 1.

Curriculums

The Ministry of Education and Culture (MOEC) devises, supervises, and publishes numerous curriculums according to "orientational" track, type of school, and educational sectors (Hebrew and Arab). Beyond this, the Department of Religious Education under the MOEC is responsible for ensuring the religious standards in the curriculum in State Religious schools.

The MOEC-prescribed curriculums consist of various schedules listing the number of instructional units required in compulsory and elective subjects. One instructional unit is defined as approximately 90 (50 minute) hours of instruction over a period of three years or one weekly class hour each year for three years, or the equivalent. The elective subjects usually represent approximately 25% of the curriculum and are determined by the individual school, the desires of its constituency, and its financial resources. The MOEC-prescribed curriculums are presented in Tables 3.2–3.5.

Within the prescribed curriculum requirements, students are allowed to select the scope and level of the subjects they will study as well as the pace at which they will study to prepare for a particular level of matriculation examination in each subject area according to their ambition and/or ability. Selection is normally consistent with the student's ability and the teacher's assessment.

Grade 10 is designed to expose students to the extensive array of subjects from which an inclination or capability might be identified. Students are in class 32-36 hours weekly and usually study up to 15 subjects at one time. This would indicate breadth of exposure, but not necessarily depth of knowledge. Depth, on the other hand, can be assessed by examining units and grades on the Matriculation Certificate (see "Diplomas, Certificates, and Examinations" below). Examination of the subjects and units will indicate whether the student has identified the arts versus the sciences as the direction to be pursued in higher education *or*, in the case of a "combination of subjects," reflects a general college preparatory program.

Table 3.2. MOEC Prescribed Secondary Curriculum—Compulsory Instructional Units for the General Theoretical Orientation in the Hebrew Sector

Subjects	State	State-Religious Boys	State-Religious Girls	Independent Boys	Independent Girls	"*Yeshiva* High School"
Jewish/Israeli Studies	**(9)**	**(14)**	**(13)**	**(15)**	**(14)**	**(17)**
Bible	2	3	3	3	4	3
Civics	1	1	1	1	1	1
Hebrew Lang. & Literature	3	3	3	3	3	3
Hist. of Israeli Nation	2	2	2	2	2	2
Talmud	1	5	4	6	4	8
General Studies	**(7)**	**(7)**	**(7)**	**(7)**	**(7)**	**(7)**
Foreign Lang. (English)	4	4	4	4	4	4
General History	1	1	1	1	1	1
General Literature	1	1	1	1	1	1
Social Studies (Economics/Sociology)	1	1	1	1	1	1
Sciences	**(7)**	**(7)**	**(7)**	**(7)**	**(7)**	**(7)**
Biology	1	1	1	1	1	1
Chemistry	1	1	1	1	1	1
Geography	1	1	1	1	1	1
Mathematics	3	3	3	3	3	3
Physics	1	1	1	1	1	1
Miscellaneous	**(3)**	**(3)**	**(3)**	**(3)**	**(3)**	**(3)**
Home Econ. (Guidance)	1	1	1	1	1	–
Physical Education	2	2	2	2	2	2
Total Compulsory Units	26	31	30	32	31	33
Total Elective Units	8	6	7	6	7	6–7
Grand Total (Units)	34	37	37	38	38	39–40

SOURCE: Ministry of Education and Culture, Israel. (in Hebrew)

Table 3.3. MOEC Prescribed Secondary Curriculum—Compulsory Instructional Units for the General Technological Orientation (MASMAT), Technical and Vocational Trends in the Hebrew Sector

Subjects	State Technical	State Vocational	State Religious Technical R	State Religious Technical Y	State Religious Vocational
General Subject Units	**22**	**19⅔**	**26**	**29**	**23⅔**
Bible	2	2	3	3	3
English	4	4	4	4	4
Hebrew (Grammar, Composition & Jewish Literature)	4	4	3	3	4
History of Israeli Nation, Civics	3	3	3	3	3
Mathematics	4	2	4	4	2
One Science: Biology or Chemistry or Physics	2	1⅔	2	2	1⅔
Talmud	–	–	4	9	3
Homeroom (Guidance)	1	1	1	–	1
Physical Education	2	2	2	1	2
Technical Subjects incl. Workshops & Laboratory	**18**	**20⅓**	**18**	**18**	**20⅓**
Grand Total (Units)	40	40	44	47	44

SOURCE: Ministry of Education and Culture, Israel. (in Hebrew)
Note: R = Religious, Y = "*Yeshivah* High School."

Secondary Education by "Orientational" Track with Statistical Profiles

Table 3.1 summarizes current school and enrollment statistics in the Hebrew and Arab sectors according to type of secondary school and orientational program.

The Agricultural and Rural Orientation

The agricultural and rural orientation under the Department of Agricultural and Rural Education (formerly the Department of Agricultural Education) provides general education as well as agricultural education and accounts for approximately 3% of all secondary enrollment. Graduates of state agricultural schools are eligible to take the Matriculation *(Bagrut)* Examinations and in recent years more students from rural schools have been presented for them. Agricultural education is offered in both the Hebrew and Arab sector schools.

Schools offering this type of education include a network of rural agricultural schools, usually residential, as well as those run by *kibbutzim* and *moshavim*. While the egalitarian philosophy held by some *kibbutzim* and *moshavim* is not consistent with the structure, prescribed curriculum, and assessment practices inherent in the state system, all *kibbutzim* and *moshavim* schools are official state schools. This is no doubt due to the financial reality stemming from government resources being tied to compliance with government curriculum requirements. Contrary to the presumed background of students in this orientation, many agricultural students come from an urban setting, large families, and broken homes where the subsidized school and living arrangements fulfill an economic necessity for some segments of society.

THE HEBREW SECTOR. In 1959-60, enrollment in agricultural schools represented 9% of the total Jewish secondary enrollment; in 1983-84, the enrollment fell to 4,698 (2.8% of all Hebrew secondary enrollment). The number of agricultural schools decreased from 30 to 26 during the same time period. In 1983, 1,146 agricultural students were presented for Matriculation Examinations (3% of all students registering for examinations that year). See Table 3.1.

THE ARAB SECTOR. In 1959-60, 23 agricultural students registered in agricultural education (1.2% of all Arab secondary enrollment in 1956, the closest available year). In 1983-84, 584 students (2% of all Arab secondary students) were enrolled in agriculture. In 1983, agricultural students represented 3% of all Arab students registered for Matriculation Examinations that year. Where there was one Arab agricultural school in 1959-60, two exist today (1984). See Table 3.1.

Table 3.4. MOEC Prescribed Secondary Curriculum—Compulsory Instructional Units for the Agricultural Orientation in the Hebrew Sector

Subjects	Settlement Schools	State	State Religious	
			Boys	Girls
Jewish/Israeli Studies and General Studies	**(13)**	**(13)**	**(19)**	**(18)**
Bible	2	–	3	4
Bible and *Talmud*	–	2	–	–
Foreign Language (English)	4	4	4	4
Hebrew Language & Literature, General Literature	4	4	4	4
History of Israeli Nation, Gen. History, Civics	3	3	3	3
Sciences	**(10)**	**(12)**	**(12)**	**(12)**
Agricultural Biology or Life Science & Agriculture	3 } 7	3 } 9	3 } 9	3 } 9
Agriculture	3	5	5	5
Chemistry	2	2	2	2
Physics	1	1	1	1
Mathematics	3	3	3	3
Miscellaneous	**(3)**	**(3)**	**(3)**	**(3)**
Homeroom (Guidance)	1	1	1	1
Physical Education	2	2	2	2
Total Compulsory Units	26	28	34	33
Total Elective Units	8	6	3	4
Practical Work in Agri.	14	14	14	14
Grand Total (Units)	48	48	51	51

SOURCE: Ministry of Education and Culture, Israel. (in Hebrew)

The Technological/Vocational Orientation

Technological/vocational education (also referred to as technical, professional, technological and/or vocational education) provides general education as well as technological/vocational education and training. Technological education is further subdivided into tracks which represent degrees of academic orientation and levels of instruction. For an indepth discussion of technological education, see Chapter 7.

Technological/vocational education in Israel is popular and widely available. In the Hebrew sector, it is found in State, State Religious, and Independent

Table 3.5. MOEC Prescribed Secondary Curriculum –Compulsory Instructional Units for All Orientations in the Arab Sector

GENERAL/THEORETICAL ORIENTATION

Subjects	Arab	Druze
Jewish/Israeli Studies	**(6)**	**(5)**
Hebrew (Language, Literature & Bible)	4	3
History of Jewish People & Civics	2	2
Arab Studies	**(7)**	**(8)**
Arabic Language & Literature*	4	4
Arab History (incl. General History)†	2	2
Islamic & Christian Culture‡	1	2
General Studies	**(5)**	**(6)**
English	4	4
General Literature	—	1
Soc. Studies (Econ./Sociol.)	1	1

Subjects	Arab	Druze
Sciences	**(7)**	**(7)**
Biology	1	1
Chemistry	1	1
Geography	1	1
Mathematics	3	3
Physics	1	1
Miscellaneous	**(3)**	**(3)**
Homeroom (Guidance)	1	1
Physical Education	2	2
Total Compulsory Units	28	29
Total Elective Units	7	6
Grand Total Units	35	35

GENERAL TECHNOLOGICAL ORIENTATION (MASMAT)

Subject	Technical Trends	Vocational Trends
General Subjects	**(23)**	**(20 ⅔)**
Arabic Language & Literature*	4	4
English	4	4
Hebrew Language, Literature & Bible	3	3
Arab History (incl. Gen. History)†	3	3
Mathematics	4	2
Physics or Chemistry or Biology	2/2/2	1⅔/1⅔/1⅔
Physical Education	2	2
Homeroom (Guidance)	1	1
Technical Subjects (incl. Workshop & Labs)	**18**	**20⅓**
Grand Total (Units)	41	41

continued

AGRICULTURAL ORIENTATION

Subjects	Units	Subjects	Units
Jewish/Israeli Studies —and General Studies	**(14)**	**Sciences**	**(12)**
Arab History (incl. Gen. History)†	3*	Agriculture	5
Arabic Lang. & Literature*	4	Biology for Agriculture or Life Sciences & Agriculture	3
English	4	Chemistry	2
Hebrew (Lang., Literature & Bible)	3	Physics	1 (Agriculture through Physics bracketed: 9)
Miscellaneous	**(3)**	Mathematics	3
Homeroom (Guidance)	1	Total Compulsory Units	29
Physical Education	2	Total Elective Units	5
		Grand Total (Units)	34

SOURCE: Ministry of Education and Culture, Israel. (in Hebrew)
Note: It is recommended that General History, History of the Jewish People, and Arab History be taught together and/or, instead of Arab History, History of the Muslims, Christians or Druzes. It is recommended that General Literature be taught with Arab Literature.
*In Arab schools, includes General Literature.
†For Muslims, includes History of Islamic Nations; for Christians, includes Christian History and Christian History in the Middle East; for Druzes, includes History of the Druze.
‡For Druzes, Druze Heritage.

schools, in "*yeshivah* high schools," in agricultural schools, and in schools belonging to *kibbutzim* or *moshavim* where any of these schools may be one-track or comprehensive. Technological/vocational education is also offered in the Arab sector to a lesser extent.

THE HEBREW SECTOR. In 1959-60, students in technical schools represented 18.4% of all Hebrew sector enrollment; in 1983-84, the 79,713 students in technical education represented 48% of all Hebrew secondary enrollment, higher even than the 44.8% in general (academic) schools. Government officials state that technological education represents 60% of all secondary enrollments which indicates that they discount continuation classes in their calculation. The 305 technical schools represent a 400% increase in schools of this type in the past 24 years. In 1983, 16,295 technical students were presented for Matriculation *(Bagrut)* Examinations (43.9% of all students registering for Matriculation Examinations that year). See Table 3.1.

THE ARAB SECTOR. In 1959-60, there was no reporting of Arab technical education. In 1983-84, the 4,651 students in 36 technical schools represented 15.8% of the 29,462 total Arab secondary enrollment. In 1983, there were 674 vocational students registering for Matriculation Examinations (12.3% of all Arab students registered for Matriculation Examinations in that year). *The Jerusalem Post* in November 1985 reported that a local committee of Arabs had established the Fund for the Development of Technological/Vocational Education in the Arab sector to promote fund raising to increase facilities for vocational training. The committee indicated that 20 (one-track) schools provide 20% of Arab pupils, aged 15 and over, with technical education as compared with some 60% of students in the Hebrew sector enrolled in technical schools. They further state concern over the lack of employment opportunities and the difficulty Arab technical school graduates encounter due to the selective hiring practices of industry, many of which handle defense contracts.

The General (Academic, Theoretical) Orientation

General secondary education is primarily directed towards preparing students for postsecondary or higher education and involves study of traditional academic subjects, as well as those unique to Israel. While this orientation leads to the Matriculation Certificate *(Teudat Bagrut)*, there are students in general schools who have no expectation of reaching the achievement level required for the *Bagrut*. General education programs are found in one-track and comprehensive schools, in Hebrew State (secular), State Religious, and Independent schools and within the Arab sector.

THE HEBREW SECTOR. In 1959-60, students in general education comprised 59.7% of all Hebrew secondary enrollment; in 1983-84, the 74,413 students in general education represented 44.8% of all Hebrew secondary enrollment, an approximate 15% decline over the past 24 years. There are some 3% more students in technical education than in general education (1983). The 278 general schools represented 41.9% of all secondary institutions. General schools presented 17,731 students for Matriculation Examinations (47.7% of all Jewish students from all schools in 1983). See Table 3.1.

THE ARAB SECTOR. In 1959-60, there were 1,933 students reported in general schools; in 1983-84 there were 24,227 students in 75 general schools, or 82.2% of all Arab secondary enrollment. General schools presented 4,476 students for Matriculation Examinations, 84.3% of all Arab students submitted for exams in 1983. See Table 3.1.

Table 3.6. Sample School Programs—Prescribed Units in Compulsory and Optional Major Subjects

All program options include at least the minimum compulsory units required by the MOEC for the Matriculation Certificate in the General/Theoretical Orientation as follows: Bible (2), English (3), Hebrew Expression (Composition—1, Grammar—1) (2), Hebrew Literature (2); History of the Israeli Nation (2), Civics (1), Math (3)

Biology Option. *Compulsory:* Bible (2), Biol. (5), Civics (1), Engl. (3,4,5), Hebrew Expres. (2), Hebrew Lit. (2), History of the Nation (2), Math (3,4,5). *Compulsory Study but not Compulsory Bagrut Exam:* Chem. (3). *One of the following:* Econ. (2) or Sociol. (2) or Hebrew Lit. (1*) or Geog. (3), or Computers (1), or Physics (3), or History of Art (2), or Bible (1*). Total 20–25.

Social Studies Option. *Compulsory:* Bible (2), Civics (1), Engl. (3,4,5), Hebrew Expres. (2), Hebrew Lit. (2), History of the Nation (2), Math (3,4,5), Soc. Studies (incl. Econ.—2, Sociol.—2, Project—1) (5). *One of the following:* Geog. (3) or Computers (1), or Hebrew Lit. (1*) or Bible (1*). Total 21–25.

Chemistry Option. *Compulsory:* Bible (2), Chem. (5), Civics (1), Engl. (3,4,5), Hebrew Expres. (2), Hebrew Lit. (2), History of the Nation (2), Math (3,4,5). *Compulsory Study but not Compulsory Bagrut Exam:* Biol. (3). *One of the following:* Physics (3) or Geog. (3) or History of Art (2) or Econ. (2). Total 22–25.

Physics Option. *Compulsory:* Bible (2), Civics (1), Engl. (3,4,5), Hebrew Expres. (2), Hebrew Lit. (2), History of the Nation (2), Math (3,4,5), Physics (5). *Compulsory Study but not Bagrut Exam:* Chem. (3). *One of the following:* Geog. (3) or Computers (1), or Hebrew Lit. (1*) or Bible (1*). Total 21–25.

Hebrew Literature Option. *Compulsory:* Bible (3), Civics (1), Engl. (3,4,5), Hebrew Expres. (2), Hebrew Lit. (5), History of the Nation (2), Math (3,4,5). *One of the following:* Physics (3) or Geog. (3) or History of Art (2) or Econ. (2). Total 21–25.

History Option. *Compulsory:* Bible (3), Civics (1), Engl. (3,4,5), Hebrew Expres. (2), Hebrew Lit. (2), History of the Nation (2), History (completion to 5 total units) (3), Math (3,4,5). *Compulsory Study but not Bagrut Exam:* Geog. (3). *One of the following:* Econ. (2) or Sociol. (2) or Hebrew Lit. (1*). Total 20–25.

Physical Education Option. *Compulsory:* Bible (2), Civics (1), Engl. (3,4,5), Hebrew Expres. (2), Hebrew Lit. (2), History of the Nation (2), Math (3,4,5), Phys. Educ. (4). *Compulsory Study but not Bagrut Exam:* Biol. for Phys. Educ. (2–3). *One of the following:* Physics (3) or Geog. (3) or History of Art (2) or Econ. (2). Total 21–25.

Note: Study in Mathematics and English is tracked according to ability, performance and the teacher's recommendation; the track determines the exam level (3,4, or 5). The maximum units allowed are 25.

*Combined with compulsory units and reported as one subject.

Continuation Classes

Statistics for "continuation classes" (Hebrew sector only) refer to students studying in schools offering two and four years of school (grades 9-10 and 9-12, respectively), usually located in rural settlements, *kibbutzim,* and *moshavim.* These schools do not give examinations or specifically prepare students for the Matriculation *(Bagrut)* Examinations. Individuals who wish to take Matriculation Examinations may do so as "external" examinees. Almost identical enrollment figures are given for continuation classes over the past 24 years (see Table 3.1 below).

Diplomas, Certificates, and Examinations

N.B. *Teudat* is a Hebrew word translated as either certificate or diploma, *gemer* as final or completion. When *Teudat* is used in conjunction with the word "matriculation" *(Bagrut),* it is almost always translated as "certificate"; when used in connection with technical/vocational, teaching, and other credentials, it is most frequently translated as "diploma." All references to "final diplomas" could correctly be translated as "certificate of completion" or "final certificate" and are frequently translated as such.

Secondary School Final Diploma *(Teudat Gemer Tichonit)*

The Secondary School Final Diploma represents the satisfactory completion of the MOEC-prescribed curriculum of required and elective courses through grade 12 according to the "orientational" track followed and type of school attended. In general secondary schools, agricultural/rural schools and continuation classes, a distinction is made between matriculation examinations and final diploma examinations. Final diploma exams in these schools and classes usually refer to final subject examinations administered by the school at the end of grade 12. Technical/vocational schools likewise offer the option to sit for matriculation and/or final exams (see discussion in Chapter 7).

Also spelled *Teudat Hagamar Hatichonit* and frequently referred to as a "certificate of completion" of secondary studies, the Secondary School Final Diploma is a formal MOEC certificate giving recognition for completion of grade 12. This diploma is not meant to identify a minimum number of subjects passed at the matriculation level nor are matriculation results reported on the diploma. However, since several low level matriculation exams such as Bible, Civics, and Hebrew Grammar are frequently taken after grade 10 or 11, it would not be unusual for diploma holders to have passed at least several matriculation exams in these subjects as well as perhaps others passed after grade 12. Students may continue to study, sit or resit for matriculation examinations, and eventually qualify for the Matriculation Certificate *(Teudat Bagrut)*.

Matriculation Certificate *(Teudat Bagrut)*

The Matriculation Certificate is the basic qualification required for admission to universities, nonuniversity institutions of higher education, teachers' training colleges, and selective technical colleges. Recipients of this certificate include students who have been educated in any of the various types of secondary schools (agricultural, general [academic], technological high schools, or "*yeshivah* high schools"), as well as independent external examinees. Sample variations of *Bagrut* certificates and examination results for internal and external examinees in Hebrew with translations are provided at the end of this chapter. Due to the complications of conversion from the old to the new examination system, the issuance of official certificates has been delayed. Individuals are usually successful in obtaining the certificate if they contact the Examination Division of the MOEC (Jerusalem) in person.

Bagrut examinations are devised, supervised, and graded by the Ministry of Education and Culture (MOEC) with the administrative assistance of the high schools. A few minor, lower standard examinations are administered through the schools. According to the established practice at individual schools, students may be tested in one or more minor examinations at the end of grades 10 and/or 11, while the balance of examinations are given over a period of several weeks in the early summer after the completion of grade 12. Required subjects include Bible, Civics, English Language, Hebrew Grammar and Composition, Hebrew Literature, Jewish History, and Mathematics (or Science).

Based upon the curriculum followed, the student then elects other subjects in which to be tested. Students may write a final paper on a topic or project in a certain subject rather than take the matriculation exam in that subject. The paper, which must be written in grade 11, may replace any required subject except Bible and History (unless the topic is not covered in the syllabus) and emphasizes independent work. A paper or project may not be done by more than one person or as a group project. Papers written in lieu of an examination are recorded on the examination report along with other examination results.

In 1976, the MOEC announced extensive revisions in the matriculation examination system. These changes included 1) subject examinations differentiated by level of proficiency according to an assigned unit value of from 1-6 units, 2) greater flexibility in the choice and levels of subject examinations, 3) the option of substituting a second science for mathematics (later rescinded), and 4) the option of substituting a written paper on a certain topic or project in place of an examination.

THE UNITS SYSTEM. The units system has been in effect for internal school candidates (as opposed to external candidates) since 1976. Each subject examination carries a particular value of from 1-6 units which reflects the level of difficulty or extent of subject matter involved. Beyond the minimum unit standard set by the regulations of the examination, the level at which the student has studied determines the unit level of examination. Not all subjects are offered at every level. For example, Civics is offered at a lower level only, while Biology is offered at only the intermediate and higher levels. Levels are designated as regular (1-2 units), intermediate or middle (3-4 units) and upper or high (5-6 units).

A unit is roughly defined as 90 hours of study, approximately three hours per week for one year, or variations thereon, but is not simply related to class hours. Beyond that, units represent different types of examinations or levels of examinations. For example, Biology, 5 units, comprises 3 units based on a written exam, 1 unit based on an oral exam, and 1 unit based upon a laboratory exam; Biology, 4 units, comprises 3 units based upon a written examination (the same as Biology 5 units), and 1 unit based upon a laboratory exam; Biology, 3 units, comprises 2 units based upon a written examination of a lower level than that for Biology 4 or 5, combined with a lower level laboratory exam, and 1 unit based upon an oral exam.

CONDITIONS FOR AWARD OF THE *Bagrut*. Academic requirements for the current *Bagrut* Certificate state that the minimum number of units required is 20, within a range of 20-25 units, stipulated according to orientation, type of school, sector (Hebrew or Arab) and including compulsory subjects (see Tables 3.7-3.14). A minimum of 15 units in compulsory subjects is required, as follows: Bible (2 units); Civics (1); English Language (3); Hebrew Language (2) (Grammar, 1; Composition, 1); Hebrew Literature (2); and Mathematics (or Science) (3). In 1986, the option to take a science exam in lieu of mathematics was rescinded and math is now required. An additional subject of at least 1 unit is required. At least one subject examination must be taken for 5 units.

A grade of at least 6 must be achieved in all the major and compulsory subjects except under certain conditions (see "Grading Practices" below).

Those who sat for Matriculation Examinations as internal school candidates prior to 1976 as well as those who have taken the examination as external (independent) examinees since then generally have no units assigned to subject examinations. Instead, those subjects studied and examined at an advanced level will be designated as "A" level, advanced, intensified, expanded, or extended, depending upon the translation. Minor subjects studied and examined at a lower level, usually after grade 11, will be designated as restricted, condensed, or reduced, depending upon the translation. Recent external candidates may have examination results which designate a unit value assigned to some subjects, usually Mathematics and English. This is done to facilitate university admission in light of new requirements (see "University Reaction" below).

The compulsory subject examinations for school candidates following the original certificate regulations prior to 1976 include Bible, Foreign Language, Hebrew (Grammar, Composition, and Literature), and Mathematics. A fifth examination is elected usually from the student's major trend or track. (Arab students replaced Bible with Arabic.) Those five examinations are set and marked by the MOEC. Four subjects are taken at a regular level, one at an advanced level. Also required are two elective lower level subject examinations

Table 3.7. Required Units/Examinations for the Matriculation Certificate—General/ Theoretical Orientation (Hebrew Sector)

	State Schools	Religious Schools			
		State	Independent		"*Yeshivah*
	Secular	Relig.	Boys	Girls	High Schools"
Total Compulsory Units	14–15	17–18	18–20	18–20	19–21
Total Elective Units	6–11	3–8	2–7	2–7	1–6
Grand Total (Units)	20–25	20–25	20–25	20–25	20–25

Subjects and Compulsory Units of Study for All Hebrew Sector Schools

Jewish/Israeli Studies		**General Studies**	
Bible	2*	Foreign Language (English)	3
Civics	1	**Sciences**	2–3
Hebrew Language	2	Biol. (2), or Chem. (2) or	
History of the Israeli Nation	2	Math (3) or Physics (2)	
Literature (or Israeli Thought in Religious Schools)	2		
Talmud	†		

SOURCE: Ministry of Education and Culture, Israel. (in Hebrew)

Note: In 1986, the MOEC changed the 2-unit science/3-unit math option to a 3-unit math requirement that affects the total compulsory and elective units cited above.

*Except in Indep.-Girls, 2–3 units

†State Secular = 0 units, State Relig. = 3 units, Indep.-Boys = 4–5, Indep.-Girls = 4, "*Yeshivah* H.S." = 5–6.

Table 3.8. Required Units/Examinations for the Matriculation Certificate and Final Diploma (MASMAT)—General Technological Orientation (Hebrew Sector, State Secular Only)

Subject	Matriculation Certificate Option 1	Option 2	Option 3	Option 4	FD (MASMAT)
Bible	2	2	2	2	2 or FD
English	3	3	3	3	2 (FD)
General Literature	2	2	2	2	2 or FD
Hebrew Language	2	2	2	2	2 or FD
History	2–3	2–3	2–3	2–3	2 or FD
Mathematics	3–4	5	4–5	4	3 or FD
Physics	–	–	3	4	–
Technical Subject 1	3 or 5	5	5	5	3 or 5
Technical Subject 2	3	3	–	–	3 or FD
Technical Drawing (Electricity Trend)	*	*	*	*	*
Total Compulsory Units	20–24	24–25	23–24	24–25	–
Total Practical Units	2	2	2	2	2

SOURCE: Ministry of Education and Culture, Israel. (in Hebrew)
Note: FD = Final Diploma Examination.
*The exam in Technical Drawing in the Electricity Trend is an external exam at the FD level.

set and marked by the school with approval by the MOEC. These seven subject exams were required for the *Bagrut* (pre-1976 format). Regulations for external examinees prior to 1976 stipulated four required subjects (Bible, a Foreign Language, Hebrew [Language and Literature] and Mathematics) and two optional subjects (Biology, Chemistry, Geography, a second Foreign Language, History, Physics or *Talmud).*

Non-academic requirements for the Matriculation Certificate exist as well. Students must participate in a two-hour per week supervised volunteer work program in grade 10. They must also participate in physical education and contribute to the homeroom sessions each year in order to receive the Certificate.

Other measures have been taken to introduce flexibility in the examination system. Where *bagrut* grades previously reflected the results on the Matriculation Examinations (with school marks considered under certain circumstances), the grades now reflect equal consideration for external and internal assessment. See "Grading Practices" below.

Further concessions have been authorized by the Ministry of Education and Culture for three categories of students: the *oleh* (immigrant or temporary resident); the returning student "A"; and the returning student "B" defined below. Although concessions have been authorized, implementation or approval is not automatic.

1. The *oleh.* A student is considered an *oleh* for a period of four complete school years from the first of September after the date of his immigration.

Table 3.9. Required Units/Examinations for the Matriculation Certificate and Final Diploma (MASMAT)—Technological Orientation Excluding Nontechnical Trends (Hebrew Sector, State Religious and "*Yeshivah* High School")

		State Religious Technical H.S.						Technical "*Yeshivah* H.S."				
Subjects	Options:	1	2	3	4	5	FD	1	2	3	4	FD
Bible		2	2	2*	2	2	1, 2 or 3	2	2	2	2	1 or 2
English		3	3	3	3	3	2 (FD)	3	3	3	3	2 (FD)
Hebrew Language		2	2	2	2	2	2 or FD	2	2	2	2	2 or FD
History of Israeli Nation, History of the State of Israel, Civics		2–3	2–3	2–3	2–3	2–3	2 or FD	2–3	2–3	2–3	2–3	2 or FD
Mathematics		3–4	5	3–4	4–5	4	3 or FD	3–4	4	3	4–5	3 or FD
Physics†		–	–	–	3	4	–	–	3	–	–	–
Talmud		2	2	3‡	2	2	2 or FD	3	3	4	4	2
Technical Subject 1		3 or 5	5	3 or 5	5	5	3 or 5	3 or 5	5	5	3	3–5
Technical Subject 2		3	3	3	–	–	3 or FD	3	–	3	3	3 or FD
Technical Drawing# (Electricity Trend)		#	#	#	#	#	#	#	#	#	#	#
Total Compulsory Units		20–24	24–25	21–24	23–24	24–25	–	21–24	24–25	24–25	23–24	–
Total Practical Units		2	2	2	2	2	2	2	2	2	2	2

SOURCE: Ministry of Education and Culture, Israel. (in Hebrew)

Note: FD in the column head refers to Final Diploma (as opposed to the Matriculation Certificate) requirements and in the body of the table to Examinations at the FD level.

*In the State Religious schools, Bible may be taken on the level of 3 units in Option 3.

†In the Technical "*Yeshivah* High School," Physics may be taken on the level of 3 units instead of Technical Subject 2.

‡In the State Religious schools, *Talmud* may be taken on the level of 2 units in Option 3.

#This exam in Technical Drawing in the Electricity Trend is an external exam at the Final Diploma level.

2. Student "A." A student who was abroad for at least eight complete school years is considered for this category for a period of four years from the first of September after his return to Israel.
3. Student "B." A student who was abroad for at least four complete school years is considered for this category for a period of two school years from the first of September after his return to Israel.

The *oleh* or student "A" may choose to study for the *Bagrut* examination in certain subjects (Bible, Hebrew Language and Literature, Jewish History and *Talmud)* according to one of three criteria: a special curriculum for immigrant students prepared by the MOEC; a curriculum prepared by the school and approved by the Ministry; or, the regular curriculum. The grade for the *oleh* who chooses the latter option will be reported as 1 point above the grade actually achieved if a minimum grade of 3.5 is obtained.

In the first year in Israel, *olim* may request to be examined in their native language. During the next three years, they may be examined in certain

Table 3.10. Required Units/Examinations for the Matriculation Certificate and Final Diploma (FD) in the Technological Orientation, Nontechnical (Vocational) Trends (Hebrew Sector, State and State Religious)

	State Secular Schools			State Religious Schools		
Subjects / Options	1	2	FD (MASMAT)	1	2	FD (MASMAT)
Bible	2*	2*	2 or FD	2*	2*	1 or 2 or 3
Civics	1	1	1	1	1	1
English†	3	3	–	3	3	–
Hebrew Language	2	2	2 or FD	2	2	2 or FD
Hebrew Literature	2	2	2 or FD	–	–	–
History of Israeli Nation	2	2	1 or FD	2	2	2 or FD
Mathematics	0 or 3	0 or 3	–	0 or 3	0 or 3	–
Sciences (Physics or Chemistry or Biology)	2	–	–	2	–	–
Talmud‡	–	–	–	2–3‡	2–3‡	1 or 2 or 3
Technical Subject 1	3	5	3 or 5	3	5	3 or 5
Technical Subject 2	3	3	3 or FD	3	3	3 or FD
Practical Work						
Total Compulsory Units	20–23	20–23	–	20–24	20–24	–
Total Practical Units	2	2	2	2	2	2

SOURCE: Ministry of Education and Culture, Israel. (in Hebrew)
Note: FD in the column head refers to Final Diploma (as opposed to the Matriculation Certificate) requirements and in the body of the table to Examinations at the FD level.
*Bible in Options 1 and 2 may be taken at the level of 3 units.
†In order to receive a Final Diploma (MASMAT) in the Secretarial Trend, English must be taken at the level of 2 units.
‡*Talmud* in Options 1 and 2 may be taken at the level of 2 units.

Table 3.11. Required Units/Examinations for the Matriculation Certificate, Agricultural Orientation (Hebrew Sector)

Subject	Settlement Schools	Agri./Rural Schools State	Agri./Rural Schools State Religious
Jewish/Israeli/General Studies			
Bible	2	2	2
Civics	1	1	1
Foreign Language (English)	3	3	3
Hebrew Language & Literature	4	4	3
History of the Israeli Nation	2	2	2
Talmud	–	–	3
Sciences			
Agri. or Agri. Biol. and Agri. or Life Sci. and Agri. (or project)‡	–*	4–5†	4–5†
Math (3 units) or Physics (2 units) or Chem. or Agri. Chem. (2 units) and/or those exempt from Agri. opts. above must take Agri. Biol. or Life Sci. & Agri. (2–3) units)	2–3	2–3	2–3
Total Compulsory Units	14–15	18–20	20–22
Total Elective Units	6–11	2–7	0–5
Total Practical Units#	–	–	–
Grand Total (Units)	20–25	20–25	20–25

SOURCE: Ministry of Education and Culture, Israel. (in Hebrew)
Note: In 1986, the MOEC changed the 2-unit science/3-unit math option to a 3-unit math requirement that affects the total compulsory and elective units cited above.
*In settlement schools, the exam in biology and/or agriculture or life sciences and agriculture may be declared compulsory.
†In agricultural schools, a student must take an exam in the agricultural science field.
‡A project may be taken at the level of 1 unit in agricultural sciences field or in the electives.
#Exam in practical work in agricultural schools is an external *Bagrut* exam but is not included in the number of units required for the Matriculation Certificate.

subjects in the native language, and, in certain subjects, may be examined orally. In addition, native speakers of English can take the English (subject) *Bagrut* exam in grade 10 instead of grade 12. These concessions are not automatic; permission must be granted.

A student "B" has the same choice of curriculums as an *oleh,* but the option for an oral exam or testing in the native language is not available.

UNIVERSITY REACTION TO NEW MATRICULATION REGULATIONS. The Inter-University Committee on Admissions Policies, a representative body of all Israeli universities, responded with concern to the "liberalization" of the Matriculation regulations announced by the Ministry of Education and Culture in 1976. In response, the Committee issued a set of minimum conditions (concerning *Bagrut* examinations) for eligibility to university studies as follows: 1)

Table 3.12. Required Units/Examinations for the Matriculation Certificate, General/Theoretical Orientation (Arab Sector)

Subjects	Arab	Druze	Subjects	Arab	Druze
Arabic Lang. & Lit.	4	3–4	Math (3 units) or Physics (2 units) or Chem. (2 units) or Biol. (2 units)	2–3	2–3
Arab/Druze History	2	2	Religion	–*	1
Civics	1	1	Total Compulsory Units	14–15	15–17
English	3	3	Total Elective Units	6–11	5–10
Hebrew Lang. & Lit.	2	3	Grand Total (Units)	20–25	20–25

SOURCE: Ministry of Education and Culture, Israel. (in Hebrew)
Note: In 1986, the MOEC changed the 2-unit science/3-unit math option to a 3-unit math requirement that affects the total compulsory and elective units cited above.
*In the future in Arab high schools, 1 unit in Islamic/Christian Religion or Islamic Culture will be included in the compulsory units; schools that have already submitted and received approval for such a program will be able to examine in this subject by the Ministry of Education and Culture.

All candidates must pass English at level 4 or above; 2) all candidates must take an additional subject (other than English) on a minimal 4-unit level; and 3) all candidates must pass Mathematics at the 3-unit level or above. Further, in order to encourage students to test at the 4-unit level or above, the universities now tend to give additional weight to test results for additional subjects passed at the 4-unit level. The MOEC has responded to the universities' concern by bringing the Matriculation Certificate regulations in line with university requirements.

Grading Practices

The grading scale used on yearly transcripts and on Matriculation *(Bagrut)* Examination results, regardless of when the examination was taken, is described below. Because verbal translations and interpretations of numerical grades vary widely, it is advisable to focus on the numeric grades. The scale reflected at the bottom of the Matriculation Certificate is as follows:

Excellent	=	95-100	(10)	(rarely given)
Very Good	=	85-94	(9)	
Good	=	75-84	(8)	
Almost Good	=	65-74	(7)	(also Fair, Fairly Good, Nearly Good)
Satisfactory	=	55-64	(6)	(also Sufficient, Pass, Adequate, Fair)
Almost Satisfactory	=	45-54	(5)	(also Almost Sufficient, Hardly Satisfactory, Hardly Adequate)
Fail, Unsatisfactory	=	0-44	(4)	

SOURCE: The Matriculation Certificate *(Teudat Bagrut)*.

Table 3.13. Required Units/Examinations for the Matriculation Certificate and Final Diploma (MASMAT), Technical/Vocational Orientation (Arab Sector)

	Technical Trends		Nontechnical Trends	
Subjects	*Bagrut*	FD (MASMAT)	*Bagrut*	FD (MASMAT)
Arabic Language & Literature	3–4	3 or FD	3–4	3 or FD
Arab/Druze History	2	2 or FD	2	2 or FD
Civics	1	1	1	1
English	3	2 (FD)	3	2 (FD)
Hebrew Language & Literature	2	2 or FD	2–3	2 or FD
Mathematics	3–4	3 or FD	0 or 3	–
Sciences (Physics or Chem. or Biol.)	–	–	0 or 2	–
Technical Subject 1	3 or 5	3 or 5	3 or 5	3 or 5
Technical Subject 2	3	3 or FD	3	3 or FD
Technical Drawing (Electricity Trend)	*	*	*	*
Total Compulsory Units	20–24	–	20–24	–
Total Practical Units	2	2	2	2

SOURCE: Ministry of Education and Culture, Israel. (in Hebrew)
Note: FD in the column head refers to Final Diploma (as opposed to the Matriculation Certificate) requirements and in the body of the table to Examinations at the FD level.
*The exam in Technical Drawing in the Electricity Trend is external on the Final Diploma level.

The grades on the Matriculation Certificate *(Teudat Bagrut)* since 1976 reflect an average calculated on the basis of internal and external assessment. The grade for internal assessment is derived from an average based on overall performance in the classroom and an internal final examination called the *magan*. The *magan* prepares students for the *Bagrut* examination and is similar to the *Bagrut* in both content and structure. The *magan*, a term used with reference to the internal examination as well as the total internal assessment, is then averaged with the score on the Matriculation *(Bagrut)* Examination to become the score commonly considered the *Bagrut* grade, or that subject grade reflected on the Matriculation Certificate. For example, if the *magan* (overall internal assessment) grade of 85 is averaged with a *Bagrut* examination score of 60, the reported *Bagrut* grade is 7, calculated as 60 + 85 = 145 ÷ 2 = 72.5 = 73 = 7 (standard rounding off practice is used, i.e., 74.4 = 70 = 7 and 74.5 = 75 = 80 = 8). A minimum grade of 6 is required in order to qualify for the *Bagrut* except under the following conditions: one subject grade of 5 is permitted if this score is only in one subject, if the subject carries a value of 1-3 units, if the subject is not Hebrew Grammar or Composition, if the student received a grade of 8 in two 4-unit subject exams (or higher), and all other scores are at least 6; one subject grade of 4 or less is permitted if the result is only in one subject, if the subject carries a value of no more than 4 units, if the subject is not Hebrew Grammar or Composition, and if the student received at least one score of 8 and at least one score of 9 in the 4-unit subject exams.

Table 3.14. Required Units/Examinations for the Matriculation Certificate in the Agricultural Orientation (Arab Sector)

Subject	Units	Subject	Units
Arabic Language & Literature	4	Hebrew Language & Literature	2
Arab/Druze History	2	Math (3 units) or Physics (2 units) or Chem. (2 units) or Agri. Biol. (2 units)	2–3
Agri. or Agri. Biol. and Agri. or Life Sci. and Agri. (or project)	4–5	Total Compulsory Units	18–20
Civics	1	Total Elective Units	2–7
English	3	Grand Total (Units)	20–25

SOURCE: Ministry of Education and Culture, Israel. (in Hebrew)
Note: In 1986, the MOEC changed the 2-unit science/3-unit math option to a 3-unit math requirement that affects the total compulsory and elective units cited above.

In order to qualify for the pre-1976 *Bagrut* as a school candidate, one grade of 5 in one subject was permitted provided it was not Hebrew for candidates from the Hebrew sector or Arabic for candidates from the Arab sector. If a student received one failing grade (4 or less), other conditions similar to those stated above for students under current regulation were considered.

External examinees under both pre- and post-1976 regulation are required to have a grade of 6 in all examinations to qualify for the *Bagrut* or may have no more than one mark of 5. If one subject is failed (grade of 4 or less), a certificate may be awarded by compensation if the sum of all marks is at least 40, if there are at least two subject marks of 8, if no other mark is less than 6, and if the failure was not in Hebrew (or Arabic for Arab students), the Foreign Language, Math at the Advanced Level, or *Talmud* at the Advanced Level.

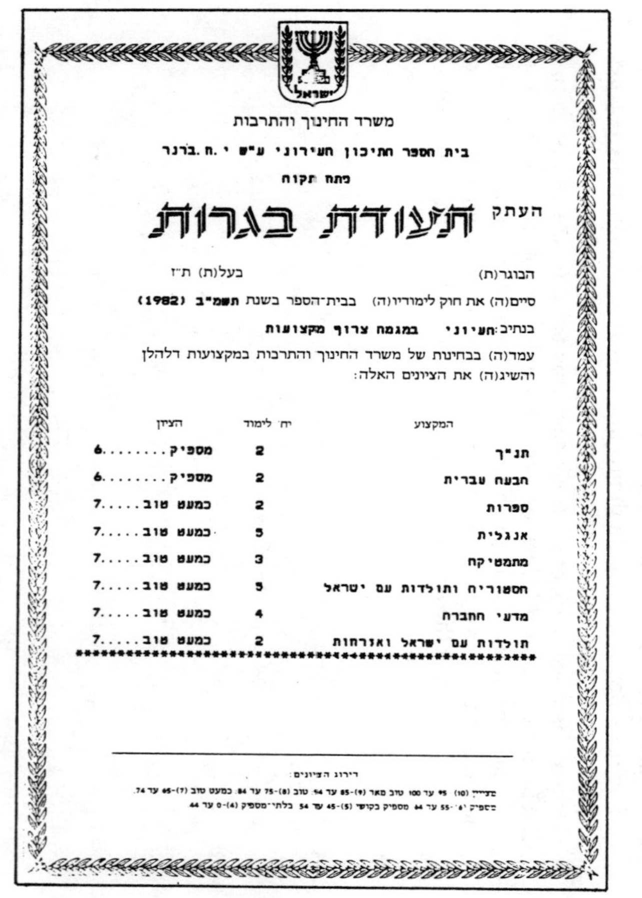

משרד החינוך והתרבות
בית הספר התיכון העירוני ע"ש י.ח.ברנר
פתח תקוה

העתק **תעודת בגרות**

הבוגר(ת) בעל(ת) ת"ז

סיים(ה) את חוק לימודיו(ה) בבית־הספר בשנת תשמ"ב (1982)

בנתיב: עיוני במגמה צרוף מקצועות

עמד(ה) בבחינות של משרד החינוך והתרבות במקצועות דלהלן
והשיג(ה) את הציונים האלה:

המקצוע	יח' לימוד	הציון
תנ"ך	2	מספיק........6
הבעה עברית	2	מספיק........6
ספרות	2	כמעט טוב.....7
אנגלית	5	כמעט טוב.....7
מתמטיקה	3	כמעט טוב.....7
הסטוריה ותולדות עם ישראל	5	כמעט טוב.....7
מדעי החברה	4	כמעט טוב.....7
תולדות עם ישראל ואנרחות	2	כמעט טוב.....7

דירוג הציונים:
מצויין (10) 95 עד 100 טוב מאד (9) 85 עד 94 טוב (8) 75 עד 84 כמעט טוב (7) 65 עד 74.
מספיק (6) 55 עד 64 מספיק בקושי (5) 45 עד 54 בלתי־מספיק (4) 0 עד 44

בית הספר התיכון העירוני ע"ש י.ח.ברנר
פתח תקוה

הנהלת בית־הספר מאשרת בזאת כי

הבוגר(ת) בעל(ת) ת"ז

השלים(ה) את לימודיו(ה) בבית־הספר גם במקצועות דלהלן והשיג(ה)
בהם את הציונים הסופיים האלה:

המקצוע	יח' לימוד	הציון
גיאוגרפיה	1	מספיק..........(6)
תלמוד	1	מספיק..........(6)
ערבית.	1	כמעט טוב.......(7)
כימית.	1	מספיק.........(6)
ביולוגיה	1	מספיק..........(6)
פיסיקה	1	כמעט טוב.......(7)
חינוך גופני	2	מספיק..........(6)

חלק זה של התעודה מודפס בבית־הספר

על־יסוד לימודיו(ה) והשגיו(ה) בבית־הספר ובבחינות־הבגרות ניתנת לבוגר(ת)
תעודת בגרות זו, המזכה את בעליה להתקבל ללימודים במוסדות להשכלה גבוהה
ובמוסדות להכשרת עובדי הוראה, בכפיפות לתנאי הקבלה הנהוגים בהם.

חתימת המנהל וחותמת ביה"ס משרד החינוך והתרבות

ירושלים, 1 באב תשמ"ו
8 באוגוסט 1986

3.1a. Matriculation Certificate *(Teudat Bagrut)*, Current Format, 1982

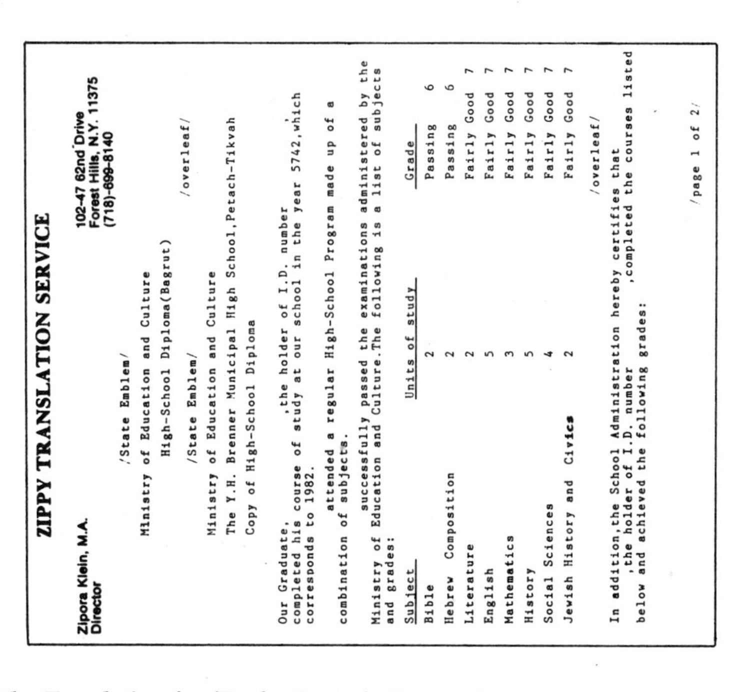

ZIPPY TRANSLATION SERVICE

Zipora Klein, M.A.
Director

102-47 62nd Drive
Forest Hills, N.Y. 11375
(718)-699-8140

/State Emblem/

Ministry of Education and Culture

High-School Diploma(Bagrut)

/overleaf/

/State Emblem/

Ministry of Education and Culture

The Y.H. Brenner Municipal High School,Petach-Tikvah

Copy of High-School Diploma

Our Graduate, ,the holder of I.D. number , completed his course of study at our school in the year 5742,which corresponds to 1982.

attended a regular High-School Program made up of a combination of subjects.

successfully passed the examinations administered by the Ministry of Education and Culture.The following is a list of subjects and grades:

Subject	Units of study	Grade
Bible	2	Passing 6
Hebrew Composition	2	Passing 6
Literature	2	Fairly Good 7
English	5	Fairly Good 7
Mathematics	3	Fairly Good 7
History	5	Fairly Good 7
Social Sciences	4	Fairly Good 7
Jewish History and Civics	2	Fairly Good 7

/overleaf/

In addition,the School Administration hereby certifies that ,the holder of I.D. number ,completed the courses listed below and achieved the following grades:

/page 1 of 2/

ZIPPY TRANSLATION SERVICE

Zipora Klein, M.A.
Director

102-47 62nd Drive
Forest Hills, N.Y. 11375
(718)-699-8140

Subject	Units of Study	Grade
Geography	1	Passing 6
Talmud	1	Passing 6
Arabic	1	Fairly Good 7
Chemistry	1	Passing 6
Biology	1	Passing 6
Physics	1	Fairly Good 7
Gym	2	Passing 6

This High-School Diploma is awarded to based on the above subjects and grades.This High-School Diploma entitles to apply to Institutions of Higher Learning,subject to the admissions requirements of those institutions.

School Principal:(name - illegible) /School Seal/

Ministry of Education and Culture:(name - illegible)

Jerusalem,Av 3,5746
August 8,1986.

I certify that this is a true and accurate translation of the original document in Hebrew.

Zipora Klein,Translator

Subscribed and sworn to before me this October 28,1986.

EDWARD MANN
NOTARY PUBLIC, State of New York
No. 41-7698410 - Queens County
Term Expires March 30, 1984

/page 1 of 2/

3.1b. Translation for *(Teudat Bagrut)*, Current Format, 1982

(STATE EMBLEM)
MINISTRY OF EDUCATION & CULTURE
MUNICIPAL HIGH SCOOL "A" (RIGHT FACE)
BAT-YAM

CERTIFICATE OF MATRICULATION
MAJOR: MATHEMATICS - PHYSICS

, I.D. # HAS COMPLETED IN THE YEAR (HEBREW CALENDAR EQUIVALENT OF 1967) THE COURSE OF STUDIES IN THE UPPER GRADE (THE TWELFTH YEAR OF STUDIES) OF THE INSTITUTION AND HAS PASSED THE EXAMINATIONS OF THE MINISTRY OF EDUCATION AND CULTURE IN THE SUBJECTS

BIBLICAL STUDIES
HEBREW
ENGLISH - A LEVEL
MATHEMATICS - ADVANCED LEVEL
PHYSICS

AS WELL AS EXAMINATIONS ACCORDING TO THE REDUCED PROGRAM IN THE SUBJECTS

HISTORY OF THE JEWISH PEOPLE - (CIVICS)
CHEMISTRY

(LEFT FACE)

THE GRADUATE HAS ACHIEVED AT THE COMPLETION OF HIS STUDIES AT SCHOOL AND AFTER PASSING THE MATRICULATION EXAMINATIONS, THE FOLLOWING GRADES:

SUBJECTS	GRADES	SUBJECTS	GRADES
BIBLE	VERY GOOD 9	HISTORY	GOOD 8
HEBREW	VERY GOOD 9	PHYSICAL ED	ALMOST GOOD 7
ENGLISH	EXCELLENT 10		
MATHEMATICS	VERY GOOD 9		
PHYSICS	EXCELLENT 10		
MODERN HISTORY OF ISRAEL	VERY GOOD 9		
CHEMISTRY	VERY GOOD 9		
ARABIC	VERY GOOD 9		
BIOLOGY	VERY GOOD 9		
TALMUD	VERY GOOD 9		
GEOGRAPHY OF ISRAEL	GOOD 8		

ON THE BASIS OF HIS STUDIES IN THE INSTITUTION AND THE RESULTS OF THE MATRICULATION EXAMINATIONS THE GRADUATE IS AWARDED THIS CERTIFICATE WHICH ENTITLES ITS HOLDER TO BE ADMITTED WITHOUT ENTRANCE EXAMINATIONS TO AN ACADEMIC INSTITUTION.

SEAL OF THE MINISTRY OF EDUCATION

SIGNED
PRINICPAL
(DR. M. MERON)

SIGNED
TEACHERS

JERUSALEM, JUNE 1, 1967
SEAL OF SCHOOL

SIGNED
DIRECTOR GENERAL #

3.2. Matriculation Certificate *(Teudat Bagrut),* Pre-1976 Format

משרד החינוך והתרבות

העתק

תעודת בגרות

בעל/ת תעודת זהות מס'

סיים(ה) בשנת ... כנבחן(ת) חיצוני(ת) את בחינות הבגרות
של משרד החינוך והתרבות וקיבל(ה) את הציונים הבאים:

על סמך האמור, ניתנת תעודה זו, המקנה לבעליה את הזכות להתקבל
למוסדות להשכלה גבוהה, בכפיפות לתנאי הקבלה הנהוגים בכל
אחד מהם

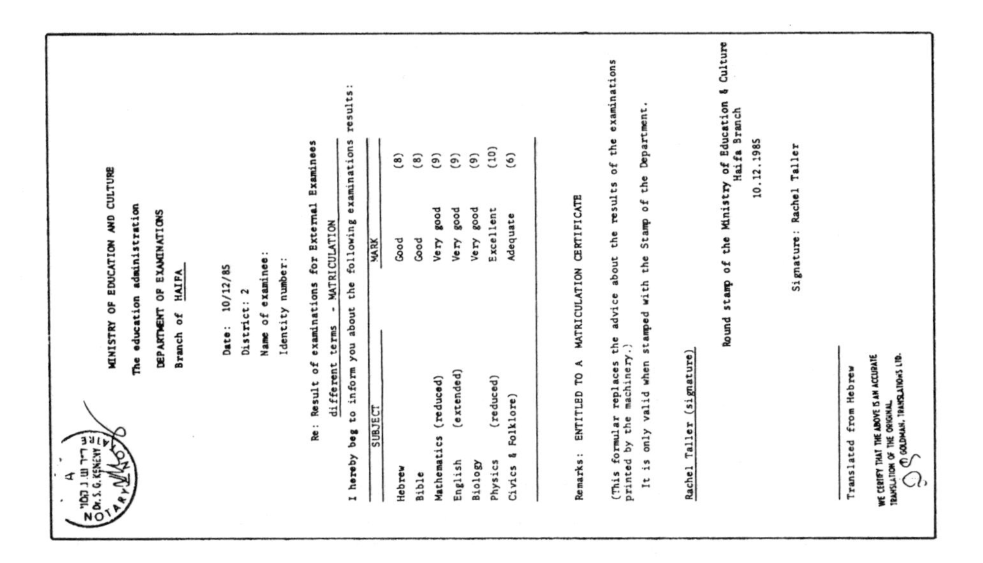

MINISTRY OF EDUCATION AND CULTURE

The education administration

DEPARTMENT OF EXAMINATIONS

Branch of HAIFA

Date: 10/12/85

District: 2

Name of examinee:

Identity number:

Re: Result of examinations for External Examinees different terms - MATRICULATION

I hereby beg to inform you about the following examinations results:

SUBJECT	MARK	
Hebrew	Good	(8)
Bible	Good	(8)
Mathematics (reduced)	Very good	(9)
English (extended)	Very good	(9)
Biology	Very good	(9)
Physics (reduced)	Excellent	(10)
Civics & Folklore)	Adequate	(6)

Remarks: ENTITLED TO A MATRICULATION CERTIFICATE

(This formular replaces the advice about the results of the examinations printed by the machinery.)

It is only valid when stamped with the Stamp of the Department.

Rachel Taller (signature)

Round stamp of the Ministry of Education & Culture
Haifa Branch

10.12.1985

Signature: Rachel Taller

Translated from Hebrew

WE CERTIFY THAT THE ABOVE IS AN ACCURATE TRANSLATION OF THE ORIGINAL.
GOLDMAN, TRANSLATIONS LTD.

Dr. S. G. KENENY NOTARY

3.3. Matriculation Certificate *(Teudat Bagrut)*, External Examination Results, 1985

Chapter 4

Teacher Training and the Education Profession

Teacher training in Israel is supervised and financed by the Ministry of Education and Culture (MOEC). Most teacher training programs up until recently have been provided in postsecondary teacher training colleges. It is the announced policy of the MOEC, however, to greatly reduce the number of teacher training colleges and to "academize" the profession, in part, through the support of nonuniversity "academic" institutions for teachers, of which there are presently five. This chapter describes teacher training programs and professional education programs in postsecondary institutions as well as institutions of higher education. Technology teacher training is discussed in Chapter 7.

An Overview

Preschool, primary and intermediate secondary school teachers are trained for the most part in postsecondary teacher training colleges. These institutions are under the administration and supervision of the Department of Teacher Training within the MOEC. They are categorized in accordance with the state educational system as State (secular), State Religious, or Arab. *Hinuch Atzma'i* or "Independent" teacher training colleges (for the ultra-orthodox) are permitted to operate also, but are outside the supervision of the MOEC. In addition, teacher training programs for preschool through the intermediate grades are offered by five accredited nonuniversity institutions of higher education. Teachers for this level have completed two-, three-, or four-year programs leading to teacher certification.

Secondary school teachers for academic subjects have normally completed bachelor's degree programs from an institution of higher education as well as one-year post-baccalaureate teacher certification programs frequently conducted through these same institutions. In addition, several postsecondary teacher training colleges offer secondary teacher certification programs for baccalaureate holders. In special subjects, such as art, music, physical education, and technology, graduates of three-year programs are qualified to teach these subjects in secondary schools.

In 1983-84, there were 41 teacher training colleges in the Hebrew sector enrolling 12,248 students (see Table 4.1). Enrollment was represented by 67% in State (secular) colleges, 22% in State Religious, and 11% in Independent (ultra-orthodox) Religious. There were two teacher training colleges in the Arab sector with 386 students. (See "Arab Education" in Chapter 1.) In the Hebrew sector, 84% were women, 16% men. In the Arab sector, 47% were women, 53% men. (*Statistical Abstract*, No. 35, p. 656)

Table 4.1. MOEC Teacher Training Colleges

Colleges Sponsored and Financed by the MOEC*

Jerusalem District

Michlalah, Jerusalem College for Women, Bayit Vegan, P.O. Box 16078, Jerusalem 91160 (SR)
The Efrata State Religious College (Beit-Midrash), Ben Yefuna 17, P.O. Box 10263, Jerusalem 91102 (SR)
The Beit-Yakov Institute for Teachers (Brandeis), P.O. Box 551, Jerusalem 94397 (I)
The David Yellin Teachers College, Bet Hakerem, Shdarot Herzel 89, P.O. Box 3578, Jerusalem 91035 (S)
The "Ram Lipschuetz" State Religious College for Teachers (men), Hillel 17 St., P.O. Box 2308, Jerusalem 91022 (SR)
The Teacher Training Institute for Independent Education, Kafach 6 St., Jerusalem 95200 (I)
The Yakov Herzog Institute for Teacher Training (Alon Shvot), Gush Etzion, Jerusalem 90805 (SR)

North and Haifa District

School of Education of the Kibbutz Movement, Oranim, Kiryat Tivon 36910 (S)
The A.D. Gordon College of Education, Tchernichovski 73, P.O. Box 1165, Haifa 35705 (S)
The Beit-Yakov Seminar in Haifa, Bar Cochva 5, Haifa 33127 (I)
The Oholo State College (Beit-Midrash), P.O. Emek Hayarden 15110 (S)
The Nahalal State College (Beit-Midrash), Nahalal 10600 (S)
The Neri Blumfield Hadassa-Vizu-Canada College, The School for Education and Teacher Training, Chana Sanesh 12, P.O. Box 4131, Haifa 31040 (S)
The Shaanan Religious College for Women, Derech Habbanim 101, Haifa 32162 (SR)
The State College (Beit-Midrash) for Arab Teachers, Ahhashmal 22, Haifa 33145 (S)

Tel-Aviv and Central District

Beit-Yakov Seminar, 4 Isacc Elhanan, Tel-Aviv 65250 (I)
College (Beit-Midrash) for Teachers Majoring in Judaism, Hraz 18, Rechovot 76110 (SR)
State Teachers College for Academicians, Borchov 3, Givatayim 53201 (S)
State Teachers College Seminar HaKibbutzim, Derech Haifa 149, Tel-Aviv 62507 (S)
The "Aliyah" Midrasha for Music, The Rav Herzog St., Petah-Tikva (SR)
The Beit-Berl Teachers Training College and the Institute for Arab Education, Beit-Berl Post 44905 (S)
The Beit-Rivka College (Beit-Midrash) for Teachers and Kindergarten Teachers, Kfar Habad B. 60978 (SR)
Levinsky Teachers College, Sushana Perasis 15, P.O. Box 48130, Tel-Aviv 61480 (S)
The "Or Chaim" College (Beit-Midrash) for Kindergarten and Vocational Teachers, P.O. Box 62, Bnai-Brak 53203 (I)
The "OROT Israel" State College for Women, 4 Aloff D. Markus St., P.O. Box 1033, Petah Tikva 49110 (SR)
The Religious College for Kindergarten Teachers and Teachers of Physical Education, P.O. Shkamim, Givat Washington 79860 (SR)
The Shein College for Education, Kaplan 42 St., Neva Oz, Petah-Tikva (S)
The State College (Beit-Midrash) for Teachers of Crafts, Patai 14, Givatayim 53203 (S)

The State College (Beit-Midrash) for Teachers of the Arts, Beit Fovrin 7 Ramat Halharon 47280 (S)
The State College (Beit-Midrash) for Administration Professions, Antiganos 6, Tel-Aviv 62664 (S)
The Talpiot State Religious College, 16–18 Dov Oz St., Tel-Aviv (SR)
The Zinman College of Physical Education at The Wingate Institute, Wingate Post Office, Netanya 42902 (S)

South District

The "Achavah" State College (Beit-Midrash), P.O. Shkamim, P.O. Box 85, Kiryat-Malachi, Beer-Tovia 84100 (S)
The Azta Religious State Beit-Midrash, P.O. Box 412, Nativot 79800 (SR)
The Kay and Hng. College for Education, P.O. Box 65, Yauda Halevi St., Beer-Sheva 80200 (S)

Institutions Sponsored but not Financed by the MOEC

"Kerem" Institution for Jewish Humanities Education, 7 Harav Avida St., Jerusalem 94268
The Centre for Technological Education in Holon, 52 Golomb St., Holon 58102
The "Gour" Orthodox Institute in Bnei-Brak, 28 Herzog St., Bnei-Brak 51125
The High (Postsecondary) School for Technology, 21 Avad Aleumi, P.O. Box 16031, Jerusalem 91160
The Rubin Academy of Music, 7 Peretz Smolenskin St., Jerusalem 92101
The "Vizniz" Orthodox Institute in Bnei-Brak, 3 Tal Chaim St., Bnei-Brak 51125

*I = Independent, S = State, SR = State Religious.

Teacher Training Qualifications

The qualifications of teachers reflect a transition from two-year to three-year to four-year programs. Minimally, a two-year pedagogical program is required for certification to teach in day-care centers, nursery schools, and kindergartens. In the past, primary school teachers also have been qualified upon completion of a two-year program. Since 1980, however, most primary and intermediate school teachers have completed a three-year program. At the same time, it is possible to complete a four-year Bachelor of Education (B.Ed.) program qualifying a teacher at these same levels (preschool through grade 10). This is a reflection of the "academization" of the teaching profession.

Teacher qualifications at this level are basically represented by two types of certification. Two-year programs lead to certification as a Qualified Teacher *(Teudat Horahah)*. Three-year programs lead to certification as a Senior Qualified Teacher *(Teudat Horahah Bachir)*. A four-year B.Ed. program leads to a Senior Qualified Teacher Certificate in addition to the degree. The certificate itself states the length of the program and the level and/or subject specialization the teacher is qualified to teach.

Note: Teacher qualifications are presented on a document which uses the word *teudat*. *Teudat* is translated as certificate or diploma. Translators will use the phrases "teacher's certificate," "teacher's diploma," and "teacher's certification" interchangeably with reference to the one and only document designating certification.

Entrance Requirements

Since 1980, more stringent requirements for acceptance to teacher training colleges (except for intending nursery and kindergarten teachers) have been established. Most institutions require the Matriculation Certificate *(Teudat Bagrut)* or at least four examinations passed at the matriculation level. In addition, a national entrance examination and definitive conditions for acceptance have been instituted. Advancement to the final year of study is now conditional upon completing these requirements for admission. In 1982-83, 72.5% of students enrolled in teacher training colleges had the Matriculation Certificate, including some 1,100 students who were tested for a full series of matriculation examinations but had not received the results (13.5% had passed at least four matriculation exams). The remaining 14% had either no subjects passed at the matriculation level or less than four, and were accepted on the basis of other qualifications. *(Statistical Abstract,* No. 35, p. 657)

Teacher Training Programs

There are eight main categories of teacher training programs offered by teacher training colleges, including the teacher training colleges that are also institutions of higher education.

- Preschool Teachers for children 3-6 years of age.
- Early Childhood Teachers for grades K-2.
- Primary School Teachers for grades 3-6.
- Special Education Teachers.
- Intermediate School Teachers for grades 7-9 specializing in two subjects, a major and a minor subject.
- Intermediate School Teachers for grades 7-10 for individuals with a Bachelor of Education.
- Teachers for Art, Music, Physical Education, and Technology for grades 1-12.
- Secondary School Teachers for grades 7-12 in special subjects: Bible, Jewish History, Religious subjects, and Torah, where teacher training is completed in religious institutions.

According to the categories for statistical reporting, the 12,248 students in Hebrew sector teacher training colleges were registered in programs as follows: kindergarten teachers (509), teachers for grades 1-2 (1,676), teachers for grades 3-6 (2,377), special education teachers (1,105), intermediate school teachers (3,185), vocational teachers (3,396). Arab sector enrollment by program was not reported. *(Statistical Abstract,* No. 35, p. 656)

While the MOEC prescribes minimum standards and curriculums for teacher training programs, each institution has a degree of autonomy beyond MOEC guidelines and, therefore, variance among institutional programs exists. Generally speaking, the MOEC prescribes a minimum percentage of time allotted to the various aspects of teacher training. These areas include courses in professional education and didactics (30% or 9 weekly hours), specialization courses (40% or 12 weekly hours), an experiential component including methods, microteaching and practice teaching (20% or 6 weekly hours) and preparation for special units (10% or 3 weekly hours). This represents a minimum of 30 weekly hours each year for two, three, or four years. A sample three- and four-year program in teaching physical education in grades 1-12 is provided in sample document 4.1. Programs for preschool special education and other program categories are briefly described in the nonuniversity institutional profiles in Chapter 8 for the institutions listed below.

Teacher Training Programs in Four-Year Institutions

The scope of teacher training programs in the nonuniversity institutions of higher education encompasses all categories of programs listed above and programs for Qualified and Senior Qualified Teachers. Their programs do not qualify secondary school teachers of academic subjects, but do qualify special subject teachers (art, music, physical education, and technology). Programs offered include the two-, three- and four-year programs as well as post-baccalaureate certification programs and post-diploma programs. The five nonuniversity institutions of higher education include Beit-Berl Teachers Training College, Levinsky Teachers College, Michlalah-Jerusalem College for Women, the David Yellin Teachers College and The Zinman College of Physical Education at the Wingate Institute. In addition, the Jerusalem College of Technology (men) is an accredited nonuniversity institution involved in teacher training programs for technology teachers. The State Teachers College Seminar HaKibbutzim offers three- and four-year diploma programs in teacher training and has applied for accreditation and approval to award a Bachelor of Education degree (see the institutional profiles in Chapter 8).

The five nonuniversity institutions are accredited and authorized by the Council for Higher Education to award a Bachelor of Education. In these institutions, the degree program is offered in addition to other certification and diploma programs. The application and approval process for accreditation by the Council required these institutions to enhance the "academic" thrust of the curriculum and to extend the length of programs from three to four years. Now that these institutions are permitted to award the B.Ed., Senior Qualified Teachers may enroll for an additional year and earn this degree. This situation is exemplified by sample document 4.1 from Zinman which also illustrates how institutions "academize" and upgrade their programs.

Credits, Examinations, Grading and Transcripts

Examinations in teacher training colleges are both internal and external. Most transcripts report subjects and grades for the entire program, grouped according to areas of study rather than on a year-by-year basis. It is, therefore, difficult to assign a credit or weighting factor to grades unless class hours are also provided. If class hours are provided, they do not designate lecture, exercise, or practical components. The best source for the evaluation of credits and course content is a detailed course and program description. Since all such information is usually accessible only in Hebrew, English translations are not readily available. Such details are sometimes provided upon request.

Grading is usually reported on a 0-100 or 0-10 point scale. Normally a breakdown of the grading scale, minimum passing grade, or transcript legend is not indicated. See traditional grading practices in "Grading Practices," Chapter 3 for guidelines.

Teacher Training and Professional Education Programs in the Universities

University programs in education offered at the baccalaureate level are in professional education rather than teacher training. Professional education includes optional majors such as Counselor Education and Vocational Guidance, Didactics and Administration (Instruction and Curriculum Planning), Special Education, and Theory (History, Philosophy, Sociology and/or Psychology of Education).

Education for teacher certification in university institutions is normally an optional post-baccalaureate program to train teachers for secondary schools (grades 7-12). Some departments permit students to enter a teacher certification program after completion of the second year of the bachelor's program, thereby extending the bachelor's program one year beyond its normal length (usually three years). In such instances, an example of the pedagogical content for the two-year program is as follows: First Year—Fundamentals in Educational Psychology, Theory of Education and Instruction, tutorials, workshops, practice teaching, and additional courses related to the student's subject area of instruction. Second Year—Didactic Seminar (in the teaching discipline), Selected Topics in Education, Sociological Aspects of Education, The Underprivileged Child, workshops in the subject of instruction. Other programs for teacher certification for the secondary level are described as requiring an additional 12 annual hours (approximately 24 semester credits) during or after completion of the degree program. University teacher certification program requirements vary from department to department and from institution to institution. It is, therefore, advisable to request specific program information directly from the faculty, department, or university academic secretary of the institution concerned.

Universities with schools or faculties of education may also offer master's degree programs to train educators in educational research, pedagogy, or as teachers for teacher training colleges. Master's degree programs in professional education are also provided in educational administration and supervision, educational planning; academic, personal and vocational counseling;

school psychology; school sociology; and other professional areas. These programs, like most master's degree programs, extend over a minimum two-year period.

In-Service Training Programs

In-service training programs provide professional growth and opportunities for upgrading or enhancing qualifications along with commensurate salary increments. In-service programs are available to all education personnel throughout the system in 45 regional, district, and national Pedagogic Centers. These Centers may be located in schools, teacher training colleges, institutions of higher education, other public institutions, or in self-contained facilities. They are all funded through the MOEC but are operated variously by professional teacher organizations, teacher training colleges, public institutes specializing in such programs or by the MOEC itself.

The principal areas of in-service training are *subjects of instruction*—updating knowledge, innovations in science and practical experience in instruction; *innovative teaching techniques*—theoretical background and philosophical concepts of techniques, experiential workshops for implementing new techniques; *support sciences for education*—study of recent developments in anthropology, psychology, sociology, research methods, etc.; *enrichment* subjects—meriting repeated scientific research or repeated press coverage, e.g., history of the Land of Israel, history of Jewish philosophy, regional problems; *technological subjects*—theoretical innovations, experiential workshops, instruction in new technologies.

In-service programs are scheduled to accommodate the working teacher, and, therefore, reflect numerous patterns. The most common program schedules are weekly meetings of 2-4 hours during the school year after school hours (total 60 hours); bi-weekly meetings of 2-4 hours during the school year after school hours (total 30-45 hours); one day/all day seminars (5-8 hours); concentrated courses for 5-9 hours daily for 5-10 consecutive days during vacation periods (total 25-45 hours per week); one weekly day of study throughout the school year (approximately 200 hours). The MOEC also encourages independent study through correspondence courses and/or Everyman's University by granting tuition scholarships.

All teachers have an opportunity to belong to two funds that provide financing for in-service programs. After 6-8 years of service, teachers may elect to take a sabbatical leave for professional study. Approval for sabbatic leave is partially dependent upon the amount of money that has accrued as a result of monthly contributions by the teacher to the fund, as well as by the MOEC's sizeable contribution. In 1980, 3,000 teachers were on sabbatic leave due to the adoption of this fund and program.

THE ZINMAN COLLEGE OF PHYSICAL EDUCATION AT THE WINGATE INSTITUTE

RECORD OF STUDIES

This is to certify that ________ ______________

was registered as a regular student in this College during

the academic year(s) ______1978/79; 1979/80; 1980/81__________

and attended the courses specified hereunder:

COURSE	NATURE OF COURSE	NO. OF WEEKLY HOURS	GRADE
1) BASIC STUDIES			
a) Hebrew	L	3	8 (Good)
b) Selected Studies in Judaism	L	2	8 (Good)
c) English	Ex	4	8 (Good)
d) Science: Chemistry, Biochem.	Lab	2	7 (Fair)
e) Science: Mathematics, Physics	Lab	1	9 (Very Good)
f) Music Appreciation	Lab	1	9 (Very Good)
g) First Aid	Lab	1	8 (Good)
2) EDUCATION			
a) History, Philosophy and Principles of Education	L	2	9 (Very Good)
b) Educational Psychology	L&Ex	2	7 (Fair)
c) Developmental Psychology	L&Ex	2	9 (Very Good)
d) Research Methods in Education & Physical Education	L&Ex	2	7 (Fair)
3) PHYSICAL EDUCATION SCIENCES			
a) Anatomy	L&Lab	3	7 (Fair)
b) Physiology	L&Lab	2	8 (Good)
c) Physiology of Work	L&Lab	2	8 (Good)
d) Kinesiology	L	1	8 (Good)
e) Biomechanics	L&Lab	2	8 (Good)
f) History, Philosophy and Principles of P.E.	L&Ex	2	10 (Excellent)

(Continued - P.2)

ABBREVIATIONS:
L - Lecture
Ex - Exercise
S - Seminar
Lab - Laboratory

LIST OF GRADES AND THEIR NUMERICAL EQUIVALENT:
Excellent = 10
Very Good = 9
Good = 8
Fair = 7
Passed = 6
Failed = 5 or under

PHYSICAL EDUCATION TEACHERS COLLEGE At The Wingate Institute Israel

ZINMAN COLLEGE OF PHYSICAL EDUCATION AT THE WINGATE INSTITUTE

COURSE	NATURE OF COURSE	NO. OF WEEKLY HOURS	GRADE
g) Sociology of Sports	L&Ex	2	8 (Good)
h) Psychological Aspects of Competitive Sports	L&Ex	2	8 (Good)
i) Physical Fitness	L&Lab	2	6 (Passed)
j) Organization of P.E.	L&Ex	1	8 (Good)
k) Methods of P.E. in Elementary Schools and Junior H.S.	L&Ex	2	9 (Very Good)
l) Methods of P.E. in H.S.	L&Ex	2	8 (Good)
m) Street Groups & Youth Clubs	S	2	8 (Good)
n) Final Term Paper			8 (Good)
4) PRACTICE AND STUDENT TEACHING			
a) Grades 1-3		1	8 (Good)
b) Elementary and Junior H.S.		10	9 (Very Good)
c) Senior H.S.		5	9 (Very Good)
5) MINOR SPECIALIZATION AREA P.E. for Grades K-3		7	9 (Very Good)
6) SKILLS			
a) Basic Gymnastics		6	7 (Fair)
b) Olympic Gymnastics		3	6 (Passed)
c) Track & Field		3	7 (Fair)
d) Swimming		3	8 (Good)
e) Basketball		2	9 (Very Good)
f) Volleyball		2	8 (Good)
g) Handball		2	8 (Good)
h) Folk Dance		2	7 (Fair)
i) Soccer		1	8 (Good)
j) Movement & Rhythm		1	7 (Fair)
k) Recreation Games		2	9 (Very Good)
l) Advanced Basketball		2	9 (Very Good)

This student is entitled to receive his physical education teaching diploma for elementary and high schools.

PHYSICAL EDUCATION TEACHERS COLLEGE At The Wingate Institute Israel

DATE: April 21, 1985

SIGNED: J. Ben-Yoseph, Ph.D.
Certification Officer

PHYSICAL EDUCATION TEACHERS COLLEGE At The Wingate Institute Israel

WINGATE POST OFFICE NETANYA ISRAEL — TELEPHONE 053-38044

4.1a. Four-Year B.Ed. Degree with Three-Year Teaching Diploma, The Zinman College of Physical Education at The Wingate Institute, pages 1 and 2

THE ZINMAN COLLEGE OF PHYSICAL EDUCATION AT THE WINGATE INSTITUTE

RECORD OF STUDIES

TO WHOM IT MAY CONCERN:

This is to certify that (I.D. No.) was registered as a fourth year student at our College during the academic year 1984/85 and attended the courses specified hereunder:

	COURSE	NO. OF WEEKLY HOURS	GRADE
1)	Psychology: Abnormal Behavior	2	9 (Very Good)
2)	Motor Learning	2	8 (Good)
3)	Management of Leisure and Recreation Services	2	9 (Very Good)
4)	Introduction to Computers	1	7 (Fair)
5)	Sociology of Sport	2	9 (Very Good)
6)	Organizational Behavior & Administration P.E.	2	9 (Very Good)
7)	Sociology	2	8 (Good)
8)	Tests and Measurement in Education and P.E.	2	7 (Fair)
9)	Exercise Physiology	2	7 (Fair)
10)	Final Term Paper		8 (Good)

This student has completed all course requirements and is entitled to receive his B.Ed. degree.

DATE: October 2, 1985

SIGNED: ____________

J. Ben-Yoseph, Ph.D.
Certification Officer

PHYSICAL EDUCATION TEACHERS COLLEGE
The Wingate Institute Israel

WINGATE POST OFFICE NETANYA ISRAEL — TELEPHONE 053-38044

4.1b. page 3

Chapter 5

Nursing and Other Health Professions

Nursing

The Ministry of Health, Nursing Division, is responsible for authorizing the establishment of schools of nursing, administering and supervising nursing education programs, establishing standards, and overseeing registration and licensing examinations. Inquiries concerning Nursing may be addressed to the Nursing Division, Ministry of Health, Rehov Ben Tabai 2, Jerusalem 93591, Israel. Telephone: (02) 638212.

Nursing is taught as an optional trend in technological secondary schools, schools of nursing, and in three universities. The three levels of nursing training in Israel are categorized as Basic Nursing Education (including transition programs), Post-Basic Nursing Education, and Baccalaureate Nursing Education. Nursing education leads to the qualifications of Practical Nurse, Registered (Qualified Professional) Nurse, Bachelor of Nursing, Bachelor of Nursing Science and post-basic nursing diplomas in specialization courses.

Schools of Nursing are recognized and supervised by the Ministry of Health (see list below). Since 1976, all Schools of Nursing have been independent and, therefore, charge for tuition, fees, and room and board. All schools observe the laws of *Kashrut* (dietary laws); however, only Jerusalem's Shaare Zedek Hospital and its School of Nursing observe orthodox customs and traditions.

1. The Jelin School of Nursing, Rambam Hospital, Haifa
2. Seide School of Nursing, Rothschild Hospital, Haifa
3. Natius School of Nursing, Hillel-Yafe Hospital, Hadera
4. "Scheinbrun" School of Nursing, Tel-Aviv
5. Dina School of Nursing (formerly Beilinson School of Nursing), Beilinson Medical Center, Petah Tikva
6. Henrietta Szold School of Nursing, The Hebrew University-Hadassah Medical Center, Ein Kerem, Jerusalem
7. The Harry and Abe Sherman School of Nursing, Emek Yezreel Medical Center, Afula
8. Recanati School for Health Professions in the Community, School of Nursing, Ben-Gurion University of the Negev, Beer-Sheva
9. School of Nursing, Hasharon Hospital, Petah Tikva
10. School of Nursing, Assaf Harofe Hospital, Sarafand
11. School of Nursing, Kaplan Hospital, Rehovot
12. School of Nursing, Barzilai Medical Center, Ashkelon
13. School of Nursing, Shaare Zedek Hospital, Jerusalem

14. Tessler Nursing School (formerly Kiryat Sanz Laniado School for Registered Nurses) also known as Laniado School of Nursing, Kiriyat Sanz Hospital, Netanya
15. School of Nursing, Chaim Sheba Medical Center, Tel Hashomer Hospital, Ramat Gan

Basic Nursing Education

Practical Nursing

Practical nurses in Israel work under the supervision of a Registered Nurse and/or a doctor. Their duties include admitting new patients, easing patients' discomfort and attending to their needs, serving meals, collecting material for tests, dispensing medicine, and preparing medical treatment. The Practical Nurse is expected to observe professional medical behavior.

From 1947-54, practical nursing education was a 12-month hospital nursing program requiring eight years of education for admission. In 1954, the program was extended to 15 months, then increased to 18 months. Since 1981, the minimum education requirement has been increased from 8 to 10 years. The program leads to registration as a Practical Nurse by the Ministry of Health.

In 1978-79, compulsory education was extended to 10 years. The Ministry of Education and Culture and the Ministry of Health considered nursing education (as an optional vocational trend) a vehicle for expanding the general education qualifications of Practical Nurses while at the same time generating opportunities for young women in vocational education. The high school practical nursing program actually began in 1973 on a very limited basis with three participating high schools. Today, 18 schools offer practical nursing as a vocational trend option under the joint supervision of the Ministry of Education and Culture and the Ministry of Health. At the same time, hospital nursing school programs for practical nurses are still offered through the Ministry of Health. In either case, both programs require the same government examination, earn the same title, and are considered professionally equivalent.

HIGH SCHOOL PROGRAM. The three and one-half year high school practical nursing program consists of general (academic) and nursing education beginning in grade 10. The program combines general, theoretical, and practical education throughout grades 10, 11, and 12 and continues for six months beyond the end of grade 12 with study in professional subjects and clinical experience. Some graduates of this program may earn the Matriculation Certificate (*Teudat Bagrut*), while others may receive the Secondary School Final Diploma (*Teudat Gemer Tichonit*, also called the Leaving Certificate). Graduates of the practical nursing program are required to pass at least three matriculation examinations and government examinations in order to qualify for the Diploma and registration as a Practical Nurse by the Ministry of Health.

18-MONTH HOSPITAL PROGRAM. The 18-month program requires applicants to have completed at least 10 years of education and generally caters to an older student. The nursing curriculum is essentially the same but no high school subjects are taken. Completion of the course and government examinations results in registration as a Practical Nurse by the Ministry of Health.

Practical nurses may be eligible to continue to one post-basic diploma program in Operating Theatre Nurse and/or may enter an 18-month transition course to be upgraded to Registered Nurse.

Registered Nurse (Qualified Professional Nurse)

Training for Registered (Qualified or Professional) Nurses in Israel is offered through 15 schools of nursing recognized and supervised by the Ministry of Health. Admission to schools of nursing in the Registered (Professional) Nursing program requires successful completion of 12 years of general education. Preference is given to those who hold a Matriculation Certificate (*Teudat Bagrut*). An interview, psychometric, and/or aptitude tests are generally required. Applicants must be between the ages of 17-35, have an adequate (if not fluent) knowledge of Hebrew, a good knowledge of written English, and be in good health.

The three-year program includes approximately 30-40 class hours per week, 46-48 weeks per year. Study in the first year is mostly theoretical. Study in the second year and first half of the third combines theory and practice. The last half of the third year is practical clinical experience. Coursework is grouped into Basic Sciences, Social Sciences, and Medical and Nursing Topics. The number of hours of clinical practice may vary according to field and the resources of the individual school. The standard curriculum for Registered Nurses (R.N.'s) is illustrated in Table 5.1.

The transition program is a supplementary course for Practical Nurses who meet the general admission standards of the R.N. program. The duration of the course is 18 months, adjusted to the individual's previous experience.

Government qualifying examinations for Registered Nurse are both written and practical, and are held at the same time in all nursing schools throughout the country. Unsuccessful candidates may retake the examination on the failed subject(s) twice, depending on the student's scholastic and practical performance during the program. Successful examinees receive certificates and are registered with the Nursing Division, Ministry of Health.

Post-Basic Nursing Education

The following certificate courses are supplementary courses for promotional upgrading that lead to specialized qualifications. Each course is open to Registered Nurses. In addition, a license in midwifery and a diploma in operating theatre nurse are offered.

NURSING EDUCATION (NURSE-INSTRUCTOR). The Nurse-Instructor certificate course is a nine month program that includes 500 hours of study in addition to group projects and practice teaching. The curriculum includes coursework in critical reading, general psychology, group dynamics, introduction to statistical research, principles of administration, psychology of learning, selected

Table 5.1. Registered Nurse—Standard Three-Year Curriculum, 1985–86

Subjects	Hours	Subjects	Hours
Theoretical Subjects		*Clinical Nursing Theory continued*	
Basic Sciences	*(444)*	Obstetrics & Gynecology	54
Anatomy & Physiology	152	Obstetrical Nursing	26
Gen. & Organic Chemistry	97	Operating Room	9
Microbiology	65	Pediatric	34
Nutrition & Dietetics	33	Psychiatric	45
Pathology & Histology	40	Public Health	45
Pharmacy & Med. Materials	57	Surgery	124
Social Sciences	*(437)*	Surgical Nursing	28
Anthropology	56	Well and Sick Child	78
Developmental Psychology	56	**Clinical Experience**	
Organiza. & Mgmt. Intro.	56	*Nursing Practice*	*(2,150)*
Psychology Introduction	94	Community Health	150
Social Psychology	56	Emergency Room	96
Sociology	63	Maternity	240
Stats. & Research Meth.	56	Medical	384
Nursing Background	*(291)*	Nursing Fundamentals	160
Communication	36	Operating Room	160
Concepts	36	Out-Patient Clinic	144
Fundamentals	183	Pediatric	240
Procedures	36	Psychiatric	192
Clinical Nursing Theory	*(640)*	Surgical	384
Disaster & First Aid	31		
Internal Medicine	107		
Medical Nursing	59		

SOURCE: Nursing Division, Ministry of Health, Israel.

nursing subjects, sociology, theory and methods of teaching, and written and oral communication. Successful completion of the course results in certification as Nurse-Instructor.

PUBLIC HEALTH NURSING (PUBLIC HEALTH NURSE). The Public Health Nurse certificate course is a 12-month program that includes 500 hours of study in addition to 36 weeks of extensive field work in all segments of public health nursing. The curriculum includes coursework in chronic disease nursing, demography, epidemiology, group dynamics, growth and development, health education, instruction and teaching methods, introduction to psychology, introduction to public health, introduction to sociology and anthropology, introduction to statistical research, maternal and child nursing, mental health nursing, methods of self-instruction and expression, nursing principles in public health, nutrition and human health, occupational nursing, old age and nursing care of the aged, principles of administration, rehabilitation, religious and traditional customs, sanitation, and school health problems. The practice period includes 13 weeks of community and family nursing, 12 weeks of school nursing, one week in homes for the aged, 2 weeks for chronically ill patients in the hospital and community, six weeks in psychiatric hospitals and clinics, one and one-half weeks in epidemiology in the hospital and community, and one-half week in occupational health. Successful completion of the course results in certification as a qualified Public Health Nurse.

NURSING SERVICE ADMINISTRATION (NURSE ADMINISTRATOR). The Nursing Service Administration course is a nine-month program that requires 500 hours of study in addition to group projects and practice teaching. The curriculum includes general psychology, group dynamics, introduction to statistical research, nursing service management and supervision, principles of administration, management and supervision, selected nursing subjects, sociology, theory and methods of adult education, and written and oral communication. Successful completion of the course results in certification as a Nurse Administrator.

MENTAL HEALTH NURSING (MENTAL HEALTH NURSE). The Mental Health Nurse certificate course is a 12-month program requiring 500 hours of theory in addition to extensive practical training. The first six months of study include theoretical coursework taken concurrently with three days of practical training. The last six months involve supervised practical training. Successful completion of the course results in certification as a Mental Health Nurse.

MIDWIFERY. The course in Midwifery is now open only to female Registered Nurses and requires passing of government examinations as well as applying for a license. Midwives may not practice without a license. Practical nurse-midwifery programs have been phased out. The nine-month program requires 317 hours of theory taken concurrently with 38 weeks of practice. The curriculum includes theoretical coursework in anesthesia, anthropology, communication, gynecology, health education, obstetrics, obstetric nursing, pediatrics, psychology, religious laws and customs, and statistics and national insurance regulations. Midwifery is offered at the Ministry of Health's School of Nursing, Chaim Sheba Medical Center, Tel Hashomer Hospital in Ramat Gan; and the Henrietta Szold School of Nursing, The Hebrew University-Hadassa Medical Center, Ein Kerem, Jerusalem. A license in Midwifery is awarded upon successful completion of the program and passing the government examination.

OPERATING THEATRE NURSE. The supplementary course in Operating Theatre (O.T.) Nurse is open to both Practical and Registered Nurses who meet the general admission standards. The seven-month course includes 20 weeks of concurrent practice in the operating theatre. Course content covers guidance and teamwork, principles and use of electricity, principles of supervision, psychological aspects of O.T., radiation and special instruments used in the modern O.T., and safety measures in the operating theatre. Successful completion of the course leads to a diploma and registration as an Operating Theatre Nurse.

Other post-basic nursing courses are offered in gerontology, growth and development, and psychology but there is no registration certificate awarded upon completion of these courses.

Baccalaureate Nursing Education

The nursing profession in Israel has become increasingly academic just as it has in the United States. The Bachelor of Nursing (B.Nurs.) and Bachelor of Nursing Science (B.Nurs.Sc.) are degrees in nursing offered by three universities: the Ben-Gurion University of the Negev, The Hebrew University of Jerusalem, and Tel-Aviv University. Baccalaureate nursing education is discussed in "Nursing," in Chapter 8.

Medical Laboratory Technology and Medical Registration

Medical Laboratory Technology is a paraprofessional program offered at postsecondary technological institutions. The program leads to certification and licensing under the supervision of the Ministry of Health and the National Institute for Technological Training. The two-year program leads to the title of Certified Medical Laboratory Technician. (See "Technological Education" in Chapter 7.)

Medical Registration is a paraprofessional program offered at postsecondary technological institutions. This program leads to certification and licensing under the governance and supervision of the Ministry of Health and the National Institute for Technological Training. (See "Technological Education" in Chapter 7.)

Occupational Therapy

Occupational Therapy is available at two universities in Israel. The Hebrew University of Jerusalem, Faculty of Medicine, School of Occupational Therapy awards a three year Bachelor of Occupational Therapy (B.O.T.).

Tel-Aviv University, School of Occupational Therapy awards a two-year post-baccalaureate Certificate in Occupational Therapy for students with a bachelor's degree in a field other than Occupational Therapy. The program is two years in length (24 months) and includes a five-month field work component (1,022 hours). In addition, the School offers a Master's in Occupational Health (M.Occ.H.). This program includes coursework in occupational medicine, occupational hygiene, and occupational behavioral sciences.

Physiotherapy (Physical Therapy)

In July 1982, the Israel National Council for Advanced Studies (for Higher Education) approved the opening of a Department of Physical Therapy in the Tel-Aviv University, Sackler Faculty of Medicine, and authorized a four-year program leading to the degree of Bachelor of Physical Therapy. The University was authorized to award the degree to graduates from the last four classes of students (1978-1981) who have studied according to this program.

Prior to 1982, there were three Schools of Physical Therapy which awarded three year diplomas in Physical Therapy, but not degrees. These three Schools, which have now been incorporated into the Tel-Aviv University Department of Physical Therapy, are the School of Physical Therapy (Ministry of Health), Assaf Harofe Hospital, Sarafand; the School of Physical Therapy (Kupat Holim, Workers Sick Fund), Zinman College of Physical Education at the Wingate Institute; and the School of Physical Therapy (Ministry of Health), Chaim Sheba Medical Centre, Tel Hashomer Hospital, Ramat Gan.

Admission to the program requires the Matriculation Certificate (*Teudat Bagrut*), the psychometric examinations, Israeli residency, and a minimum level of English and Hebrew proficiency as evaluated by the psychometric examination. Selection is made on the basis of the matriculation examination results and the psychometric exam. Applicants must be 18-35 years of age.

First year studies take place on the Tel-Aviv University campus. After the first year, students are assigned to one of the three Schools of Physiotherapy, listed above, taking into account the students' preference. Studies from the second to the fourth year take place at the Schools, with students returning to the Tel-Aviv campus for a small number of courses, and to hospitals, clinics, and other institutions for their clinical affiliations. One set of final examinations is held for the students from all three Schools. See Tables 5.2 and 5.3 for three- and four-year programs in physiotherapy, respectively.

Table 5.2. Three-Year Curriculum in Physiotherapy, School of Physiotherapy, Zinman College of Physical Education, Wingate Institute

Subjects	Theory	Prac.	Subjects	Theory	Prac.
Basic Courses	**(594)**	**(204)**	**Related Medical Subjects**	**(374)**	**(–)**
Anatomy	170	68	Diseases of Skin, Eyes,		
Chemistry	42	17	Ears, Nose & Throat	34	–
Developmental Psych.	34	–	Fundmntls. of Geriatrics	34	–
Intro. to Pathology	34	–	Fundmntls. of Internal		
Intro. to Psychology	34	–	Medicine & Microbiology	51	–
Intro. to Sociology	51	–	Fundmntls. of Neurology	85	–
Kinesiology	68	68	Fundmntls. of Obstetrics &		
Physics	42	17	Gynecology	68	–
Physiology	85	34	Fundmntls. of Orthopedics	68	–
Psych. of Disabled	34	–	Fundmntls. of Surgery	34	–
Professional Courses	**(513)**	**(595)**	**Practical Experience**	**(–)**	**(1,782)**
Hydrotherapy	8	17	Physical Fitness	(–)	192
Electromechanics	92	17	Clinical Observation	–	46
Electrother./Actinother.	51	102	Clinical Practice	–	1,510
Intro. to Methods of					
Admin. & Research	34	–	**Specialization Electives**		
Manual Muscle Test. &			(Two from the following):	(34)	–
Body Measurements	25	51	Pre- & Postnatal Exercises,		
Massage	40	85	Specializ. in Treatment of		
Rehab./Daily Activities	25	17	Cerebral Palsy, Sport &		
Therapeutic Exercises	85	102	Recreation for Disabled,		
Therapeutic Procedures	102	102	Sport & Work Injuries,		
Practicum-Spec. Meth.			Treatment of the Aged,		
in Therapeut. Exer.	51	102	Treatment of Respiratory		
			Diseases (17 hrs. each)		
			Grand Totals	(1,515)	(2,581)

SOURCE: School of Physiotherapy, Wingate Institute, and Kupat-Holim, Health Insurance Institute (also called Central Workers Sick Fund).

Table 5.3. Bachelor of Physical Therapy Curriculum, Department of Physical Therapy, Sackler Faculty of Medicine, Tel-Aviv University

Subject	Hours	Subject	Hours
	Basic Studies		
Anat./Physiol. of Nervous Sys.	52	Intro. to Psychology	60
Child Development	40	Intro. to Sociol. & Antro.	60
Compara. Vertebrate Anatomy	60	Intro. to Stats. & Rsrch. Meth.	76
Genetics	30	Pathological Chemistry	50
Histology & Pathology	72	Physics	130
Human Anatomy	150	Physiology	95
Instruct. for Seminar Work	30	Total	920
Interview Techniques & Communica.	15		
	Medical Studies		
Clinical Geriatrics	30	Pediatrics	30
Epidemiol. & Public Health	30	Rehab. Psychology	30
Intens. Care & Respira. Diseas.	45	Rheumatology	30
Internal Medicine	45	Select. Med. Subjs. (Dermatol., E.N.T., OB/GYN, Opthalmology)	45
Intro. to Psychiatry	30		
Neurology	60	Surgery	45
Orthopedics	120	Total	540
	Physical Therapy & Allied Subjects		
Cardiac Rehabilitation	15	Nursing Techniques	10
Electrodiagnostics	30	Pathophysiol. of Exertion	30
Electrother. & Thermother.	90	Posture	30
First Aid	20	Rehab. in Spinal Cord Injuries	30
Gymnastics & Movement I	30	Rehabilitation of Amputees	45
Kinesiology	75	Rehabilitation Techniques	30
Massage	60	Sport Injuries	30
Neurology Rehabilitation	45	Tests & Measurements	30
Neuropediatrics	30	Therapeutic Exercise	180
		Total	810
	Physical Therapy Electives*		
Family Med. & Primary Care	30	Intro. to Gerontology	30
Intro. to Community Health	30	Sport/Leisure Activ. in Rehab.	30
		Total	90
General University Electives	240		
Clinical Affiliations	1,050		
Grand Total	3,650		

SOURCE: Department of Physical Therapy, Sackler Faculty of Medicine, Tel-Aviv University.
*Each affiliate School of Physical Therapy offers three electives.

Chapter 6

Overseas Student Programs in Israel

The many study abroad programs available in Israel are classified in this chapter as accredited or non-accredited—i.e., "academic" or "nonacademic"—in accordance with the status of the institution within Israel.

Accredited "Academic" Overseas Student Programs (OSP's)

One-Year and Other Special Programs for Overseas Students

The One-Year Program (O-YP) is designed for overseas students who want a "study abroad," credit-bearing educational experience in Israel and do not intend to study towards an Israeli degree. Student status is that of a visiting student. While the program is designed as a one-year academic experience, some students complete only one semester; others remain for more than one year. Ben-Gurion University of the Negev, Bar-Ilan University, The University of Haifa, The Hebrew University of Jerusalem, Jerusalem Rubin Academy of Music and Dance, Jerusalem College of Technology, Michlalah-Jerusalem College for Women, and Tel-Aviv University all offer One-Year Programs.

Other special programs offered to overseas students include summer session and one-semester programs, joint *kibbutz*-university programs, one-semester or one-year graduate programs, and programs for mid-year and high school graduates, all of which issue transcripts designating credits or hours and grades. While there are many other special educational or experiential opportunities offered to foreigners on the university campuses, normally transcripts are issued only for credit-bearing courses or programs.

The University of Haifa and the Hebrew University of Jerusalem require applicants to have completed one year of university-level study at an accredited institution of higher learning prior to enrolling. Bar-Ilan University, Ben-Gurion University of the Negev, Jerusalem College of Technology, Michlalah-Jerusalem College for Women, and Tel-Aviv University accept students without prior university attendance. Students are admitted on the basis of prior academic performance (generally, a "B" grade point average or better), letters of recommendation, the U.S. Scholastic Aptitude Test (SAT) or aptitute tests and, sometimes, an interview.

Familiarity with Hebrew is an advantage but not a prerequisite to participation in the program. Intensive Hebrew language study *(ulpan)* is required of all students during the summer prior to the academic year, unless an exemption is otherwise determined. Continued study in Hebrew throughout the academic year is normally mandatory.

Courses are offered in Archaeology; Art; Bible; Hebrew language and language electives; Jewish and Israeli Literature; Jewish Philosophy; and Israel, Middle East and Islamic Studies (Anthropology, Geography, History, International Relations, Political Science, Social Work, Sociology, and Urban Studies, all as they relate to Israel). Most are taught in English. If the student has sufficient proficiency in Hebrew, departmental permission to take regular departmental courses may be granted. Courses are normally taught by faculty members of the institution. Coursework may be selected from the Overseas Student or Four-Year Program, and, under certain circumstances, from regular academic departments (subject to departmental approval). Most courses are at an introductory level, or sequential by semester within the year. A few "advanced" courses are found in well established programs with catalogs and course descriptions verifying that courses are beyond the normal one-year program level.

Transcripts are available in English under the normal transcript format used by the university, some with the clear designation that the study was within the framework of the OSP (the Hebrew University of Jerusalem), others without the designation (Tel-Aviv University). Grading may vary from that used by the university for its regular degree programs and also may vary from institution to institution. OSP grading scales known to be different from that used by the institution offering the program are given in the institutional profiles at the end of this chapter. Otherwise, the grading scale is assumed to follow the regular grading scale of the institution and will be found in the institutional profiles section of Chapter 8.

Ulpanim and Hebrew Language Coursework

Ulpan (sing.) and *ulpanim* (pl.) are terms used for intensive Hebrew language training. The intent of *ulpanim* varies from language and cultural orientation for new immigrants to attainment of language proficiency to facilitate study in Israeli institutions of higher education.

Ulpanim may be offered under the auspices of universities and non-university institutions of higher education, through *kibbutzim* work/study or immigrant programs, or in absorption centers (residential centers for new immigrants). The university *ulpanim* for overseas students are normally mandatory late summer programs preceding the academic year which begins in late October or early November; *kibbutz ulpanim* and *ulpanim* offered through absorption centers are structured according to the needs of the group or individuals concerned.

The academic intent and the affiliation of *ulpanim* govern the "academic" recognition of the study. As such, only institutions of higher education may offer *ulpanim* for academic credit, usually doing so if the student subsequently enrolls in the university. Transcripts, credits, and grades are presented on the institutional transcript with the course identified as "*ulpan.*"

Academic *ulpan* classes are usually offered at six levels of proficiency, each level requiring normally one semester of study. Proficiency levels from lowest to highest are: Lower Beginners—*Aleph* or A, Upper Beginners—*Beth* or B, Lower Intermediate—*Gimmel* or C, Upper Intermediate—*Daleth* or D, Lower Advanced—*Hé* or E, Upper Advanced—*Vav* or F.

For OSP students, the study of Hebrew does not end with the summer *ulpan,* nor is completion of *ulpan* study up through the advanced levels required. Students are normally required to continue study of Hebrew throughout the academic year of the study abroad program. Placement in a Hebrew language course(s) is based upon the student's level of proficiency. Overseas students who decide to continue in a regular degree program after the OSP must meet the level of Hebrew proficiency set by each institution and determined by means of an exemption examination. Once the level of required proficiency is met, a note is made on the transcript, generally without reference to weekly hours, credit, or grade.

The Four-Year Program

The Four-Year Program was designed for qualified immigrant and foreign-educated secondary school graduates who intend to enter an Israeli university's regular (three-year) bachelor's degree program. Students generally come from countries where the secondary school graduation diploma is not considered equivalent to an Israeli Matriculation Certificate and/or the secondary curriculum did not include Jewish studies, Hebrew language instruction, and/or English language instruction. This program should not be confused with degree programs which required Israelis four years to complete.

The curriculum is described as a "freshman year of general studies on a university level, as well as Hebrew and English language studies." The program is divided into five types of courses: Hebrew language, Hebrew language electives, English language, Jewish and Israeli studies, and introductory (departmental) studies. The introductory courses for those intending to study in mathematics or sciences are at the preparatory level and are comparable to courses offered in the *mechina* (see Chapter 8). Many courses are cross-referenced with the courses taught in English in the One-Year Program and are the same. Not infrequently, U.S. students start in this program with the intention of completing a degree program, but for various reasons transfer back to the United States after the first or second year. The Hebrew University of Jerusalem clearly indicates Four-Year Program as the department on the School for Overseas Program record of studies. Other institutions use their One-Year Program to serve the purpose of the Four-Year Program, i.e., as a prerequisite one year of study in Israel at the university level prior to admission to a regular degree program.

Non-Accredited "Nonacademic" Overseas Student Programs

Many students choosing a study abroad experience in Israel select one of the smaller, more intimate programs, each projecting a unique nonsecular philosophy. The character of each program reflects the ideals of the program's originator or sponsors, religious or social movements, or particular Zionist, orthodox or ultra-Orthodox groups. By Israeli standards, these programs are considered nonacademic and religious in nature. Because of the separation of church and state in the United States, the word "religious" elicits a more specific response in the U.S. than is normally the case in Israel. From an American perspective, "philosophy" might be a more accurate description of what Israelis refer to as religion in those instances where the inspiration is more socio-political, cultural, or ethnic. At the same time, religious study, in the traditional sense, of a more classical nature exists for overseas students in *Yeshivot* and institutes for Jewish and religious studies. Almost all programs outside the *Yeshivot* enroll only non-Israelis. *Yeshivot,* on the other hand, are primarily Israeli-based with some providing opportunities for foreigners, particularly in instances where a branch or affiliated *Yeshivah* exists in another country, e.g., the United States.

Most non-accredited programs base their admission on character references and the intent of the student rather than on particular academic credentials. Programs exist for all levels of students, but most programs are directed towards the high school graduate. For more advanced religious studies, particularly in the *Yeshivot,* a traditional background in religious schooling (Hebrew and Jewish studies) is expected.

Curriculums vary considerably due to the basic differences in intent of the numerous programs. Most students in the same program, however, participate in the same courses or activities, the extensiveness depending mostly upon the size of the program and qualifications of the instructors.

Programs that enroll primarily or exclusively U.S. foreign students provide transcripts in English and use a U.S. letter grading scale of "A" to "F" to facilitate the transfer of credit. Another frequently used grading system is based on a scale of 10-0 with 6 the minimum passing grade (the traditional Israeli grading system is discussed in Chapter 3).

The more established programs have transcripts with legends that clearly explain the grading system and define the credit system. While the majority of programs define a credit as one hour (50 minutes) of lecture each week for one semester, students generally accumulate well beyond the 15 credits which would be earned each semester by fulltime students at a U.S. college or university. In some instances, the total may be as high as 30 credits each semester. This reflects the intensive and submersive nature of these programs.

Yeshivot traditionally give no grades, examinations, or transcripts. To accommodate U.S. students who want to request transfer credit from their home institution, some *Yeshivot* will provide their students with reports or transcripts. Since these documents are intended only for use by U.S. institutions, the reporting of subjects, credits and grades usually follows the U.S. grading and semester credit systems. (See *Yeshivot* discussion above.)

Institutional and Program Profiles

The profiles in this section relate only to institutional programs offered for overseas students. The programs are categorized into two groups according to the status of the institution within the Israeli educational system. The first group represents selected programs affiliated with institutions recognized and accredited as institutions of higher education by the Israeli Council for Higher Education. (See the accreditation process in Chapter 8.) Detailed information on these institutions is provided in the profiles section of Chapter 8. The second group represents other institutions or programs. Descriptions of programs are extracted from program catalogs, brochures, and/or transcripts.

I. Accredited "Academic" Overseas Programs

BAR-ILAN UNIVERSITY, Friends of the Bar-Ilan University, 853 Seventh Ave., New York, NY 10019. Tel.: (212) 315-1990. Brochure avail. from NY office.

ONE-YEAR PROGRAM. A study abroad, credit-bearing program incl. reqd. summer *ulpan.* Instruction in Engl. and Hebrew. Offers up to 36 credits. SUMMER PROGRAM. A study abroad, credit-bearing program offering college-level courses + *ulpan.* Offers 6 credits. KIBBUTZ PLUS. A 14-week sem. for high school grads. and undergrads. in the fall and/or spring. Combines living/working on relig. *kibbutz* with *ulpan* and study at Bar-Ilan.. Offers 16 credits per semester. PROGRAM 13. A spring + summer study program for high school seniors. Incl. organized tours. Courses in English. Offers 16 credits in Jew. Stud. and 14 credits in Liberal Arts.

BEN-GURION UNIVERSITY OF THE NEGEV OVERSEAS STUDENT PROGRAMS, American Associates of the Ben-Gurion University of the Negev, 342 Madison Ave., Suite 1924, New York, NY 10173. Tel.: (212) 687-7721. Brochure avail. from NY office.

ONE-SEMESTER (FALL AND SPRING) AND ONE-YEAR PROGRAM (O-YP). Credit-bearing study abroad experience for freshmen, sophomores, and juniors. Freshman applicants must provide a copy of U.S. college acceptance with transcripts and U.S. SAT scores (minimum acceptable score—850); sophomore applicants submit high school and fall sem. college transcripts with U.S. SAT scores. Hebr. lang. proficiency not required. A 6-7 week *ulpan* is required; those fluent in Hebr. must attend *ulpan* orientation and field trip components. Instruction in English. Students fluent in Hebr. may take regular courses if prereqs. met and permission of instructor and OSP Advisor is granted. Courses offered in Desert Stud., Hebr. Lang., Israel Society, Jew. Stud., Politics &

Zionism, Sci. and Technol. Programs req. 12 credits + 3 Hebr. lang. credits per sem. or min. 15 sem. credits without Hebr. each sem. beyond the 6-credit *ulpan* course. Classes meet twice wkly. for two 1½ hour sessions. Credits determined by number of class hours. Most courses 3 credits. Grading (different from regular univ. grading) is as follows: A = 90-100, B = 80-89, C = 70-79, D = 60-69, F = 0-59. Transcripts only avail. directly from OSP Office in Israel upon student's request. Calendar (1986-87): Fall/Spring *ulpan*—8/11 - 9/26, and 1/12 - 2/27, respectively. Fall/Spring sems.—10/27 - 1/30 and 3/2 - 6/19, respectively. Fall/Spring exams—2/2 - 2/13 and 6/21 - 6/30, respectively.

ULPAN. Mandatory for all Sem.- and O-YP students unless exempted by exam. Course offered at elem., intermed., advd. levels. Fall/Spring *ulpans*—160 hrs., 6 days/wk., (5 hrs./day Sunday - Thursday; 2 ½ hrs., Friday) for 6 credits. KIBBUTZ WORK-STUDY PROGRAM. A credit-bearing work-study program. Reside/work in one of 10 *kibbutzim;* study at P. Sapir R.C. of the Negev. Courses in Human. & Soc. Sci. academic unit of P.Sapir are 2-3 credits each, for 11-12 total credits per sem. Students study 2 ½ days; work 3 ½ days each week. SUMMER ARCHAEOLOGY FIELD COURSE. A 4-wk. (5 days/wk.) excavation course. Involves lectures, field work, research paper (if taken for credit). SUMMER FIELD WORKSHOPS IN GEOGRAPHY & DESERT RESEARCH. Courses in Geomorph. of Arid Zones, Nomadism & Modern State, Rural & Urban Development in Sparsely Populated Areas for 6 credits each. Classes and field activities in English 5 days/wk. for 3 wks. (gen. tour, 4th wk.). MASTER'S OF SCIENCE IN MANAGEMENT (MSM). Sponsored jointly by Boston University and Ben-Gurion University in Beer Sheva. FT program reqs. 10 (4 credit hr.) courses. Students may take 12-16 credits per sem. Bach.'s degree or equiv. reqd.; major from any field acceptable. Two grad. courses (8 credit hrs.) may be accepted as transfer credit. Instruction in English. Program bulletin available from either institution upon request.

MICHLALAH-JERUSALEM COLLEGE FOR WOMEN, MACHAL-OVERSEAS STUDENT PROGRAM, American Friends of the Michlalah-Jerusalem College for Women, 1350 E. 54th St., Brooklyn, NY 11234. Tel.: (718) 531-9090.

ONE-YEAR PROGRAM. Estd. 1968 offering advd. program in Jew. Stud. (Judaica & Hebraica, Hebr. Lang., Biblical Geog.), intro. course in computers. Overseas enrollment of 85 (U.S.), other (15). Grades reported numerically on scale from 0 to 100 with 60% pass. One credit = 1 sem. hr. or 2 lab hrs.; programs reflect 48-60 credits a year.

TEL-AVIV UNIVERSITY OVERSEAS STUDENT PROGRAM, Student Dormitory, Bldg. B., Ranat Aviv 52100. Tel.: (03) 420639. U.S. Address: Office of Academic Affairs, 360 Lexington Ave., New York, NY 10017. Tel.: (212) 687-5651. OSP catalog available annually in English.

OSP's differentiated by length (sem., yr., etc.), level of programs (mid-yr. high school grad., undergrad., grad., etc.), and program of studies (gen., lang. stud., or specific). In general, programs are fulltime, open to high school grads. regardless of Hebr. lang. proficiency, and yield academic credit.

ONE SEMESTER PROGRAM. For univ. students whose leave of absence cannot exceed 1 sem. Offered fall and spring; spring sem. coincides best with U.S. academic calendar. *Ulpan* mandatory prior to sem. ONE-YEAR PROGRAM. Consecutive 2-sem. program open to entering college freshmen. *Ulpan* mandatory prior to first sem. ULPAN. Required of all One-Sem. and One-Yr. students unless exempt by exam. Fall *Ulpan*—160, 30 hrs./wk., 6 credits; Spring *Ulpan*—100, 30 hrs./wk., 6 credits; Summer Session (not for One-Sem. or One-Yr. students)—120, 30 hrs./wk., 6 credits. Levels: Beginners (A, B); Intermed. (C, D); Advd. (E, F). SUMMER SESSION. A 4-week July program for academically qualified college students who study Hebr. (listed above) for 6 credits or two 3-credit courses in Middle East and/or Jew. Stud. Instruction in English. SUMMER ARCHAEOLOGY PROGRAMS. Credit and noncredit 3-4 wk. programs under auspices of Tel-Aviv Univ.'s Insti. of Archaeol. in coop. with several U.S. univs. MID-YEAR HIGH SCHOOL GRADUATE PROGRAM. Spring sem. *kibbutz* and study program. Live/work on *kibbutz* with 6-month *kibbutz ulpan* under supervision of Tel-Aviv Univ.'s Hebrew Dept. (6 credits.), and two intro.-level courses from the OSP (6 credits).

GRADUATE MIDDLE EAST STUDIES PROGRAM. Nondegree, credit-bearing grad. program for those with bach.'s ave. of "B" who are enrolled (or intend to enroll) in U.S. master's program. Major in M.E. Stud. not necessary. *Ulpan* reqd. prior to program. Courses in Engl. incl. seminars, indep. study, Arabic & Hebr.; undergrad. courses from OSP allowed. Credit may apply towards subsequent M.A. in Israel. M.D. PROGRAM FOR NEW YORK STATE RESIDENTS. N.Y. State/Tel-Aviv Univ., School of Medicine's 4-yr. program offering basic pre-clin. courses. Instruction in Engl. Admission reqmts. follow med. schools in N.Y. For details, contact Office of Admissions, Sackler School of Medicine, 17 East 62nd St., New York, NY 10021. (212) 688-8811. SUMMER LAW PROGRAM. Sponsored jointly by Temple University Law School and Tel-Aviv Univ., Fac. of Law for qualified U.S. law students. Six-wk. courses in English taught by both faculties. Three 2-credit courses in law and legal aspects of the Middle East. ARABIC LANG. PROGRAM. One sem. or 1-yr. Elem. Arabic for beginners. JOINT PROGRAM WITH KIBBUTZ RESEARCH CENTER. Classes (courses and seminars), field work, and *kibbutz* visits in conjuction with Yad Tabenkin Kibbutz Research Center—EFAL.

INDEPENDENT STUDY. For junior and senior undergrads. with study proposal and approval from applicant's Dean of Students and advisor. COURSES TAUGHT BY TEL-AVIV UNIV. FAC. in Engl. on intro., upper, and advd. levels identified by 100-, 200-, 300-level course numbers, respectively. Freshmen and mid-year high school grads. may enroll in only intro. courses. Sophomores, juniors and seniors may enroll in intro. and upper level courses. Advd. honors seminars req. junior or senior standing with B+ or better ave., sometimes an interview and approval of instructor. Courses meet twice wkly. Courses in Arts Stud., Bus., Gen. Stud., Hebr. Lang. Stud., Israel Stud., Judaic/Jewish Stud., Labor Relns. & Mgmt. Stud., and Middle East Studies. Credit determined by hrs. of instruction. Program reqs. 12 credits + 4-6 credits Hebr. lang. each sem. (min. 15 credits if no Hebr. is reqd.). Summer Session (1985)—7/1 - 7/26;

Spring *Ulpan*(1986)—1/27 - 2/21; Fall/Spring sems. (1985- 86)—10/21-1/24 and 2/24 - 6/11, respectively. Fall/Spring exams (1986)—1/27 - 2/7, 6/12 - 6/20, respectively. Grading system differs from regular grading system described in transcript legend as: A+ = 95-100, A = 90-94, B = 80-89, C = 70-79, D = 60-69, and F = 0-59. Transcripts avail. only through OSP Office in Israel at student's request. "Overseas Student Program" is indicated on the document.

THE HEBREW UNIVERSITY OF JERUSALEM OVERSEAS STUDENTS PROGRAM, The Rothberg School for Overseas Students, Goldsmith Bldg., Mount Scopus, Jerusalem 91905. Tel.: (02) 882-607. U.S. American Friends of The Hebrew University of Jerusalem, 1140 Avenue of the Americas, New York, NY 10036. Tel.: (212) 840-5820. Rothberg School OSP Bulletin published in English annually.

Admission reqmts. and level of study programs vary—One-Sem., One-Year, Undergrad., Grad., etc. One-Year Program (O-YP) is primary program. Programs follow current univ. calendar; OSP always followed sem. system. Exams for O-YP, F-YP and Preparatory Program (PP) are 1 wk. after end of each semester. All programs follow univ. grading system.

ONE-YEAR PROGRAM (O-YP). Credit-bearing academic, study abroad experience for undergrad. or grad. students. Undergrad. admission reqs. sophomore-level standing with "B" or better ave. for admission; grad. admission reqs. bach.'s degree or U.S. grad. matriculated status. Grad. student classified as visiting student (those with bach.'s degree), visiting grad. student (those enrolled in master's program), and visiting research student (those enrolled in doctoral program). Summer *ulpan* reqd. prior to enrollment; continued Hebr. lang. study reqd. during academic year unless exempted by exam.

Instruction in Engl.; in Hebr. for those proficient in Hebrew. Undergrads. select from courses in the O-YP, F-YP, or regular program (if Hebr. and dept. permit). Wide range of courses in Israel Stud., Jew. Stud., Middle East Stud., and, in Fall 1985, Bus. Admin. Some courses for pre-med. and sci. major avail. All O-YP courses considered Upper Div. except those listed as "Introduction." Prereqs. for 300 and 400 level courses; 200-level courses have no prerequisite. Program reqs. min. 16-18 hrs./wk. each sem., according to level of Hebr. proficiency; 4-6 hrs. of Hebr. lang. + at least 1 course in Jew. or Israel Stud. each sem. Student taking 8 or more hrs. in Hebr. Lang. must take 2 addl. 4-hr. courses each sem. (1 in Jew. or Israel Stud.).

FOUR-YEAR PROGRAM (F-YP) AND PREPARATORY PROGRAM (PP). Intended for overseas high school grads. without previous Jew. Stud. or Hebr. lang. instruction who expect to complete bach.'s degree in Israel. The F-YP consists of 1 yr. of prep., lang. and Jew./Israeli Stud. attached to 3-yr. regular B.A./B.Sc. program, not regular Israeli degree program requiring 4 years. Admission based on secondary school record or matriculation grades and the U.S. Scholastic Aptitude Test (SAT) and/or Israeli Psychometric Exam. Secondary school grads. who do not meet reqmts. for admission to the F-YP may be admitted to PP. Required courses in Jew. and Israel Stud. and Math for Soc. Sci. offered in Engl., Fr., Span., easy Hebr. during autumn sem. Sci. courses during autumn offered in all above langs. except French. Spring sem. courses given in Hebrew. Academic calendar and grading same throughout university. Course of studies for both programs is the same with slight modifications made for PP; both incl. Hebr. and Engl. Lang. study and Jew. and Israel Stud. Other courses determined by anticipated field of study.

SEMESTER PROGRAM OF JEWISH AND ISRAELI STUDIES. One-sem. course given twice yearly for overseas high school grads. Syllabus designed to foster a better understanding of Judaism, Jew. Hist., Jew. people, and the State of Israel. SUMMER COURSES AND SPECIAL ACADEMIC PROGRAMS. Courses in Judaica, Israel-Past and Present, Middle East politics, lang. and culture "intended to provide intellectual stimulation and cultural immersion." Instruction in English. Admission reqs. sophomore standing. Generally, 15 hrs. of crswrk. equals 1 sem. credit. Transcripts provided if attendance and course reqmts. met. Courses offered in two 3-wk. sessions; Hebr. lang. course in 6 wks. Other special programs incl. 2-wk. noncredit Faculty Seminar; noncredit mini-courses for Sabbatical Professors and Engl.-Speaking Residents; noncredit Elderhostel; noncredit 1-2 wk. Continuing Educ. Program. SUMMER *Ulpan.* (Note the difference between this program and the *Ulpan* preceding the O-YP, F-YP and PP.)

THE UNIVERSITY OF HAIFA, DEPARTMENT OF OVERSEAS STUDENT PROGRAMS, American Friends of Haifa University, 41 E. 42nd St., New York, NY 10017. Tel.: (212) 818-9050. The N.Y. office annually publishes and distributes program and course descriptions in English.

Summer (1986) *Ulpan*—7/23 - 9/25. *Kibbutz*/Univ. Fall/Spring (1986-87) program—7/23 - 2/13 and 12/26 - 6/19, respectively. Fall/Spring sems. (1986-87)—11/2 - 2/13 and 3/8 - 6/19, respectively. Reported grading scale: A (Excellent), B (Good), C (average), P (Pass), F (Fail).

SEMESTER AND ONE-YEAR PROGRAM. Credit-bearing academic study abroad experience open to students with sophomore standing from an accredited U.S. college or univ. Knowl. of Hebr. not prereq. Summer *ulpan* prior to enrolling not reqd. but recommended. Instruction in English. Those with sufficient level of Hebr. may request permission to take regular courses, seek tutorial services, and be examined and submit papers in English. Courses incl. Art, Hebr. & Arabic Lang. & Lit., Hist. & Intl. Relations., Jew. & Israeli Hist., Natural Sci., Oceanogr. & Maritime Stud., Relig. Stud. (Judaism & Islam). Credits reported and correspond to wkly. hrs. per sem. except in lang. where credits are less than hrs. Indep. stud. can be arranged. KIBBUTZ/UNIVERSITY SEMESTER. Six-month combined work/study program for those with sophomore standing. Incl. 8 or 10 wks. on a *kibbutz* combining 5 hrs. work daily and Hebr. lang. study for 4 credits. Students may elect indep. study or research a topic related to the *kibbutz* for 3 credits. Students then join the regular overseas program. SUMMER ULPAN. Intensive 10-wk. program (5 hrs./day, 4 days/wk.) + wkly. field trip integrated with lang. study (8 sem. credit). Offered on 5 levels. DIVING COURSE. Non-credit, basic scuba diving course offered each sem. in coop. with the Center for Maritime Stud. Leads to certification by

(U.S.) Natl. Assn. of Underwater Instructors. INTERNSHIP PROGRAM. Credit-bearing supervised internship (which may be taken concurrently with courses in overseas program) in academic or voc. fields. Length of internship flexible within 1 month work reqmt. Applicants submit proposal, resume, etc.

II. Non-Accredited "Nonacademic" Overseas Programs

AISH HATORAH COLLEGE OF JEWISH STUDIES, 70 Misgav Ladach St., P.O. Box 14149, Jewish Quarter, Old City, Jerusalem 91141. Tel.: (02) 273 191. U.S. Address: 900 Forest Ave., Lakewood, NJ 08701. Tel.: (201) 370-9053.

Estd. 1974. *Programs*—Jewish Stud. for high school grads. vary from 2-wk. introductory course to 4-yr. program, from rabbinical ordination to a women's division (named Eyaht) located in the Kiriyat Sanz section of Jerusalem. FT students complete 15 credits per sem. (max. 18). *Enrollment*—3,000 students in various programs yearly; about 200 FT (Men—25 Israeli, 105 U.S., 15 other, foreign; Women—35 U.S.). *Branches*—Los Angeles, St. Louis (U.S.), Tel-Aviv, and Toronto (Canada). *Grading*—Reported as A = 4, B = 3, C = 2, D = 1, F = Failure. *Calendar*—Sept.-Jan., Feb.-June, July-Aug. *Library*—10,000 vols.

BEIT-MIDRASH L'TORAH (B.M.T., JERUSALEM TORAH COLLEGE, COLLEGE FOR JEWISH STUDIES), Givat Mordechai, Jerusalem 93 721. U.S. Address: Torah Educ. Dept., World Zionist Organization, 515 Park Ave., New York, NY 10022.

Estd. 1969 by Dept. of Torah Educ. and Culture in the Diaspora of the World Zionist Organization. Tradit. higher academy for Torah studies (men). Capacity for 150; 950 have completed studies since 1969. *Programs*—Jew. Stud. (1-2 yrs.) at beginning, intermediate, advd. levels; Teacher Train. (2-yr. program for Jew. Stud. for grades 6-12 in the Diaspora); Pre-Rabbinic Program; Other Special Programs as arranged with overseas Jewish high schools and colleges. *Grading*—Reported as 10 (Outstanding), 9 (Excellent), 8 (Good), 7 (Fair, lowest passing grade for overseas students), 6 (Poor, lowest passing grade for transfer to local institutions), 5 (Failed).

BET-EL YESHIVA CENTER, Bet El D.N. Mizrach Binyamin, Jerusalem 90801. Tel.: (02) 976192.

Tradit. higher academy for Torah studies (men), primarily for Israelis. Letter grades and "credit hours" reported by sem.; over 70 credit hrs. per semester.

B.M.T. See Beit-Midrash L'Torah

BNEI AKIVA SCHOLARSHIP INSTITUTE IN ISRAEL—HACHSHARA, P.O. Box 700, Tel-Aviv. Tel.: (04) 264153. U.S. Address: 200 Park Ave., South., New York, NY 10013. Tel.: (212) 889-5260.

Organized 1956 to give young men/women exposure to Israeli society, values, and culture in a work/study program on a religious *kibbutz*. Affiliated with Kvutzat Yavneh, Kvutzat Sa'ad, and Kibbutz Ein Hanatziv. Some 700 participants to date; mostly American. *Admission Requirements*—High school grad., letters of reference, strict physical exam, and interview. If not fluent in Hebr., must attend summer *ulpan*. *Program*—Incl. 50% work on relig. *kibbutz* or in development town; 50% study at various sites (Kibbutz Maale Gilboa, Kibbutz Yavne, Michlelet OROT). Agri., Home Econ., and Phys. Educ. crswk. is practical; other courses (Educ., Hebr. Lang. & Lit. [Bible I, II, Conv. & Comp., Lit.], Jew. Hist., Jew. Philos., Judaica [relig. law, prayer, *Talmud*], Music & Dance of Israel, Sociol. of the *Kibbutz)* listed as hrs./wk. over 15 wks./ sem. or yr. + 500 total hrs. in Agri. or Home. Econ. and 120 hrs. in Phys. Educ.

B'NOT CHAYIL, P.O. Box 16048, Jerusalem. Tel.: (02) 410215.

Reports under letterhead of Nevé Yerushalayim Institutions. *Program*—Relig. Stud. for women (Bible, *Halacha* [Daily Law, Relig. Customs], Hebr. Lang., Jew. Hist., Philos., etc.). *Transcript*—Indicates class hrs./wk. and credits (approx. 23/sem.), "A-F" letter grades.

B'NOT TORAH INSTITUTE, 27 Rechov Yam Suf, Jerusalem. Tel.: (02) 814382. U.S. Address: 1040 E. 10th St., Brooklyn, NY 11230. Tel.: (212) 253-4579.

Opened 1977. Also known as "Sharfman's" and Beit-Midrash L'Nashim. Small women's relig. program. Goals incl. development of relig. textual ability; study of Jew. philos., hist., and Bible; and development of self in relig. context. Recog. by the Ministry of Relig. Affairs, Israel. *Ave. Class Size*—12. *Faculty*—25 PT. *Enrollment*—70 (U.S.). *Admission Requirements*—High school graduation; commitment to intensive study and relig. observance. *Programs*—Offers 1- and 2-yr. programs. Beit-Midrash method of group study; lect., seminars, and wkshps. Courses in Bible, Torah, Hebrew, Jew. Hist., *Halacha* (Daily Law, Relig. Customs), Philos., Liturgy. Second yr. incl. advd. courses on same topics + educ. Not all courses req. exams. or papers. *Transcript*—Legend indicates 1 credit = 1 hr./wk. for 15-wk. sem. incl. exams and study periods. Ave. credits per year = 45-48. "A-F" letter grades used.

DIASPORA YESHIVA OF JEWISH STUDIES (DIASPORA YESHIVA TORAS YISRAEL), Mt. Zion, P.O. Box 6426, Jerusalem 91063. Tel.: (02) 716841. U.S. Address: c/o Gitlin, 662 Lefferts Ave., Brooklyn, NY 11203.

Estd. 1967 by American Rabbi M. Goldstein. Tradit. higher academy for Torah studies (men). *Program*—For begin. and advd. Torah studies. Recog. by Ministry of Relig. Affairs, Israel; authorized to ordain rabbis. Specializes in transla. of Torah studies from Hebr. to Engl. Women's Div.—The Roni Goldstein Teacher's Institute. *Kollel* for married students. *Enrollment (Men)*—10 Israelis, 100 U.S., 25 other foreign.

DIASPORA INSTITUTE OF TORAH STUDIES-WOMEN'S DIVISION (THE RONI GOLDSTEIN TEACHER'S INSTITUTE), Jewish Quarter (Address/ Tel. same as above).

Estd. 1969 as the Women's Torah Educ. Division of Diaspora Yeshiva of Jewish Studies (see above). *Enrollment*—10 Israelis, 80 U.S., 25 other foreign.

DVAR YERUSHALAYIM. See Yeshivat Dvar Yerushalayim.

GOLD COLLEGE FOR WOMEN. See Machon Gold.

HASHACHAR—YOUNG JUDEA'S YEAR COURSE. See The Jerusalem Institute.

INSTITUTE FOR YOUTH LEADERS FROM ABROAD. See The Jerusalem Institute.

ISRAEL TORAH RESEARCH INSTITUTE, Bethelehem Rd., Jerusalem.

Estd. 1959 as grad. institute for religious studies; advd. program opened 1964 (described as undergrad.). Under the Ministry of Relig. Affairs; authorized to ordain rabbis. Branches in Bet Safafa, Romema, Hadera, other areas of Jerusalem, and New York (U.S.). *Calendar*—Sept.-Jan., Jan.-June, June-Aug. *Program*—Ave. 15-20 credits per semester. *Grading*—A = 90-100, B = 80-89, C = 70-79, D = 60-69, F = 0-59 with 4-point system (A = 4, B = 3, etc.).

KIRIYAT HATEFUTSOT (HAIM GREENBERG HEBREW COLLEGE), Ha'askan St., Talpiot, Jerusalem 93557. Tel.: (02) 714731. U.S. Address: Dept. of Educ. and Culture, Jewish Agency, 515 Park Ave., New York, NY 10022.

JERUSALEM ACADEMY OF JEWISH STUDIES. See Yeshivat Dvar Yerushalayim.

JERUSALEM TORAH COLLEGE. See Beit-Midrash L' Torah (B.M.T.).

THE JERUSALEM INSTITUTE, P.O. Box 24111, Jerusalem 91240. Tel.: (02) 817341. U.S. Address: Hadassah Zionist Youth Commission, 50 W. 58th St., New York, NY 10019. Tel.: (212) 303-8262. Detailed program and course descriptions available from New York office.

Sponsored by Hadassah Zionist Youth Commission and Youth and Hechalutz Dept. of the World Zionist Organization, Jerusalem. Provides formal educ. program for Hashachar—Young Judaea's Year Course in Israel, an umbrella title for various yr. programs offered by Hadassah Youth Center. Program is values-oriented; goal is to produce enlighted Jews with life-long commitments to Judaism, the Jew. people, and to Israel. *Programs*—Hashachar offers *The Jerusalem Program* and the *Community Service Program* options, as well as the *Institute for Youth Leaders from Abroad* (a concurrent part of the Year Course). The Institute is a leadership program for Zionist youth movements, Jew. youth organizations, etc. *Transcripts*—Provide total contact hrs., credit hrs., and grades on "A - F" grading scale. Reverse side gives detailed course, credit, and grade information.

MACHON DEVORAH, P.O. Box 16020 Jerusalem 91160. Tel.: (02) 417886. See Nevé Yerushalayim College for Women.

MACHON GOLD, 36 Haturim, Jerusalem 94662. Tel.: (02) 521752. U.S. Address: c/o Torah Educ. Dept., World Zionist Organization, 515 Park Ave., New York, NY 10022. Tel.: (212) 752-0600. Catalog with course descriptions available.

Estd. 1958 by World Zionist Organization, Dept. of Torah Educ. and Culture to provide relig. Zionist educ. experience for non-Israeli women. Faculty: 8 FT, 22 PT. *Enrollment*—100 (U.S.). *Programs*—Teacher's College offers program for teaching relig. and Jew. stud. in Jew. schools in the Diaspora (1-2 yrs.); School of Jew. Stud. offers program for enrichment of Jew. knowl. and identity (1 yr.). Crswk. in Art, Bible/Torah Stud., Gen. Stud., Hebr. Lang. & Lit., Israel Stud., Jew. Hist., Jew. Liturgy, Jew. Phil., Music, and Phys. Activity. *Transcripts*—List sem. and yr. courses, credit hrs. (65 min./hr. for 16 wks.); legend with 10-0 grading scale; approx. 30 credits a semester. *U.S. Linkages*—Stern College, Brooklyn College, Touro College.

MICHLELET BNEI AKIVA. See "OROT Israel."

MICHLELET BRURIA, Ben Zion 19, Kiriyat Moshe, P.O. Box 15091, Jerusalem 91150. Tel.: (212) 496-1618. See Yeshivat Hamivtar.

MIDRESHET YERUSHALAYIM, Nevé Schechter, P.O. Box 196, Jerusalem 91001. Tel.: (02) 663261. U.S. Address: Midreshet Yerushalayim, Jewish Theological Seminary, 3080 Broadway, New York, NY Tel.: (212) 78-8832.

NEVE YERUSHALAYIM COLLEGE FOR WOMEN, Beer Mayim Chayim, Bayit Vegan, P.O. Box 16020, Jerusalem. Tel.: (02) 532598.

Estd. 1970 as Nevé Yerushalayim to offer Engl.-speaking women with little or no background in Jew. stud. a high quality Jew. educ. *Nevé Shoshana* program (estd. 1976) replicated this program for Israeli women. The school expanded in 1979 by opening *Machon Devorah Seminar*, a O-YP for Jew. Relig. High School grads. to further their relig. stud. and qualify them to teach in Hebr. schools in the Diaspora. In 1980, *Ohr Somayach Women's School* was absorbed by Nevé Yerushalayim. The consolidation of the two schools resulted in the name *Nevé Yerushalayim College*, also identified as *Nevé Yerushalayim College for Women*. The umbrella name is *Nevé Yerushalayim Institutions* or simply *Nevé Yerushalayim*. Catalogue available.

The Nevé Yerushalayim College offers several programs—the *Mechina* for mature beginners with little or no background in Jew. Studies (usually 6 wks. but determined by the student); the *Nevé* program, regular prog.; *Shalhevet*, an advd. course for univ.-aged women. The levels are identified by course numbers as *Mechina* (1000 numbers), *Nevé* (2000-3000), *Shalhevel* (4000). *Enrollment*—Some 400. *Transcript*—Reflects class hrs./wk., credits, and letter grades "A-F."

NEVE YERUSHALAYIM INSTITUTIONS. See Nevé Yerushalayim College for Women

NEVEH ZION, Kiriyat Telshe-Stone, D.N. Harei Yehuda 90840. U.S. Address: American Friends of Neve Zion, 3 West 16th St., New York, NY 10011. Tel.: (212) 929-1845.

A tradit. higher academy for Torah stud. (men). Prior to 1981, Neveh Zion was named Neveh Yehoshua, a branch institution of the Israel Torah Research Institute (ITRI) from Sept. 1977-June 1981. As of Sept. 1981, Neveh Yehoshua became Neveh Zion and disaffiliated with ITRI. *Transcripts*—Report credits averaging 16/sem. with "A-F" letter grades.

OHR SOMAYACH INSTITUTIONS—TANENBAUM COLLEGE, 22-24 Shimon Hatzadik St., P.O. Box 18103, Jerusalem 91180. Tel.: (02) 810 315. U.S. Address: 39 Broadway, Suite 3304, New York, NY 10006. Tel.: (292) 344-2000.

OHR SOMAYACH WOMEN'S SCHOOL. See Nevé Yerushalayim College, Nevé Yerushalayim College for Women

"OROT ISRAEL" COLLEGE FOR WOMEN, 4 Aluf David Marcus, P.O. Box 1033, Petach Tikva 49100. Tel.: (03) 918478. U.S. Address: American Friends of Yeshivot Bnei Akiva, 50 W. 34th St., New York, NY 10001. Tel.: (212) 947-6787.

Estd. 1979 under sponsorship of Merkaz Yeshivot Bnei Akiva, a State Relig. Teacher's seminar offering several study abroad programs, the most popular being "Bat Zion." Intensive Jew. Stud. program that may lead to qualifying for teaching in Hebr. schools in the Diaspora. *Enrollment*—350.

ULPAN AKIVA NETANYA (INTERNATIONAL HEBREW STUDY CENTER), Green Beach Hotel, P.O. Box 256, Netanya 42102. Tel.: (053) 52312/3.

WORLD UNION OF JEWISH STUDENTS (WUJS INSTITUTE), Arad 80700.

YESHIVAT AISH HATORAH. See Aish Hatorah College of Jewish Studies

YESHIVAT DVAR YERUSHALAYIM (THE JERUSALEM ACADEMY OF JEWISH STUDIES), 8 Rechov HaYeshiva, P.O. Box 5454, Jerusalem. Tel.: (02) 288645. U.S. Address: 1542 Coney Island Ave., Brooklyn, NY 11230. Tel.: (212) 258-3311. Woman's Seminary Div., 18 Rechov Blau, Jerusalem. Tel.: (02) 817647. Other U.S. and foreign offices.

Estd. 1971. Tradit. higher academy for Torah stud. (men) and Seminary div. (women). *Nontradit. Requirements*—No previous knowl. of Judaism reqd. *Cal-*

endar—Oct.-Mar., May-Aug., Aug.-Oct. Summer Session, July-Oct. *Courses*—Ethics/Philos.; *Hassidism;* Hist.; Legal Codes; *Talmud;* Legal Codes; Relig. *Ulpan.;* Torah, Prophets, Writing. Programs offered PT/FT in summer. *Grades*—Reported with "credits" and "A-F" letter grades.

YESHIVAT HAKIBBUTZ HADATI.

YESHIVAT HAKOTEL, Old City, P.O. Box 603, Jerusalem 91006.

YESHIVAT HANEGEV, Netivot.

YESHIVAT HAMIVTAR/MICHLELET BRURIA, Sderot HaMeiri 11, Kiriyat Moshe, P.O. Box 15091 Jerusalem 91150. U.S. Address: 1 W. 85th St., Apt. 2F, New York, NY 10024. Tel.: (212) 496-1618.

Estd. 1976 as Yeshivat Hamivtar (for men)/Michlelet Bruria (for women). Indep. of one another and housed separately. *Combined Enrollment*—Over 200 with fac. of 35. Tradit. higher academy for *Talmudic*/Torah stud. Open to relig. high school grads. *Yeshivat Hamivtar*—Offers 3 levels of programs accord. to educ. background: *Yeshiva* Division, a 3 consecutive yr. program; the *Kollel,* the advd. Torah Research Division for those who have completed Yeshivat Hamivtar, Yeshiva staff and transfers; Project Return, for beginners with limited relig. stud. background operating on 3-month cycles. *Michlelet Bruria*—Offers courses in 4 divisions: Michlalah Division, a 3-yr. multi-level curriculum for women of differing educ. backgrounds; *Kollelet,* advd. stud. in Torah Research; Project Return (as above); and Israel Program, for Israeli and Hebr.-speaking women.

YESHIVAT HAR ETZION, P.O. Box 7447, Jerusalem 91073. Tel.: (02) 931456.

YESHIVAT KEREM B'YAVNEH, Doar Na: Shiqmim 79855. Tel.: (055) 31192.

YESHIVAT SHA'ALVIM, Joseph and Faye Tanenbaum Campus, D.N. Ayolon near Ramlah. Tel.: (054) 226161. U.S. Address: 156 5th Ave., New York, NY 10010.

Chapter 7

Technological Education

Technological education in Israel is a distinct operational entity maintained and supervised for the most part by the Department of Technological Education/DTE (within the Ministry of Education and Culture/MOEC) and the National Institute of Technological Training/NITT (under the Ministry of Labor and Social Welfare/MOLSW). All matters relating to technological education—whether in primary, secondary, or postsecondary schools—represent a centralized and coordinated effort. The framework under which technological education operates and the extensive educational programs emanating from it are the topics of this chapter.

Literature and credentials associated with Israeli technical education use the terms "professional," "technical," "technological," and "vocational" simultaneously and interchangeably. Variance is usually the result of translation inconsistency or style and carries no implied distinction. In this text, the words "technical," "technological," and "vocational" are also used interchangeably and without intended distinction. The word "technological/vocational" expands the concept of technological education by interjecting the distinction made between technical and nontechnical (general vocational) fields called trends.

Background Information

The first Jewish vocational school in Palestine was founded by the Kol Israel Havarim Society in Jerusalem in 1882 to train craftsmen within a practical workshop setting. While there were several such schools established during these early years, the system of technological education under a government inspectorate began after establishment of the State of Israel in 1948. The waves of Jewish immigration which followed had a decisive impact on the educational system, especially technological education. The number of fulltime Jewish students in technological education went from 2,002 in 1948 to over 79,000 in 1983-84. (*Statistical Abstract*, No. 35, 1984)

While Jewish immigration to Palestine under the British primarily originated from Europe and Eastern Europe, more than half of the immigrants to Israel after 1948 came from "underdeveloped, semi-feudal, traditional societies in the Middle East and Northern Africa." (*Statistical Abstract*, No. 18, 1967, p. 89) The European element (Ashkenazim) who were the leaders and developers of the new state, did not envision the impact that the Oriental element (Sephardim) would have on their expectation of Israel becoming the Western, industrialized capital of the Middle East. Israeli society and its educational system thus took on the challenge of "*Misug-Galuyot*, or the fusion and integration of the exiles," with the goal of rapid modernization and westernization of the Sephardim who were *a priori* socially, politically, and economically disadvantaged. (Iram and Balicki 95) Extensive social welfare programs and free and compulsory education were perceived as the most effective route to social, cultural, and political integration.

The mere expansion of education institutions and opportunity alone did not alleviate the disparity in educational achievement between children of Middle Eastern or African origin and those of European or American origin. (Iram and Balicki 97) Instead, a new philosophy of education superceded the notion that educational structures and programs should be uniformly pitched at a high and demanding level. This change in philosophy had ramifications throughout the educational system, but was most significant in the area of technological education. In the technological high schools, new or modified programs were introduced through a pyramid of tracks reflecting high to less demanding levels of academic orientation. In addition, a wide variety of vocational fields (trends) allowed children with advanced technical abilities as well as those with less academic inclination to complete 12 years of formal education. One result of these changes has been a reduction in the dropout rate, which, for Sephardim children, went from 83% in 1956-57 to 50% in 1970. (*Statistical Abstract*, No. 21, 1970, p. 560)

Since 1950, technological education has been the mutual concern of the MOEC, Department of Technological Education/DTE and the MOLSW, represented by the National Institute of Technological Training/NITT. Together, they have established goals, standardized programs, and supervised schools. The authority of the DTE and the NITT encompasses all technological/vocational education outside the universities, designated according to the following criteria: The MOEC/DTE has jurisdiction over technological/vocational education for youth through the age of 18 and for those beyond that age who continue directly from secondary into postsecondary technological programs as a result of deferment or exemption from military service. DTE postsecondary programs are referred to as "Youth" programs. The MOLSW/NITT has jurisdiction over technological/vocational education for young adults who have fulfilled their military obligation, as well as for those whose age places them outside the responsibility of the MOEC. NITT postsecondary programs are referred to as "Adult" programs. In addition, but outside traditional fulltime education, the MOLSW is responsible for apprenticeship schools, industrial schools, and short courses in vocational training.

An impressive increase in enrollment has been seen since the resumption of supervision of technological/vocational education by the DTE. In 1962-63, technical enrollment in the Jewish sector constituted 20% of all secondary education; in 1969-70, it represented 35%; and in 1982-83 it involved 60% of all Jewish secondary students. (See Chapter 3 for the statistical profile of technological education in the Hebrew and Arab sectors, Tables 3.1 and 7.1.)

The Israeli educational system operates by legislative mandate under the auspices of the MOEC. The Ministry is headed by the Pedagogical Secretariat who, in turn, operates the Commissions for Primary Education, Secondary

Table 7.1. Twelfth Grade Enrollment in Technological Programs* by Track and Trend (1981–82)

	Total	Track (% of Enrollment)						% of
	Enroll.	# MASMAT	%	# MASMAR	%	# MASMAM	%	Enroll.
Arab Sector†	691	215	31.1%	302	43.7%	174	25.2%	100.0%
Boys	392		30.1%		47.5%		22.4%	56.7%
Girls	299		32.4%		38.8%		28.8%	43.3%
Hebrew Sector	15,436	8,511	55.1%	4,691	30.4%	2,234	14.5%	100.0%
Boys	8,342		57.6%		28.3%		14.1%	54.0%
Girls	7,094		52.3%		32.8%		14.9%	46.0%
Trends†	(15,310)							
Applied Arts	303		64.6%		18.2%		17.2%	2.0%
Automa. Data Proces.	219		100.0%		—		—	1.4%
Bldg. & Architecture	375		85.4%		11.7%		2.9%	2.4%
Clerical Admin. & Secretar. Trades	3,494		49.5%		38.9%		11.6%	22.8%
Draw. & Planning	336		65.8%		34.2%		—	2.2%
Elect., Instrumental Mechanics & Refrig.	1,710		59.5%		32.3%		8.2%	11.2%
Electronics	2,088		95.5%		4.5%		—	13.6%
Fashion & Sewing	1,408		37.1%		35.4%		27.5%	9.2%
Hotel., Housekpg., & Tourism	576		64.2%		16.5%		19.3%	3.8%
Lab Assistants	370		69.2%		30.8%		—	2.4%
Mechanics	1,267		32.7%		46.8%		20.5%	8.3%
Metal Work	2,106		37.3%		35.3%		27.4%	13.8%
Nursing	698		50.8%		35.0%		14.2%	4.6%
Woodworking	217		4.1%		40.1%		55.8%	1.4%
Other Subjects‡	143		33.6%		63.6%		2.8%	1.0%

SOURCE: Adapted from *Statistical Abstract of Israel*, No. 35, 1984, p. 649.
*Including students in technological schools and technological tracks of multi-track schools.
†Breakdown of Arab sector by trend not reported.
‡Including Printing and Maritime Trades.

Education, and Technological Education. The chairman of the Commission for Technological Education is also the head of the Department of Technological Education. The Commission is concerned with the policies and day-to-day operations of technological education within the jurisdiction of the MOEC.

The plenary Commission of Technological Education includes 22 national inspectors responsible for the various vocational trends.Other members include the Assistant Commissioner; the heads of the four district supervisory teams; the head of the Technological Curriculum Department; the Coordinators of Technological Education for the Departments of Religious Schools, Education of Agricultural and Rural Schoools, and the Arab Sector; the Inspector for In-Service Training; the Examiner; and the Inspector for shop classes in intermediate schools.

The Department of Technological Education

The Department of Technological Education/DTE is responsible for supervising technological education in coordination with various other ministries and bodies. The areas of supervision under the DTE include any and all educational frameworks under the jurisdiction of the MOEC, as follows: Crafts classes in primary schools; shop classes (technical and general) in intermediate schools; technological/vocational training in secondary schools; and postsecondary training at the grade 13 and 14 levels in Technician and Practical Engineering programs when the study immediately follows grade 12 and is permitted on the basis of deferment of or exemption from military service.

In addition, the DTE has responsibility for preparing curriculums and teaching materials for all technological subjects, planning and developing programs in coordination with other ministries and bodies, initiating studies in technological fields, conducting follow-up studies of technology graduates, and conducting in-service teacher training for vocational instructors and technical education teachers through established educational institutions.

Technological Education in Primary Schools

Technological education in primary schools is provided once or twice a week in crafts classes of most Hebrew and Arab sector schools. From grades 1-4, crafts classes are usually integrated into general education classes and are taught by regular classroom teachers. After grade 4, arts and crafts teachers conduct crafts classes of approximately 20 students per class.

Technological Education in Intermediate (Junior High) Schools

The primary aim of technological education in junior high schools is to familiarize students with the technical realities of their environment, to provide them with the wherewithall to function as future consumers and parents, and to influence attitudes towards possible careers. This is accomplished through the teaching of technical and domestic skills for three hours per week in grades 7, 8, and 9.

Technical skills are taught to boys in grades 7 and 8 and include drafting, metalworking, plastics, and woodworking and, in grade 9, electricity and electronics. Girls are taught domestic skills which include textiles in grade 7 and home economics in grades 8 and 9. Consideration is being given to teaching both boys and girls domestic and technical skills.

A 30-hour program entitled "Industry and the Economy in Israel" for grade 9 students in Hebrew sector intermediate schools includes lectures, visits to industrial plants, simulation games, and a final paper tracing a specific product from the design through the marketing stage. This course aims to introduce students to the functions and challenges of industry, to change attitudes about industry, thereby developing an appreciation for it, and to familiarize students with occupational opportunities.

Technological Education in Secondary (Senior High) Schools

Technological/vocational education is one of three so-called "orientational" options, along with general or agricultural education, available to senior high school students. The technological orientation provides both general education and technical/vocational education. Students in the Secondary Technological/Vocational Track (also called the General or Expanded Technological/Vocational Track) study at the highest academic level of the various tracks available. Streaming is introduced through a hierarchy of tracks representing degrees of academic orientation and levels of instruction. The Hebrew names for these tracks, referred to commonly by their abbreviations—MASMAT, MASMAR, MASMAM—are given below. These tracks with their Hebrew names are listed in descending order of academic orientation with the proportion of general education to technical/vocational education indicated parenthetically:

MASMAT *(Maslul Miktzoi Ragil Marchav)* Secondary Technical/Vocational Track (60/40)
MASMAR *(Maslul Miktzoi Ragil)* Regular Technical/Vocational Track (50/50)
MASMAM *(Maslul Miltzoi Ma'asi)* Practical Technical/Vocational Track (40/60)
Guidance Track (not reported)

Besides the general education subjects offered within each of these tracks, there are two categories of technological/vocational subjects which are referred to as trends: technical vocational trends and general (nontechnical) vocational trends.

Technological/vocational education in Israel is popular and widely available. In the Hebrew sector it is found in state, state religious, "*yeshivah* high schools," and independent religious schools; in agricultural, general, and technological schools; and in regional schools serving *kibbutzim* and *moshavim*, wherein most of these schools may be either one-track or multi-track (comprehensive) schools. Technical education is also offered in the Arab sector to a lesser extent.

The Ministry of Education and Culture, Department of Examinations, sets the examinations for all general (academic) and technological subjects, but does not administer exams for practical subjects. For each track and trend (specialization) there is a different series of examinations. The two highest levels of examinations are referred to as Matriculation Level and Final Diploma Level, of which the former is higher. In addition to these external examinations, students sit for internal examinations set by their school, primarily in technological subjects. The level of internal examinations corresponds to the level of the track in which the student has studied.

N.B. *Teudat* is a Hebrew word translated as both "certificate" and "diploma." When used in combination with the word "matriculation," it is most commonly translated as "certificate"; when used in connection with other vocational track credentials, it is most frequently translated as "diploma." All references to "final diplomas" could as correctly be translated "certificate of completion" or "final certificate."

Those students who do not pass either the Matriculation Examinations or the Final Diploma Examinations of any track are issued neither a Matriculation Certificate nor a Final Diploma. Instead, the student may receive certification indicating knowledge of a trade which is used for employment purposes and a union salary grade.

Technical/Vocational Tracks in Senior Secondary School

Secondary Technical/Vocational Track—MASMAT

The Secondary Technical/Vocational Track is available for students with high academic achievement and is provided for those students who intend to take a complete or partial series of matriculation examinations upon completion of the program. Those students who pass all examinations for the Matriculation Certificate *(Teudat Bagrut)* and consequently qualify for receipt of the *bagrut* are eligible to continue their education at institutions of higher education or postsecondary technical institutions; those who pass a partial series of matriculation examinations and receive the Final Diploma of the Secondary Technological/Vocational Track (described below) are eligible to continue their education at postsecondary technological institutions. Students in this latter group who do not go directly into military service may continue immediately into programs for Technicians or Practical Engineers, sometimes as a continuation of their secondary technical program in the same institution, sometimes in postsecondary technical colleges or institutions of higher education.

Secondary technical education no longer seeks to train skilled laborers for the job market. The goal today—to provide a broad technological education—is reflected in a curriculum that places greater emphasis on theoretical technology and general studies in exchange for a reduction in hours of practical work.

EXAMINATIONS. Students in the Secondary Technical/Vocational Track (MASMAT) sit for a full or partial series of Matriculation Examinations or Final Diploma examinations depending upon their academic performance in school. The full series of Matriculation Examinations leading to the *Teudat Bagrut* includes the following required general subjects: Bible, English, Hebrew (Grammar and Literature), Jewish History, and Mathematics. Alternatively, students may sit for these examinations at the Final Diploma level. Students in the general (nontechnical) vocational trends are not required to sit for Mathematics, but instead are examined in either Biology, Chemistry, or Physics. Examinations in vocational subjects include two examinations in technological subjects, a practical examination, and Fundamentals of Technical Drawing for those in a technical (rather than general) trend. See Chapter 3 for more details on the *Bagrut* examination schedules for technical education in the Hebrew and Arab sectors.

DIPLOMA. Technological students who sit for and pass the full series of matriculation examinations will be awarded a Matriculation Certificate *(Teudat Bagrut)* entitling them to continue their education at higher education institutions or postsecondary institutions. A Matriculation Certificate from a technological school is considered the equivalent of one from a general (academic) school. Students who sit for and pass a partial series of matriculation examinations along with the lower level Final Diploma examinations are awarded a Final Diploma of the Secondary Technological/Vocational Track *(Teudat Gemer Maslul Miktzoi Ragil Marchav,* MASMAT) issued by the MOEC/DTE.

Regular Technical/Vocational Track—MASMAR

The Regular Technical/Vocational Track is designed for students of average academic ability and is a program generally considered terminal. Students who complete their studies in this track sit for final examinations and receive a Regular Technological/Vocational Final Diploma (described below) which entitles them to a certain professional (trade) rating.

EXAMINATIONS. Students in the Regular Technical/Vocational Track sit for examinations at a final examination level lower than that taken by students in the Secondary Technical/Vocational Track. In general (academic) subjects, students in the technical trends (as opposed to general or nontechnical trends) sit for examinations in Hebrew Composition, Jewish History, and Mathematics. Students in the general (nontechnical) vocational trends are not required to sit for the examination in Mathematics. Examinations in vocational subjects are the same as those listed above for students in the Secondary Technical/Vocational Track.

Diploma. Students who sit for and pass the series of final examinations prescribed for the MASMAR track (which are at a level lower than that of the Secondary Technical/Vocational Track) are awarded the Final Diploma of the Regular Technological/Vocational Track *(Teudat Gemer Maslul Miktzoi Ragil,* MASMAR) issued by the MOEC/DTE.

Practical Technical/Vocational Track—MASMAM

The Practical Technical/Vocational Track is designed for students of low academic ability and is a program which is terminal. The Practical Track is the only one for such students that affords an opportunity for a diploma after grade 11. Students completing this program sit for a shorter series of final examinations and receive a Practical Technological/Vocational Final Diploma (described below) which entitles them to a certain professional (trade) rating.

Examinations. Students in the Practical Technical/Vocational Track sit for only three examinations: Hebrew Composition, one technological subject, and practical work.

Diploma. Students who sit for and pass the final examinations prescribed for this track at the end of grade 12 are awarded the Final Diploma of the Practical Technological/Vocational Track *(Teudat Gemer Maslul Miktzoi Ma'asi,* MASMAM) issued by the MOEC/DTE. Students who complete their studies at the end of grade 11 are entitled to sit for final examinations in a limited number of subjects. Those who pass receive a diploma. Students who complete their studies after grade 10 may receive an informal certificate from their school, but will receive no government diploma.

Guidance Track

For those students whose low academic achievements make it difficult to enter a secondary school, one-, two-, and three-year programs at a "level of guidance" provide general education and basic vocational training. More advanced students in the Guidance Track may transfer to the Practical Technical/Vocational Track.

Major Secondary Vocational Trends

Secondary vocational trends are categorized as either Technical Vocational or General Vocational. Technical vocational trends train personnel for work in industry and services of a technical nature; general vocational trends train personnel for work in industry and services of a nontechnical nature. Table 7.1 provides data on the number of grade 12 technical students according to vocational trend.

Secondary Vocational Curriculum

A reorganization of the Department of Technological Education/DTE has resulted in changes in the curriculum and syllabi which reflect the desire to teach a broad technological education in the early years and introduce specialization in the final year. The program prescribes a unified syllabus for grades 9 through 11 and the introduction of specialization subjects for the trend in grade 12. The field of specialization (trend) is determined on the basis of academic performance and the student's preference. The Department is planning a unified course of studies for groups of technical/vocational trends which have common technological features. Implementation of this program has begun for grade 9 where all classes study a common program according to one of two categories of vocational trends—technical or general (i.e., non-technical). This differs from the former structure where students from the onset (grade 9) were divided into separate classes according to trend.

There were several reasons behind the restructuring by the DTE. With the increased flexibility introduced in 1976 by reform regulations for the matriculation examinations, it became possible for students of average ability to acquire a Matriculation Certificate *(Teudat Bagrut)*. While many students in the secondary and regular technical tracks (MASMAT and MASMAR) wanted to sit for Matriculation Examinations, the heavy study load prescribed by the technological curriculum prevented them from having the time necessary to prepare for the examinations. Other factors prompted the reorganization and curriculum changes—a reduced study load would allow for other educational, extracurricular, and social activities; a reduction in study hours would bring technological programs in line with other orientations; and there was a need for cutbacks due to rising deficit spending attributed to the costs of wages and equipment. For these reasons, the following changes have occured:

1. The number of study hours per week has been reduced from an average of 44 hours to 38 in grade 9, 40 in grade 10, 39 in grade 11, and 38 in grade 12. The reduction in study hours in the Secondary Technical/Vocational Track has been taken from practical work and emphasis placed on theoretical technological studies and general academic studies.
2. The Regular Technical/Vocational Track was reorganized to advance average and above-average students to the Secondary Technical/Vocational Track.
3. Classes in the Secondary Technical/Vocational Track are now heterogeneous until grade 12 when classes are conducted on two levels, called Study Groups; for each course the student is assigned to one of two Study Groups at the appropriate ability level.

See Tables 3.3 and 3.5 for MOEC prescribed curriculums for technical and general trends in the Hebrew and Arab sectors and Table 7.2 for the curriculums for the Technical Vocational Trends and the General Vocational Trends—MASMAT, MASMAR, MASMAM.

Subjects in each vocational trend (technical and general) are categorized as either GENERAL (academic) STUDIES including humanities and science or VOCATIONAL STUDIES which vary according to trend (field of study).

General Studies include the following subjects: Bible; Biology, Chemistry, or Physics; English; Hebrew (including Literature); History and Civics; Mathematics; Physical Education; Homeroom (for discussion of topics of general interest and current events) and *Talmud* (in religious schools). The number of hours prescribed to the humanities is the same for all trends. The number of hours devoted to science and mathematics is greater in the Technical Trends than in the General Trends and the nature of science study differs between the Technical and General Trends.

Vocational Studies include theoretical and practical subjects, some of which are particular according to the trend and some of which are common to all technically-based trends (e.g., Technical Drawing, Introduction to Computers, Theory of Electricity and Electronics).

Transcripts

While yearly transcripts are available upon request, the standardization provided by the Ministry's external Matriculation and Final Diploma Examinations provides a more accurate assessment of a student's achievement level.

Postsecondary Technological Education

Postsecondary technological education in Israel is available in postsecondary technical colleges, regional colleges, and nonuniversity institutions of higher education. This segment will discuss postsecondary institutions only, including those attached to secondary schools. See Appendix A for a list of NITT postsecondary technological/vocational institutions. Selected institutional profiles from all types of institutions are provided at the end of this chapter.

Governance

The Government of Israel has designated the Ministry of Education and Culture/MOEC, Department of Technological Education/DTE and the National Institute of Technological Training/NITT, on behalf of the Ministry of Labor and Social Welfare/MOLSW, as the authorities responsible for the administration and supervision of postsecondary technological education. The division of responsibility between these two ministries is determined by the age of the student and military service status. The DTE serves (pre-military) youth who are continuing directly from grade 12 into postsecondary schools attached to existing secondary technological schools or in separate postsecondary institutions in programs for technicians and practical engineers. The NITT serves adults who have completed military service and are thus beyond the jurisdiction and responsibility of the MOEC; NITT also provides programs for technicians and practical engineers. The Ministry of Education and Culture, DTE programs are referred to as "Youth Programs"; Ministry of Labor and Social

Table 7.2. General Vocational and Technical/Vocational Curriculum Schedules for MASMAT, MASMAR, MASMAM

Subjects	Hours per Week													
	Secondary (MASMAT)						Regular (MASMAR)				Practical (MASMAM)			
	10	11	12		Total		10	11	12	Total	10	11	12	Total
			Study Group†											
			1	2	1	2								
General Vocational Trends														
Bible	2	2	2	–	6	4	2	2	–	4	2	1	–	3
English	4	4	4	3	12	11	3	2	2	7	3	1	–	4
Hebrew	4	4	4		12		3	3	3	9	3	3	3	9
History and Civics	3	2	3	2	8	7	3	2	2	7	3	2	2	7
Mathematics	3	3	–		6		2	2	1	5	2	1	–	3
Physical Education	2	2	2		6		2	2	2	6	2	2	2	6
Physics/Chemistry/Biology	3	2	–		5		2	1	–	3	2	–	–	2
Home Room	1	1	1		3		1	1	1	3	1	1	1	3
General/Academic Studies	22	20	16	12	58	54	18	15	11	44	18	11	8	37
Technical/Vocational Studies*	18	19	22	26	59	63	22	24	27	73	22	28	30	80
Grand Total	40	39	38		117		40	39	38	117	40	39	38	117
Technical/Vocational Trends														
Bible	2	2	2	–	6	4	2	2	–	4	2	1	–	3
English	4	4	4	3	12	11	3	2	2	7	3	1	–	4
Hebrew	4	4	4		12		3	3	3	9	3	3	3	9
History and Civics	3	2	3	2	8	7	3	2	2	7	3	2	2	7
Mathematics	4	4	4		12		3	2	3	8	3	2	2	7
Physical Education	2	2	2		6		2	2	2	6	2	2	2	6
Physics	3	3	–		6		2	2	–	4	2	1	–	3
Home Room	1	1	1		3		1	1	1	3	1	1	1	3
General/Academic Studies	23	22	20	16	65	61	19	16	13	48	19	13	10	42
Technical/Vocational Studies*	17	17	18	22	52	56	21	23	25	69	21	26	28	75
Grand Total	40	39	38		117		40	39	38	117	40	39	38	117

SOURCE: *Technological Education in Israel*, MOEC/DTE, 1984, pp. 27–28.

*Technological/Vocational Studies category subjects vary in accordance with the trend.

†In grade 12, classes are conducted on two levels called study groups.

Welfare/NITT programs are referred to as "Adult Programs." The DTE and the NITT are each responsible to their constituencies for setting curriculums, administering and grading external examinations, allocating financial aid, and awarding diplomas.

The Roof Commission

The Roof Commission is responsible for policy-making with respect to the training of technicians and practical engineers. The Commission is a public body comprised of member representatives from the MOEC, MOLSW, the Union of Technicians and Practical Engineers, the Ben-Gurion University of the Negev, the Technion-Israel Institute of Technology and ORT Israel. The chairman of the Commission is also the Head of the Department of Technological Education in the MOEC.

The Roof Commission approves new trends reflecting economic and educational considerations, approves curriculums, determines qualifications of teaching and instructional staff, and determines minimum entrance requirements for technician and practical engineering programs. Decisions made by the Roof Commission are implemented by the DTE and the NITT reflecting uniform but not identical curriculums, syllabi, examinations, and trends.

The National Institute of Technological Training

The National Institute of Technological Training/NITT (frequently translated as the Government Institute of Technological [Technical] Training) was established in the early fifties in response to the national needs of educating, training, and absorbing immigrants in order to better serve the labor and economic sectors of society. Specific concern was expressed over the gap between the functioning levels of vocational school graduates and graduate engineers. As a result, the MOLSW along with the MOEC approached the United Nations for advice and assistance. The U.N. through its affiliated organization, the International Labor Organization (the ILO), established the Institute and assisted in its development during the first five years through the provision of modern equipment, qualified personnel, and bursaries.

NITT is under the auspices of the Israeli government and is responsible for the technical training of adults at levels of certification below that of graduate engineers and above that of skilled laborers. The Institute is also charged with the training of vocational instructors and teachers of technical subjects in secondary schools and various training centers. The Institute is authorized by both the MOLSW and the MOEC and is operational under a Board of Directors. This Board consists of the Head of the Division of Vocational Training and Proficiency in the MOLSW, the Head of the Department of Technological Education in the MOEC, the Head of the Institute, and heads of several colleges. Funding is divided between the two ministries, while management policy is carried out by the Head of the Institute according to directives set forth by the Institute's Board of Directors.

The Institute is divided into four main operational units—the Division of Vocational Instructors, Technology Teacher Training; the Division for Advanced Studies; the Division for Research and Planning; and the Professional-Pedagogical Division. The Professional-Pedagogical Division is divided into the Curriculum Unit, the Examinations Unit, and the Supervision Unit—which together standardize the training and qualifications of Practical Engineers, Technicians, Laboratory Technicians, and Draughtsmen. The Institute itself is not directly involved in the education and training of individuals but instead directs these functions through the various technical colleges and training schools, regional colleges, ORT-sponsored schools and other schools.

Accreditation

The notion of "accreditation" for postsecondary technological schools and colleges does not exist. Accreditation is by law a function of the Council of Higher Education and applies only to universities, nonuniversity institutions of higher education, and certain programs within regional colleges. There are, however, accredited institutions of higher education and regional colleges which offer postsecondary technological programs for Technicians and Practical Engineers in addition to academic programs. All postsecondary institutions providing programs for Technicians or Practical Engineers have authorization from the DTE or the NITT and are under their jurisdiction; the program offered, not the proprietorship of the institution, is the factor determining the source of authorization.

Postsecondary Technological Programs

Postsecondary technological programs provide trained technical personnel who serve as links between the academic engineer and skilled laborers. There are two levels of training offered by these programs:

Technicians—The first (lower) level of training provides a connecting link between the Practical Engineer and skilled laborers. Technicians complete either a fulltime day program of 40-42 study hours per week for one year, *or* an accumulative part-time afternoon or evening program requiring one and one-half to two years to complete. Technicians fulfill a wide range of functions in industry and other sectors such as management of production and maintenance departments, supervision of work and efficiency methods, acquisition of equipment and materials, and laboratory testing. Qualified, licensed Technicians are referred to as *Technaim (Technai,* sing.).

Practical Engineers—The second (higher) level of training provides a connecting link between the Graduate Engineer and the Technician or skilled laborer. Practical Engineers complete either a fulltime day program of 36-44 study hours per week requiring about one and one-half years if proceeding directly from a technical secondary program, *or* about two years if there is a break in attendance after secondary school, *or* an accumulative part-time afternoon or evening program requiring about four years (it is theoretically a two-year program). Practical Engineers provide senior functions in industry and other sectors such as research assistants to engineers and scientists, design and calculation, technical planning and technical supervision of production and maintenance operations. Qualified, licensed Practical Engineers are referred to as *Handassaim (Handassai,* sing.).

In the Ministry of Education's Youth Programs, schools for Technicians and Practical Engineers are attached to existing secondary technical schools and constitute a postsecondary framework for the continuation of secondary technological education. Youth Programs exhibit a definite continuity of curriculum from secondary technical education to technician programs through practical engineering programs. Grade 13 for both Technicians and Practical Engineers in the same trend is identical and serves as the basis for grade 14. Those who successfully complete the grade 13 Technicians program receive the qualification of Certified Technician *(Technai)*; those who continue and successfully complete the grade 14 Practical Engineering program receive the qualification of Certified Practical Engineer *(Handassai)*.

In the Ministry of Labor's Adult Programs, Technician and Practical Engineering programs may be found operating alongside Youth Programs in technological schools, as described above, or more frequently are provided through separate postsecondary colleges, regional colleges, or nonuniversity institutions of higher education. Because of the time lapse between secondary schooling and Adult Programs (normally the result of obligatory military service), the same Technician and Practical Engineering program may be more intensive or extensive. The resulting qualification of Certified Technician or Certified Practical Engineer, however, is the same and considered equivalent.

Technician and Practical Engineering programs are designated by trend (field of specialization) and exhibit a certain degree of uniformity resulting from the prescribed curricula established by the member representatives of the Roof Commission. While flexibility is granted to the various schools providing these programs, minimum standards are met by compliance with prescribed curricula; external examinations which are designed, administered, supervised and graded by the DTE or the NITT; and national supervision and coordination of programs.

Postsecondary Technical Trends (Fields of Specialization)

Trends in technician and practical engineering programs reflect a continuation of specializations introduced in secondary technical schools. The postsecondary trends and subtrends available are displayed in Table 7.3.

Entrance Requirements to Postsecondary Technical Programs

The Roof Commission, comprised of representative members from the Ministry of Education and Culture, the Ministry of Labor and Social Welfare, the

Table 7.3. Postsecondary Technical/Vocational Trends in Technician and Practical Engineering Programs Offered by DTE and/or NITT

Technicians		Practical Engineers	
Main Trends	Subtrends	Main Trends	Subtrends
Agricultural Engineering	Mechanization, Water & Ground	Agricultural Engineering	Mechanization, Water & Ground
Agriculture (Agronomics)	Animals, Citricult., Control. & Protec. Crops, Field Crops, Plantations	Agriculture (Agronomics)	Animals, Field Crops, Plantations
Architecture	–	Architecture	–
Bldg. & Construc.	–	Building	Civil Engineering
Chemistry	Food Proces., Food Proces. (milk), Indus. & Lab. Chem.	Chemistry	Food Proces., Food Proces. (milk), Indus. & Lab Chem.
Data Processing (Computers)	–	–	–
–	–	Ecology	–
Electricity	–	Electricity	–
Electronics	Indus. Electron., Medical Electron., Telecommunications	Electronics	Computers, Indus. Electron., Medical Electron., Telecommunications
Instrumentation & Control	–	Instrumentation & Control	–
Landscape Architecture	–	Landscape Architecture	–
Management	Indus., Production	Management	Industrial
Mechanics (Machines)	Aeromech., Automation (Instrumen.) & Control, Automech., Machine Construc. & Materials Proces., Maritime, Metallurgy, Refrig. & Air Condit.	Mechanics (Machines)	Aeromech., Automation (Instrumen.) & Control, Machine Construc. & Materials Proces., Metallurgy, Refrig. & Air Condit.
Nuclear Technology	–		–
–	–	Physics	Electronics, Electro-Optics
Plastics & Synthetic Materials	–	Plastics & Synthetic Materials	–
Technical & Scientific Photography	–	Technical & Scientific Photography	–

SOURCE: Adapted from *Technological Education in Israel*, MOEC/DTE, 1984, p. 50; and information obtained in an interview with the director of NITT, Israel.

Union of Technicians and Practical Engineers among others, is responsible for establishing minimum entrance requirements for Technician and Practical Engineering programs. These requirements are as follows:

1. A Matriculation Certificate, regular or external, or
2. Graduation from a four-year (Pre-Reform) general (academic) or technological secondary school, or its equivalent under the Reform System.
3. Graduates of a three-year (Pre-Reform) technological program or others completing grade 11 may be accepted after a preparatory course when that course results in successfully passing an external Ministry of Education examination.

These requirements represent a general framework under which schools determine eligibility for admission. Competitive admission requirements such as entrance examinations, a certain level of examination results, specified subjects, an interview, portfolio, or a Matriculation Certificate may be required when space limitations and high demand exist. Admission requirements may differ from one department to another within a single institution.

Transcripts, Grades, and Assessment

Transcripts are provided in English and indicate subjects, numerical grades, and study hours. Courses may be one term (usually a semester) or one year in length. Sometimes grade reports list subjects studied each semester; frequently, however, transcripts simply list all subjects taken within a designated time frame. In either case, the total number of study hours per subject is normally indicated. Since a credit system is not used, the number of study hours is the key indicator for establishing credit equivalency. The number of study hours, however, includes both theoretical and practical components of the course without further clarification. A breakdown is difficult to determine because the practical component is an integral part of the course. See various sample documents at the end of this chapter.

Grading is based upon homework, tests, term papers, and final examinations. The grade may represent either internal or external assessment, sometimes both. Internal assessment refers to institutional assessment, while external assessment refers to examinations which are developed, supervised, and graded through the government-designated ministry. Internal examinations are held at the end of each term; external examinations are held at the end of those courses which are designated by the ministry as requiring external examination. Both Technician and Practical Engineering programs include a prescribed number of external examinations (usually five to seven) as well as a Final Project, which is also externally evaluated. Both internal and external assessments are reported by the institution; some institutions designate those subjects for which an external examination was given while other institutions make no distinction.

The grading system most frequently employed for both internal and external assessment is on a scale of 0-100 with a minimum passing mark of 55. Other institutions may use a 54 or 50 as the lowest passing mark. Grades are reported as an absolute number without further descriptive remarks. Those institutions using a 0-100, 55 pass scale follow a traditional Israeli breakdown:

95 - 100	=	Excellent	65 - 74	=	Fair
85 - 94	=	Very Good	55 - 64	=	Poor
75 - 84	=	Good	0 - 54	=	Fail

Diplomas

In order to qualify for the Diploma of Certified Technician and Diploma of Certified Practical Engineer all students must complete the prescribed program and pass the external examinations administered by the Department of Technological Education (Ministry of Education and Culture) or the National Institute of Technological Training (Ministry of Labor and Social Welfare). In addition, all students for either diploma are required to submit and defend a Final Project.

Registration as a Certified Technician or a Certified Practical Engineer requires no further examination but does involve filing an application and supporting documentation to the Unit for Registration of Practical Engineers, Technicians, Laboratory Technicians and Draughtsmen. This Unit is authorized by the Government and the Federation of Practical Engineers to verify the qualifications and diplomas of applicants and to register and license individuals in the appropriate field.

The Diploma indicates the level of Technician *(Technai)* or Practical Engineer *(Handassai)* and the field of specialization. See sample documents at the end of this chapter.

Articulation

There are no formal articulation agreements between postsecondary technological institutions offering Technician or Practical Engineering programs and institutions of higher education offering degree programs in related fields. One known exception to this is a two-year (24-month) B.Sc. program for *Handassaim* offered by the Faculty of Engineering at Tel-Aviv University. Practical Engineers may be granted transfer credit or exemption from coursework, but such matters are dealt with on an individual basis and consideration rarely results in recognition of more than one year.

The reason cited for the lack of recognition by institutions of higher education is that the practical nature of technological programs is not consistent with the theoretical nature of university-level programs, a traditional opinion expressed in countries where tracking of technological education is separate from university education. In fact, the ramifications of recognition and coordination lie at least as much in the financial and political arena as problems resulting from this situation having national economic repercussions. Individuals emigrate for want of higher educational opportunities which causes not only a short-term loss of qualified manpower but in many cases a permanent one.

The Organization For Rehabilitation Through Training (ORT)

The Organization for Rehabilitation Through Training (ORT) is a global network of schools and training programs which provides secondary and postsecondary technical education by and for the Jewish community. Founded in St. Petersburg, Russia in 1880 by a group of wealthy, philanthropic Jews, ORT was first established as a system of cooperative workshops and agricultural settlements for Jews of limited economic means. In the decades that followed, a network of ORT schools spread throughout Eastern Europe providing basic skills training for industry and agriculture. Today ORT serves some 116,000 men and women through informal and formal technical education programs in 15 countries: Argentina, Brazil, Chile, France, India, Israel, Italy, Mexico, Morocco, Peru, South Africa, Switzerland, the United Kingdom, the United States, and Uruguay. Funding for the near $100 million 1984 budget was provided by the American Jewish Joint Distribution Committee, the American ORT Federation, Women's American ORT, other ORT groups throughout the world, and various foreign governments; however, over 78% of total costs are met within the local communities ORT serves.

The ORT program in Israel, ORT Israel, is the largest of all ORT operations. It is also the largest network of technical/vocational schools in Israel, second only to schools under the proprietorship of local authorities. In 1983, ORT Israel reported a total enrollment of 80,431 students, including those involved in informal and formal technical education programs. The diversity of their institutional settings includes intermediate and secondary schools, "*yeshivah* high schools," and other religious schools, industrial schools and classes, adult programs, apprenticeship programs, and colleges and other postsecondary institutions. In 1985-86, ORT Israel claimed 55,000 students registered in 105 schools, all but 14 of which were secondary. In addition, enrollment in their 13 postsecondary institutions (ORT Moshinsky excluded) was reported as 5,763 (1983) in 10 localities throughout the country. At the postsecondary level ORT provides both Youth and Adult programs, thereby functioning under the MOEC/DTE and the MOLSW/NITT.

ORT Israel is a broad-based network operating throughout the country. ORT Israel is present in cities and suburbs, inner city quarters, development towns and settlements, industrial plants, *kibbutzim*, and military bases. It claims to provide an educational opportunity for almost every kind of student from the high achiever excelling in advanced technology to the slow learner or problematic student who is looking for a skill with which to directly enter the job market. ORT describes its educational institutions and programs as follows:

1. Special Education Centers for children with learning and social problems and low self-esteem, offering a carefully designed curriculum of general education with a trade specialization.
2. Industrial and Military Base Schools and Apprenticeship Centers: non-selective admission, emphasizing on-the-job training combined with general education; vocational skills diploma.
3. Vocational High Schools: selective entry; students work for a full or partial series of Matriculation *Bagrut* Examinations, or a Final Diploma; program combines vocational study with general education.
4. Technical High School and Comprehensive Schools: selective entry; graduation with a Matriculation Certificate *(Teudat Bagrut)* giving access to higher education; program of general education with technological specialization.
5. Technical Colleges: postsecondary one-year and two-year courses for Technicians and Practical Engineers.
6. Pedagogical and Technological Research and Development Center: (ORT Moshinsky) for teacher up-grading, development of new curricular and teaching methods.
7. ORT Adults: training, retraining or upgrading for men and women terminating military service. Courses include matriculation preparation, post-secondary Technician and Practical Engineering programs, and a drug rehabilitation center operated in conjunction with the Ministry of Health to provide assistance in breaking addiction while providing vocational training and social support.

Teacher Training for Technological Education

Every teacher/instructor in a secondary school must have a Teaching Diploma (license) from the Ministry of Education and Culture (MOEC). The qualifications required for a license are determined by the grade, track, and level of the course (basic or advanced). The required qualifications are also dependent upon the trend in which the course is taught, i.e., technical/vocational trends or general (nontechnical) vocational trends. These requirements are briefly described below according to trend and teacher qualifications.

Technical Vocational Trends

1. An engineer or person with an M.Sc. is eligible to be licensed to teach basic and advanced technological subjects within the speciality for all grades and tracks once the pedagogical and Hebrew studies courses specified by the regulations have been completed.
2. A Practical Engineer *(Handassai)* is eligible to be licensed for basic and advanced technological subjects within the specialty for all grades and tracks excluding advanced subjects in grades 11 and 12 in the secondary technical/vocational track, once the pedagogical and Hebrew studies courses as prescribed have been completed.

3. A Technician *(Technai)* with a minimum of two years' industrial experience in the field is eligible for a license as an instructor in all grades and tracks and as a teacher of basic technological subjects within the speciality for all tracks in grades 9 and 10 only, once completing the pedagogical and Hebrew studies specified by the regulations. A technician is eligible for a teacher license only after the instructor's license has been obtained.
4. An instructor's license can be obtained by a person holding certification from the inter-ministerial committee for the field specified on the certification.

General (Nontechnical) Vocational Trends

1. A person with a B.A. or B.Sc. in a general technological subject is eligible to be licensed for basic and advanced technological subjects in the specialty for all grades and tracks once the pedagogical and Hebrew studies courses specified in the regulations have been completed.
2. A graduate of a four-year teacher training college or program in general vocational subjects may be licensed for basic and advanced technological subjects within the specialty for all grades and tracks. There are conditions set for graduates of three-year teacher training programs who wish to qualify for a license. A person with a high professional rating and five years of experience in the field may, at the discretion of the proper authorities, also be licensed if the person is "academically" educated in any subject and completes a minimum of 700 hours of professional pedagogical and Hebrew studies courses at a recommended institution.
3. A graduate of a three-year teacher training college in a general vocational subject may be licensed for all grades and tracks excluding advanced technological subjects in grades 11 and 12 in the secondary technological/vocational track. Conditions for licensing professionals with five years of experience in the profession, at least 12 years of schooling, and at least 700 hours of coursework in pedagogical and Hebrew studies also exist.
4. An instructor's license may be granted to a graduate of a three-year teacher training program in a general vocational subject for the specialty.

Technological teachers are trained in institutions supervised by the MOEC or jointly by the MOEC/MOLSW. Programs exist in teacher training colleges, in postsecondary technological colleges, and institutions of higher education. Through the MOEC, teacher training colleges educate teaching personnel for certain subjects: computers, fashion trades, nutrition sciences, secretarial trades, shop, and technical and general trades. The MOLSW through the NITT trains vocational instructors and practical engineers as teachers. In the teacher training departments of institutions of higher education, engineers are trained to teach science and technological subjects. The MOEC, Departments of Teacher Training and Technological Education, have together developed a combined training program for teachers of technology on the level of practical engineer. Other teachers become qualified as a result of retraining courses for individuals with degrees in engineering and natural sciences or through in-service training programs.

Technical Institutional Profiles

The following alphabetical listing of selected institutions offering technical/vocational programs includes the name, address, type of institution by designator, date of establishment, affiliation, fields of study, and diplomas and degrees awarded. Other names by which an institution is known are included in parentheses after the institution listing. See also Appendix B which lists all postsecondary technological colleges under the Ministry of Labor and Social Welfare/National Institute for Technological Training.

The following abbreviations (in parentheses) have been used to indicate the type of institution: **IHE** = Institution of Higher Education accredited by the Council for Higher Education; **IHE-A** = IHE-affiliated institution; **ORT** = Organization for Rehabilitation Through Training institution; **OTHR** = Other, unaffiliated institutions; **RC** = Regional Colleges. Types of programs and diplomas awarded are indicated by the following: **PC** = preparatory course; **PE** = Practical Engineer *(Handassai)*; **T** = Technician *(Technai)*; **TT-TI** = Technology Teacher-Technology Instructor; **B Tech** = Bachelor of Technology; **OYP** = One-Year Program; **FT/D** = fulltime/day; **PT/E** = part-time/evening.

ACHAVAH REGIONAL COLLEGE, P.O. Box 85, Kiriyat Malachi. (RC) *Fields of Study:* Electronics, Mechanics. Extension courses in Mech. and Pre-Engr. estd. and offered by the Practical Engineering College of Beer-Sheva. *Programs:* PC, T, PT/E. *Diploma:* T.

PRACTICAL ENGINEERING COLLEGE OF BEER-SHEVA (BEER-SHEVA TECHNOLOGICAL COLLEGE). (IHE-A) Estd. 1961. Capacity: 3,000. Affiliated with Ben-Gurion University of the Negev. Extension courses held at Achavah R.C., Arab Youth Center, Offakim College (for religious girls), Ashdod Technological Training College. *Fields of Study:* Architecture, Bldg./Construc., Chemistry, Comput. Engr., Electricity, Electronics, Electro-Optics, Indus. Mgmt., Instrument. & Control, Mech., Nuclear Technol., Teach. & Instruction. *Programs:* PC, Pre-Engr. PC, PE, FT/D (4-5 sems., 40 hrs./wk.), PE-PT/E (8 sems., 16-20 hrs./wk.), T-FT/D (3 sem. extended yr., 40 hrs./wk.), T-PT/E (5 sems., 16-20 hrs./wk.). *Grading:* 95-100 (Excellent), 85-94 (Very Good), 75-84 (Good), 65-74 (Fair), 56-64 (Poor), 0-55 (Fail). *Diplomas:* PE, T, TT-TI.

TEL-AVIV UNIVERSITY TECHNICAL COLLEGE (COLLEGE OF PRACTICAL ENGINEERING, TEL-AVIV; SCHOOL FOR ENGINEERS), 30 University Rd., Ramat Aviv 69975. (IHE-A) Estd. 1962. Affiliated with and located near Tel-Aviv University campus. *Enrollment:* 3,000 FT/D + PT/E. Adult and Youth programs, Tech. H.S., and Educ. Development Center. *Fields of Study:* Comput. Sci., Electronics, Indus. Mgmt., Instrument. & Control, Mech., Technol. Educ. (Teach. & Instruction). *Programs:* PC, PE, TT-TI, FT/D, PT/E. *Diplomas:* PE, TT-TI.

COLLEGE FOR SCIENTIFIC PHOTOGRAPHY (COLLEGE OF PHOTOGRAPHY), Kiriyat Ono near Tel-Aviv. (OTHR) *Fields of Study:* Scientific Photography. *Programs:* T, PT/E. *Diplomas:* T.

THE MUNICIPAL COLLEGE OF EILAT (EILAT REGIONAL COLLEGE). Affiliated with Ben-Gurion University of the Negev. (RC) *Fields of Study:* Instrument. & Control, Machines. *Programs:* PC, T, PT/E. *Diplomas:* T.

SCHOOL FOR TECHNICAL LANDSCAPE (SCHOOL FOR GARDENING AND LANDSCAPE), Petah Tikva. (OTHR) *Fields of Study:* Gardening & Landscap. *Programs:* T, FT/D. *Diplomas:* T.

HADASSA COMMUNITY COLLEGE, 37 Haneviim St., Jerusalem. Tel.: (02) 222-291. (OTHR) Estd. 1969. Adult programs only. Selective admission based upon Matriculation Certificate, entrance exams, interviews (variable by dept.). *Grading:* 95-100 (Excellent), 85-94 (Very Good), 75-84 (Good), 65-74 (Fair), 55-64 (Pass), 0-54 (Fail). *Fields of Study:* Computers, Dental Technician, Ecology, Electronics (discontinued), Lab Tech., Med. Secretaries, Printing Technician (2 yrs.), Technical/Scientific Photogr. (2 yrs.), X-Ray Technician. *Programs:* PE, T, FT/D. *Diplomas:* PE, T.

JERUSALEM COLLEGE OF TECHNOLOGY (JERUSALEM HIGHER SCHOOL OF TECHNOLOGY, JERUSALEM INSTITUTE OF TECHNOLOGY, JERUSALEM SCHOOL OF APPLIED SCIENCES), 21 Havaad Haleumi, Givat Mordechai, P.O. Box 16031, Jerusalem. Tel.: (02) 423131. (IHE) Estd. 1970. *Enrollment:* Approx. 200 (all Male). Tradit. academy for advanced Torah studies with technol. programs. *Fields of Study:* Appl. Physics/Electro-Optics, Computers, Electronics, Technol. Teach. & Instruction. *Programs:* OYP, PC, PE, TT-TI, B Tech, FT/D. *Diplomas:* PE, B Tech, TT-TI (see also institutional profiles in Chapter 8).

THE ISRAELI INSTITUTE OF PRODUCTIVITY, SCHOOL OF INDUSTRIAL ENGINEERING (LABOR PRODUCTIVITY INSTITUTE), 4 Henrietta Szold St., P.O. Box 33010, Tel-Aviv 61330. Tel.: (03) 422411. (OTHR) Estd. 1953. A public institution chartered by the government, the Histadrut, the Manufacturers' Assn., Technion-Israel Institute of Technology, and the Engineers' Assn. *Fields of Study:* Practical Indus. Engr., Production Technician. *Programs:* PC, PE, T, FT/D, PT/E. *Diplomas:* PE, T.

MICHLALAH-JERUSALEM COLLEGE FOR WOMEN, Bayit Vegan, P.O. Box 16078, Jerusalem. Tel.: (02) 91160. (IHE) Estd. 1964. *Fields of Study:* Computers. *Programs:* PE, T, FT/D. *Diplomas:* PE, T (see institutional profile in Chapter 8).

VINICK INSTITUTE (MIKVE YISRAEL). (OTHR) *Fields of Study:* Agri. *Programs:* T, FT/D. *Diplomas:* T.

THE NATIONAL SCHOOL FOR HANDASSAIM (TECHNION JUNIOR TECHNICAL COLLEGE), P.O. Box 4459, Technion City, Haifa 31043. (IHE-A) Estd. 1963. Affiliated with Technion-Israel Institute of Technology. Adult and Youth programs. Competitive admission; Matriculation Certificate required. Grades reported each sem. on 0-100 scale with 55 passing. *Fields of Study:* Architecture, Bio-Med., Chem., Computers, Bldg. & Construc., Electricity, Indus. Mgmt., Mech., Physics/Electro-Optics. *Programs:* PE, T, FT/D, PT/E. *Diplomas:* PE, T.

NERI BLUMFIELD HAIFA INSTITUTE. (OTHR) *Fields of Study:* Architecture. *Programs:* PE. *Diplomas:* PE.

ORT AFULA, 1 Hatzaftsefot St., Afula 18367. *Fields of Study:* Electronics. *Programs:* PE. *Diplomas:* PE.

ORT ARANNE COMPREHENSIVE HIGH SCHOOL, (Religious)—P.O. Box 25; (Secular)—P.O. Box 66, Beit Sha'an 10900. *Fields of Study:* Mechanics. Programs: PE, T. *Diplomas:* PE, T.

MAX A. BRAUDE ORT INTERNATIONAL SCHOOL, Carmiel. Municipal support from development town of Carmiel in Western Galilee. *Projected Secondary and Postsecondary Programs:* Biochem., Computer-Aided Design, Comput. Sci., Electronics & Robotics, Electro-Optics. For Israeli ORT students and students worldwide. Proposal to offer part of training for teaching of technol. educ. currently under consideration. Scheduled to open Fall of 1986 with 300 students.

ORT GIVATAYIM TECHNICAL JUNIOR COLLEGE (TECHNICAL JUNIOR COLLEGE ORT GIVATAIM) 15 Golumb St., Givatayim 53466. Adult and Youth programs. *Fields of Study:* Air Condit. & Refrig., Architecture, Construc., Data Proces., Electronics, Mechanics. *Programs:* PE, T, FT/D. *Diplomas:* PE, T.

ORT HANEVIIM (ORT TECHNICAL SCHOOL, JERUSALEM), 42 HaNeviim St., Jerusalem 95103 (with branch in East Jerusalem). *Fields of Study:* Architecture, Bldg. & Construc., Electromech., Mechanics. In East Jerusalem—Bldg. Construc., Electromech., Technology Teach. & Instruct. *Programs:* PE, T, TT-TI, PT/E. *Diplomas:* PE, T, TT-TI.

ORT LANE TECHNICAL HIGH SCHOOL (ORT LAINE SCHOOL), 2 Giborey Israel St., Rehovot. *Fields of Study:* Electronics, Mechanics. *Programs:* PE. *Diplomas:* PE.

ORT LEVINSON (ORT TECHNICAL SCHOOL, KIRYAT BIALIK), Hagalil St., Kiryat Bialik 2700. *Fields of Study:* Bldg. & Construc., Data Proces., Electronics, Instrument. & Control, Mechanics. *Programs:* PC, PE, T, FT/D, PT/E. *Diplomas:* PE, T.

ORT LOD. P.O. Box 301, Lod 71103. *Fields of Study:* Electronics. *Programs:* PE. *Diplomas:* PE.

ORT LVOVITCH JUNIOR TECHNICAL COLLEGE (ORT TECHNICAL COLLEGE, NETANYA), New Industrial Zone, Netanya 42379. *Fields of Study:* Electromech., Electronics, Instrument. & Control, Mechanics. *Programs:* PC, PE, T. *Diplomas:* PE, T.

ORT MOSHINSKY, 28 Derech Hatayasin, Yad Eliahu, Tel-Aviv 67299 (on the campus of ORT Syngalowski). Estd. 1976. A Technical and Pedagogical Research Institute serving entire ORT Israel network and contributing to worldwide network. Has staff of 24 and 7 operational units: Library used by staff, teachers, practical engineers for research; Technical Publishing House; Graphics Dept. for in-house magazines, textbooks, animated teach. film; Audio-Visual Dept. used in textbooks, teach. film and public relations; Course Development Dept. served by Computers, Electronics, Mechanics units to develop new courses as technol. emerges (e.g., Robotics, Digital & Satellite Communica., Fiber & Electro-Optics); In-Service Teacher Train. for new courses; In-Service Teacher Upgrading as technol. evolves and changes occur in various fields. *Programs:* In-Service Teacher Train. *Diplomas:* TT-TI.

ORT SCHOOL OF ENGINEERING (ORT SCHOOL OF ENGINEERING AT THE HEBREW UNIVERSITY OF JERUSALEM), 12 Shefa Tal St., Givat Ram (near The Hebrew University), Jerusalem 94384. Tel.: (02) 533-141. Estd. 1976. *Enrollment:* 150. Secondary/postsecondary programs. Adult and Youth programs. Selective admission. *Fields of Study:* Data Proces., Electronics, Technol. Teach. & Instruction. *Programs:* PC, PE, T, TT-TI, FT/D. *Diplomas:* PE, T, TT-TI.

ORT SHAPIRO JUNIOR TECHNICAL COLLEGE (ORT PRACTICAL ENGINEERING SCHOOL, KFAR SABA), Main Rd., Kfar Saba 42269. *Fields of Study:* Ecology, Electromechanics. *Programs:* PC, PE, T, FT/D, PT/E. *Diplomas:* PE, T.

ORT A. SYNGALOWSKI JUNIOR TECHNICAL COLLEGE (ORT YAD SYNGALOWSKI JUNIOR TECHNICAL COLLEGE), (sometimes spelled Sy[i]ngalov[w]ski[y]). Technical H.S. division estd. 1949 in Jaffa; moved to present location 1959. Junior Tech. College estd. 1977. Selective admission to Tech. H.S. section with eligibility determined by entrance exams in math, Engl., other subjects, along with intermediate school grades; matriculation cert. required for junior college. *Enrollment:* Secondary School—1,284; Junior College—1,500. *Fields of Study:* Comput. Sci., Electricity, Electronics, Mechanics. *Programs:* PE, T, FT/D. *Diplomas:* PE, T.

P. SAPIR REGIONAL COLLEGE OF THE NEGEV (SHA'AR HANEGEV REGIONAL COLLEGE), Mobile Post, Hof Ashkelon 79165. Tel.: (051) 97161. (RC, IHE-A) Estd. 1976. Affiliated with Ben-Gurion University of the Negev. *Fields of Study:* Bldg. & Construc., Computers, Electronics, Indus. Mgmt., Mechanics. *Programs:* PC, PE, T, FT/D, PT/E. *Diplomas:* PE, T.

SCHOOL FOR PRACTICAL ENGINEERS, RUPPIN INSTITUTE OF AGRICULTURE. (OTHR) Affiliated with Ruppin Institute of Agriculture, Emek Hefer 60960. Tel.: (053) 95131-7. *Fields of Study:* Agri., Bldg. Construc., Chem., Indus. Mgmt., Mechanics, Technol. Teach. & Instruction. *Programs:* PC, PE, T, TT-TI, FT/D. *Diplomas:* PE, T, TT-TI (see Ruppin Institute of Agriculture profile in Chapter 8).

SEMINAR FOR TECHNICAL TEACHERS AND TUTORS, TEL-AVIV. (OTHR) *Fields of Study:* Bldg. Metals, Electricity, Electronics, Indus. Mgmt., Instrument Control. *Programs:* T, FT/D, PT/E. *Diplomas:* T.

TEL-AVIV ORT JUNIOR COLLEGE FOR TECHNICIANS (ORT TECHNICAL SCHOOL, TEL-AVIV), 12 Shefa Tal St., Tel-Aviv. *Fields of Study:* Electromech., Electronics, Indus. Mgmt., Mechanics. *Programs:* PE. *Diplomas:* PE.

TEL-HAI RODMAN REGIONAL COLLEGE, Upper Galilee,Tel Hai 12210. Tel.: (069) 40969 or 43731. (RC, IHE-A) Estd. 1957 as arts and crafts center. Affiliated with Haifa University. Sem. sys. (Oct.-March, April-July). Library: 40,000 vols., 600 periodicals. Faculty: 40 FT, 55 PT. *Fields of Study:* Agri., Architecture, Bldg. Construc., Computers, Electronics, Indus. Mgmt., Machines, Robotics, Technol. Teach. & Instruction. *Programs:* PC, PE, T, TT-TI, FT/D, PT/E. *Diplomas:* PC, PE, TT-TI, T.

THE SHENKAR COLLEGE OF TEXTILE TECHNOLOGY AND FASHION, 24 Anne Frank St., Ramat Gan. (IHE) See institutional profile in Chapter 8 for more information.

WESTERN GALILEE COLLEGE, YAD NATAN. (OTHR) *Fields of Study:* Agriculture. *Programs:* PE. *Diplomas:* PE.

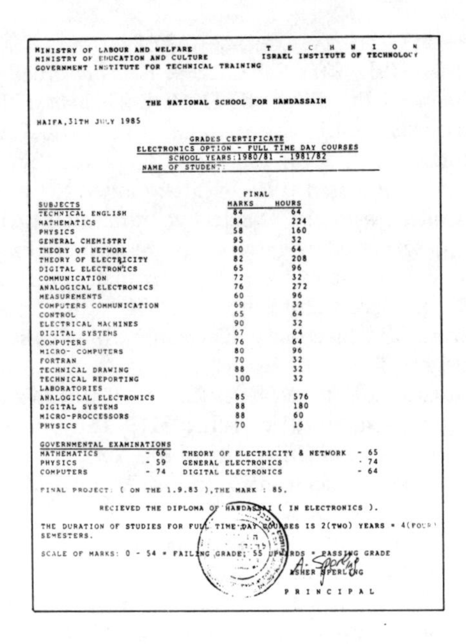

MINISTRY OF LABOUR AND WELFARE
MINISTRY OF EDUCATION AND CULTURE
GOVERNMENT INSTITUTE FOR TECHNICAL TRAINING

T E C H N I O N
ISRAEL INSTITUTE OF TECHNOLOGY

THE NATIONAL SCHOOL FOR HANDASSAIM

HAIFA,31TH JULY 1985

GRADES CERTIFICATE
ELECTRONICS OPTION - FULL TIME DAY COURSES
SCHOOL YEARS:1980/81 - 1981/82
NAME OF STUDENT:

SUBJECTS	FINAL MARKS	HOURS
TECHNICAL ENGLISH	84	64
MATHEMATICS	84	224
PHYSICS	58	160
GENERAL CHEMISTRY	95	32
THEORY OF NETWORK	80	64
THEORY OF ELECTRICITY	82	208
DIGITAL ELECTRONICS	65	96
COMMUNICATION	72	32
ANALOGICAL ELECTRONICS	76	272
MEASUREMENTS	60	96
COMPUTERS COMMUNICATION	69	32
CONTROL	65	64
ELECTRICAL MACHINES	90	32
DIGITAL SYSTEMS	67	64
COMPUTERS	76	64
MICRO- COMPUTERS	80	96
FORTRAN	70	32
TECHNICAL DRAWING	88	32
TECHNICAL REPORTING	100	32
LABORATORIES		
ANALOGICAL ELECTRONICS	85	576
DIGITAL SYSTEMS	88	180
MICRO-PROCCESSORS	88	60
PHYSICS	70	16

GOVERNMENTAL EXAMINATIONS

MATHEMATICS	- 66	THEORY OF ELECTRICITY & NETWORK	- 65
PHYSICS	- 59	GENERAL ELECTRONICS	- 74
COMPUTERS	- 74	DIGITAL ELECTRONICS	- 64

FINAL PROJECT: (ON THE 1.9.83),THE MARK : 85.

RECIEVED THE DIPLOMA OF HANDASSAI (IN ELECTRONICS).

THE DURATION OF STUDIES FOR FULL TIME DAY COURSES IS 2(TWO) YEARS = 4(FOUR) SEMESTERS.

SCALE OF MARKS: 0 - 54 = FAILING GRADE; 55 UPWARDS = PASSING GRADE

A. Sperling
ASHER SPERLING
P R I N C I P A L

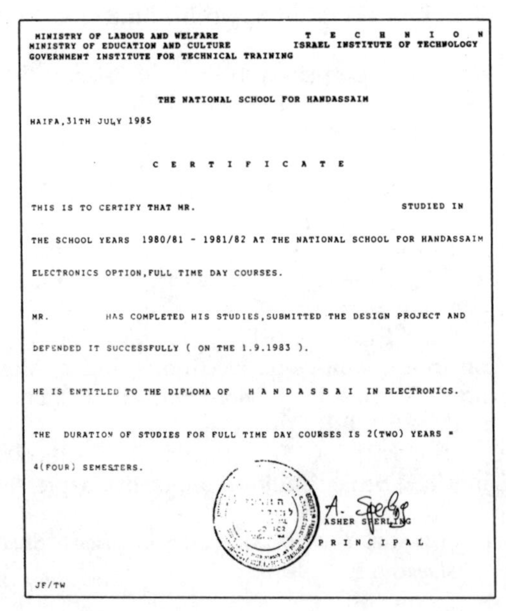

MINISTRY OF LABOUR AND WELFARE
MINISTRY OF EDUCATION AND CULTURE
GOVERNMENT INSTITUTE FOR TECHNICAL TRAINING

T E C H N I O N
ISRAEL INSTITUTE OF TECHNOLOGY

THE NATIONAL SCHOOL FOR HANDASSAIM

HAIFA,31TH JULY 1985

C E R T I F I C A T E

THIS IS TO CERTIFY THAT MR. STUDIED IN THE SCHOOL YEARS 1980/81 - 1981/82 AT THE NATIONAL SCHOOL FOR HANDASSAIM ELECTRONICS OPTION,FULL TIME DAY COURSES.

MR. HAS COMPLETED HIS STUDIES,SUBMITTED THE DESIGN PROJECT AND DEFENDED IT SUCCESSFULLY (ON THE 1.9.1983).

HE IS ENTITLED TO THE DIPLOMA OF H A N D A S S A I IN ELECTRONICS.

THE DURATION OF STUDIES FOR FULL TIME DAY COURSES IS 2(TWO) YEARS = 4(FOUR) SEMESTERS.

A. Sperling
ASHER SPERLING
P R I N C I P A L

JF/TW

7.1. Transcript and Diploma of *Handassai* (Electronics), The National School for Handassaim, 1980–81

TEL-AVIV UNIVERSITY
TECHNICAL COLLEGE

אוניברסיטת תל-אביב
בית הספר להנדסאים

28 March 1982

CERTIFICATE

This is to certify that the student Mr. , I.C. No. has completed his studies in our Technical College in the Mechanical Department, and has received the following marks:

First Year - 1979/80

Semester I

Course	No. of Hours	Mark
Geometry and Trigonometry	40	75
Algebra	40	67
Chemistry	24	exempted
Physics	55	88
Descriptive Geometry	60	74
Technical Mechanics	45	70
Strength of Materials	45	80
Technical English - advanced	24	80
Technical Drafting	40	80
Computer Programming	30	60
Automation + Laboratory	30	90
Theory of Materials	24	70
Chemistry of Laboratory	30	exempted
Physics of Laboratory	30	75
Workshop Practice 1	100	exempted
Mechanical Measurements	20	90

Semester II

Course	No. of Hours	Mark
Mathematics - Analytic Geometry	45	60
Calculus 2	45	60
Physics	30	76
Technical Mechanics	60	72
Strength of Materials	45	85
Materials 2	30	70
Descriptive Geometry	50	90
Automation + Laboratory	30	90
Metal-Cutting Theory	30	75
Technical Drafting	40	exempted
Technical English	30	Exempted
Computer Programming	30	65
Physics Laboratory	50	70
Strength of Materials Laboratory	30	80

TEL-AVIV UNIVERSITY TECHNICAL COLLEGE

../2

UNIVERSITY ROAD, RAMAT-AVIV, TEL-AVIV, ISRAEL

TEL-AVIV UNIVERSITY
TECHNICAL COLLEGE

אוניברסיטת תל-אביב
בית הספר להנדסאים

\- 2 -

Name: Mr. I.C. No.

Second Year - 1980/81

Semester I

Course	No. of Hours	Mark
Thermodynamics	45	65
Chipless Mechanical Processes	45	80
Plastic Materials	30	75
Fluid flow	45	65
Manufacturing Processes	45	85
Electricity Theory	40	75
Technical Drafting	30	80
Machine Elements	90	82
N.C. Machines + Laboratory	20	80
Materials Laboratory	30	76
Workshop Practice 1	100	80
Measurement Laboratory	20	95

Semester II

Course	No. of Hours	Mark
Transportation and Conveying Equipment	20	88
Chipless Mechanical Processes	45	65
Metal Cutting Theory	40	85
Control Systems + Laboratory	35	80
Technical Drafting	30	65
Electric Machines	50	60
Machine Elements	80	92
Thermodynamics	40	100
Manufacturing Processes	45	80
Theory of Machines	30	90
Hydraulic Systems	55	64

Final Government Examinations

Course	Mark
Restricted Mathematics	56
Restricted Physics	78
Machine Elements	65
Production Theory	75
Chipless Forming Processes	71
Hydraulic Systems	64
Final Project	Not Submitted

TEL-AVIV UNIVERSITY TECHNICAL COLLEGE

B. EILAT M.Sc.
Principal

UNIVERSITY ROAD, RAMAT AVIV, TEL-AVIV, ISRAEL

7.2. Certificate from Tel-Aviv University, Technical College

Chapter 8

Higher Education in Israel

Tertiary-level education in Israel is designated as either postsecondary education or higher education. Postsecondary education is under the Ministry of Education and Culture (MOEC) and/or the Ministry of Labor and Social Welfare (MOLSW) and includes education offered by either Teacher Training "Seminars," Colleges and Institutes (see Chapter 4, "Teacher Training") or Technical Colleges (see Chapter 7, "Technological Education"); postsecondary education does not lead to an academic degree. Higher education, on the other hand, is under the direct jurisdiction of the Council for Higher Education which is responsible for accrediting and authorizing institutions of higher education to award degrees. It is this jurisdiction which makes higher education distinguishable from postsecondary education. Institutions of higher education comprise eight universities and twelve, other nonuniversity institutions of higher education which together constitute the scope of accredited, degree-granting institutions in Israel today. These institutions are listed in Table 8.1 and include those that are in the process of becoming accredited or have limited accreditation. Also under the Council are university-affiliated programs located on the campuses of regional colleges.

Historical Development of Higher Education

The idea of an institution of higher education in the "Land of Israel" was conceived in the late nineteenth century by European Zionists. Hermann Schapira, a professor at the University of Heidelberg, proposed such an institution at the First Zionist Congress in 1897. A proposal to explore the possibilities was submitted to the Fifth Zionist Congress in 1901. A petition requesting permission for its establishment in Palestine was submitted to the Ottoman sultan for approval. Not until the Eleventh Zionist Congress in 1913 was it resolved to implement the establishment of a Hebrew university in the city of Jerusalem, an institution which was later to become known as The Hebrew University of Jerusalem.

Development of The Hebrew University of Jerusalem was suspended during World War I. In 1918, foundation stones for the university were laid on Mount Scopus, an area in East Jerusalem, and on April 1, 1925, formal dedication of the university took place. The university functioned as a research institute until 1928, at which time it became a teaching institution offering four-year programs leading to a first degree of master. The first degrees were awarded in 1931. In the early fifties, a three-year bachelor's degree program and two-year master's degree program were instituted, replacing the four-year master's degree.

Table 8.1. Institutions of Higher Education—Enrollment and Accreditation Status, 1983–84*

Universities	Code†	Bachelor	Master	Doctorate	Diploma	Nondegree	Total
Bar-Ilan University	3	7,105	1,460	275	130	1,000	9,970
Ben-Gurion University of the Negev	3	4,070	570	150	80	110	4,980
Everyman's (Open) University	3B	13,595#	—	—	—	—	3,500
Technion-Israel Institute of Technology	3	5,870	1,600	340	60	400	8,270
Tel-Aviv University	3	12,750	3,750	750	190	950	18,390
The Hebrew University of Jerusalem	3	9,480	3,645	1,225	200	1,500	16,050
The University of Haifa	3	5,540	675	25	190	35	6,465
The Weizmann Institute of Science	3	—	180	300	—	—	480
Subtotal		48,315	11,880	3,065	850	3,995	68,105

Other, Nonuniversity Institutions of Higher Education

Teacher Training Colleges‡	Code†	Bachelor	Other Nonuniversity Institutions	Code†	Bachelor
Beit-Berl Teachers Training College	3B	—	Bezalel Acad. of Art & Design	3B	616
Levinsky Teachers College	3B	—	College of Administration (Tel-Aviv branch)	1	—
Michlalah-Jerusalem College for Women	3B	650	Jerusalem College of Technology	3B	215
State Teachers College Seminar HaKibbutzim	1	—	Jerusalem Rubin Acad. of Music & Dance	3	305
The David Yellin Teachers College	3B	—	Ruppin Institute of Agriculture	3B	177
The Zinman College of Phys. Educ. & Sport	3B	—	Shenkar-College of Textile Technology & Fashion	3B	308

SOURCE: Adapted from Samuel Halperin, *Any Home a Campus: Everyman's University of Israel*, 1984; *PGC Annual Report No. 11*, 1985.

*Including overseas students, primarily in the nondegree category.

†Code: 1 = Licensed institutions not yet accredited or authorized to award degrees; 3 = Licensed, accredited, and authorized to award degrees; B = Licensed, accredited, and authorized to award bachelor's degree only.

‡See teacher training college profiles for additional enrollment information.

#Enrollment at Everyman's University is primarily part-time and represents the approximate equivalent of 3,500 fulltime students, about half of whom are pursuing a degree.

Upon establishment of the State of Israel on May 14, 1948, war erupted and activity on the Mount Scopus campus ceased. Mount Scopus became part of the demilitarized zone and Jerusalem was declared "international" by virtue of the United Nation's partition plan. Jerusalem and its inhabitants were divided by a so-called Green Line into East Jerusalem (Palestinian) and West Jerusalem (Jewish). Academic activities of the university continued in facilities in West Jerusalem rented from the Franciscan Monastery of Terra Sancta as well as in other buildings scattered throughout that part of the city. In 1958, the newly-built campus at Givat Ram, a section of West Jerusalem, was dedicated and still functions as an integral part of The Hebrew University. After the 1967 War, Israel declared "reunification" of East and West Jerusalem and the Mount Scopus campus resumed activities. Another branch, The Hebrew University-Hadassa Medical School, was inaugurated in 1963 in the East Jerusalem suburb of Ein Kerem.

The Technion-Israel Institute of Technology was, in fact, the first Jewish institution of higher education operating in Palestine. Conceived in 1907 by a member of the Hilfsverein der Deutschen Juden (Aid Association for German Jews) in Germany, the Institute's cornerstone was laid on the slopes of Mount Carmel near Haifa in 1912, and opened for instruction December 14, 1924 on property acquired from the Hilfsverein by the Zionist Organization.

Before its official opening, the Technikum, as it was then named by its German founders, was the center of what has become known as "the Language War." A controversy among the governing board arose out of the Zionist minority's demand that Hebrew be the language of instruction while the German majority insisted on the use of German. Debate and controversy accompanied by strikes and demonstrations erupted throughout the educational community with those favoring Hebrew proving victorious. The name of the institute was therefore changed from the Technikum to the Hebrew Technical College, was later renamed the Hebrew Technical Institute, and finally took on its present name, the Technion-Israel Institute of Technology. The outcome of the "Language War" served to establish Hebrew as the language of instruction at all levels of education in Israel.

The Weizmann Institute of Science developed out of the Daniel Sieff Research Institute, founded in Rehovot in 1934. With a staff of ten scientists headed by Dr. Chaim Weizmann, and ten technicians, it was first established as a research institute. The Sieff Research Institute became the Weizmann Institute of Science in 1949. In 1958, it initiated a graduate teaching and research institute awarding advanced degrees (master's and doctorates). It remains today strictly a graduate research and teaching institution.

Thus, when the State of Israel was established in 1948, three institutions of higher education existed: 1) The Hebrew University of Jerusalem, 2) a technological institute, now known as the Technion-Israel Institute of Technology, and 3) a graduate research institute in Rehovot, which later became the Weizmann Institute of Science. Higher education grew rapidly as waves of immigrants arrived in the newly established state. The institutions of higher education which followed—Tel-Aviv University (1953), The University of Haifa (1963), and Ben-Gurion University of the Negev (1969)—developed out of local initiative and, in some instances, under the academic tutelage of the first three. Bar-Ilan University, established in 1953, was an exception in that it was founded by the Mizrahi Organization in the United States to advance knowledge of Jewish studies, general science and research in accordance with the ideology of *Torah im Derech Ertz* ("Torah with general knowledge"). Everyman's University (the open university), established in 1974 by the Rothschild Foundation, was accredited and granted permission to award the Bachelor of Arts degree by the Council for Higher Education in 1980; it is the only institution designed for "distance teaching" and independent study. (Note: Since its inception, all references to the university in English have used the name "Everyman's University." Israelis, however, have always called it "Ha'Universita Ha'Ptucha," which translates as The Open University.) (Halperin 27)

The Council for Higher Education: Academic Authority and Accreditation

The Council for Higher Education is the statutory body created as a result of the Council for Higher Education Law passed by the Knesset on August 5, 1958, and is the "State institution charged with Higher Education in Israel." As such, its authority includes, but is not limited to, the following: 1) recommending to the Government that a proposed institution of higher education's operating license be granted or revoked; 2) recommending to the Government that a proposed institution of higher education's partial or full accreditation be granted or revoked; 3) authorizing accredited institutions to award academic degrees, and the title of professor; 4) permitting the use of recognized academic nomenclature such as "academic," "institutions of higher education," "professor," and "faculty"; 5) proposing, after consultation with accredited institutions, the consolidation, development, improvement, and advancement of scientific research; 6) recommending allocations of public funds to budgets of accredited institutions; and 7) approving or disapproving requests for new academic programs and building projects.

The Council is composed of not fewer than 19 and not more than 25 members, including the Minister of Education and Culture who serves as *ex-officio* chairman. At least two-thirds of its membership are academics of standing (about 95% full professors, 5% associate professors), recommended by the Minister in consultation with the institutions of higher education. Council members are appointed *ad personam* for a five-year term by the President of the State on the basis of approval by the Government.

Accreditation and Other "Academic" Activity Restricted by Law

Note: "Academic" (Hebrew, *Academi)* is a status and word associated only with higher education in Israel. When the word is used in this context, it will appear in quotation marks; otherwise, it may be interpreted in the general context of academic or theoretical versus technical or practical.

The authority vested in the Council by the 1958 Council for Higher Education Law provides specific reference to procedures involved in the recognition (accreditation) and licensing of institutions of higher education. Official Israeli literature on this topic uses the words "recognition" and "accreditation" interchangeably. The accredition process, as it is most frequently referred to in written and verbal translation, is a three-stage process.

Stage One: The first requirement for opening and operating an institution of higher education is a license or permit, the issuance of which is recommended by the Council and subject to Government approval. The final decision rests with the Government.

Stage Two: The second stage is that of recommended recognition or accreditation by the Council on the basis of rules prescribed by it . A decision by the Council to recognize an institution is subject to approval by the Government. If the Council refuses recognition to a petitioning institution, the institution may present the application to the Government which may, in turn, refuse it or return it to the Council for reconsideration. In situations where the Government has recommended reconsideration, the decision of the Council upon reconsideration shall be final.

Stage Three: The final stage entails the Council granting authorization to institutions to award degrees. Institutions that are not universities usually are authorized to award only the bachelor's degree. This decision is made exclusively by the Council.

"Academic" nomenclature is restricted by law to use by accredited institutions that operate under permit by the Council. These restrictive designations include use of the words *academi* ("academic"), *universita* ("university"), *academia* ("academy"). (Note: Two institutions of higher education incorporate the word "academy" in their names: Bezalel Academy of Arts and Design, and the Jerusalem Rubin Academy of Music and Dance. Because "academy" is now associated with higher education, the use of this word is restricted.) Additional "academic" nomenclature includes *beit sefer gavoach* (literally, "high school," i.e., school above the level of a secondary school), *mosadot le haskala gevohah* ("institutions of higher education") *haskala gevohah* and *hinukh gavoach* (both "higher education"), either separately or in combination with another word or as an adjectival or nounal adjunct to another designation, either in Hebrew or in a foreign language. The designation "*beit sefer gavoach*" may only be used by an institution of higher education which awards a bachelor's degree or offers courses which an institution authorized to award academic degrees has recognized for the purpose of credit. Even reference to the awarding of "credits" *(mekudot zchut)* is restricted to recognized institutions of higher education.

The law further stipulates the illegality of opening or maintaining an institution that awards or promises to award an academic degree (or credits towards a degree) without that institution having Council recognition and operating under a license granted by the Council. Promotional material by institutions that are not accredited by the Council may not refer to "academic courses," "credits," or the awarding of degrees. Admissions officers should be alert to any institution not mentioned in Table 8.1 which makes use of such terminology. Inquiries concerning the status of such institutions should be addressed to the Council for Higher Education, 12 Hanassi Street, Jerusalem, Israel 91040.

The Planning and Grants Committee: Financing of Higher Education

The law creating the Council for Higher Education stipulated that accredited institutions are autonomous in academic and administrative matters within the limits of their budgets. This caveat assigned undeniable influence to the Government—the principal source of funding—and left the Council with an incentive to create a budget manager. The Council designated a committee with the charge of recommending criteria for the allocation of funds to institutions of higher education and establishing a grants committee to be patterned after the British University Grants Committee. What evolved was the Planning and Grants Committee.

The Planning and Grants Committee (PGC) officially began functioning in March 1974 with "unprecedented powers to plan and budget for accredited higher education institutions." (Halperin 13) The PGC is a "body coming between the Government and the universities protect(ing) both Government and the public from producing one more sector creating deficits . . . and also protect(ing) the universities against edicts and regulations by Government. . . ." (Council for Higher Education, PGC, *Annual Report No. 7)* Inasmuch as the PGC regulates the majority of funding dispersed to the universities, it is a most influential body. The extent of its authority lies within Government Decision No. 666 (1977) (see below).

The PGC is the planning and executive arm of the Council for Higher Education. The PGC has six members and is headed by the chairman, who is appointed by the Minister of Education and Culture with the approval of the Council. The chairman is also an *ex-officio* member of the Council. Four of the members, including the chairman, are academics of standing (full professors), while the other two come from the economic sector.

Terms of Reference of the Planning and Grants Committee
Government Decision No. 666, June 5, 1977

1. To be an independent body coming between the Government and the national institutions and the institutions of higher education in all matters relating to allocations for higher education.
2. To submit the ordinary and development budget proposals for higher education, taking into account the needs of society and the State, while safe-guarding academic freedom and assuring the advancement of research and learning.
3. To have exclusive authority to allocate to the institutions of higher education the global approved ordinary and development budgets.
4. To submit to the Government and to the Council for Higher Education plans for the development of higher education, including financing.
5. To encourage efficiency in the institutions of higher education and coordination between them with a view to preventing superfluous duplication and encouraging economy.

6. To ensure that budgets are balanced and that there are no deviations from them.
7. To express its opinion to the Council for Higher Education before the Council reaches a decision on the opening of a new institution or new unit having financial implications in an existing institution. . . .The PGC will determine whether the opening of the new unit has or has not financial implications. (Council for Higher Education, PGC, *Annual Report No. 11*, 2)

While the PGC's allocation of funds from public monies to institutions in 1982-83 was a substantial 69% of all monies spent by institutions of higher education, they are not state, municipal, or "public" institutions, and their staff, with the exception of staff of teacher training colleges or departments, are not civil or municipal employees. Institutions of higher education are corporate bodies made up of a Board of Governors, a President (the administrative head), and a Rector (the academic head).

The PGC's budget is reported in terms of ordinary and development budget items. The ordinary budget includes monies allocated to accredited academic study programs, research programs, and complementary administrative and service units. Expenditures reflected in the ordinary budget include wages and related expenses, purchase of scientific and other equipment, books, periodicals, materials and expendable supplies, routine maintenance and repairs, and renovations of existing buildings and infrastructure systems. In 1983-84, these activities were financed from the following sources: PGC direct allocations (47.8%); tuition fees (4.3%); donations (7.7%); and miscellaneous, including PGC special allocations and deficit financing (40.2%). In the same year, the PGC's allocations were distributed as follows: direct allocations to universities (86.7%); direct allocations to other institutions of higher education (2.4%); special allocations for research, equipment, scholarships, and student aid (10.6%); and PGC's operation budget (0.3%). (Council for Higher Education, PGC *Annual Report No.11*, 60) Development budget expenditures reflect monies spent on construction in the higher education system. Recently, however, 20% of the development budget has been allocated for renovation of buildings and systems and adaptation of existing structures rather than new construction.

The government, in consultation with the Ministry of Finance, the MOEC, and representatives from the universities and student organizations, annually sets a tuition fees schedule which is uniform throughout the country, regardless of university, program of study, or level of study. Tuition covers approximately 20% of the actual cost of instruction and about 7% of institutional ordinary operating costs. In 1983-84, annual tuition for a fulltime student was the approximate equivalent of U.S. $615. More recently, the Ministry of Finance has recommended an increase of tuition to $1,000 as well as subsequent increases to set tuition at a rate which would eventually approach half of the cost of education. (Halperin 16)

From the individual's perspective, education and its related costs are principally met from personal resources. A 1978-79 profile of 39,010 undergraduate students indicates that 72.9% were fulltime students, 18.7% at least halftime students, and 6.5% were studying less than halftime. At the same time, 61.7% were employed, including 24.4% fulltime. The main source of income for

36.5% was income from employment; for 28.6%, parents and relatives; and for 14.2%, spouses' work. Only 7.6% indicated scholarship as their mainstay. Other sources such as veterans benefits involved 13.1%. Finally, an estimated 10% receive approximately 60% tuition remission through the Perach Tutorial Project, a program whereby partial tuition waivers are granted in exchange for tutoring high school students in "disadvantaged schools." (Halperin 16-17)

Higher Education: Present Conditions and Future Considerations

In the past decade, enrollment at universities has increased 30%. During the same time, the number of faculty positions decreased 3%, technical and administrative personnel by 11%. Expenditures other than salaries fell 26% in real terms. The share of higher education in the national budget (excluding defense and debt repayments) fell by some 44%. The ratio of students to teachers was satisfactory at the end of the seventies, but deterioriated in recent years, reaching limits which give cause for concern. Worse hit were funds required for the purchase of scientific equipment, libraries, basic research and maintenance. On the average, the amount of space is satisfactory. (The Council for Higher Education, PGC, *The Higher Education System in Israel,* 4)

In 1982-83, the Council for Higher Education and the Planning and Grants Committee presented guidelines for the planning and development of higher education for the 1983-88 period, along with their forecasts and recommendations. Highlights of their conclusions provide insight from their perspective into the present and future status of higher education in Israel.

1. Existing figures and forecasts indicate Israel will need no additional universities up to the end of the eighties; all study and research objectives can be handled by existing institutions.
2. By 1988, total university enrollment is predicted to increase 12% above that of 1983 to an estimated 70,000; this increase can be absorbed by existing institutions. Estimates indicate that by 1995 there will be some 85,000 students in the universities. Expansion and investment in existing universities or the establishment of new universities in the early nineties will be needed to absorb this increase.
3. While forecasts through 1988 indicate that existing faculties of the universities will fill the needs of the country and its economy, there is room, however, for additional units at the departmental level and below.
4. The structure of undergraduate university curriculums should be reviewed. The possibility for expanding general and interdisciplinary studies should be examined as well as the length of time required to study for the bachelor's degree, the use of technologically advanced teaching aids, and the study framework for older students reaching universities for a "second round" of studies.
5. Equilibrium in supply and demand for academically qualified manpower within Israel is predicted for the next five years.
6. A shortage of university graduates is foreseen in the fields of computers, dentistry, and electrical engineering; a surplus is seen in medicine.
7. Engineering and scientific professions needed for high-technology industries must have the highest priority in the higher educational system over the next five years.

Specific fields include bio-technology, computers, electronics, electro-optics, genetic engineering, and robotics. Student enrollment, academic and technical staff, scientific equipment, computers, and space must be considerably expanded in faculties dealing with computers and electronics.

8. No effort must be spared to increase the number of Jewish students from abroad coming to study at universities in Israel.
9. Pre-academic preparatory courses must be expanded to facilitate access to university studies by the widest possible range of population.
10. Academic staff at universities must be increased by 12%-20% by 1988 in order to maintain the desirable ratio of students to teachers. (Council for Higher Education, PGC, *Annual Report No. 11*, 25-28)

Institutional Organization and Administration

Higher educational institutions are autonomous bodies each administered through a Board of Governors. Supreme authority is vested in each institutional Board whose membership comprises both academic and public figures from Israel and abroad. Each Board exercises ultimate control in matters of major policy, development, annual budgets, and the establishment or abolition of faculties and departments within the institution. The Board of Governors also appoints the president of the university, who is the administrative head, and vice-presidents. The Executive Council, made up of both academic and nonacademic members, is responsible for the conduct of university affairs between annual meetings of the Board. Day-to-day operations are managed by a permanent committee appointed by the Executive Council and consisting of a membership which is approximately two-thirds nonacademic.

The academic senate is the supreme academic body of the university. The senate is chaired by the Rector, the academic head of the university, who is elected by members of the senate holding the rank of full professor. Within each faculty, academic matters are dealt with by a faculty board, which elects the dean. The Rector is an *ex-officio* member of each such board. Academic appointments and promotions are determined by special committee.

The configuration of academic entities in Israeli universities follows a familiar pattern not unlike that found in the United States. In descending order of size, the university is organized according to faculties, departments, schools, institutes, centers, and units. Faculties normally house any or all of these entities according to the academic discipline. Departments and schools are normally engaged in research and study within the structure of degree programs while institutes and centers focus on specialized interests or scholarly activities and research alone. Units are entities offering coursework ("academic" and "nonacademic") in fields where there is no department or degree program available. For example, units exist for courses in some foreign languages, physical education, and *mechinot*.

The university faculty—referred to in Israel as academic staff—is represented according to title and position. In descending order of stature, these are as follows: Professor, associate professor *(professor haver)*, senior lecturer *(martze bachir)*, lecturer *(martze)*, instructor *(madrich)*, and assistant.

The Academic Calendar

There is no uniformity among institutions of higher education with respect to the date of commencement or conclusion of the academic year; such decisions are within the purview of each institution. The nonuniversity teacher training institutions are an exception since teacher training falls under the Ministry of Education and Culture; their academic year extends from September 1 through June 20. Generally speaking, the academic year for the other institutions begins in late October or early November and ends sometime in June. The summer vacation, therefore, extends from July through most or all of October. Final examinations, which are given in two sessions, are scheduled during this time.

Classes are in session five and one-half to six days each week, Sunday through half or all of Friday. No classes are held on religious or national holidays, of which there are many. (See Chapter 1, "Academic Calendar.")

Institutions vary in terms of the type of system they operate—trimester, semester, or annual. While the trend is toward the semester system, institutions have changed their system back and forth. A trimester represents approximately nine weeks, and a semester approximately 14 weeks. Despite religious holidays advancing 11-12 days each year due to the 354-day lunar cycle, the academic calendar is adjusted so that the length of the term remains constant.

The Credit System

The credit system employed by Israeli universities and nonuniversities is expressed in terms of 50-minute "hours," sometimes qualified as "semester hours," "yearly hours," or "annual hours." Unless otherwise specified, reference to hours is assumed to be calculated on a yearly basis regardless of whether the course met for a trimester, semester, or year. In order to convert annual hours to total semester hours for the year, the number of annual hours reported may be multiplied by two. Caution is recommended, however, before automatically multiplying all hourly entries by two. Not all institutions report in the same fashion nor is institutional reporting consistent. Each institutional profile explains how to interpret transcripts for that institution and reports any known irregularities.

The Course System

Israeli transcripts reflect various types of course offerings. Transcripts frequently identify the type of course by use of an abbreviation, shown below parenthetically.

- Lecture *(She'ur)*—usually involves a single final examination (L).
- Exercise *(Targil)*—requires student participation (E).
- Lecture and Exercise *(She'ur vet targil)*—requires student participation and one or two term papers (L and E).

- Proseminar *(Kdamseminar)*—an annual course on a selected topic, usually on a second-year or third-year level, which requires a less extensive paper (averaging 10-20 pages) than that required in a seminar course (PS, ProS). Degree requirements generally include several proseminars and a minimum of two seminars. One-third of the course is devoted to lecture and two-thirds to research, writing, presenting and defending a proseminar/seminar paper before the professor and class. The paper is corrected or revised as needed. The course grade is generally based on the seminar paper but may include an exam on the lecture component. The student elects to take the course as a proseminar or seminar, the distinction being essentially the extensiveness and depth of the paper.
- Seminar *(Seminar*—an annual course on a selected topic, usually on a second-year, third-year, or graduate level, which requires an extensive paper of 30-60 pages (S). See "Proseminar" discussion above.
- Research Seminar *(Seminar Mechkara)*—(RS).
- Tutorial *(Hadracha)*—a period of individual instruction (T).
- Preparatory Course *(Mechina)*—a pre-university, noncredit course (PC, M).
- Field Trip *(Siyur)*—a study trip off campus (FT).
- Field Work *(Avodat Sadeh)*—includes work in the field, observation, and practical experience (FW).
- Guided Readings *(Kri'a Mudrechet)*—usually a short course on research and use of the university library (GR).
- Laboratory *(Ma'abada)*—an integral part of most science and some language courses (Lab).
- Workshop *(Sadna)* usually requires student-initiated projects (WK).
- *Ulpan*—intensive Hebrew language and Israeli culture program for foreigners usually preceding the regular coursework of a study abroad program.

The Grading System

The university grading system is reminiscent of the 10- or 100-point scale implemented throughout primary and secondary education. The grading scale used by universities is normally explained in the legend on the transcript and is based upon a five-grade pass system reported numerically on a scale of 0-100. The descriptive and letter grade interpretation is provided in the transcript legend. The numerical cut points for the five passing grades and the minimum passing mark vary slightly among the universities, but the most common scale presented on legends appears as follows:

95 - 100	=	Excellent (A+)	65 - 74	=	Fair (C)
85 - 94	=	Very Good (A)	50 - 64	=	Pass (D)
75 - 84	=	Good (B)	0 - 49	=	Fail (F)

The past and present grading scales used by each university are described within the "Institutional Profiles" section at the end of this chapter.

Nonuniversity institutions of higher education and postsecondary institutions tend not to report a legend or other interpretive information. Unless otherwise indicated, it is fair to interpret their numerical grades in terms of the scale provided above.

The Examination System

There are two official examination periods: one from the end of June through August *(Moed Aleph)*, the other from the end of August through October *(Moed Beth)*. Examinations may be divided between the two sessions, but students are advised to take as many examinations as possible during the first session. In case of failure, it is possible to retake the examination during the second session. Students enrolled in semester courses which end midyear are examined at the end of the course. All regular students must take their examinations at the scheduled time. (Rothberg School bulletin 11)

In annual lecture courses, grades are usually determined on the basis of a single, final examination given at the end of the academic year. In courses designated exercise or lecture and exercise, some departments may require examinations and/or papers during or at the end of every trimester or semester. At the completion of a program, the student's major department computes a cumulative weighted average which appears towards the end of the transcript.

Each institution sets its own examination regulations. In addition, the examination regulations for the overseas program division of a particular institution may differ from examination regulations of the regular academic program at the same institution. See individual institutional profiles for specific regulations.

Pre-Academic Preparatory Programs *(Mechinot)*

Preparatory programs *(mechina* [sing.], *mechinot* [plur.]) are noncredit, pre-"academic," pre-university programs instituted for students who are ineligible to continue their education in postsecondary or higher educational institutions. *Mechinot* are administratively distinct from the universities, nonuniversities, and regional colleges to which they are affiliated. These programs are jointly sponsored by the MOEC and the Council for Higher Education. In 1983, the direction of pre-academic preparatory courses was entrusted to the Association for the Advancement of Education, an organization of the MOEC. In the near future, the MOEC is expected to appoint a public council and directorate made up of representatives from the MOEC and the universities to establish a common policy for *mechinot*.

Mechinot have been instituted to provide a second chance or an opportunity to bridge the gap for high school graduates (and some nongraduates) by preparing them for university admission. With the exception of the Weizmann Institute of Science, all universities house a *mechina*. *Mechinot* are also available for students intending to further their education in other institutions of higher education. The David Yellin Teachers College, the Zinman College of Physical Education at the Wingate Institute, and Beit-Berl Teachers Training College provide pedagogic *mechinot*. The technological *mechina* in Beer Sheva offers a preparatory program for those interested in postsecondary technical education. Regional colleges involved in this level of preparatory education are Alperin R.C. of the Jordan Valley; Emek Yisrael R.C. "Ohel Sarah"; Sha'ar Hanegev R.C., P. Sapir (the Negev); and Tel Hai Rodman R.C.

Beyond academic preparation, *mechinot* aim to facilitate integration of the socially, culturally, and economically disadvantaged into mainstream Israel; they also serve as an orientation for new or prospective Jewish immigrants. As such, there are other features which complement *mechinot*: intensive academic, career and personal counseling; tutorial services; scholarships; and culturally-enriching extracurricular activities.

Mechinot can be categorized conceptually into two groups based upon the origin of the participants' previous education: foreign or Israeli. The first group consists of new or prospective Jewish immigrants who are eligible for admission to university-level study in their home country but who require intensive preparation in order to be eligible for admission to higher education in Israel. The objectives in this instance are to improve the student's knowledge of the Hebrew language, to provide a basic knowledge of the history of the Jewish people and the State of Israel, to acquaint the student with the Israeli educational system, and to strengthen skills in basic academic disciplines.

The second group is the most representative of students enrolled in *mechinot*. This group characteristically includes Israelis with weak or partial matriculation examination results from *kibbutzim* (usually agricultural), discharged soldiers, and the socially-economically disadvantaged. In 1983-84, approximately 61% of the students in *mechinot* came from disadvantaged economic backgrounds (mostly Sephardim) and had completed military service. (See Chapter 1, "The Impact of Cultural Origin, Political Persuasion, and Religious Belief.") The preparatory and compensatory nature of this category aims to strengthen knowledge in basic areas such as language, mathematics, science, and social science while developing abstract thinking ability and study skills. In general, however, it can be said that the aims of both programs are to admit students who demonstrate potential for achieving normal university-level admission standards and to prepare them to compete and succeed in the regular academic milieu.

ADMISSION. Israeli applicants to *mechinot* may be typically characterized as students who have completed 12 years of education, have passed some matriculation *(bagrut)* examinations, or have a weak Matriculation Certificate *(Teudat Bagrut)* and are not qualitatively eligible to continue their education at the next higher level. In general, immigrant applicants should have completed no more than one year of university-level study outside Israel, should have a very basic knowledge of Hebrew, and, for some programs, must have completed military service in the Israeli Defense Forces. Admission to *mechinot* is not "open," nor are criteria and standards for acceptance uniform. Eligibility is determined on the basis of several factors such as entrance examinations, psychometric examinations, socio-economic status, and military status; eligibility varies in accordance with the requirements of the institution under which the *mechina* is housed and the program for which the student is being prepared.

DURATION OF PROGRAM. The normal length of *mechinot* is one year, but in fact may vary from seven to 11 months. An experimental 18-month program lasting for two academic years also exists for discharged soldiers who have completed 10 to 11 years of education.

PROGRAM STRUCTURE. *Mechinot* for the foreign-educated are intensive programs requiring 36-40 classroom hours per week. Coursework includes compensatory study of Hebrew, Judaica, History of Israel, and subjects in traditional academic disciplines which provide a foundation for the intended field of study. The nature of *mechinot* for Israelis is described above.

Institutions offering preparatory programs do not award credit for this study or for the purpose of transferring credit to foreign institutions. As a result, coursework and grades from study in these programs are normally not reflected on institutional transcripts. Results from study in these programs are used by Israeli institutions to determine applicants' eligibility for admission. Students do have access to these reports, however, and may present them to U.S. institutions with a request for transfer credit. See sample document 8.1.

Advanced Preparatory Programs (TAKA)

Students who have studied outside Israel and who have been accepted directly into an undergraduate or graduate degree program are required to participate in the Advanced Preparatory Program known as *Tochnit Klita Academic* (TAKA). TAKA is also referred to as the Academic Absorption Program. TAKA is a noncredit-bearing cultural and language orientation program generally beginning in April or September and extending over a period of five months. The program includes intensive Hebrew study, Judaica, and English (for nonnative English speakers). Since 1978, TAKA has been conducted at the Ben-Gurion University of the Negev.

The Hebrew University of Jerusalem, however, offers its own Academic Absorption Program for students who have completed at least two years of university-level study outside Israel and are candidates for admission. TAKA students have a special student status which does not guarantee subsequent admission to regular university studies. The program consists of intensive Hebrew and/or English and two required courses in Jewish and Israeli studies. It is offered during the spring and summer semesters, according to demand.

Regional Colleges

Regional colleges were originally established as far back as the 1950's to extend "nonacademic" educational opportunities to segments of the population living in areas outside the urban centers. The regional colleges are primarily financed by the MOEC, by various regional authorities, and, in certain instances, by the MOLSW. The "nonacademic" programs offered by regional colleges include pre-academic preparatory programs *(mechinot)*, high school classes for adults and discharged military personnel, postsecondary technological programs, arts and crafts classes, and forums dictated by regional and community needs. The more recent introduction of "academic" units into regional college programs has added another dimension to their mission.

Regional colleges, while not institutions of higher education, have "academic" units which are under the academic supervision of an affiliated university and thereby function indirectly under the authority of the Council for Higher Education. All "academic" features, including admission requirements, course offerings, teaching, examinations, and reporting, are under the supervision of the university with which a given college is affiliated. The regional colleges and their university affiliation are listed below:

1. Achavah Regional College near Sderoth (Everyman's [Open] University)
2. The Municipal College of Eilat (Ben-Gurion University of the Negev)
3. Emek Hayarden Regional College, the Alperin Regional College of the Jordan Valley (Bar-Ilan University)
4. The Menashe Regional College (Tel-Aviv University)
5. Emek Yisrael Regional College - "Ohel Sarah" (The University of Haifa)
6. Ramat Hanegev Regional College (Everyman's [Open] University)
7. Sha'ar Hanegev Regional College, the P. Sapir Regional College of the Negev (Ben-Gurion University of the Negev)
8. Tel Hai Rodman Regional College (The University of Haifa)

The involvement of the Council for Higher Education in regional college programs relates directly and exclusively to the "academic" courses offered by the regional colleges under the supervision of the universities. The Council has appointed a special committee to oversee "academic" considerations, including determination of the distribution of funds in support of "academic" responsibilities. This support involves the fostering of local teaching staff whose primary employment is in the regional college as well as assistance with the college's overhead, administrative expenses, and wages of the academic coordinator.

The "academic" status of specified courses in regional colleges is the result of affiliated university supervision: the teaching staff is part of the university staff; the program of study is determined by the university; admission requirements are determined by the university and students are considered students of the university; course requirements are the same as the university departmental requirements; coursework and grades are transmitted on official university transcripts; and the degree, which involves a residency requirement at the university, is awarded by the university. Students may complete up to two-thirds of the degree program in the regional college. The third and final year of the program must be completed in residence at the university.

University versus Nonuniversity Institutions

Institutions of higher education are designated as either universities or other, nonuniversity institutions of higher education. A further distinction is made within the nonuniversity category: one group represents institutions that are neither universities nor teacher training colleges; the other group represents the accredited, degree-granting teacher training colleges. Characteristics which distinguish universities from nonuniversity institutions are summarized below.

1. All universities (except Everyman's University) are fully accredited and authorized to award degrees through the doctorate; Everyman's University is fully accredited but awards only the bachelor's degree.
2. Nonuniversity institutions of higher education may be either fully or partially accredited; i.e., some institutions, in addition to Council-approved programs leading to degrees, may conduct other courses or programs which do not lead to a degree. For example, other programs may lead to diplomas for teacher certification through the MOEC or for technicians and practical engineers (*technaim* and *handassaim*, respectively) through the MOEC/DTE and/or MOLSW/NITT. Of the 12 nonuniversity institutions, only three are not fully recognized (Beit-Berl Teachers Training College, Ruppin Institute of Agriculture, and the David Yellin Teachers College) and the status of two (State Teachers College, Seminar HaKibbutzim and The College of Administration, Tel Aviv) has yet to be determined.
3. Nonuniversity institutions are not authorized to award master's or doctoral degrees. The Jerusalem Rubin Academy of Music and Dance is the only exception; it conducts a joint program with The Hebrew University of Jerusalem which leads to a Master of Music (M.Mus.).
4. University bachelor's degree programs are generally three years in length (see Table 8.2 for exceptions); all nonuniversity degree programs are four years in length. A distinction may be made between university four-year degrees and nonuniversity four-year degrees. See "Duration of Programs" below.
5. Nonuniversity institutions focus on teaching rather than research.
6. Only the universities are permitted to award the degrees of Bachelor of Arts (B.A.) and Bachelor of Science (B.Sc.). The nonuniversity institutions award degrees of Bachelor of (profession) (the degree includes the name of the professional field, e.g., Bachelor of Education [B.Ed.], Bachelor of Technology [B.Tech.], etc.). Note the difference in bachelor's degrees according to the type of institution and field or profession in degrees labeled "A," "B," and "BB" in Table 8.2. An example of this distinction is seen in The Hebrew University-Rubin Academy of Music and Dance joint bachelor's degree program where, upon completion of the program, a student is awarded both a Bachelor of Arts in Music (B.A.Mus.) by The Hebrew University and a Bachelor of Music (B.Mus.) by the Rubin Academy.
7. Because the government has assigned the responsibility of teacher training to the MOEC, the nonuniversity group of teacher training colleges and teacher training programs within the universities are financed through the MOEC, rather than through the budget allocations of the PGC. Among other things, this affects statistical reporting of the Council for Higher Education and PGC and accounts for the omission of teacher training institutions in the Council and PGC statistics reported in this chapter.

Table 8.2. Length of Degree Programs in Institutions of Higher Education

	Primary–Secondary	Higher Education								
Years in	1–12	13	14	15	16		17	18	19	20
School		1	2	3	4	½	5	6	7	8
				A	B	C	D	E	F	G
					BB			EE		

A— Three (3) Years: Bachelor's Degrees
Bachelor of Arts (B.A.)
Bachelor of Arts in Music (B.A.Mus.)
Bachelor of Arts (B.A.) (Accounting & Economics, Statistics, or Math; Business [since 1986])
Bachelor of Medical Sciences (B.Med.Sc.)
Bachelor of Occupational Therapy (B.O.T.)
Bachelor of Science (B.Sc.)
Bachelor of Science in Agriculture (B.Sc.Agr.)
Bachelor of Science in Nutritional & Domestic Sciences (B.Sc.N.D.S.)
Bachelor of Social Work (B.S.W.)

B— Four (4) Years: Bachelor's Degrees
Bachelor of Arts (B.A.) (Accounting towards Certified Public Accountancy, Management & Economics; Business [prior to 1986])
Bachelor of Education in Technology & Sciences (B.Ed.Tech.Sc.)
Bachelor of Engineering (B.Eng.)
Bachelor of Landscape Architecture (B.L.Arch.)
Bachelor of Laws (LL.B.)
Bachelor of Nursing (B.Nurs.)
Bachelor of Nursing Science, 3–5 years (B.Nurs.Sc.)
Bachelor of Pharmacy (B.Pharm.)*
Bachelor of Physiotherapy (B.P.T.)
Bachelor of Science (Technion) (including Engineering) (B.Sc.)
Bachelor of Science (Technological Science) (B.Sc. [Tech.Sci.]) (only at Ben-Gurion University/B.G.U.)

BB—All Degrees from Nonuniversity Institutions of Higher Education:
Bachelor of Administration of the Kibbutz Economy (B.Admin.Kibbutz)
Bachelor of Design (B.Des.)
Bachelor of Design (Fashion) (B.Des.[Fash.])
Bachelor of Design (Textile) (B.Des.[Tex.])
Bachelor of Education (B.Ed.)
Bachelor of Fine Arts (B.F.A.)
Bachelor of Music (B.Mus.)
Bachelor of Technology and Applied Science (B.Tech.&App. Sc.)
Bachelor of Technology (Textile) (B.Tech.[Tex.])

C— Four and One-Half (4.5) Years: Master of Science (M.Sc.)

D— Five (5) Years: Bachelor's and Master's Degrees.
Bachelor of Architecture & Town Planning (B.Arch.T.P.)
Master of Arts (M.A.)
Master of Criminology (M.Crim.)
Master of Library Science (M.L.S.)
Master of Management Science (M.S.M., B.G.U. only, Overseas Student Program)

Master of Occupational Health (M.Occ.H.)
Master of Public Administration (M.P.A.)
Master of Public Health (M.P.H.)
Master of Science (M.Sc.)
Master of Science in Agriculture (M.Sc.Agr.)
Master of Science in Basic Medical Sciences (M.Med.Sc.)
Master of Social Sciences (M.Soc.Sc. or M.S.S.)
Master of Social Work (M.S.W.)

E— Six (6) Years: Master's Degrees.
Master of Business Administration (M.B.A.)
Master of Laws (LL.M.)
Master of Pharmacy (M.Pharm.)
Master of Science (Technical Sciences) (M.Sc. [Tech. Sci.])(B.G.U.)

EE— Six (6) Years: Doctoral Degrees.
Doctor of Dental Medicine (D.M.D.)†
Doctor of Medicine (M.D.)†
Doctor of Veterinary Medicine (D.V.M.)

F— Seven (7) Years: Doctoral Degrees.
Doctor of Philosophy (Ph.D.)
Doctor of Science (D.Sc.)
Doctor of Science in Technology (D.Sc.[Tech.])

G— Eight (8) Year Doctor of Laws (Doctor Juris, Dr. Jur.)

*Includes six months' internship
†Plus one year internship.

Degree Programs

First Degrees

The first university-level degree in Israel is the bachelor's degree. This degree is awarded by all the universities (except the Weizmann Institute of Science which awards only graduate degrees) and all nonuniversity institutions, including the accredited teacher training colleges. The names of these institutions, their accreditation status, and enrollment are listed in Table 8.1.

In 1982-83, 7,164 bachelor's degrees were awarded by Israeli universities and approximately 400 more by nonuniversity institutions. Table 8.3 lists the number of bachelor's degree recipients by institution for all accredited institutions except accredited teacher training institutions and shows the distribution of university bachelor's degrees according to field of study.

DURATION OF PROGRAMS

The university degree program usually extends over a period of three years. Exceptions to the three-year university degree exist in some university degree programs such as Architecture, certain Business programs, Dentistry, Engineering, Law, Medicine, Nursing, Pharmacy, Physiotherapy, and Veterinary Medicine, each of which requires more than three years.

All accredited nonuniversity institutions award degrees requiring four years of study. Historically their upgrade from postsecondary to "academic" institutions became possible as the professional fields they offered became more theoretically developed and academically recognized. A parallel situation in the United States might be seen in the transition and eventual incorporation of normal schools into U.S. college and university departments or faculties of education as the theoretical approach to the profession developed. In most instances, what was an Israeli three-year postsecondary professional program (i.e., pedagogy, technology, and the arts) became "academized," or recognized by the Council for Higher Education after these institutions proposed a four-year program which expanded and strengthened the academic, theoretical content of the curriculum. The four-year nonuniversity program, therefore, is not one year better than a university three-year program, nor is it designed to replicate a three- or four-year university program. In fact, it is the discipline which dictates the length and nature of the program, the type of institution it is housed in, and the degree awarded. Consequently, each degree program should be considered on its own merits in light of the nature or intent of the discipline or profession. See the following sections for further clarification.

1. "Physiotherapy" in Chapter 5 and Tables 5.2 and 5.3, which illustrate the former three-year postsecondary diploma program in Physiotherapy from Zinman College and the current four-year B.P.T. program at Tel-Aviv University;
2. Teacher education, Chapter 4, and discussions on the three-year postsecondary diploma program, the four-year nonuniversity B.Ed. program, and the university programs in professional education along with sample document 4.1;
3. Tables 8.2. for the length of degree programs in Israel, and 8.6, and 8.8 for sample four-year bachelor's degree curriculums from a university and nonuniversity.

THE THREE-YEAR BACHELOR'S DEGREE—A DISCUSSION

The three-year bachelor's degree is the most commonly awarded university degree in Israel. The distribution of degrees by field (see Table 8.3) indicates that approximately 73% of all university bachelor's degrees are in fields which award three-year bachelor's degrees: Agriculture; Jewish Studies and Humanities; Math, Natural and Physical Sciences; and Social Sciences, including some Business programs. Exceptions, therefore, constitute 27%, but include professional programs (Law, Nursing, Medicine, Pharmacy, and Veterinary Medicine [approximately 10%] as well as Architecture, other Business programs, and Engineering and Technology [about 17%]).

Examination of the three-year degree entails consideration of various factors, some of which are discussed more extensively in other sections of this chapter or other chapters. These factors include admission standards, the structure of degree programs, student characteristics, access to further education, and duration of degree programs immediately above.

Table 8.3. Bachelor's Degree Recipients by Institution and Distribution of Degrees According to Field of Study, 1982–83

Institution	Degrees Awarded	Institution	Degrees Awarded
UNIVERSITIES		NONUNIVERSITIES*	
Bar-Ilan University	1,066	Bezalel-Academy of Arts and Design	39
Ben-Gurion University of the Negev	610	Jerusalem College of Technology	30
Everyman's (Open) University	40	Jerusalem Rubin Academy of Music and Dance	39
Technion-Israel Institute of Technology	972	†Ruppin Institute of Agriculture	18
Tel-Aviv University	1,815	†Shenkar-College of Textile Technology and Fashion	30
The Hebrew University of Jerusalem	1,732		
The University of Haifa	929		

Distribution of University Degrees According to Field of Study

Agriculture	4.3%	Medicine & Pharmacy Professions	4.6%
Engineering & Architecture	17.4%	Math, Natural & Physical Sci.	13.0%
Jewish Studies & Humanities	24.6%	Social Sciences (incl. Business)	30.8%
Law	5.2%		

SOURCES: Adapted from the *Statistical Abstract of Israel,* No. 35, 1984, pp. 666, 667; and The Planning and Grants Committee, *Annual Report* No. 11, 1983–84, p. 55.
*Excluding accredited teacher training institutions.
†Degrees are awarded only every two years. Previous number of degrees awarded were 10 (Ruppin) and 73 (Shenkar).

Admission to university programs is in general selective and competitive, more so in some institutions and fields than in others (see "Admission to First Degree Programs" later in this chapter). While changes in the structure of the matriculation *(bagrut)* examinations have allowed more students to earn the *Bagrut,* the units system of the new *Bagrut,* in conjunction with the scores from the Psychometric Entrance Examination and departmental exams, allow institutions to implement admission cutoffs in more exacting terms. Furthermore, the Council for Higher Education and the PGC exert influence over enrollment through budget allocations and their ability to recommend the opening of new institutions, expansion of facilities, and the establishment of new programs. The Council, the PGC, and the universities have been known to freeze enrollment, especially in fields representing oversubscribed professions. The size of the country and the university community, along with fiscal constraints of the economy in general and the PGC in particular, are conducive to a much more controlled and competitive academic environment than exists in the United States. (See also "The Council for Higher Education," "The Planning and Grants Committee," "Higher Education: Present Conditions and Future Considerations," and "Professional Programs.")

The program structure of the three-year degree involves several features, mainly the course and credit system. The course system provides course offerings at lower, intermediary, and upper levels, described variously as introductory, basic, complementary, supplementary, standard, advanced or accelerated, even though these levels are not regularly reported on transcripts. Each department structures its program in a logical sequential pattern of introductory and theoretical coursework, followed by specialized, indepth, advanced study. Therefore, much of the work in the second half of the second year and all of the third year would be considered advanced upper level instruction. Proseminars and seminars are required in most, if not all, programs and frequently prevent students from completing degree requirements within the prescribed three years (see also the discussion on proseminars and seminars in "The Course System" earlier in this chapter).

The single major versus dual major options provide another, although not necessarily definitive, perspective from which to view the strength of the student's preparedness. The single major offers diversified coursework outside the department in conjunction with extensive studies in a single major. A dual major, on the other hand, provides indepth study in two majors throughout the three-year program. In either case, the number of hours devoted to the major usually exceeds the requirements of a departmental major in the United States. Not all programs, however, offer an option between the dual and single major, nor are all programs structured along these lines. (See also "First Degree Program Structure" in this chapter.)

The examination of courses and credits should be based on the general guideline that regular fulltime students are registered for an average of 20 hours each semester, or 40 hours each year based upon a six-day week. The reported hours or credits, however, are not necessarily defined in terms of the U.S. semester credit system. For example, seminar hours or credits are usually reported in excess of the actual class hours met and reflect, instead, a weighting factor. Laboratory hours, on the other hand, may not always reflect the U.S. standard of three hours equating to one credit and frequently are reported literally hour for hour. On balance, it is possible for students to meet the program schedule of 20 weekly hours while fulfilling out-of-class preparation requirements that are expected in U.S. higher education. In addition, narrower, more indepth degree programs such as those that exist in Israel may effectively proceed at an accelerated pace due to the reinforcement of knowledge resulting from study of an extensive amount of interrelated subject matter. (See also "The Credit System" and program/credit specifics within the "Institutional Profiles" section in this chapter.)

A comparison of Israeli students and traditional U.S. undergraduates must take into account the unique characteristics of Israeli students and society. Dimensions such as student age, military obligations, seriousness of purpose, the political and economic climate, and a national atmosphere generally lacking in frivolity play an integral part in the attitude of students and the atmosphere on campuses. To some degree, Israeli students may be said to share similar characteristics with the U.S. "nontraditional," adult student population. While strengths and weaknesses may be attributed to any one of these factors, their impact should be considered when evaluating the overall effectiveness of the three-year degree. (See also "The Military and Education" in Chapter 1 and "The Planning and Grants Committee" in this chapter.)

The determination of the number of years required for Israeli degrees is based upon the field of study. In fields where the three-year degree is awarded, options such as "honours" or four-year degrees, which are alternatives in other educational systems where three-year degree programs exist, usually are not available in Israel. Consequently, the three-year bachelor's degree provides direct access to graduate-level study in the same or related fields in Israel. An exception to this can be noted in the Technion-Israel Institute of Technology profile under the degrees and admission requirements section. Technion awards a three- and four-year degree in some departments, consequently affecting the requirements for admission to their master's degree program in these departments.

Statements of degree equivalencies are infrequently made in terms of absolutes. Not only do various factors under consideration lack U.S. counterparts, but the diversity of universities and individual departments negates the validity of blanket statements about the three-year degree. It is generally observed, for example, that "up front" liberal arts requirements are lacking in the three-year Israeli degree rather than a weakness in the major (a feature not uncommon in foreign degrees). However, this is not entirely valid: most degree programs require study and proficiency in a foreign language (usually English), physical education, (both not-for-credit), and include introductory, complementary, or elective courses outside the major department.

Israelis are openly discussing at the highest level the structure of undergraduate studies: Can students in the humanities, social sciences, and law continue to graduate without any exposure to scientific and technological subjects? Can students in the natural sciences forego study in the humanities and social sciences? Should the length of undergraduate studies be altered? *(Higher Education in Israel* 81) The political, economic, and financial implications of altering the structure of programs and adding one more year of study to degree requirements, however, in a country that has recently witnessed demonstrations and resistance over tuition increases, makes a change in this direction seem unlikely in the near future. (See also "The Planning and Grants Committee: Financing of Higher Education" and "Higher Education: Present Conditions and Future Considerations" in Chapter 8.)

ADMISSION TO FIRST DEGREE PROGRAMS

Admission of most students, women and men, is usually delayed two to three years, respectively, due to mandatory military service. Exceptions to this may be granted on religious grounds, but, otherwise, deferring military service results in an extension of the total obligation by one year for every year deferred. Consequently, most high school graduates go directly to military service and, as a result, are two to three years older than the traditional U.S. undergraduate. (See "The Military and Education" in Chapter 1.)

The standard minimum requirements for admission to first degree programs include the Israeli Matriculation Certificate *(Teudat Bagrut)* or its equivalent, the Israeli Psychometric Entrance Examination (see below), proficiency in Hebrew, and, in some instances, a personal interview. Acceptance to the institution or program of choice is not open or guaranteed, except in the case of Everyman's University which has open admission. Admission is not a centrally administered State allocation process but rather is decentralized at the institutional level with acceptance of applicants determined according to the demand and selectivity of individual faculties and departments. Students usually select two major departments and receive approval by each before admission is finalized. The more competitive departments are Accounting, Aeronautical Engineering, Biology, Business Administration, Computer Engineering, Computer Science, Dentistry, Electronics and Electrical Engineering, Industrial Management, Law, Medicine, Pharmacy, Psychology, Social Work, and Veterinary Medicine. Israeli citizenship is also a requirement of those accepted to Dentistry, Medicine, Pharmacy, and Veterinary Medicine. (See also "Professional Programs" in this chapter for comments on selectivity and "The Three-Year Degree," above.)

In 1983, the Council for Higher Education approved institutional discretion in the exemption of basic admission requirements, on an individual basis, for applicants who are 30 years of age or older and can demonstrate other achievement meriting consideration. Normally, however, applicants not meeting admission requirements are advised to apply to the pre-academic preparatory programs *(mechinot)* discussed earlier in this chapter.

The Psychometric Entrance Examination

The Psychometric Entrance Examination, designed and administered by the National Institute for Testing and Evaluation (NITE), Israel, is the examination used by institutions of higher education, preparatory programs, and other educational institutions in conjunction with matriculation examination results to determine eligibility for admission. In 1983, NITE began administering this examination for all institutions which, up until that time, had administered their own psychometric tests.

The examination evaluates cognitive abilities for the purpose of predicting academic success. It consists of a battery of tests measuring cognitive abilities utilized in academic study: verbal, quantitative-numerical and spacial. The five separate examinations cover: 1) General Knowledge—familiarity with various fields such as art, history, natural sciences, the social sciences, etc.; 2) Forms—spacial logic and perception of graphic relationships; 3) Reasoning—ability to analyze data, comprehension of texts, comprehension of the relationships between words and concepts, and verbal logic; 4) Mathematical Comprehension—elementary knowledge at the ninth and tenth grade curricula level of Israeli schools; and 5) English—ability to comprehend texts and sentences in English. With the exception of the test in English, the examination does not test knowledge, but ability.

The Psychometric Entrance Examination is a multiple-choice examination consisting of approximately 60 questions per test and offered in several languages: Arabic, English, French, Hebrew, Russian, Spanish, or a combination of two of the above. The examination is valid for three academic years.

FIRST DEGREE PROGRAM STRUCTURE

The traditional university bachelor's program in the arts, humanities, and social sciences involves study concentrated in two major departments for the duration of the program (normally three years). This program structure is referred to by some institutions as a dual or double major program. Each year students normally register for approximately 10 annual hours in each department for a total of 20 annual hours (or approximately 40 semester hours each year). Some institutions will prepare separate transcripts for each department; others simply group the coursework according to the two major departments year-by-year.

In those degree programs mentioned above, an alternative to the traditional dual major program is the single major program. This option is not offered by every department, nor is it usually available until the second year of studies. As a result, students who study in the single major program—like dual major students—normally will have studied in two departments during the first year. In this instance, approval to follow a single major program involves satisfactory completion of first year advancement requirements in both departments *or* at least a passing grade in all required courses of one department and grades 5 points above advancement requirements in the department chosen for the single major. In the single major program, students concentrate their studies in one major department to which approximately 50%-60% (30-36 annual hours) of the program is devoted, and will take "sections" in two or three other departments for the remainder of the program. (A section [*hativa*] consists of a required group of courses from one field taken over a two-year period.) This program structure tends to give more breadth to the overall program than does the dual major program. (See Tables 8.4 and 8.5.)

Degrees based on the dual major program and single major program are viewed with equal regard.

The structure of programs in Agriculture; Business Administration and other business fields; Engineering; and Mathematics, Natural and Physical Sciences does not follow the dual and single major programs in the Humanities and Social Sciences described above. See the discussion below and in the "Institutional Profiles" section at the end of this chapter. See Tables 8.6 through 8.9 for curriculums in engineering and business.

AGRICULTURE. Agriculture is offered by one institution—The Hebrew University of Jerusalem—in a three-year degree program leading to a B.Sc.Agr. Students study in one of six departments (e.g., Animal Science, Horticulture, Soil and Water Science). The first year consists of required courses from the Faculty of Math and Natural Sciences, and includes Biology, Chemistry, Economics, English, Mathematics, Physics, and Zoology. The program includes basic, elective, and specialization courses and requires 100-104 study units beyond the first year's coursework—where a unit is defined as one weekly hour per semester. The Department of Agricultural Economics and Management requires a total of 105 study units including first-year compulsory courses.

Table 8.4. Sample Dual and Single Major Programs in the Faculties of Humanities, and Social Sciences, The Hebrew University of Jerusalem, 1985–86

Faculty of Humanities

Dual Major	Annual Hours	*Single Major*	Annual Hours
First Major Subject	26–28	Major Subject	26–28
Second Major Subject	26–28	First year of second major subject or intro. courses	6
Prep. Lang. Studies	4–8	Two Sections (*hativot*)	12
		Additional study in major dept. and/or aux. studies	8–10
Total (includes tutorials, lang. studies, etc.)	56–60*	Total	56–60*

Faculty of Social Sciences

Dual Major	Annual Hours	*Single Major*	Annual Hours
First Major Subject	22–26	Major Subject	24–32
Second Major Subject	22–26	One of the Following:	
		1) Suppl. Stud. other subjs.	22–28
Total (includes tutorials, lang. studies, etc.)	48–56*	2) One Section *(hativa)*	7–8
		Two Intro. Courses	6–8
		Elective Courses	6
		3) Two Sections *(hativot)*	14–16
		One Intro. Course	3–4
		Elective Course	2
		Total (approx.)	48–56*

*Figures are those reported by the institution and do not necessarily reflect the totals of all lower or higher numbers.

BUSINESS. Undergraduate business-related programs (and the number of universities offering the programs) include Accounting (offered by three universities), Business Administration (two), Economics (six), Management (one), and Management/Economics (one). The *Accounting* program is usually a three-year, dual-major only program with the second department being either Economics, Statistics, or Computer Science or other options. The basic program in accounting at The Hebrew University of Jerusalem includes Commercial Law, Computers and Information Systems, Corporate Accounting and Special Problems, Costing of Management Accounting, Financial Accounting, Fundamentals of Behavioral Science, Fundamentals of Finance, Fundamentals of Law, Introduction to Accounts Auditing, Introduction to Economics, Introduction to Tax Law, Labor Relations, Organizational Behavior, Preparatory Course in Computers, Selected Problems in Accounting in addition to the other major. Usually a fourth year of 10 annual hours in accounting is offered to accounting majors who want to qualify as a Certified Public Accountant. A sample three-year B.A. dual major program in Accounting and Economics is given in Table 8.9.

Table 8.5. Sample Major/Minor vs. Expanded Major Program at Bar-Ilan University, 1985–87

Most students are required to complete both a "major" and a "minor" subject. The concept behind this terminology is comparable to that used in U.S. institutions. However, certain subjects must, and others may, be taken as "expanded" majors, i.e., without a minor. Major and minor subjects are usually chosen from the same faculty. Natural Sciences and some Social Sciences departments require additional hours of laboratory and recitation. Total hours do not include Hebrew Expression or Physical Education. The following represents the program structure in all faculties except Law.

Major Subject	30 Annual Hours
Minor Subject	16 Annual Hours
or	
Expanded Major	46 Annual Hours
Basic Jewish Study Requirements: Bible, *Talmud*, Oral Law, Jewish History, Jewish Philosophy	16 Annual Hours (men)
	or
	14 Annual Hours (women)
Electives	2–4 Annual Hours
Physical Education	1–2 Annual Hours
Total Required Annual Hours	64 Annual Hours*

*Figures are those reported by the institution and do not necessarily reflect the totals of all lower or higher numbers.

Table 8.6. Sample Program: Four-Year B.Sc. (Tech.Sc.), Ben-Gurion University of the Negev, Faculty of Technological Sciences, Department of Industrial Engineering and Management

First Semester	Second Semester
	First Year
Computer Programming	Engineering Graphics
Engineering Graphics	English
English	General Chemistry
General Chemistry	General Physics
General Chemistry Lab	Mathematics II
General Physics	Physics Lab
Humanities	Probability Theory for Sci.
Mathematics I	Statistics
Physics Lab	Technical Report Writing
	Second Year
Economic Control	Economic Control
Fndn. of Thermodynamics	Industrial Statistics
Industrial Statistics	Intro. to Materials
Intro. to Numerical Methods	Intro. to Modern Physics
Lab	Mathematics IV
Mathematics III	Physics Lab
Metal Cutting	Strength of Materials
Strength of Materials	
Technical English	

continued

	Third Year
Digital Systems Simula.	Automatization
Electron. & Elect. Engr.	Behavioral Sci. in Mgmt.
Engineering Design	Electronics in Industry
Industrial Economics	Humanities
Intro. to Economics I	Intro. to Economics II
Motion & Time Study I	Mini Computers
Operations Research I	Motion & Time Study II
Productn. & Plan. Control I	Operations Research II
Quality Control	Productn. & Plan. Control II
	Fourth Year
Analysis of Systems	Adv. Operations Research
Case Studies in Indus. Engr. I	Case Studies in Indus. Engr. II
Construction Management	Comput. Applica. in Indus. Engr.
Health Occupa. Hazards	Digital Systems Simula.
Industrial Sociology	Econ. & Indus. Structure in Israel
Marketing Management	Financial Management
Organization & Mgmt. in Indus.	Mini Computers in Industry
Plant Layout/Materials Handling	Seminar II
Seminar I	

Table 8.7. Sample Program: Four-Year B.Sc. (Tech. Sc.), Technion-Israel Institute of Technology, Faculty and Department of Electrical Engineering (165 credits required)

First Semester	Credits	Second Semester	Credits
	First Year		
Algebra I	2.5	English	2.0
Descriptive Geometry	2.0	Differen. & Integr. Calculus II	4.0
Differen. & Integr. Calculus I	3.5	General Chemistry II	2.0
English	2.0	General Chemistry Lab II	1.0
General Chemistry I	2.0	Intro. to Ordin. & Diff. Equa.	2.0
General Chemistry Lab I	1.0	Physical Education I	1.0
Hebrew	2.0–3.0	Physics II	3.5
Physics I	3.5	Physics Lab II	1.5
Physics Lab I	1.5	Programming 1 (PL/1)	3.0
	Second Year		
Algebra II	3.5	Complex Functions	2.0
Electrical Engineering I	4.5	Electrical Engineering II	3.0
Electrical Engineering Lab I	2.0	Intro. to Materials Engineering	2.0
Ordin. & Part. Diff. Equa. I	2.0	Ordin. & Part. Differen. Equa. II	2.0
Physical Education II	1.0	Physics Lab IV	1.0
Physics III	3.5	Programming II	3.0
Physics Lab III	1.0	Technical Mechanics	3.5
Semiconductor Devices	4.5	Thermodyna. & Statis. Physics	3.5

	Third Year		
Digital Systems	3.0	Elect. Engr. Lab III-Electronics	1.5
Electrical Engineering Lab II	2.0	Elect. Engr. Lab III-Energy Con.	1.5
Electromagnetic Fields	3.5	Electronic Devices I (MOS)	3.0
Energy Conversion	3.5	Electronic Switching Circuits	3.5
Foreign Language I	2.0	Foreign Language II	2.0
Linear Electronic Circuits	3.5	Intro. to Probability	2.0
Systems I	3.5	Waves & Distributed Systems	3.0
		Systems II	3.5
	Fourth Year		
Analog Communication	3.0	Electronic Instrumentation	3.0
Electrical Engineering Lab IV	3.0	Filters Synthesis & Design	3.0
Electronic Devices II (Bipolar)	3.0	Integrated Circuits	3.0
Instrumentation	3.0	Lab Project B	3.0
Lab Project A	2.5	Medical Electronics	3.0
Pass. & Active Networks & Circ.	3.0	Special Electronics Circuits	3.0
Receiv. & Transmit. Techniques	3.0		

Table 8.8. 4-Year Curriculum for B.Tech. (Tex.) in Industrial Management, Shenkar-College of Textile Technology and Fashion

Subject	Lect.	Tut./Lab	Subject	Lect.	Tut./Lab
		Year 1			
1st Term	(30 total hours)		2nd Term	(30 total hours)	
English 1	4	–	Advd. Technic. Draw.	2	–
Intro. Economics	2	1	Chemistry 1	3	1
Intro. Spin. Technol.	2	2	English 2	4	–
Intro. Weav. Technol.	2	2	Intro. Garment Technol.	2	2
Mathematics 1	4	2	Intro. Knit. Technol.	2	2
Physics 1	3	2	Mathematics 2	4	2
Technical Drawing	2	2	Physics 2	4	2
		Year 2			
1st Term	(33 total hours)		2nd Term	(32 total hours)	
Mathematics 3	3	1	Organiza. Sys.	3	–
Work Method Analy.	2	2	Time & Motion Study 2	2	2
Statistics 1	2	1	Data Proces. Sys.	2	1
Intro. Computers	2	1	Accounting 2	2	1
Dyeing & Finishing	3	2	Statistics 2	2	1
Accounting 1	2	1	Textile Testing	1	3
Textile Engr. 2	3	4	Textile Engr. 3	4	4
English 3	4	–	English 4	4	–
		Year 3			
1st Term	(29 total hours)		2nd Term	(25 total hours)	
Communica. & Report Writing	2	–	Human Resources 2	2	–
Computer File Organiza.	2	–	Intro. Mktg.	3	–
Engr. Economics	3	–	Oper. Research 2	2	1

continued

Year 3 *continued*

Human Resources 1	2	–	Plant Design	2	1
Oper. Research 1	2	1	Systems Analysis I	2	–
Plant Layout	2	1	Textile Econ. of Israel	2	–
Production Mgmt. 1	3	–	Textile Engr. II 2	4	4
Textile Engr. II 1	4	4	Elective Course 1	2	–
Work Study Wkshp. & Project	1	2			
		Year 4			
1st Term	(20 total hours)		2nd Term	(12 total hours)	
Financial Mgmt.	3	–	Computers in Indus.	2	–
Indus. Case Stud. (Seminar)	4	–	Stat. Quality Control	2	–
Intro. Final Project	2	–	Final Project 2 Seminar	2	–
Personnel Training	2	–	Elective Course 4	2	–
Production Mgmt. 2	3	–	Elective Course 5	2	–
Systems Analysis 2	2	–	Elective Course 6	2	–
Elective Course 2	2	–			
Elective Course 3	2	–			

SOURCE: Shenkar-College of Textile Technology and Fashion catalog.

Table 8.9. Sample B.A. Program: Dual Major in Economics (Faculty of Social Sciences) and Accounting (Faculty of Management)

Economics	Sem. Hrs.	Accounting	Sem. Hrs.
Intro. to Econ. I, II	8	Intro. to Data Proc.	2
Intro. to Statistics I, II	6	Mgmt. Acct.	4
Math for Soc. Sci. I, II	8	Principles Acct.	4
Advd. Calculus	4	Principles of Bus. Law	2
Intro. to Econometrics	4	Principles of Law	3
Macro-econ. I, II	4,2	Commercial Law I	2
Price Theory I, II	8	Corporate Law	3
Principles of Finance I, II	4	Finan. Commun. in Bus. & Indus.	4
Tax System/Israel	2	Finan. Struct., Spec. Acct. Issues	4
The Econ. of Israel I, II	4	Principles Auditing	4
Economic Growth	2	Quant. Meth. for Accts.	4
Econ. of the Middle East	2	Report Sys./Measurement Problems	4
Energy & Natural Resources	2	Taxation Law I	4
Inflation I, II	4	Acct. Theory	3
Intro. Labor Econ.	2	Advd. Managerial Acct.	2
Issues in Econ. Backwardness & Growth	2	Commercial Law II	2
Public Finance	2	Corporate Tax	4
Social Decisions	2	Seminar—Bus. Plng. & Control	2
Seminar	–	Struct. of Acct. Sys.	2
		Taxation Law II	4

SOURCE: Tel-Aviv University transcript, 1978–81.
Note: Auxiliary Studies include English, and Sport.

Graduate Degrees

Graduate programs in Israel lead to the master's and doctoral degrees. A master's degree program usually extends over a period of one and one-half to two years; a doctoral degree usually requires a minimum of two additional years beyond the master's degree. Seven universities have been authorized to award master's and doctoral degrees by the Council for Higher Education. The data related to graduate degrees awarded is provided in Table 8.10.

THE MASTER'S DEGREE

Master's degree programs are designed to provide the student with indepth knowledge and research capabilities in a particular subject area.

DURATION OF PROGRAM. The length of master's degree programs varies according to the field of study and from institution to institution. Programs in the Humanities and Social Sciences generally require a minimum of two years of study while programs in Mathematics, Natural and Physical Sciences usually require four to six trimesters or one to two years of study. Students admitted at the master's level with course deficiencies are required to complete supplementary coursework which extends the length of their program. Many students register on a part-time basis which also tends to give a misleading impression of the length of the program. (See Table 8.2 and "Program Structure" below.)

ADMISSION REQUIREMENTS. Admission to a master's degree program requires a bachelor's degree from a recognized university or college and an average of "B" (75-80), or "Good." Individual departments may in actuality require more or less than the stated minimum grade average, entrance examinations, and/ or an interview. Applicants are expected to have an appropriate undergraduate background when applying for admission to a graduate program. When an exception to this is made, the applicant is accepted conditionally, subject to completion of supplementary courses which are taken (not-for-credit) before beginning, or concurrently with, the master's program. Proficiency in Hebrew language is required.

PROGRAM STRUCTURE. The structure of master's degree programs varies from institution to institution, faculty to faculty, and department to department, with each choosing its own terminology to describe degree requirements. Components of the program may include one or more of the following: coursework, laboratory work, theoretical or practical research or a project, seminars or research seminars, a thesis (usually incorporating results of research or the project), and a comprehensive or final examination. Coursework, laboratory work, research seminars, seminars, and projects are usually valued in terms of "hours" or "credits" but may be expressed in a variety of ways. (See also "The Course System" and "The Credit System" earlier in this chapter.) Coursework is normally concentrated in the first year, while research or a project is undertaken in the remaining time.

Master's programs in the Humanities and Social Sciences tend to be offered at two levels referred to as tracks or plans. Track or Plan A involves coursework

Table 8.10. Distribution of Master's and Doctoral Degrees by Institution and Field of Study, 1982–83

Institution	Master's Degrees (% of Total)		Doctoral Degrees (% of Total)	
Bar-Ilan University	180	(9.3%)	28	(8.4%)
Ben-Gurion University of the Nevev	89	(4.6%)	6	(1.8%)
Technion-Israel Institute of Technology	291	(15.0%)	61	(18.2%)
Tel-Aviv University	568	(29.2%)	44	(12.8%)
The University of Haifa	76	(3.9%)	–	–
The Hebrew University of Jerusalem	679	(34.9%)	136	(40.6%)
Weizmann Institute of Science	60	(3.1%)	61	(18.2%)
Total Degree Recipients	1,943		336	

Field of Study Percentages	Master's	Doctoral
Agriculture	3.3%	3.0%
Engineering and Architecture	10.7%	9.8%
Jewish Studies and Humanities	14.0%	20.0%
Law	0.8%	0.9%
Medicine and Paramedical Professions	19.0%	2.7%
Mathematics, Natural and Physical Sciences	17.6%	55.3%
Social Sciences (including Business)	34.6%	8.3%

SOURCE: *Statistical Abstract of Israel*, No. 35, 1984, p. 666.

and a written thesis and allows access to further study at the doctoral level. Track B requires more coursework than Track A, several seminar papers, and sometimes a project, but no thesis; Track B does not permit continuation at the doctoral level. There is no stated distinction between the two plans in terms of admission requirements. In addition, there is a mechanism for changing from one track to the other.

Brief program descriptions are provided below to acquaint the reader with the different terminology used by departments or faculties in defining program requirements. These descriptions also serve to illustrate the usual structure of master's degree programs within a particular field. Parenthetical information has been added by the author to clarify or standardize terminology. All descriptions except the M.B.A. are taken from bulletins of The Hebrew University of Jerusalem, the institution awarding the largest percentage of graduate degrees; deviations, when known, are found within individual institutional profiles.

M.A. (Faculty of Humanities). Track or Plan A. Program for those intending to proceed to doctoral studies. Involves 16-20 weekly hours of coursework (16-20 clock hours each week for one academic year, or 8-10 clock hours each year for two years, or the equivalent of 32-40 semester hours total), including one to two seminar papers, a thesis, and final examination. *Track or Plan B.* Program includes 20-24 weekly hours of coursework (20-24 clock hours a week annually, or 10-12 clock hours each week for two academic years, or 40-48 semester credits) over two years distributed as 12-16 hours in the department, 8-12 hours in other departments, three seminar papers (not-for-credit), and a final examination.

M.A. (Faculty of Social Sciences) Track or Plan A. Program includes coursework for 20 weekly hours over two years (20 annual hours or about 40 total semester credits) distributed as 10-14 weekly hours (year 1) and 6 to 10 hours (year 2), including research seminars, a research paper of limited scope, and a final examination. *Track or Plan B.* Program includes 24 weekly hours over two years (or 48 total semester credits), 18-20 annual hours in the department and 4-6 outside the department, plus a final examination.

M.B.A. (Faculty of Management, The Leon Recanti Graduate School of Business Management Administration). A master's program in Business Administration is offered by The Hebrew University of Jerusalem and Tel-Aviv University. The Tel-Aviv University program is a four-semester program requiring 34 semester units (where 1 unit represents one 75-minute weekly session for one semester) plus 11 units of noncredit preparatory courses. The program assumes no previous business study. The four-phase curriculum is divided into *noncredit preparatory courses* (English for Business Administration, Introduction to Data Processing, Mathematics for Business Administration, Principles of Economics, Principles of Statistics); *basic courses* (17 units total including 6 units of basic management[Business Law, Organizational Systems Management, Principles of Accounting I, Principles of Finance I, Principles of Marketing Management I]); 8 units of disciplinary studies [Group Functions in Organization, Macro-economics, Micro-economics, Models in Operations Research I and II, Statistics for Business Administration I and II, Structures and Process in Organization], 3 of 9 units optional basic courses in the specialization); *specialization studies* (9 units from specializations in Finance and Accounting, Financial Management and Capital Markets and Banking, Information Systems, Insurance and Risks Management, International Management, Marketing, Operations Research, Organizational Behavior, Production Management, Public Sector); *elective studies* (4 units in general elective courses and a seminar); *integrative courses* (4 units in Business Game and Business Policy). Students may elect to write a thesis in place of 5 semester units in advanced studies.

M.Sc. (Faculty of Mathematics and Natural Sciences). Program includes coursework in the field of specialization and related courses, extending over 4-6 trimesters, and comprises 400-500 hours, or 40-50 credits (10 clock hours = one trimester credit, 40-50 trimester credits, or approximately 27-34 semester credits in total), plus a thesis and a comprehensive examination.

M.Sc. (Department of Computer Science, Faculty of Mathematics and Natural Sciences). Program includes 45 trimester hours (45 trimester credits or about 30 semester credits) of lecture and laboratory, a research project which is summarized in the thesis, and participation in a colloquium or research seminar.

M.Sc. (Department of Physics, Faculty of Mathematics and Natural Sciences). Program extends over 5-6 trimesters and comprises 50 trimester hours (approximately 34 semester credits), participation in a weekly colloquium and a divisional seminar (not-for-credit), a thesis, and a final comprehensive examination.

M.Sc. (Faculty of Agriculture). Program includes 32 or 28 credits for Agriculture or Agricultural Economics, respectively; active participation in two seminars (not-for-credit); a thesis; and a final examination which is a defense of the thesis. (The Faculty of Agriculture uses a semester calendar and a "credits" system.)

THE DOCTORAL DEGREE

The doctorate represents the highest level of academic achievement within the Israeli educational system. The doctoral program focuses on a scientific paper or dissertation which is expected to make an original and substantial contribution to the advancement of knowledge. The various doctoral degrees awarded in Israel are identified in Table 8.2, but the Doctor of Philosophy (Ph.D.) is by far the most common doctorate. Seven universities are approved by the Council for Higher Education to award this degree. The Hebrew University of Jerusalem was the first university to award the doctorate and to date (1984-85) has awarded a total of 3,360 Ph.D.'s. Israel has graduated approximately 300 doctoral candidates each year for the past decade, the details of which for 1982-83 are provided in Table 8.10.

DURATION OF PROGRAM. The doctoral program extends over a minimum of two years beyond the master's degree.

ADMISSION REQUIREMENTS. Applicants to doctoral programs must normally have a master's degree from a recognized university with a grade average of at least "B" or "Good" in master's level coursework and a thesis grade of "Very Good." Applicants from departments offering Track (Plan) A and B programs are required to have completed the Track A option (see the master's degree "Program Structure" section above). At the discretion of university doctoral committees, applicants who do not meet normal admission criteria but appear to be able to meet the requisite standard within one year may be admitted provisionally. Provisional candidates follow a prescribed program of supplementary studies for one year, after which time the qualifications of the applicant are re-evaluated. Previous scientific work, research, and publications are taken into consideration.

THE DIRECT DOCTORAL DEGREE PROGRAM. A program for exceptional students who have a bachelor's degree with a grade average of at least 90 in the department of their intended doctorate, and an average of at least 80 in other coursework. The first year of the program is an accelerated master's program. If high achievement is maintained, the student may bypass the second year of the master's program and proceed directly to doctoral studies.

PROGRAM STRUCTURE. Requirements for the doctorate are regulated by individual university doctoral committees which work in conjunction with the university department and/or faculty through which the degree will be recommended. As a result, program structure varies slightly from institution to institution and from department to department. In general, doctoral programs comprise coursework, a language requirement, and focus on an original research dissertation carried out within the framework of the department.

Within six months of being accepted into a program, the student must seek out a senior member of the faculty who will supervise the research and dissertation. A research proposal must be submitted to and approved by the university doctoral committee. Research work is usually carried out through the department of the university but, under certain circumstances, may be conducted in part or in its entirety at another scientific center in Israel or abroad. During the course of the program, students meet with their advisor, submit written progress reports, and lecture to a research seminar or similar forum. The dissertation is evaluated by a committee of three, one of whom is the advisor; the written evaluation submitted by the committee serves as the basis for the award of the degree. The dissertation is normally written in Hebrew, although special permission may be granted for its submission in another language. If it is prepared in Hebrew, an abstract in English or French must be submitted; if it is in a foreign language, a Hebrew abstract must be attached.

Coursework generally consists of 180 hours (18 trimester hours or 12 semester hours). Some institutions do not specifically require registration in courses but assume student attendance and participation in courses which have been determined in consultation with the advisor.

Doctoral candidates must pass an examination in English or Hebrew (whichever is not the native language) and one additional language (French, German, or Russian). While the language requirement is subject to waiver by the doctoral committee, the committee, on the other hand, in consultation with the advisor, may require the candidate to acquire a foreign language deemed essential to the preparation of the dissertation.

Certificates and Diplomas

In addition to degrees, institutions of higher education offer programs leading to certificates and diplomas. These programs vary in length from one to three years and may represent post-baccalaureate undergraduate-level, or post-baccalaureate graduate-level study. The evaluation of these programs involves determination of entrance requirements, entrance qualifications of the student, the objective of the program, the content of the coursework, and the quantity and quality of study completed. It is also appropriate to ascertain the significance between a degree and diploma or certificate programs from the same institution in the same field, as well as if, or to what extent, the institution recognizes the diploma or certificate coursework towards a degree. This information is usually available upon written request from the Academic Secretary of the institution.

Areas of study from which certificates and/or diplomas may be presented include Criminology, Dietetics, Family Medicine, Librarianship and Archive Studies, Local Government, Ophthalmology, Polymer and Textile Chemistry, Teacher Certification, Training of Community Center Directors and Senior Personnel (Social Work), Training Directors of Early Childhood Programs for Children and Their Parents (Social Work), and Translation and Interpretation. (For details, see "Institutional Profiles" at the end of this chapter.)

Professional Degree Programs

Professional education leading to degrees in Dentistry, Law, Medicine, Nursing, Pharmacy, Social Work, and Veterinary Medicine commences in the first year of university study (third year in Veterinary Medicine) and does not require a first degree as a prerequisite.

DENTAL MEDICINE

The professional study of Dental Medicine (Dentistry) is provided at the Faculty of Dental Medicine, Hadassah Medical Center at The Hebrew University of Jerusalem; and the School of Dentistry, Sackler Faculty of Medicine at Tel-Aviv University. The program is six years in length, plus a one-year internship. The degree of Doctor of Dental Medicine (D.M.D.) is awarded by the university upon completion of the program. The license to practice is issued by the Ministry of Health without further examination. The dentistry profession is under the governance and supervision of the Ministry of Health and the universities.

ADMISSION. Admission is highly competitive and restricted to Israeli citizens. The Council for Higher Education and the PGC have made provisions to increase the capacity of the two dental schools hoping that by 1988 the annual number of graduates will have increased by 50%. Admission to the program begins with the first year of university study and does not require a first degree. Eligibility for admission is based upon the following criteria: the Matriculation Certificate *(Teudat Bagrut)* with appropriate academic subjects (Mathematics and Science); the Psychometric Entrance Examination; additional examinations in Mathematics and two of the following subjects—Biology, Physics, and Chemistry; a personal interview; proficiency in Hebrew; Israeli citizenship; and proficiency in English.

PROGRAM OF STUDIES. The six-year Dentistry program is divided into three stages: Pre-Medical Studies, Pre-Clinical Studies, and Clinical Studies.

1. *Pre-Medical Studies.* Conducted within the Faculty of Mathematics and Natural Sciences and the Faculty of Medicine and Dental Medicine. Includes coursework in Behavioral Sciences, Biology, General Chemistry, Organic Chemistry, Mathematics, Basic Programming, Statistics, English, and Hebrew for non-native Hebrew speakers.
2. *Pre-Clinical Studies.* Conducted in the Faculties of Medicine and Dental Medicine. Includes coursework in Anatomy, Biochemistry, Oral Chemistry, Genetics, Growth and Development, Histology, Dental Histology, Immunology, Microbiology, Dental Morphology, Nutrition, General Pathology, Oral Pathology, Pharmacology, Physiology, Oral Physiology, Psychopathology, and Statistics.

   The pre-medical and pre-clinical stages together require three years of study. Upon successful completion of these first two stages, the student is awarded the Bachelor of Medical Science (B.Med.Sc.). Eligibility to continue into the final clinical stage requires a three-year weighted average of 75. Those with a weighted average between 71-74 are reviewed individually. Students with an average of 70 or below are not allowed to continue their studies in Dentistry.
3. *Clinical Studies.* Includes practical training, treatment of patients, and study in the following areas: Diagnosis, Endodontics, Epidermiology, Dental Materials, Community Dental Medicine, Hospital Dental Medicine, Oral Medicine, Orthodontics, Pedodontics, Periodontics, Radiology, Oral Rehabilitation, and Oral and Maxillofacial Surgery. The D.M.D. degree is awarded upon completion of this stage.

GRADUATE DENTAL PROGRAM. The Hebrew University of Jerusalem, Faculty of Dental Medicine offers graduate studies in Dental Medicine Sciences leading to a Master of Medical Sciences (M.Med.Sc.). This degree is academic rather than professional. The two- to four-semester program is based upon a first university degree in Biology or Medical Sciences with a minimum final grade of "Good" or "B." Normal studies include approximately 400 lecture hours, laboratories, seminars, and a final experimental paper. Students with a B.Med.Sc. require less time (300-350 course hours) to complete the degree.

LAW

The professional study of law is provided at Bar-Ilan University, The Hebrew University of Jerusalem, and Tel-Aviv University. The four-year Bachelor of Laws (LL.B.) program commences with the first year of university studies. The three faculties of law admit but a small fraction of those students who apply. Admission is therefore quite selective.

The 1983-84 report by the Council for Higher Education and the PGC states that it is difficult to accurately determine the demand for lawyers in the economy and society. The main factor limiting the capacity of the existing law faculties is the difficulty in recruiting suitable academic staff. This limitation prevents serious thought being given to any new faculties or to a significant expansion of existing ones. The little more than 500 law degrees (all levels) awarded in 1983 represented 5.2% of all degrees awarded in that year. (Statistical *Abstract*, 1984)

A sample four-year curriculum from the Faculty of Law, Tel-Aviv University is as follows: First Year—Constitutional Law, Criminal Law, English, Historical Introduction to Jewish Law, Introduction to the Israeli Legal System (with Bibliography), Introduction to Jurisprudence, Principles of Common Law, and electives. Second Year—Administrative Law; Criminal Procedure; English; International Law; Law of Contracts; Law of Persons, Family, and Succession; Law of Tort; Moot Trials; and electives. Third Year—Civil Procedure, Corporate Law, Jewish Law, Labor Law, Law of Property, Taxation Law, Seminar, and electives. Fourth Year—Law of Evidence, Law of Negotiable Instruments, Private International and Interreligious Law, Seminar, and electives.

The Master of Laws (LL.M.) program normally extends over a period of two years although special permission may be granted to complete the program in one year or three years. The program involves 16 annual hours of coursework (32 semester hours) including 10 annual hours of seminars and six annual hours of electives. In addition to coursework, degree requirements include a final examination, master's dissertation and oral defense. In special cases, *magna cum laude* and *summa cum laude* graduates with an LL.M. and LL.B. degree may be admitted for the highest degree, Doctor of Laws *(Doctor Juris),* not to be confused with the first American law degree—*Juris Doctor* (J.D.).

MEDICINE

The professional study of medicine is provided at Ben-Gurion University of the Negev; The Hebrew University of Jerusalem, Hadassah Medical Center in Ein Kerem; Technion-Israel Institute of Technology; and Tel-Aviv University. The length of the program is six years, plus a one-year internship. The degree of Doctor of Medicine (M.D.) is awarded by the universities upon completion of the program. The license to practice is issued by the Ministry of Health without further examination. The profession is under the governance and supervision of the Ministry of Health and the universities.

Based upon a 1981 study completed by the Economic Planning Authority, the Council for Higher Education and the PGC report that a considerable surplus of doctors is expected by 1989 (2,000 above the expected demand of some 13,000). About one-third of the doctors in Israel are educated in Israel; the rest are either immigrant doctors or Israelis who have studied abroad. As a result of the predicted surplus, the PGC and the four medical schools in Israel have agreed to freeze the total number of medical students at the present level until future studies indicate a need to change this practice.

ADMISSION REQUIREMENTS. Requirements for admission are the same as those for the program in Dental Medicine described above.

PROGRAM OF STUDIES. The seven-year program of study and internship is divided into five stages: Pre-Medical Studies, Pre-Clinical Studies, Clinical Studies, Electives, and Internship.

five stages: Pre-Medical Studies, Pre-Clinical Studies, Clinical Studies, Electives, and Internship.

1. *Pre-Medical Studies (1 year).* Conducted within the Faculty of Mathematics and Science. Includes coursework in Behavioral Sciences, Biology, Chemistry, Computer Science, English, Hebrew, Mathematics, Physics, and Statistics.
2. *Pre-Clinical Studies (2 years).* Includes coursework in Anatomy, Biochemistry, Introduction to Clinical Medicine, Microbiology, Pathology, Pharmacology, Physiology, Electives, and a seminar paper.

Upon successful completion of the pre-medical and pre-clinical stages, the student is awarded the Bachelor of Medical Sciences (B.Med.Sc.). In order to advance to the final stages, the student is required to have a minimum average of 75. Students with an average between 71-74 are reviewed individually. Those with an average of 70 or below may not continue their studies in medicine.

3. *Clinical Studies (3 years).* Year Four—Emphasizes practical work in various clinical departments of the hospital along with clinical case studies, lectures, and seminars. Year Five—Studies in Pediatrics and Internal Medicine at various hospitals. Year Six—Studies in other hospital departments (Dermatology; Ear, Nose and Throat; Gynecology; Preventive Medicine; Neurology; Ophthamology; Psychiatry; Surgery; and Traumatology).
4. *Elective Studies.* One month of the sixth year is devoted to elective courses in para-clinical and clinical fields, determined by the student's area of specialization.
5. *Internship (1 year).* Rotation in an accredited hospital.

GRADUATE MEDICAL PROGRAMS. The Hebrew University of Jerusalem, Faculty of Medicine offers a Master of Science in Basic Medical Sciences, Microbiology, Neurobiology, Pharmaceutical Sciences, and Public Health. This degree is an academic rather than professional degree. Admission is based upon a Bachelor of Science, Bachelor of Medical Sciences or the equivalent. In general these two-year programs include 400-450 lecture hours, laboratories, seminars, and a final experimental project and/or thesis. Program structure and degree requirements vary slightly according to the program. Areas of specialization within the programs cited above are extensive.

NURSING

The Council of Higher Education and the PGC, along with the Ministry of Health, the Hadassah Medical Center and the medical schools, favor gradual "academization" of the nursing profession. The bachelor's degree in nursing is available at Ben-Gurion University of the Negev, The Hebrew University of Jerusalem, and Tel-Aviv University. These institutions offer two kinds of nursing degrees: a four-year Bachelor of Nursing (B.Nurs.) and a three- to five-year Bachelor of Nursing Sciences (B.Nurs.Sc.) for Registered Nurses.

The Bachelor of Nursing program is a four-year university program for students entering directly after secondary school or military service, not for individuals with other nursing qualifications. Applicants to this program must meet the general admission requirements of the university: the Israeli Matriculation Certificate *(Teudat Bagrut),* the Psychometric Entrance Examination, Israeli citizenship, English proficiency, Hebrew proficiency at level *Hé,* (level 4, lower advanced) and possibly additional examinations and/or a personal interview. An English proficiency examination must be passed by the end of the first year in order to continue. See Table 8.11 for a sample B.Nurs. program.

Graduates of nursing programs are required to pass the Ministry of Health Board Examination to receive a license to practice as a Registered Nurse.

The Bachelor of Nursing Sciences (B.Nurs.Sc.) program is the university program for applicants who are Registered Nurses (R.N.'s). The length of time required to complete

Table 8.11. Sample Curriculum for a Bachelor of Nursing Program, Faculty of Medicine, The Hebrew University of Jerusalem

Course	Type	Ann. Hrs.	Course	Type	Ann. Hrs.
Year 1			*Year 3*		
Anatomy	L	1⅓	Holidays in Jewish Subcultures	E	1
Biochemistry	L	3	Intro. to Research	L	⅔
Fndn. of Nursing A	LE	2⅔	Marriage Customs Among North Africans	E	1
Gen. Chem. (Level A)	LE	3⅓	Nurs. in Chronic Ill.—1	LE	17
Human Growth & Develop.	LE	3	Nurs. in Acutely Ill.—2	LE	8⅓
Inorganic Chem. Lab	Lab	1	Nutrition	L	⅔
Intro. to Nursing	L	1	Psychiatric Nursing	LE	1⅓
Intro. to Zoology	LLab	2⅔	Reprod. Health Nursing	LE	1⅓
Psychology	L	2	Statistics	L	1⅓
Sociology	L	2	Clin. Research Seminar	S	⅔
Year 2			*Year 4*		
Developmental Anatomy	LE	⅔	Clin. Nurs. Experience	–	–
Fndn. of Nursing B	LE	8	Community Health Nurs.	LE	4⅔
General Pathology	L	1	Comm. Mental Health Nurs.	LE	2⅔
Microbiology	L	1⅓	Environmental Health	LE	⅔
Nurs. Well Individuals & Family	–	7⅓	Health Econ.	LE	⅔
Pharmacology	L	2	Health Education	LE	1⅓
Physiology	L	5	Nursing Administration	LE	1⅓
			Nursing Seminar	L	1⅓
			Nursing Theory	LE	1⅔
			O.P.D.	E	2
			Specific Nursing	E	18

SOURCE: Transcript from School of Nursing, Faculty of Medicine, The Hebrew University of Jerusalem, 1978–82.

L = Lecture *(She'ur)*; LE = Lecture and Exercise *(She'ur vet targil)*; Lab = Laboratory *(Ma'abada)*; S = Seminar *(Seminar)*.

the program is three to five years, depending upon the student's ability to pass exemption examinations or to receive credit for prior field experience. The program is based upon the four-year B.Nurs. program described above, including identical admission requirements. In addition, applicants must present an R.N. certificate.

The Hebrew University of Jerusalem also offers two extension programs leading to the B.Nurs.Sc. degree. The admission requirements are the same as those for admission to the B.Nurs. program, mentioned above. Courses in Natural Sciences and Social Sciences are taken during the first two years in Jerusalem. The remainder of the program is completed at the extension campuses of the School of Nursing, Asaf Harofeh Hospital in Sarafand and the School of Nursing, Kaplan Hospital in Rehovot. These programs are called the "Asof Harofeh" extension and "Kaplan" extension, respectively.

The B.Nurs.Sc. program at Tel-Aviv University is a four-semester program open only to R.N.'s. There are 15-20 hours of lecture per week, plus seminars. Tel-Aviv University is awaiting approval from its University Senate to offer a three-year B.Nurs. program to applicants who are not R.N.'s. For more detailed information on nursing and licensure, see Chapter 5.

PHARMACY

Pharmacy is offered only by The Hebrew University of Jerusalem, School of Pharmacy, and is the one program that prepares licensed pharmacists. The School of Pharmacy, established in 1953, is responsible for the training of pharmacists for professional practice in the fields of community, hospital, clinical, institutional, and industrial pharmacy. Pharmacy is a four-year undergraduate program that includes a six-month period of practical training in an approved pharmacy. The program leads to a Bachelor of Pharmacy (B.Pharm.) degree as well as a license to practice.

The School of Pharmacy also awards master's and doctorate degrees in pharmacy with five optional areas of concentration: Clinical Pharmacy, Industrial Pharmacy, Medicinal Chemistry, Pharmacology, and Pharmacy. Neither of these degrees, however, leads to licensure.

The Bachelor of Pharmacy program includes basic studies in Anatomy, Botany, Chemistry, Mathematics, Physics, and Statistics; fundamental courses in Pharmacy and Advanced Pharmacy in the fields of liquids, semi-solids, solids and dispersion; advanced studies in Pharmaceutical Chemistry, Natural Products and Biochemistry; studies in Microbiology, Pharmacology, Physiology, and Processes of Illness. In the final year, courses are organized according to two trends: Community-Clinical Pharmacy and Research-Industrial Pharmacy.

Admission is selective with minimum requirements including the Israeli Matriculation Certificate *(Teudat Bagrut)*, the Psychometric Entrance Examination, additional entrance examinations as required, Hebrew proficiency level *Gimmel* (level 3, lower intermediate), and a high level of English proficiency.

SOCIAL WORK

The study of social work in Israel is treated as a regular academic program offering. The objective is to train professional social workers through a combination of theoretical instruction and practical field work in areas of social service. Social work is offered at Bar-Ilan University, Ben-Gurion University of the Negev (within the Faculty of Humanities and Social Sciences), The University of Haifa, The Hebrew University of Jerusalem, and Tel-Aviv University, and may be studied at both the undergraduate and graduate levels. Standard university admission requirements are applied.

The Council for Higher Education and the PGC report that there are contradictory forecasts concerning the supply and demand for social workers. For this reason, it was decided that the present status of social work is satisfactory and that the number of students and funds allocated to the schools of social work would be frozen at the present level.

The Bachelor of Social Work (B.S.W.) degree requires completion of a three-year undergraduate program. First year studies consist of basic courses in the social and behavioral sciences, research studies, and introductory courses in social welfare and social work. The second and third years are devoted to professional aspects of social work, including theoretical courses in social work methodology, research, courses dealing with social services (policy and administration), and field work training.

The Master of Social Work (M.S.W.) degree requires completion of a two-year fulltime graduate program including the summer in-between. At The Hebrew University of Jerusalem, three trends are available to M.S.W. students: the research trend emphasizing research projects in social work and social services with stress placed on professional intervention in social services; the management trend emphasizing social welfare and social services programs; and the supervision and guidance trend which prepares professionals in supervision, counseling, and staff development. The program consists of 24-26 annual hours. Degree requirements vary according to trend.

VETERINARY MEDICINE

The Doctor of Veterinary Medicine (D.V.M.) degree is awarded by The Hebrew University of Jerusalem, School of Veterinary Medicine, and has been available since 1985. The four-year program follows two years of fulltime study at an Israeli university in the field of Biology, Medicine, or Dental Medicine. The first two years of study in the D.V.M. program are conducted in the Faculty of Agriculture (Rehovot); the last two years are held at the Veterinary Institute at Rishon Leizion and in Rehovot. The program, which is designed to meet the needs of animal farms in Israel, examines both normal conditions and various diseases in animals (particularly farm animals) and comparative medicine for humans and animals.

Admission is selective and requires an 80 average in specific mathematics and science courses taken during two years of fulltime study in the Departments of Biology, Medicine, or Dental Medicine at an Israeli university; the Psychometric Entrance Examination, plus the possibility of other entrance examinations; and a high proficiency in English.

Institutional Profiles

Universities

BAR-ILAN UNIVERSITY, Academic Secretary, Ramat Gan, 52 100, Israel. Tel.: (03) 718274. U.S. Address: Office of Academic Affairs, Bar-Ilan University, 853 Seventh Ave., New York, NY 10019. Tel.: (212) 315-1990.

DESCRIPTION: Founded 1953; opened 1955. Considered Israel's only religious university, combining religious observance and customs with contemporary scholarship. Located on over 100 acres in Ramat Gan (Tel-Aviv suburb). Has 5 faculties, 3 schools, 32 departments, 15 research institutes and a One-Year Program plus other special programs for overseas students (see Chapter 6). Three branches—Ashkelon, Jordan Valley at Emek Hayarden Regional College (also called Alperin Regional College of the Jordan Valley), and Safed—offer "academic" programs. (See "Regional Colleges.") *Library:* Wurzweiler Library, 250,000 vols., 4,000 journals; deptl. libraries, 63,000. *Enrollment:* 9,970 (see Table 8.1).

CALENDAR: Two 15-wk. sems. (1 wk. after *Succoth* - Jan., Feb. - June), excluding 4-wk. exam period and 2-wk. mid-sem. break.

ACADEMIC STAFF: 500 FT/600 PT.

FACULTIES: FAC. OF HUMANITIES—Depts. (Arab. & Islamic Culture, Bibliogr. & Librshp., Classical Studies., Compar. Lit., Engl. Lang. & Linguis., Fr. Lit. & Culture, Gen. Philos., Jewish Philos., Musicol.). *School for Translators & Interpreters.* FAC. OF JUDAIC STUDIES—Depts. (Bible Studies, Gen. History, Hebrew & Semitic Langs., Hebrew Lit., Jew. History, Jew. Studies, Land of Israel Studies, *Talmud). Unit of Hebrew Composition & Ulpan. Institutes—* Assyriology, History of Jewish Bible Research, Judaism & Contemporary Thought, Lexicography, Post-*Talmudic* Research, Research of Religious Zionism, Research on Diaspora Jewry, Research of Oriental Jewry; Menachem Begin Institute for Research of Underground Movements, Finkler

Institute for Holocaust Research, Rivlin Institute for Research in the History of the Yishuv. YAAKOV HERZOG FAC. OF LAW. *Institute for Research in International and Comparative Law.* FAC. OF NATURAL SCIENCES AND MATHEMATICS—Depts. (Chem., Life Sci., Math & Computer Sci. including Stats., Physics). *Institute for Information Retrieval.* FAC. OF SOCIAL SCIENCES—Depts. (Criminol., Econ. including Bus. Admin. & Acct., Geog., Poli. Studies, Psych., Sociol. & Anthropol.). *Schools:* Social Work; Pinchas Churgin School of Education. *Institutes:* Local Government, Study of Ethnic & Religious Groups; Research Institute on the Economic Structure of Jewish Communities.

DEGREES AND DIPLOMAS: BACHELOR'S—*3 yrs.* - Arts (BA), Sci. (BSc).—*4 yrs.* - Law (LLB). MASTER'S—*2 yrs.* (max. 3 yrs. FT or 5 yrs. PT) - Arts (MA), Sci. (MSc). DOCTORATE—*2-3 yrs. FT or max. 6 yrs. total after MA/MSc* - PhD and title of "Doctor Philosophiae." DIPLOMAS—generally 2-yr. postbach.'s (see "Diplomas" below).

ADMISSION REQUIREMENTS: BACHELOR'S—Standard requirements (see text) + min. knowl. of *Talmud.* MASTER'S—Bach.'s from Bar-Ilan with min. ave. grade of 76%, "B" or Good, or equiv. degree and grade from another recognized institute. DOCTORATE—Master's from Bar-Ilan with min. ave. grade of 76% or Good; or, in Direct Doctoral Program, Bach.'s with min. *cum laude* honors.

GRADING AND TRANSCRIPTS: Written final exams held at end of each course during exam period at end of each yr. or semester. Third special exam session is usually first exam period in next year. Courses with grade of "D" or "F" after first exam are entitled to re-examination in second or third period. Students who twice fail course in their major or in courses leading to Teacher's Diploma are not entitled to re-examination unless they re-register and repeat the course.

Prior to 1967	Since 1968	Scholastic Index Leading to Honors
A = 90-100	A+ = 96-100	92% with Distinction . . . *Summa Cum Laude*
B = 80-89	A = 86-95	88% with Success Worthy of Honors . . . *Magna Cum Laude*
C = 70-79	B = 76-85	
D = 60-69	C = 66-75	84% with Success . . . *Cum Laude*
F = 0-59	D = 60-65	
	D* = 56-65	

*A lower passing mark is allowed for Basic Study and Elective courses.

Transcript has credit column which corresponds to sem. hrs. (1 sem. hr. = 1 (50 min.) lect., tutor., seminar session per wk. or 2-3 wkly. hrs. of lab for one 15-wk. sem. Since 1985, ann. courses studied for 1 sem. are identified by transcript cover letter listing course name and number, credit, and grade, and signed by Dean of Students.

CREDITS, PROGRAM STRUCTURE, AND DEGREE REQUIREMENTS: Requirements expressed in ann. hrs. (1 ann. hr. = 1 hr./wk. of lect., tutorial, or seminar for 1 academic yr. of 30 wks.). Depts. may determine if 1 ann. hr. of tutor. is recognized for ½ ann. hr. credit. Transcripts reflect credits on sem. basis. Univ. recommends 2 hrs. prep. for each wkly. lect. or tutor. hour.

BACHELOR'S—Students select a) dual major; b) single, i.e., expanded major; or c) 3 minor subjects. Options 2 and 3 avail. only in Senate-approved programs, subj. to early approval on indiv. basis (see Table 8.5). Except in Fac. of Nat. Sci., normal credit load represents 8-20 wkly. hrs. in major, 6 wkly. hrs. in minor, 4-6 wkly. hrs. in Judaism. All Facs. except Law require total 64 ann. hrs. (128 sem. credits) of which 2 yrs. and 50% of crswrk. are required in residence. Total ann. hrs. excludes 2 ann. hrs. in Phys. Educ., Hebrew (for non-Hebr. speakers) and Engl. (for non-Engl. speakers). Min. 25% of crswrk. required in Judaism (14-16 ann. hrs. in Bible Studies, Jew. Hist., Jew. Philos., Oral Law, *Talmud).* Submission of 2-3 seminar papers required. Some depts. require comprehen., bibliogr. or aptitude exams taken no later than 2 yrs. after completion of all crswrk.

MASTER'S—Students select Track A or Track B (see text). *Track A* (all depts.): Requires min. of 10 ann. hrs. of crswrk., research project, oral exam, and thesis based on research. In addition, all must complete 1-yr. Jew. Studies course or, if admitted from another univ., 3 courses in Jew. Studies, 1 each in *Talmud,* Bible Studies, Jew. Philos. *Track B* (some depts.): Requires min. of 25 ann. hrs. of crswrk. (6 may be undergrad.) from which student must submit at least 3 seminar papers; final deptl. exam; Jew. Studies reqmt. in Track A. No research project or thesis required.

DOCTORATE—Students conduct original, indep. research resulting in thesis and actively participate in crswrk. and seminars for min. of 3 yrs. or until studies are completed, whichever comes first. Candidates reviewed annually for approval to continue. Jew. Studies reqmt. determined by nature of crswrk. or degrees previously completed up to 4 courses. Foreign lang. reqmt. of at least 2 modern langs. determined by dept.

DIPLOMAS—*Library Science*: 2-yr. post-bach.'s program requires 26 total ann. hrs. of crswrk., knowl. of second foreign lang., practical training in library, participation in study tours. Second year students specialize in Public & School Libraries, Special & Univ. Libraries, or Bibliogr. Studies. One seminar paper required. Certified Librarian diploma awarded. —*Translation*: 2-yr. post-bach.'s program requires 32 total ann. hrs. of crswrk. + 1-3 courses in Jew. Studies. Languages of transla. are Arab., Engl., Fr., Hebrew. Certified Translator and Interpreter diploma awarded. —*Institute of Local Government*: Estd. 1968 with assistance of Israeli Ministry of Interior and Israel Union of Local Authorities. Programs include a) 2-yr. in-service training program for senior local govt. officials. Diploma awarded upon successful passing of exams; b) shorter seminars and training sessions for local govt. officials; c) research projects relative to problems of local govt. Students accepted by Dept. of Poli. Stud. are given credit for institute courses.

SPECIAL PROGRAM: INSTITUTE FOR ADVANCED TORAH STUDIES—Undergrad. degree program for "*yeshivah* high school" grads. incorporating intensive Judaic Studies with academic studies; *Yeshivah* for men, *Midrasha* for women. Both meet from 8 a.m.-1 p.m. (*Yeshivah,* 5 mornings wkly.; *Midrasha,* 3). Students are exempt from Judaism and Gen. Stud. reqmts. for graduation.

LINKAGES: Cooperative programs with City University of New York (Brooklyn College, Kingsborough Community College, Queens College) (U.S.), Concordia University (Canada), Rockland Community College, State University of New York (U.S.), Stern College (U.S.); Touro College (U.S.); University of Berne (Switzerland), University of Paris-Sorbonne (France), University of Pennsylvania (U.S.), Yeshiva University (U.S.).

BEN-GURION UNIVERSITY OF THE NEGEV, Academic Secretary, P.O. Box 653, Beer-Sheeva, 84 120. Tel.: (057) 664111 (new campus), (057) 661111 (Tuviyahu campus). U.S. Address: American Associates of the Ben-Gurion University of the Negev, 342 Madison Ave., Suite 1924, New York, NY 10173. Tel.: (212) 687-7721.

DESCRIPTION: Founded 1964 as the Institute for Higher Education. Accreditation granted in 1969 as the University of the Negev. Acquired present name in 1973. Major educational institution for the arid south region. One of 3 universities offering programs in engineering; one of 4 with programs in medicine. Functioned initially under academic tutelage of The Hebrew University of Jerusalem (for arts), of Technion-Israel Institute of Technology (for engineering), and Weizmann Institute of Science (for science). Programs structured through 4 faculties, 30 departments, 3 schools, 2 centers, and 3 units. Sde Boker campus opened 1976, 55 km. south of Beer-Sheva and houses Blaustein Institute for Desert Research, the Ben-Gurion Research Center, and the Environmental High School. Affiliated for "academic" supervision with 2 Regional Colleges (the Municipal College of Eilat and Sha'ar Hanegev R.C. (also known as P. Sapir R.C. of the Negev). Residential facilities provided. Three campuses—Tuviyahu (original), Beer-Sheva (new), Sde Boker. *Enrollment (1986-87):* 4,474 undergraduate (1,601 PT; 2,873 FT); 850 graduate (450 PT, 400 FT). Total of 5,024 includes 300 Arab. See Table 8.1. *Library:* The Aranne Library and Study Center—340,000 vols. and journals; 4,200 periodicals.

ACADEMIC CALENDAR: Two 13-wk. sems. (Oct. - Jan., Feb. - June). Previously trimester.

ACADEMIC STAFF (1986): 534.

FACULTIES, DEPARTMENTS, SCHOOLS, CENTERS: FAC. OF HUMANITIES AND SOCIAL SCIENCES—Depts. (Behav. Sci., Bible & Ancient Near East. Studies, Econ., Educ., Foreign Lang. & Lit., Geog., Hebrew Lang. & Lit., History, Philos., Soc. Work). *Centers*—Social Ecology, Studies in Sephardic Heritage. FAC. OF HEALTH SCIENCES—Depts. (Clin. Pharmacol., Epidemiology; Med. Admin. & Health Econ., Microbiol. & Immunol., Morphology, Primary Care, Physiol., Sociol. of Health, Virology). *Schools*—Allied Health Professions (Nursing, Phys. Therapy), Medicine. Fac. of Natural Sciences Depts. (Biol., Chem., Geol. & Mineralogy, Math & Computer Sci., Physics). *School*—Continuing Education (Unit for Adult Educ., Special Programs). FAC. OF TECHNOLOGICAL SCIENCES—Depts. (Chem. Engr., Electrical & Computer Engr., Industrial Engr. & Mgmt., Materials Engr., Mechanical Engr., Nuclear Engr. [Unit for Medical Engr.]).

DEGREES AND CERTIFICATES: BACHELOR'S—*3 yrs.* - Arts (BA), Sci. (BSc). —*4 yrs.* - Technological Sci. (BSc[TechSc]), Nursing (BNurs), Physiotherapy (BPT). MASTER'S—*1 yr.* - Mgmt. Sci. (MSM) (see Chapter 6, "Overseas Student Programs"). —*2 yrs.* - Arts (MA), Sci. (MSc). DOCTORATE—*4 yrs.* - Ph.D. —*6 yrs.* Medicine (MD). CERTIFICATES—*1 yr.* Postbach.'s Teacher's Certificate (secondary grades).

ADMISSION REQUIREMENTS: BACHELOR'S—Standard requirements (see text). MASTER'S—Bach.'s degree or equiv. with min. ave. grade of 75 (Natural Sci., Humanities and Soc. Sci.); min. ave. grade of 75 during last 2 yrs. (Tech. Sci.). DOCTORATE—Standard reqmts. (see text). TEACHER'S CERTIFICATE—Bach.'s degree or equiv.

GRADING AND TRANSCRIPTS: Courses offered on sem. basis with grades reported numerically on scale of 0-100. See Chapter 6, "Overseas Student Programs" for different grading scale.

Until 1972-73		From 1973-74	
91 - 100	= Excellent	95 - 100	= Excellent
81 - 90	= Very Good	85 - 94	= Very Good
71 - 80	= Good	75 - 84	= Good
61 - 70	= Fair	65 - 74	= Fair
51 - 60	= Pass	56 - 64	= Pass
0 - 50	= Failure	0 - 55	= Failure

CREDIT SYSTEM, PROGRAM STRUCTURE, AND DEGREE REQUIREMENTS: Weekly hrs. per sem. used instead of credits. Before mid-1970's, no hrs. reported.

Bachelor's—Options in 3-yr. BA/BSc program in Humanities and Soc. Sciences were single major, dual major, or major-minor. Total 120 hrs. required in all options. Single major reqmts. include 104 hrs. in deptl. studies, 16 hrs. in gen. studies. Dual major reqmt. includes 52 hrs. in each major dept., 16 hrs. in gen. studies. Major-minor reqmts. include 76 hrs. in major dept., 28 hrs. in minor dept., 16 hrs. in gen. studies. Gen. studies include 2 hrs. of Hebrew composition, 2 hrs. in first foreign lang. after exemption level, 12 hrs. selected from crswrk. designated as suitable for elective reqmts. Engr. program requires approx. 60 hrs. per yr., 240 total hrs. Courses designated by level according to year, i.e., 1st yr., 2nd yr., etc. Earlier transcripts provide no indication of wkly. hrs. or credits.

LINKAGES: *United States*—Boston University, California State University-Fresno, City University of New York, New Mexico State University, State University of New York-Stonybrook, Southern Illinois University-Carbondale, Texas Tech. University (International Center for Arid and Semi-Arid Land Studies), University of Arizona, University of California-Los Angeles, University of North Carolina-Chapel Hill (School of Public Health and Medical School), University of Maryland-College Park (Dept. of Meteorology), University of Utah. *Italy*—Universitá Degli Studi Di Udini. *Brazil*—Federal University of Alagoas Maceio, Federal University of Pernambuco-Recife, Universidade Federal Do Rios DeJaneiro. *Federal Republic of Ger-*

many—Technische Universität-Berlin, Technische Hochschule-Darmstadt, Universität Ulm, Universität Gesamthochschule-Wuppertal, Universität Heidelberg. *South Africa*—University of the Orange Free State. *Venezuela*—Universidad Central de Venezuela-Caracas, Universidad Nacional Experimental de los Llanos Centrales "Romulo Gallegos" San Juan de los Morros. *Mexico*—Universidad de Sonora-Hermosillo. *Puerto Rico*—University of Puerto Rico-Mayaguez. *Chile*—Pontificia Universidad Católica de Chile. *France*—Université de Paul Valery-Montpellier, University of Paris I, V. *Korea*—Kon-Kuk University-Seoul. *Canada*—Concordia University-Quebec, University of Alberta-Edmonton, University of Winnepeg.

EVERYMAN'S UNIVERSITY (ALSO KNOWN AS HA'UNIVERSITA HA'-PTUCHA, THE OPEN UNIVERSITY), 16 Klausner St., P.O. Box 39328, Ramat-Aviv, Tel-Aviv 61392. Tel.: (03) 422511. U.S. Address: American Friends of Everyman's University (Israel) Inc., 330 W. 58 St., Suite 6P, New York, NY 10019. Tel.: (212) 713-1515.

DESCRIPTION: Estd. 1974 by the Rothschild Foundation with approval of Israeli Government. First classes offered 1976. Only "distance" correspondence institution in Israel. Seeks to provide higher education at home to those unable to study in existing educational framework, to help elementary and junior high school teachers study towards "academic" degree, to provide second chance to those who discontinued their education, to raise population's general educational level. Recognized by the Council for Higher Education July 1980 and permitted to award B.A. degree. Some courses available (in Hebrew and/or English) to those living outside Israel. *Enrollment:* 13,595 PT (see Table 8.1).

CALENDAR: Two 18-wk. sems. (Sept. - Jan., Feb. - June), and summer.

ACADEMIC STAFF: Members of other Israeli institutions and other experts contribute to course development. Employs assts., editors, 350 PT tutors.

COURSES: Institution not organized by faculties. Instead courses are grouped by field and discipline and classified as either gen. adult educ. or "academic" educ. applicable to B.A. "ACADEMIC" COURSES—Behavioral Sci. (interdisciplinary instruction covering Israel and gen. society [Poli. Sci., Psych., Sociol.]), Econ. & Mgmt., Educ., Jew. Stud. (History, Lit., Philos.); Humanities (interdisciplinary instruction [Fine Arts, History, Lit.]); Math (Applied Math, Computer Sci., Pure Math, Stats.), Natural & Life Sci. (Biol., Chem., Geol., Nature & Life Sci., Physics). ADULT EDUCATION—Noncredit courses in areas of gen. interest, gen. knowl.; prep. courses for Matriculation Exam; vocational training.

DEGREE: Bachelor of Arts (B.A.), self-paced.

ADMISSION REQUIREMENT: None.

CREDIT SYSTEM, PROGRAM STRUCTURE AND DEGREE REQUIREMENTS: Study sys. for distance teaching is necessarily unique compared to normal Israeli program structure. Multimedia sys. approach is patterned after British Open University, modified for local needs. Central educational tool is printed text (texts for each course consist of approx. 700–900 fully illustrated pages). Courses are divided into study units (usually 12 per course). Each course text is divided into 12 wkly. units of 60–80 pages requiring an ave. of 12–17 hrs. of study for each wkly. unit. One course (expressed as 1 credit), therefore, represents 144-216 study hours. B.A. requires satisfactory completion of 18 courses or credits. In addition to textbook learning, program is enhanced and complemented by television and radio programming, study kits (science kits, maps, specimens, slides, audio cassettes, etc.), organized study tours, meetings at one of the study centers, group meeting with tutors, telephone conferences with tutors.

EXAMINATIONS AND GRADING: Each student is regularly evaluated and required to submit number of assignments which are graded and returned with tutors' comments. Multiple choice exams are computer-graded and evaluated. Each course requires final exam at Study Center under proctor supervision. Final grade reflects combination of performance on assignments and final exam. Grades reported numerically on scale of 0-100 with 60 passing.

TECHNION—ISRAEL INSTITUTE OF TECHNOLOGY, Academic Secretary, Technion City, Mount Carmel, Haifa 32000. Tel.: (04) 292111. U.S. Address: American Society for Technion—Israel Institute of Technology, 810 7th Ave., New York, NY 10019. Tel.: (212) 889-2050.

DESCRIPTION: Estd. 1912; opened 1924 as the Hebrew Technical College. Prestigious, most comprehensive technological institution. Since 1953, modern 300-acre campus of over 100 buildings overlooks Lower Galilee and Haifa Bay. Main (Technion City), Hadar HaCarmel and Bat Galim campuses. Programs primarily engineering, sciences, and technology with all 20 faculties and departments except Education offering degrees through the "Doctor." About one-third of all degree students study at the graduate level. Graduate School opened 1953; Faculty of Medicine 1971. Pre-academic program for Israelis and immigrants. No Regional College affiliation or formal overseas student program. Residential facilities available. *Library:* Elyachar Central Library, 260,000 vols.; 160,000 periodicals. *Enrollment:* 8,270 (see Table 8.1 and "Historical Development in Higher Education" earlier in this chapter).

CALENDAR: Two 15-wk. sems. (Oct. - Feb., Feb. - June). Summer session.

ACADEMIC STAFF: Profs. (159 FT), Assoc. Profs. (173 FT), Sr. Lect. (251 FT), Lect. (84 FT), Asst. (273 FT), Adjunct (96 PT).

FACULTIES (UNITS), AND DEPARTMENTS: Note: All faculties and departments have a unit in the same name as the faculty or department in addition to, in some cases, other units. FACULTIES OF AERONAUTICAL ENGR., AGRICULTURAL ENGR., ARCHITECTURE & TOWN PLANNING (Units - Landscape Arch., Urban & Regional Plan.), CHEM. ENGR., CHEM., CIVIL ENGR. (Units -

Bldg. Sci. & Construction Mgmt., Environ. Engr., Geodetic Engr., Hydraulic Engr., Mineral Engr., Municipal Engr., Soil & Highway Engr., Soil Sci. Structures, Traffic & Transport. Engr.), ELECTRICAL ENGR., INDUSTRIAL & MGMT. ENGR. (Units - Econ., Industrial Engr., Industrial Relations & Manpower Admin., Mgmt. & Behavioral Sci., Operations Research, Stats.), MATH, MECH. ENGR., MEDICINE (Pharm., Unit - Med. Sci.), PHYSICS. *Departments*—Appl. Math, Biol., Biomed. Engr., Comput. Sci., Educ. in Technol. & Sci., Food Technol. & Biotech., Materials Engr., Nuclear Engr. *Center for Pre-Academic Studies.* Twenty-four research centers and institutes.

DEGREES AND CERTIFICATES: BACHELOR'S—*3 years* - Arts (BA) (in Appl. Math, Biol., Chem., Comput. Sci., Math, Physics). —*4 years* - Science (BSc) (in Appl. Math, Biol., Chem., Comput. Sci., Landscape Architecture, Math, Physics, Engr. [all branches], Educ. in Technol. & Sci.). —*5 years* - Arch. & Town Planning (BArch). MASTER'S—*11 months FT or 2-4 years PT* -Science (MSc) (all Faculties and Departments). DOCTOR—*2 years FT or 3-6 years PT* Science (DSc), Science in Technology (DSc[Tech]). —*7 years* - Medicine (MD). CERTIFICATE—1 year postbach.'s Teacher's Certificate.

ADMISSION REQUIREMENTS: BACHELOR'S—Standard requirements (see text) plus math qualifying exam and, in some depts., other exams; competitive. MASTER'S—Technion 4-yr. BSc or equivalent; min. grade ave. of 71%-75% in final undergrad. yr. considered adequate but will consider other years. Applicant with 3-yr. BA or BSc is required to complete as a qualifying student 1 yr. of study and exams in prerequisite crswrk. equivalent to min. 1 yr. undergrad. study at Technion 4th yr. BSc level. To be accepted as regular MSc student, applicant must pass exams at level required of Technion BSc students. DOCTOR—Technion MSc or equivalent; adequate level of achievement (i.e., grade of "Good" or B or better in crswrk., thesis, final exam).

GRADING AND TRANSCRIPTS:

Prior to 1972-73			Beginning 1972-73		
A+	(91 - 100)	= Excellent	A+	(95 - 100)	= Excellent
A	(81 - 90)	= Very Good	A	(85 - 94)	= Very Good
B	(71 - 80)	= Good	B	(75 - 84)	= Good
C	(61 - 70)	= Sufficient	C	(65 - 74)	= Sufficient
D	(51 - 60)	= Barely Sufficient	D	(55 - 64)	= Barely Sufficient
F	(0 - 50)	= Failure	F	(0 - 54)	= Failure

Transcripts available in English listing each semester's courses, credits, numeric grades, and sem. grade average. Total credits required for particular degree listed. Min. pass subj. grade is 55; min. cumulative G.P.A. required for good standing is 65.

PROGRAM STRUCTURE, DEGREE REQUIREMENTS, AND CREDITS: BACHELOR'S—Sem. credit system with sem. courses, exams, and reporting. BA requires 120-123 credits, specified on transcript; BSc requires 160-165 credits, specified on transcript. Regardless of specialization, first 2 yrs. are similar and common for all students. First yr. emphasizes fundamental sci.; 2nd yr., basic engr. subj; 3rd and 4th yrs., specialization in particular program. Gen. crswrk. in Fine Arts, History, Judaism, Lit., Poli. Sci., Soc. Sci. required. MASTER'S—3 programs offered are a) study, research, thesis, final exam; b) study, comprehensive engr. project, thesis, final exam; c) in some depts., more extensive studies, final paper, final exam. Gen. program structure encompasses 36-44 credits distributed as follows— research thesis (20 credits) or engr. project thesis (20) *or* 12-credit final paper *and* balance in crswrk. Research may be theoretical or experimental, basic or applied. DOCTOR—Lect. attendance, seminar participation, independent reading, lang. reqmt. (demonstrated proficiency in Hebrew and Engl. and German or Fr. or Russian), candidacy exam (all or in part oral, as determined by Doctor Committee; may be failed once), original research and thesis.

LINKAGES: Brandeis University (U.S.), Churchill College (Cambridge, U.K.), Eidgenössische Technische Hochschule Zürich (Switzerland), Tuoro College (New York; joint MD program), University of Karlsruhe (FRG), University of Pennsylvania (U.S.).

TEL-AVIV UNIVERSITY, Academic Secretary, Ramat-Aviv, Tel-Aviv 69978. Tel.: (03) 420111. U.S. Address: Office of Academic Affairs, American Friends of Tel-Aviv University, 360 Lexington Ave., New York, NY 10017. Tel.: (212) 687-5651.

DESCRIPTION: Founded 1953 as municipal institution; estd. 1956 as university. Largest university enrollment, claiming to offer broadest scope of academic programs in Israel. Located in greater Tel-Aviv metropolitan area on 170 acres in the more rural suburb of Ramat-Aviv. Provides academic affiliation to Menashe Regional College. Has Overseas Student Program (see Chapter 6). Residential facilities available. *Library:* Sourasky Central Library (600,000 vols.); deptl. libraries (587,000 vols.). *Enrollment:* 19,600 FT, 8,600 PT nondegree.

CALENDAR: November - February, March - June.

ACADEMIC STAFF: Prof. (209 FT), Assoc. Prof. (344 FT), Sr. Lect. (443 FT), Lect. (338 FT).

FACULTIES, SCHOOLS, DEPARTMENTS, INSTITUTES, CENTERS, AND UNITS: FAC. OF ENGINEERING—Depts. (Electronic Communica., Control & Computer Sys.; Electronic Devices, Materials & Electromagnetic Radiation; Fluid Mech. & Heat Transfer; Industrial Engr. & Manufac. Technol., Interdisciplinary Stud., including Biomed. Engr.; Solid Mech., Materials & Structures). *Kranzberg Institute of Electronic Devices Research. Center*—Gordon Center for Energy Studies, Pletman Research Center for Systems Engineering. FAC. OF EXACT SCIENCES—*School of Chemistry* including Depts. (Chem. Physics & Theoretical Chem., Pure & Applied Electrochem., Phys. Chem., Organic Chem.). *School of Mathematical Sciences* comprising Depts. (Computer Sci., Pure & Applied Math, Stats.). *School of Physics and Astronomy* comprising Depts. (Astronomy & Astrophysics, Higher Energy Physics, Nuclear Physics, Pure & Applied Condensed Matter Physics). Department of Geophysics & Planetary Sciences. FAC. OF HUMANITIES—Depts. (Archaeology & Ancient Eastern Cultures, Arabic, Bible, Classics, Engl. & American Lit., Fr. Lang.

& Lit., Gen. History, Geog., Hebrew Lang., Hebrew Lit., Jew. History, Jew. Philos., Linguis., Middle East. & African History, Philos., Poetics & Compara. Lit., Psych., Semitic Linguis., *Talmud. Schools*—Education, History, Jewish Studies, Language & Literature. *Centers*—Dayan Center for Middle Eastern & African Studies, Russian & E. European Research Center, Center for Technological Education. *Units*—Auxiliary Studies (Foreign Languages), Pre-Law Studies. *Institutes*—for History & Philosophy of Science & Ideas, of Archaeology, of German History. Diaspora Research Institute, Katz Institute for Literary Research, Porter Institute for Poetics & Semiotics, Weizman Zionist Research Institute. FAC. OF LAW—Institutes (Continuing Legal Stud., Criminol. & Penal Law, Legislative Research). FAC. OF LIFE SCIENCES—Depts. (Biochem., Botany, Microbiol., Zool.). *Center*—of Biotechnology; Canadian Center for Ecological Zoology. *Institute*—for Cancer Research, for Cereal Crops Improvement, for Nature Conservation Research. FAC. OF MANAGEMENT (RECANATI GRADUATE SCHOOL OF BUSINESS ADMINISTRATION)—Accountancy, Bus. Admin., Mgmt. Sci. *Israel Institute of Business Research. Erhard Center for Higher Studies & Research in Insurance.* SACKLER FAC. OF MEDICINE—19 Clinical Divisions, 10 Basic & Pre-Clinical Science Divisions. *Schools*—Communication Disorders (Speech & Hearing), Continuing Medical Education, Dental Medicine, Nursing, Physical Therapy, Psychotherapy. *Division of Veterinary Medicine. Institutes*—Biological Research, Environmental Health, Human Reproduction & Fetal Development, Medical Research, Occupational Health, Physiological Hygiene; Eye Institute. FAC. OF SOCIAL SCIENCES—Depts. (Econ., Labor Stud., Poli. Sci., Sociol. & Anthropol.). *School of Social Work. Institutes*—for Economic Research, for Research of Developing Countries, for Social Research, of Labor & Social Sciences. *Centers*—for Development, for Urban & Regional Studies. *Graduate Program*—Public Policy. FAC. OF VISUAL AND PERFORMING ARTS—Depts. (Film & Television, History of Art, Musicol., Theatre Arts). *Samuel Rubin Academy of Music (*Lab for Electronic Music, Research Center for Movement Notation).

DEGREES AND DIPLOMAS: BACHELOR'S—*Fac. of Humanities* - 3 yrs. Arts (BA) in Arabic Lang. & Lit., Archaeology & Ancient Eastern Cultures, Bible, Classics (Archaeology, Classical Cultures, Greek, Latin), Engl., Fr. Lang. & Lit., Gen. Stud., Geog., Hebrew Lang., Hebrew Lit., History (Gen.), History of Eretz-Israel, History of Jew. People, History of Middle East, Jew. History, Jew. Philos., Linguis. (Applied, Theoretical, Semitic), Oral Law, Philos., Poetics & Compara. Lit., Psych., *Talmud. Fac. of Soc. Sci.* - 3 yrs. Arts (BA) in Econ., Poli. Sci., Sociol. & Anthropology. 3-4 yrs. in Soc. Work (BSW). *Fac. of Management* - BA in Accounting with Econ., Math, or Statistics. - 4 yrs. (BA) in Acct. towards CPA, in Mgmt. & Economics. *Fac. of Exact Sci.*- 3 yrs. Sci. (BSc). *Fac. of Life Sci.*- Sci. (BSc). *Fac. of Visual & Perform. Arts* –3 yrs. Fine Arts (BFA) in Film & Television, History of Art, Theatre Arts. - 3 yrs. Music (BMus). *Fac. of Law* -3 ½ yrs. FT or 4 ½ yrs. PT Law (LLB) after 1-yr. pre-law. *Fac. of Engr.* - 2 yrs. plus 6 sems. including summers (for *Handassaim*) in Electrical Engr. & Electronics. 4 yrs. (BSc) in Electrical Engr.

& Electronics, Industrial Engr., Mech. Engr. *Fac. of Med.* - 3 yrs. Occupa. Therapy (BOT). - 3-5 yrs. Nurs. Sci. (BNursSc). - 4 yrs. Physiotherapy (BPT). MASTER'S—2 yrs. in Arts, Bus. Admin. (MBA), Educ. Sci., Engr., Exact Sci., Fine Arts (MFA), Law (LLM), Life Sci., Mgmt. Sci. (Information Systems, Opera. Research, Organiza. Behavior), Med. Sci. (MSc), Occupa. Health (MOccH), Soc. Sci. (MA). DOCTOR—6 yrs. in Medicine (MD), Dental Medicine (DMD). DOCTORATE—2 yrs. all disciplines (PhD), Law (DrJur). DIPLOMAS AND CERTIFICATES—Noncredit, undergrad. & postbach., with variable length. See Diplomas and Certificates below.

ADMISSION REQUIREMENTS: BACHELOR'S—Standard reqmts. (see text); U.S. and Canadian applicants with Hebrew proficiency must have "B" ave. and score of 1200 on U.S. Scholastic Aptitude Test (SAT), excluding Engr. and Medicine; Israelis educated in U.S. or Canada must have "B" ave. and U.S. SAT score of 1100 or 600 in Math with less than 1100, excluding Engr. and Medicine. Also required are fac. and deptl. exams or specific reqmts. on *Bagrut, mechina,* or preparatory program results. Engr. has 2-yr., 6-sem. program for *Handassaim* (see below). MASTER'S—Standard reqmts. (see text); fac. and deptl. reqmts. may be specific and above standard reqmts. DOCTORATE—Master's degree with cumulative grade ave. of "B" and thesis grade of at least 80.

CREDIT SYSTEM AND PROGRAM STRUCTURE: Credits reported as sem. credits or wkly. hrs. per sem., usually year-by-year. Reporting varies considerably. One credit normally represents 1 hr./wk. of lect., exercise, etc. Credit in Graduate School of Bus. Admin. represents 75 min. of lecture.

Program structure varies from dept. to dept. where 1 or more than 1 option may be available. Terminology of programs includes single major/SM; two double major/DM (subjs. in 1 fac.) or two double major/DM (subjs. in 2 facs.). Bus. Admin. has double major only; Engr., Law, Life. Sci. (Biol.), and Social Work have single major only. All master's programs are designated single major only.

Special Degree and Diploma/Certificate Program Characteristics:

Business Administration. Mgmt./Econ. Option is 8-sem. double major through Fac. of Soc. Sci. and Fac. of Management. Accounting Dept. offers 5 programs—Acct. & Econ., Acct. & Stats., Acct. & Math (all 3-yr. programs including crswrk. in Acct., Auditing, Mgmt. Sci., Law, Taxation); 4-yr. program which is the 3-yr. program plus 1-yr. for those intending to become a CPA (allows exemption from part of CPA exams); a "Post-Degree Certificate" program for BA holders with min. grade ave. of "Good" that requires 2 yrs. to reach level of 3-yr. program, 1 add'l. yr. to reach level of 4-yr. program. Post-MBA Certificate program requiring MBA with min. ave. of 75. Certificate received upon completion of 8 sem. hrs. (lects. and seminars) attesting to participation and achievement and noting specialization (Banking, Information Systems, Finance & Acct., Internat'l. Mgmt., Marketing, Mgmt. & Organiza. Behavior).

Dental Medicine. Diploma program entrance reqmts. include 18 yrs. of age, 12 yrs. of educ., Psychometric Entrance Exam, personal interview. Dental Assistant Diploma (1 yr.); Dental Hygienist Diploma (2 yrs.) awarded.

Engineering. BSc in Engr. (4 yrs.) includes first 2 yrs. in math, exact sci., basic stud. in engr. Third yr. concentrates on basic engr. relevant to specific engr. field. Fourth yr. expands profes. knowl. including project planning in field of specialization. Special BSc in Electrical Engr. & Electronics for Electronics Technologists (*Handassaim*) requires 2 yrs., 6-sem. intensive program including summer studies for Electronics *Handassaim* with ave. grade of 8 on government exams, *Bagrut,* and Psychometric Exam.

Education. Certification programs for teachers at secondary level in various subjs. in Humanities, History & Soc. Sci., Exact Sci., Langs., Arts. (2 yrs. postbach.'s except for Tel-Aviv grads. in Educ. Sci. who would take 1 yr. program). Teacher certification program for intermediate/junior high school.

Journalism. Diploma program intended for BA holders or for those with practical journalism experience who hold the *Bagrut.* Theoretical and practical components. Afternoon classes, 22 hrs./wk. for 2 sems. including practical field work in second sem.

Real Estate Appraisal. Min. 2 yr., 55 credit afternoon/evening diploma program designed in cooperation with the Israel Real Estate Appraisal Council. Diploma exempts person from all exams but final exam for certification by the Council.

Social Work. Besides standard 3-yr. BSW program, 2-yr. BSW program available for grads. with majors in Criminol., Econ., Educ., Law, Poli. Sci., Psych., and Sociol., other related subjs.

Unit of External Studies. Comparable to U.S. continuing educ. depts. intended to extend services to community, including gen. interest courses and courses requested or prescribed by companies and various institutions. Not intended for acquiring "academic" credits. Certificates of participation issued. Three semesters (Oct. - Jan., Feb. - June, July - Sept.).

GRADING: The Overseas Student Program uses a different scale. See Chapter 6 profiles.

95 - 100 = Excellent	65 - 74 = Fairly Good
85 - 94 = Very Good	60 - 64 = Fair, Passing
75 - 84 = Good	0 - 59 = Failure

LINKAGES: United States—Beloit College, Boston University, City University of New York (Brooklyn College, City College, Queens College), Cornell University, Drake University, Georgetown University, Mills College, New Jersey State Colleges, Northeastern University, Northern Illinois University, Pennsylvania State University, Pomona State College, State University of New York, Syracuse University, University of Maryland, University of Miami, University of Pennsylvania, University of Pittsburgh, Vanderbilt University. Mexico—National Autonomous University of Mexico. France—University of Paris V, University of Strasbourg. FRG—University of Hamburg. Italy—University of Torino.

THE HEBREW UNIVERSITY OF JERUSALEM, Mount Scopus, Jerusalem 91905. Tel.: (02) 882111. U.S. Address: American Friends of The Hebrew University, 1140 Ave. of the Americas, New York, NY 10036. Tel.: (212) 840-5820.

DESCRIPTION: Founded 1918; opened 1925 on Mount Scopus. Other campuses: Givat Ram, Jerusalem; Rehovat; Ein Kerem, Jerusalem. Prestigious, second largest university in Israel. Campus closed 1947-67; however, teaching and research continued at sites in West Jerusalem. Givat Ram campus estd. 1955, opened 1958; Ein Kerem campus opened in 1963. Mount Scopus campus reopened June 1967 after the 1967 war. For details see "Historical Development of Higher Education" in this chapter. Overseas student programs since 1955; Rothberg School of Overseas Students opened 1971. Has 7 faculties, 13 schools, 2 institutes, 3 centers. No regional college affiliation. Residential facilities available. *Libraries:* Bloomfield Library, 400,000 vols.; other special libraries. Jewish National and University Library, Givat Ram campus (over 2,500,000 vols., including deptl. libraries), open to all Hebrew University students. *Enrollment (1983-84):* 16,050 (see Table 8.1).

CALENDAR: Effective Fall 1985 (sem. sys., two 14-wk sems., late Oct. - Jan., Jan. - June). Prior to Fall 1985 (trimester sys., late Oct. to mid-June).

FACULTIES, SCHOOLS, INSTITUTES, DEPARTMENTS, CENTERS, PROGRAMS: FAC. OF HUMANITIES (Mt. Scopus)—*Institute of Archaeology* (Dept. of Archaeol.). *Institute of Asian & African Studies* (Depts. of Arabic Lang. & Lit.; East Asian Studies; Indian, Iranian & Armenian Studies; Islamic & Mid. East. Studies; Hist. of Africa/African Studies). *Institute of Jewish Studies* (Depts. of Bible, Hebr. Lang., Hebr. Lit., Hist. of the Jew. People, Jew. Thought, Yiddish). *Institute of Languages, Literature and Art* (Depts. of Ancient Semitic Lang., Art Hist., Assyriology, Classical Stud., Egyptology, Engl., Gen. & Compara. Lit., German Lang. & Lit., Italian, Fr. Lang. & Lit., Linguis., Musicol., Romance Stud., Theatre Stud.). *Institute of Philosophy and History* (Depts. of American Stud.; Compara. Relig.; Geog.; Hist.; Hist., Philos. & Sociol. of Sci.; Philos.; Russian & Slavic Stud.; Sp. & Latin American Stud.). FAC. OF SOCIAL SCIENCES (Mt. Scopus)—Depts. (Communica., Demogr., Econ., Geog., Internatl. Relations, Poli. Sci., Psych., Public Admin., Sociol. & Soc. Anthro., Stats.). *School of Business Administration* (Bus. Admin., Acct. progs.). *Graduate Interdepartmental Programs. Area Studies (Grad.)*—West Europ. Stud., Urban & Regional Stud. *School of Social Work* (Mt. Scopus). FAC. OF LAW (Mt. Scopus)—Law, Criminol. (Grad.). GRAD. SCHOOL OF LIBRARY AND ARCHIVE STUDIES (Mt. Scopus). FAC. OF MATH AND NATURAL SCIENCES (Givat Ram)—Depts. (Atmospheric & Environ. Sci., Biol., Chem., Computer Sci., Earth Sci., Math, Physics, Sci. Instruct. [Grad.], Stats.). *School of Applied Sciences* (Givat Ram)(Grad. Programs Only)—Appl. Chem., Appl. Microbiol., Appl. Physics, Chem. Tech. Mgmt., Human Environ. Sci., Materials Sci., Polymers & Textile Chem. FAC. OF MEDICINE (Hadassah Medical School, Hadassah Hospital, Ein Kerem)—*Schools* (Med., Nurs., Occupa. Therapy, Pharm., Soc. Med. & Public Health [with Dept. of Family Med.]). FAC. OF

DENTAL MEDICINE (Ein Kerem). FAC. OF AGRICULTURE (Rehovot)—*Schools* (Nutrition. & Domes. Sci., Vet. Med.). Depts. (Agri. Econ. & Mgmt., Animal Sci., Field & Veg. Crops, Horticul., Physiol. & Biochem. [Food Sci. Trend], Plant Protect., Soil & Water Sci.). JOINT PROGRAMS WITH RUBIN ACADEMY OF MUSIC AND DANCE AND FACS. OF HUMANITIES, MATH/NATURAL SCI., SOC. SCI. ROTHBERG SCHOOL FOR OVERSEAS STUDENTS (see Chapter 6).

DEGREES, DIPLOMAS AND CERTIFICATES: BACHELOR'S—*3 yrs.* Arts (BA) (awarded by Facs. of Humanities and Soc. Sci., incl. School of Bus. Admin.), Arts in Music (BAMus, joint program with Rubin Academy), Med. Sci. (BMedSc), Occupa. Therapy (BOT), Soc. Work (BSW), Sci. (BSc), Sci. in Agriculture (BScAgr), Sci. in Nutrition. & Domes. Sci. (BScNDS). —*3½ yrs.* - Pharm. (BPharm). —*4 yrs.* - Bus. Admin. (certain progs.) (BA), Law (LLB), Nurs. (BNurs). MASTER'S—*1½-2 yrs.* - Sci. (MSc). —*2 yrs.* - Arts (MA) (awarded by Fac. of Humanities, Fac. of Soc. Sci.), Bus. Admin. (MBA), Criminol. (MCrim), Law (LLM), Library Sci. (MLS), Med. Sci. (MMedSc), Public Health (MPH), Soc. Sci. (MSocSc), Soc. Work (MSW), Sci. in Agriculture (MScAgr), Sci. in Pharm. (MScPharm). DOCTORATE—*6 yrs. + 1 yr. internship* - Dental Med. (DMD), Med. (MD). —*4 yrs. after 2 yrs. of univ. study* - Vet. Med. (DVM). —*2 yrs. after LLM* - Law (DrJur). POSTBACCALAUREATE DIPLOMA PROGRAMS—*1-2 yrs.* - Archive Stud., Family Med., Lib. Sci., Polymers & Textile Chem., Dietician. *1-2 yrs.* - Teaching (Agri., sec. school).

ADMISSION REQUIREMENTS: BACHELOR'S— Standard reqmts. (see text). Selectivity and add'l. reqmts. vary by Fac. or dept. Students in joint program with Rubin Academy must meet reqmts. of both Univ. and Academy. MASTER'S—Standard reqmts. (see text). MLS requires bach. with 80 ave. DIPLOMAS AND CERTIFICATES—Bachelor's degree.

EXAMINATIONS, GRADING AND TRANSCRIPTS: Two exam sessions, usually yearly. First exam session at end of academic yr. through Aug.; second exam session at end of Aug. through Oct. Students who fail first session may retake exam in second session. The notation "Fail" appears for grades below 50; in Fac. of Nat. Sci. for grades below 38. A final grade of 60 entitles a student to a bach.'s degree in most faculties. Phrases corresp. to final grade ave. are as follows: "Completed Academic Requirements" (74 & below); "Completed Academic Requirements . . ." with success (75-84); . . . *cum laude* (85-94); . . . *summa cum laude* (95-100).

Grading scale is as follows:

Prior to May 1972	From June 1972	From Oct. 1974
A+ = 10 (Excellent)	A+ = 95-100 (Excellent)	A+ = 95-100 (Excellent)
A = 9 (Very Good)	A = 85- 94 (Very Good)	A = 85- 94 (Very Good)
B = 8 (Good)	B = 75- 84 (Good)	B = 75- 84 (Good)
C = 7 (Fair)	C = 65- 74 (Fair)	C = 65- 74 (Fair)
D = 6 (Pass)	C− = 57- 64 (Pass/Satisfactory)	D = 50- 64 (Pass)
F = 0-5 (Fail)	D = 50- 56 (Pass/Unsatisfactory)	F = 0- 49 (Fail); 0- 37 (Fail) in Fac. of Nat. Sci.
	F = 0- 49 (Fail)	S.C. = (Satisfactory Completion) — *Ulpan* only

Transcript symbols—After course title, (A) = autumn course; (S) = spring course; (S) after Fall 1985 = summer course and (B) = spring course; (Y) = year course; (H) = taught in Hebrew (Overseas Program Transcripts only). Exempt grade given when student is exempt from course on basis of exam or previous study at another institution.

CREDIT SYSTEM, PROGRAM STRUCTURE, DEGREE REQUIREMENTS:

BACHELOR'S—Courses and reqmts. stated in assigned yearly or annual hours. Degree reqmts. consist of required and elective courses, Hebrew and Engl. lang. proficiency, prescribed number of total annual hrs. Prior to Fall 1985, annual hrs. expressed as wkly. hours, defined as the number of hrs. a course meets each wk. for 1 academic yr. For example, Course A is reported as 1 wkly. hr. (i.e., 1 hr./wk. for 3 trimesters or 1 academic yr.). One hr./wk. multiplied by three 9-10-wk. trimesters = 27-30 yearly hrs. One hr./wk. multiplied by a U.S. 15-wk. sem. for 1 academic yr. = 30 hrs. but is equiv. to 2 U.S. sem. credits. Therefore, credit equivalency is calculated by multiplying Israeli wkly. hrs. by 2. Whether course is taken for 1, 2 or 3 trimesters, the number of wkly hrs. is defined in terms of an academic yr. or 3 trimesters. Thus, a 3 hr./wk. course meeting for 1 trimester is noted on transcript as 1 wkly. hr. A 3-yr. bach.'s degree program gen. represents 56-60 yearly hrs. taken over 3 yrs., or approximately 112-120 U.S. sem. credit hrs. Effective Fall 1985, a credit point and sem. hr. system was introduced. Credit points are determined on basis of a weighting factor which corresp. to number of wkly. class hrs./sem. Normally, 1 credit point = 1 sem. hr. However, preparatory courses, workshops, tutorials = 1/2 credit point for each sem. hr. of class. Remedial courses are non-credit bearing. Some types of courses merit more credit points than wkly. hr. normally yields; e.g., a seminar paper may be 4 credit points, a proseminar paper 2 credit points. Since 1985, hrs. represent the number of hrs./14-wk. sem. rather than annual hrs. as before.

JOINT PROGRAM WITH RUBIN ACADEMY OF MUSIC AND DANCE—Simultaneous 3-yr. program at The Hebrew Univ./4-yr. program at Academy. Leads to BAMus from The Hebrew Univ. and a BMus from the Academy. Qualifies holder for admission to grad. studies.

FOUR-YEAR BACHELOR'S PROGRAMS—See Chapter 6 and discussion earlier in this chapter.

MASTER'S—Generally completed after 2 yrs. of study beyond bach.'s. MLS requires 26 yearly hrs. over 2 yrs., 2 seminar papers, thesis, and 2-month supervised internship.

DOCTORATE—Standard reqmts. (see text). Min. of 2 yrs. beyond master's.

DIPLOMAS AND CERTIFICATES—Qualified Archivist and Qualified Librarian Certificates (also referred to as Postgrad. Diploma Studies) require 23 yearly hrs. over 2 yrs., 1 seminar paper and (for Librarian only) 1-month supervised internship. Dietician's Diploma requires 3 sems. + 6-month internship. FAC. OF AGRICULTURE, SCHOOL OF NUTRITION. & DOMESTIC SCIENCES. *Agricultural Teaching Certificate (Diploma)*—Entrance reqmts. are as follows: Those who have completed or are completing 3 yrs. (6 sems.) undergrad. study or those who need complete only 3 or fewer courses and have min. ave. of 70 are eligible. Leads to a cert. (dip.) enabling students to qualify for MOEC teaching license to teach Agri. & Biol., Domestic Sci., or Nutri. & Biol. in secondary schools (grades 7-12). (Length of programs not available.) *Dietician*—Postbach. program leading to institutional dip. and profes. certification by Ministry of Health. Three sems. of theoretical studies + 6-mo. internship. FAC. OF MATH/NATURAL SCIENCE, SCHOOL OF APPLIED SCIENCE & TECHNOLOGY. *Polymers & Textile Chem.*—No description available. Bachelor's reqd. to enter. FAC. OF MEDICINE, SCHOOL OF SOC. MED. & PUBLIC HEALTH. *Family Med.*—For doctors (M.D.'s) specializing in Family Med. Entrance reqmt. is M.D. qualification specializing in Family Med. Two-yr. program of courses and workshops. Papers and exams reqd. GRADUATE SCHOOL OF LIBRARY & ARCHIVE STUDIES. *Archive Studies*—Postbach. dip. program leading to certification as Qualified Archivist. Two-yr. program req. 23 total annual hrs. and 1 seminar paper. *Library Science*—Postbach. dip. program leading to certification as a Qualified Librarian. Two-yr. program req. 23 total annual hrs., 1 seminar paper, and 1-month supervised internship.

LINKAGES: Canada—McGill University. FRG—Universities of Berlin, Bonn, Gottingen, Heidelberg, Tubingen, and others, Faculties of Theology. Italy—The Pontifical Biblical Institute, Rome. U.S.—American University; Barnard College, Columbia University; Hebrew Union College; Boston University; Brooklyn College, City University of New York; California State University System; Case Western Reserve; City College, City University of New York; Columbia University; Cornell University; Douglas College; George Washington University; Harvard University; Hunter College, City University of New York; Indiana University; Jewish Theological Seminary; New York University; Queens College, City University of New York; Rutgers University; Seton Hall University (College of Education); State University of New York System; Temple University; The University of Illinois; University of California System; University of Chicago; University of Colorado; University of Maryland; University of Massachusetts; University of Michigan; University of Pennsylvania; University of Rochester; University of Wisconsin; Yale University; Yeshiva University. Many cooperative programs with universities in France, Switzerland, and Turkey.

THE UNIVERSITY OF HAIFA, Mount Carmel, Haifa 31999, Israel. Tel.: (04) 240111. U.S. Address: American Friends of Haifa University, 41 E. 42nd St., New York, NY 10017. Tel.: (212) 818-9050.

DESCRIPTION: Founded 1963 as a university institute under academic tutelage of The Hebrew University of Jerusalem. Became autonomous and accredited 1972. Youngest of Israeli universities. School of Graduate Studies estd. 1979. Principal educational center in the North on 200 acre campus overlooking Haifa from Mt. Carmel. Serves diverse student population, including development town residents, *kibbutz* members, Arabs, and Druze. Has 2 faculties, 27 departments, 5 schools, 6 centers and 2 institutes in addition to "academic" extension divisions at Regional Colleges (Tel Hai Rodman R.C. and Emek Yisrael R.C. (also known as "Ohel Sarah" and Jezreel Valley College). Department of External Studies is "nonacademic" unit comparable to continuing education programs in United States. Has overseas student programs (see Chapter 6). On and off campus dormitories. *Library:* 700,000 vols.; 900 periodicals. *Enrollment:* 6,465 (see Table 8.1).

CALENDAR: Two 15-wk. sems. (Nov. - Jan., Feb. - June).

FACULTIES, SCHOOLS, INSTITUTES, CENTERS: FAC. OF HUMANITIES — Depts. (Arab. Lang. & Lit., Archeol., Art, Biblical Studies, Engl. Lang. & Lit., Fr. Lang. & Lit., Gen. History, Hebrew & Compar. Lit., Hebrew Lang., History of the Jew. People, History of Marit. Civiliza., History of Middle East, Jew. Thought, Land of Israel Studies, Library Studies, Philos.). FAC. OF SOCIAL SCIENCES AND MATHEMATICS —Depts. (Econ., Geog., Math, Poli. Sci., Psych., Sociol. & Anthro., Stats.). *Schools*—Educ. (Depts. of Educ.; Teacher Training; School of Education of the Kibbutz Movement, Oranim), Soc. Work, Grad. Studies. *Centers*—Holocaust Studies, Maritime Studies, Psychological Stress Studies, Rehabilitation & Human Development, Study of Kibbutz & Co-op. Idea; Arab-Jewish Center. *Institutes*—Evolutionary Biology, French Culture & Civilization.

ACADEMIC STAFF: Prof./Assoc. Prof. (60 FT, 23 PT); Sr. Lect./Lect. (163 FT, 73 PT); Asst./Instructors (16 FT, 40 PT).

DEGREES, CERTIFICATE AND DIPLOMAS: BACHELOR'S—*3* YRS. *FT*, MAX. *5* YRS. *PT* - Arts (BA). MASTER'S—*2* YRS. *FT*, MAX. *4* YRS. *PT* –Arts (MA). DOCTORATE—*2-4* YRS. Ph.D. TEACHING CERTIFICATE AND DIPLOMAS—variable (see below).

ADMISSION REQUIREMENTS: BACHELOR'S—Standard reqmts. (see text). MASTER'S—Bach.'s degree or equiv. with min. ave. grade of 76-80; indiv. deptl. reqmts. DOCTORATE—Master's or equiv. with ave. grade of 76-80 and thesis grade of 86-90.

GRADING AND TRANSCRIPTS:

95 - 100	=	Excellent	64 - 75	=	Fairly Good
85 - 94	=	Very Good	50 - 64	=	Satisfactory
75 - 84	=	Good	0 - 49	=	Failure

Transcripts list sem. courses taken yearly, separated by dept. of study, wkly. hrs., credits and numeric grades. Not all transcripts indicate credits.

CREDITS, PROGRAM STRUCTURE, AND DEGREE REQUIREMENTS: Courses assigned specific number of credits according to "credit point" system. Usually, credits correspond directly to reported wkly. hrs. per sem. (although proseminar, seminar carry more credit than hrs., and lang. courses less credit than hrs.). Courses offered on sem. basis and designated by level as 1st-, 2nd-, 3rd-yr. courses. Max. of 44 credits per yr. towards 120 required for B.A.

BACHELOR'S—All programs 3 yrs. Structured as "double" or "single" ("expanded," "extensive") major programs. Both options available in 14 depts.; double major only in 9 depts.; single major only in 1 (soc. work). Double major requires 60 credits in 2 depts. Single major requires 72 credits in primary dept. and 48 credits in 2 or 3 specified divisions of study. Most single major programs begin in 2nd yr., a few in 1st. Degree reqmts. include 120 total credits or, for transfer students, 40 credits in residence; G.P.A. of no less than 60; proficiency in Hebrew and Engl.; Phys. Educ. taken 1 hr. wkly. for 2 sems. during 1st yr. (not-for-credit).

Special honors program available. Selection based on highest scores on Psychometric Entrance Exam and interview. Honors program considered a double major program, i.e., 1 dept. selected for in-depth study, second major created interdisciplinary.

MASTER'S—Intended to broaden and deepen knowl. in undergrad. major. Three program options: a) major dept. with related studies and thesis, b) major and minor dept. with no thesis, c) specific area of concentration with crswrk. in various depts. and thesis. Major and minor programs offered by 12 depts.; major only by 9 depts. Total of 17 depts. offer M.A.

DOCTORATE—Ph.D. offered by 4 depts. (Educ., Gen. History, Math, Psych.). Requires research and includes min. of 4 courses, dissertation. Contact Depts. for detailed information.

CERTIFICATES AND DIPLOMAS—*Teacher's Certificate* Optional routes: incorporated with 3-yr. B.A. in teacher educ. program; or 1-yr. post-bach.'s; or, after completion of 2 yrs. of undergrad. study in major depts. offering subjs. taught in secondary schools and min. 20 yrs. of age. All programs qualify for teaching grades 7-12. *Diploma in Librarianship*—2-yr. post-bach.'s program requiring 80 G.P.A. in at least 1 major, fluency in Hebrew, Engl. and add'l. lang., personal interview. Diploma of Certified Librarian awarded. *Other Diplomas (post-Matriculation)* - Hotel Mgmt., Occupa. Therapy (2 yrs.), Soc. Work.

LINKAGES: Queens College, City University of New York (U.S.); State University of New York (U.S.); University of Connecticut (U.S.); University of Pennsylvania (U.S.).

WEIZMANN INSTITUTE OF SCIENCE, Academic Secretary, P.O. Box 26, Rehovot 76100. Tel.: (054) 82111. U.S. Address: American Friends of the Weizmann Institute of Science, 515 Park Ave., 7th Floor, New York, NY 10022. Tel.: (212) 752-1309.

DESCRIPTION: Estd. 1934 as Daniel Seiff Research Institute; renamed 1949 (see "Historical Development" earlier in the chapter). Feinberg Graduate School is the academic unit of the Institute. Opened 1958, offering only Ph.D.'s; since 1972, also offers M.Sc. degrees and small number of certificates for science teaching. All research facilities of Institute available to students of Graduate School. Located 15 miles southeast of Tel-Aviv. Has 5 science faculties, 1 teaching science department. Residential facilities provided. *Library:* Over 150,000 vols. *Enrollment:* 480 (180 master's, 300 doctorates). See Table 8.1.

CALENDAR: Two 15-wk. sems. (Oct. - Feb., March - June).

ACADEMIC STAFF: Prof. (86), Assoc. Prof. (100), Sr. Scientist (132), Scientist (6).

FACULTIES, DEPARTMENTS, SCHOOL: FAC. OF BIOLOGY—Depts. (Biological Ultrastructure, Cell Biol., Chem. Immunol., Genetics, Hormone Research, Plant Genetics, Virology). FAC. OF BIOPHYSICS AND BIOCHEMISTRY—Depts. (Biochem., Biophysics, Membranes & Bioregulation, Polymer Research). FAC. OF CHEMISTRY—Depts. (Chem. Physics, Isotope Research, Organic Structural Chemistry, Plastics Research). FAC. OF MATHEMATICS—Depts. (Appl. Math, Computer Sci., Theoretical Math). FAC. OF PHYSICS—Depts. (Electronics, Nuclear Physics). Dept. of Science Teaching. Graduate School.

DEGREES: MASTER'S—*2-yr.* - Master's of Science (MSc). DOCTORATE—*3- to 4-yr.* - doctorate (PhD).

ADMISSION REQUIREMENTS: MASTER'S—BSc with min. grade ave. of "Good" or the equiv. DOCTORATE—MSc with sound academic record or equiv.

GRADING AND TRANSCRIPTS:

Grade		Range	Grade		Range
A+ (Excellent)	=	95 - 100	C (Fair)	=	65 - 74
A (Very Good)	=	85 - 94	D (Pass)	=	55 - 64
B (Good)	=	75 - 84	F (Fail)	=	0 - 54

Transcripts list subjs., credits, numeric grade, and legend for grading (see above).

PROGRAM STRUCTURE, DEGREE REQUIREMENTS AND CREDITS: Credit system used (1 credit = 1 hr. lect. per wk. per sem., excluding lab and seminars). Min. credit reqmts. set by Board of Studies and include crswrk. and research, e.g., MSc Theoretical Math requires 24 grad. credits + 6 credits guided reading, noncredit crswrk. or seminars; MSc Chem. requires 32 credits; MSc Physics requires 2 yrs. lect. courses and research (1st yr.—4 courses and project, 2nd yr.—thesis research and 2 courses). MSc program includes lect., lab (where appropriate), seminars, and research project over 4 sems. Research begins after 2 sems. with results presented as thesis. Students normally work 16 hrs./wk. at the Institute as part of program. Ph.D. min. reqmts. set by Board of Studies and include lect., lab, seminar averaging 2-3 hrs./wk., research project, and dissertation over 3-4 yrs.

LINKAGES: National Autonomous University of Mexico, Swiss Federal Institute of Technology, Institute Pasteur-Paris (France), University of Wisconsin (U.S.).

Other, Nonuniversity Institutions of Higher Education

TEACHER TRAINING COLLEGES

BEIT-BERL TEACHERS TRAINING COLLEGE, Beit-Berl Post 44925.

DESCRIPTION: Major educational center providing formal and nonformal educational programs at various levels—higher, postsecondary, secondary, etc. Beit-Berl is the "academic" institution of higher education within the educational complex permitted to award B.Ed. Includes a Regional Comprehensive High School. No Overseas Student Program or affiliation with a Regional College.

CALENDAR: Sept. 1 - June 20 (Sept. - Jan., Feb. - June).

DEGREE AND DIPLOMAS: BACHELOR'S—*4 Yrs.* - Educ. (B.Ed.). DIPLOMA—*3 Yrs.* - Teacher Certification (K-6 and Special Educ.).

CENTERS, INSTITUTES, SEMINARS: CENTERS—Exhibition Center, Pre-Academic Studies Center (*mechina*), Training & Study Center for Youth Workers, Workers Education Center. SEMINARS—for Vocational School Counselors, Youth Movement Leaders, Zionist Political Seminar. INSTITUTE FOR ARAB TEACHERS. ARCHIVES OF THE ISRAEL & WORLD LABOR PARTIES. LIBRARY.

ADMISSION REQUIREMENTS: BACHELOR'S AND DIPLOMAS—Standard reqmts. (see text) or equivalent.

PROGRAMS: *Junior High Educ.*—4-yr. "academic" program for teachers in grades 7-10 and for training educational workers in nonformal education tasks leading to B.Ed. *Kindergarten, Elem. Educ. & Special Educ.*—3-yr. certification program for kindergarten, elem. and special educ. teachers. Specialization in addition to Educ. and Psych. includes Agri., Bible, Engl., Gen. Stud. in Judaism and the Labor Movement, Geog., Hebrew Lang. & Lit. (Hebrew and Gen.), History (Gen. and Jew.), "Land of Israel" Stud., Nature Stud., Soc. Sci. *Special Programs—Mechina* for Elem. School Teachers of Arabic, Elem. School Administrators, Pedagogic Programs, Training of New Immigrants for Engl. Lang. Teaching, Soc. Sci. subjs. for Trade Union Workers.

LEVINSKY TEACHERS COLLEGE, 195 Ben-Yehuda, P.O. Box 48130, Tel-Aviv 91480. Tel.: (03) 426162.

DESCRIPTION: Estd. 1913 as the first Hebrew teachers college of Tel-Aviv in Kiriyat Hachinuck. Aims to prepare teachers and educators who are conscientious citizens with awareness of their Zionist and Jewish heritage. One of the largest and most comprehensive teacher training institutions in Israel. No overseas student program or regional college affiliation. *Enrollment (1986):* 900 FT, 600 PT in-service teachers.

CALENDAR: September 1 - June 20.

ACADEMIC STAFF: 300.

DEPARTMENTS/PROGRAMS: Arabic Elem. School Educ., Early Childhood Educ., Elem. School Educ., Junior H.S. Educ., Music Educ., Special Educ.; Special Facilities–The Kipnis Children's Literature Center, pedagogical labs providing multimedia & audio-visual classroom aids, lang. lab, reading skills lab.

DEGREES AND DIPLOMAS/CERTIFICATES: BACHELOR'S—*4 yrs.* - Educ. (B.Ed.). DIPLOMA—*3 yrs.* - Educ., Teacher Certification.

ADMISSION REQUIREMENTS: All programs req. Matriculation Certificate or equivalent, entrance exams, interview.

PROGRAMS AND COURSES: *Early Childhood Educ.*—Prepares teachers for kindergarten, grade 1, 2. Humanistic approach, stresses active learning. Kindergarten attached to dept. serves as lab for new methods. *Elem. School Educ.*—Prepares gen. teachers for grades 3-6. Subjs. studied incl. Bible,

Geog., Hist., Jew. Stud., Lit., Math, Natural Sci. *Arabic Elem. School Educ.*—Prepares elem. school teachers qualified to teach Arabic in addition to other subjs. Courses incl. spoken and literary Arabic and enrichment courses in Islamic culture. *Special Educ.*—Prepares teachers to work with children in various levels of spec. educ. for remediation of those with learning disabilities. Study incl. courses in learning disabilities, mental disturbances, retardation. *Junior H.S. Educ.*—Prepares intermed. school teachers for grades 7-10 specializing in one of the following: Biol., Engl., History, Lang., Lit., Math. Study in specific course incl. recent theoret. developments, thorough grounding in subj., extensive background courses. *Music Educ.*—Prepares music and movement teachers for educ. system. Other specializations incl. music and movement in special educ., rhythmics, choir conducting.

MICHLALAH-JERUSALEM COLLEGE FOR WOMEN, P.O. Box 16078, Bayit Vegan, Jerusalem 91160. Tel.: (02) 422-481. U.S. Address: American Friends of Michlalah-Jerusalem College for Women, 1350 E. 54th St., Brooklyn, NY 11234. Tel.: (718) 531-9090.

DESCRIPTION: Estd. 1964 as State-Religious women's teachers seminar by a group of Americans. Accredited by Council for Higher Education and in 1979 was granted permission to award B.Ed. Moved to Bayit Vegan 1976, a campus city located on about 5 acres of mountainside property with residential facilities. Offers intensive One-Year program in Jewish Studies for overseas students (see Chapter 6). Educational programs at several levels—postsecondary, "academic" higher education, and postbacccalaureate teacher certification. *Enrollment:* 800 (all programs); 650 Israeli, 85 U.S., 15 other foreign. *Library:* Library Center—40,000 vols.

CALENDAR: Geared to Jewish calendar (Oct. or Nov. - Jan., Feb. - June) with 1 month break for *Chanukah.* Most courses yearly.

ACADEMIC STAFF: 31 FT, 193 PT (32% Ph.D., 40% M.A., 28% B.A.).

DEPARTMENTS AND SCHOOLS: Curriculum is categorized according to 12 major areas of study: Computer Sci., Educ. (Teacher Training, Special Educ., The Institute for the Treatment of Children with Learning Disabilities, and the Montessori Kindergarten), Educational Technol. in Audio-Visual Educ., Engl. Lang. & Lit., Guidance & Counsel., Hebraica, Hebrew Lit., School of Information Stud., Judaica, Math/Computers, Music, Science. There is also the Graduate Department of Hebraica and the Overseas Student Program.

PROGRAMS: 1 YR.—Overseas Student Program. 3 YR.—Teacher certification through grade 9 (junior high). 4 YR.—Bach. of Educ. and teacher certification through grade 10. POSTBACH.'S—Hebraica and Judaica leading to teacher certification through grade 12.

ADMISSION REQUIREMENTS: ONE-, TWO-, AND THREE-YR. PROGRAMS—Standard reqmts. (see text), letters of recommendation, personal interviews. POSTBACH.'S—One program for certified teachers and one for bach.'s degree holders.

GRADING AND TRANSCRIPTS: Credits reported as equiv. to 1 lect. hr. or 2 lab hrs. per wk. per sem. Total credits for 1 academic yr. averages 60 credits.

Course numbers are coded as follows: first 2 digits designate dept., next three numbers designate course, last number designates number of hours the course meets wkly. Overseas students have prefix number 8 replacing first digit of dept. code.

Grades are reported on scale of 0-100 with 60% passing mark.

SEMINAR HAKIBBUTZIM, 149 Haifa Rd., Tel-Aviv 62507.

DESCRIPTION: Seminar HaKibbutzim (Kibbutz Teacher's Seminar) was the school of education for the three major *kibbutz* movements in Israel—HaKibbutz Ha'artzi Hashomer Hatzair; Ichud HaKibbutzim Vehakvitzot; and HaKibbutz Hameuchad. Maintains branches in Oranim, Beit-Berl, and Tel-Aviv which are now functioning as independent institutions. Seminar HaKibbutzim in Tel-Aviv has been approved by the Council for Higher Education through the second stage of the accreditation process (described earlier in this chapter) and has been granted a permit to operate and temporary recognition but no authorization to award degrees. Offers 3- and 4-year teacher education programs leading to a diploma *(teudat)* and teacher certification.

THE DAVID YELLIN TEACHERS COLLEGE (ALSO KNOWN AS SEMINAR BEIT HAKEREM), Beit Hakerem, P.O. Box 3578, Jerusalem 91035. Tel.: (02) 533111. U.S. Address: Friends of the David Yellin Teachers College, 1501 Broadway, Suite 1613, New York, NY 10036. Tel.: (212) 686-7700.

DESCRIPTION: Estd. 1914; Beit Hakerem campus opened 1928. Major state (secular) teacher training institution offering postsecondary and (since 1979) higher education programs. Offers 11 programs including pre-academic *mechina* for new immigrant prospective teachers, for pre-service and in-service training, and for academic retraining. Operates Demonstration School, Learning Laboratories, Diagnostic Clinic. Has graduated over 5,000 students, most from postsecondary programs. *Enrollment:* 515 total (485 Female, 30 Male; 47 Arab) plus in-service program (180 Female, 20 Male). *The Library Center:* 100,000 vols.

CALENDAR: Sept. 1 - June 20 (Sept. - Jan., Feb. - June).

LANGUAGE OF INSTRUCTION: Hebrew and Arabic.

ACADEMIC STAFF: 133 PT, 61 FT.

INSTITUTES AND CENTERS: INSTITUTES—Children's Literature Institute, Jerusalem Institute for Environmental Studies, The Judaic Institute. CENTERS—Computer Tech. Center; Early Childhood Center; Instructional Materials, Pedagogic and Resource Centers; National Center for Teachers of Mentally Handicapped.

DEGREES AND CERTIFICATES: BACHELOR'S—*4 Yrs.* - Educ. (B.Ed.). DIPLOMAS—*3 and 2 Yrs.* - postsecondary Senior Qualified and Qualified Teachers Certificates. —*1 Yr.* -postdip. or postbach.'s program in Special Educ.

ADMISSION REQUIREMENTS AND PROGRAM DESCRIPTIONS BY PROGRAM:

Early Childhood Educ.—3 yr. teacher certificate and/or 4 yr. B.Ed. program (B.Ed. program pending Council for Higher Education final approval). For K-2 teachers with option to specialize in programs for children from birth to age 4 in Child Care Centers and Nurseries.

Elementary School Educ.—3 yr. teacher certificate and/or 4 yr. B.Ed. program (B.Ed. program pending Council approval). For gen. teachers in grades 3-6 or optional specializations in Adult Educ., Children's Lit., Humanities, Judaica, Math, School Library, Sci., Special Educ., Teach. Engl. as Foreign Lang.

Junior High School Educ.—4 yr. B.Ed. program for teachers in grades 7-9 with specialization in Engl., Home Econ. & Nutrition, Humanities, Math, Sci.

Technical Handicrafts—3 yr. certificate program for teachers of technical handicrafts in grades 1-6.

Arab Elem. Educ.—3-yr. certificate program for teachers in Arab elem. schools in which instruction is in Arabic.

Mentally Retarded Children in Residential Institutions—2-yr. program for certified teachers.

Institute for Remedial Educ.—1-yr. special educ. program for certified remedial elem. teachers or those with bach.'s in educ. or psych. who are to be trained as teachers of mentally retarded or learning disabled. Separate 2-yr. program for educ. of music and art therapists.

Home Econ. & Nutrition Sci.—3-yr. certificate and/or 4-yr. B.Ed. program (B.Ed. program pending Council approval) for home econ. & nutrition specialists who will teach in elem. or junior high.

In-Service Teacher Certificate Program and Retraining for University Graduates Entering Teaching—1-2 yr. program for upgrading or obtaining teacher qualification and profes. advancement.

Mechina Pre-Academic Program—1-yr. program for Israelis who have completed military service, have 12 yrs. of educ., and 3 matriculation exams.

New Immigrant Program—1-yr. program for potential teachers. Prep. course in Hebr. Lang. and Judaic Stud. Retraining program for new immigrant teachers as teachers of Engl. as a Second Lang.

GRADING AND TRANSCRIPTS:

91 - 100 = Excellent	61 - 70 = Fair
81 - 90 = Very Good	60 = Pass
71 - 80 = Good	50 = Incomplete

Transcripts list courses taken during 1 yr. with designation of hrs. per sem., sem. taken, and numerical grade.

THE ZINMAN COLLEGE OF PHYSICAL EDUCATION AT THE WINGATE INSTITUTE, Wingate Post Office, Netanya 42901. Tel.: (053) 25352.

DESCRIPTION: Estd. 1957. The Zinman College of Physical Education is a part of the Wingate Institute for Physical Education and Sport, the nation's largest center for training physical education teachers, physiotherapists and coaches. Located on 125 acres on the Mediterranean Sea, 15 miles north of Tel-Aviv, 4 miles south of Netanya. Houses the National Archives of Physical Education and Sport and the nation's largest library of books and publications on physical education and sport (20,000 vols. plus 200 publications). No regional college affiliation. No overseas student program. Residential facilities available. *Enrollment:* 1,200 (all programs and courses).

CALENDAR: Two 15-wk. sems. (Sept. 1 - June 20).

LANGUAGE OF INSTRUCTION: Hebrew.

ACADEMIC STAFF: Approximately 100.

SCHOOLS AND DEPARTMENTS: SCHOOLS—Army Physical Training Instructors, Coaches and Instructors, Physiotherapists; Physical Education Teachers College. DEPARTMENTS—National Archives (see above), Professional Publications, Research and Sports Medicine.

DEGREES, DIPLOMAS AND CERTIFICATES: BACHELOR'S—*4 yrs.* Education (B.Ed.). DIPLOMAS—*3 yrs.* - Physiotherapy (from 1961-80), Teaching. *1 yr.* - Coaching. POST-DIPLOMAS—*1 yr.* - Rehab. for holders of Physiotherapy and Teacher's Diplomas.

ADMISSION REQUIREMENTS: BACHELOR'S—Standard reqmts. (see text), letters of recommendation from Phys. Educ. instructor, medical exams.

CREDIT SYSTEM, GRADING AND TRANSCRIPTS: Courses assigned a number of wkly. hrs. where 1 wkly. hr. equals 30 class hrs. (i.e., 1 class hr. = 1 ann. hr.). No stated difference between lect. and lab hrs. Transcripts present courses according to category rather than by yr. (basic studies, educ., phys. educ. sciences, minor specialization, practice & student teach. and skills courses). Grading is on 0-10 scale with 6 the lowest passing mark: 10 = Excellent, 9 = Very Good, 8 = Good, 7 = Fair, 6 = Pass, 5 or less = Fail.

PROGRAMS: Sample document 4.1 illustrates a 3-yr. teach. diploma program combined with a 4th yr. for a Bachelor in Educ. (B.Ed.). The School of Physiotherapy (PT) is one of 3 PT programs jointly offering the Bach. of Physiotherapy in conjunction with Tel-Aviv Univ. (see table 5.3).

OTHER, NONUNIVERSITY INSTITUTIONS

BEZALEL ACADEMY OF ARTS AND DESIGN, 10 Shmuel Hanazid St., Jerusalem 94592. Tel.: (02) 225111. U.S. Address: American Friends of Bezalel Academy of Arts and Design, Inc., 655 Madison Ave., Suite 1500, New York, NY 10022.

DESCRIPTION: Opened 1906 as the Bezalel School of Arts and Crafts; closed from 1932-36. Status and name changed to Bezalel Academy of Arts and Design 1969; accredited 1976. Israel's sole academy of arts and design. Presently in various locations in Jerusalem. In process of relocating all departments to a united campus on Mount Scopus. No part-time students, summer courses or overseas student program or regional college affiliation. External Studies Unit offers "nonacademic" nonprofessional courses in evening and intends to conduct summer courses. Due to space limitations, enrollment is restricted to approximately 600 (mostly Israeli) with no more than 25% of applicants accepted. *Library:* 15,500 vols.; 110 periodicals; 34,000 slides archives. *Enrollment:* 616 (see Table 8.1).

CALENDAR: Trimester system (Oct. or early Nov. - June).

ACADEMIC STAFF: 120 FT or PT teachers and instructors.

DEPARTMENTS, UNITS, AND PROGRAM: DEPARTMENTS—Ceramics, Environ. & Indus. Design, Fine Arts, Gold- & Silversmithing, Graphic Design, Photography. UNITS—Animation, External Stud., Video. PROGRAM—Gen. Stud.

DEGREES AND DIPLOMAS: BACHELOR'S—*4 yrs.* - Fine Arts (BFA); Ceramics, Gold- & Silversmithing, Fine Arts and Photography, Designs (BDes); Environ. Design, Graphics, Indus. Design. Permission to teach architecture in Dept. of Environ. Design pending approval by Council for Higher Education. Grad. program planned; 5th yr. specialized study permitted. DIPLOMA—*4 yrs. FT*- (discontinued) in art and design.

ADMISSION REQUIREMENTS: Standard reqmts. (see text), portfolio, artistic skills tests by dept., personal interview. Fall only.

PROGRAM STRUCTURE AND COURSES: All degree programs comprise 3 components—Gen. Stud. Program, compulsory and elective deptl. courses. Curriculums published at beginning of academic yr. All students must take all courses offered by dept.; may take courses in other depts. only by special arrangement. First yr. is probationary. GEN. STUD. PROGRAM—Offers 24 2-credit courses in arts, humanities, sciences, soc. sciences. Students reqd. to complete min. of 12 of these courses in addition to deptl. courses as follows: *Dept. of Fine Arts*—Curriculum divided into 2 main study units: basic unit during first 2 yrs. dedicated to acquiring skills & command of artistic tools, developing ability to translate reality into visual lang., and methodical study of rules of that lang.; second unit—yrs. 3-4—personal and independent approach based on principle of tutoring with 4th yr. concentrating on project. Courses include Basic and Advd. Drawing (abstract, landscape, model, nature, still); Materials, Painting Techniques & Printing; Morphology & Theory of Colors, Graphic Techniques (etching, lithogr., paper wkshp., silk screen); Painting, Photogr. (advd., basic, color, studio); Sculpture; Open Wkshp.; Theoretical Wkshps. *Dept. of Graphic Design*—First 2 yrs. offer compulsory program of pract. & theoret. courses for development of analyt. skills and use of artistic tools. Third yr. incl. wider range of problem/issue-solving and integration of new subjs. Emphasizes indiv. development. Indep. project. Courses incl. design of info., design that aids functioning, teaches, explains, convinces & sells: Animation, Basic (concepts in 2-dimens. design, graphic design, typogr.); Color and 3-Dimens. Design, Descript. Geom, Drawing; Printing Wkshps.; Typograph. & Graphic Design; Illustration; Photogr.; Printing, Visualization, Video. *Dept. of Environ. & Indus. Design. Environ. Design*—For designing internal spaces, houses, phys. spaces & landscapes in consideration of soc., technical, climatic and energy factors. Curriculum divided into 5 categories: Design Studio, Communica. in Design (tool, techniq., sys.), Technol. Stud., Profes. Seminars & Theoret. Stud. + elective and recommended studies. *Indus. Design*—Approaches, stresses research, soc., indus., ergonomic, commerc. & mktg. aspects of practical projects and design for simple products or complex systems. Yr. 1—basic studies in creative and artistic abilities and skills. Yr. 2—profes. project of indep. design & technol. courses. Yrs. 3-4—specializa. in indep. design and electives. *Dept. of Gold- & Silversmithing*—Yrs. 1-2—basics of design and techniq. Yrs. 3-4—project and project team chosen with project guided by mixed teams of lecturers; each student reqd. to complete courses in other depts. and at least 1 indep. project. Compulsory courses in areas of smithing: Gemology, Descrip. Geom.; Drawing, Sculpture, Photogr.; 2- and 3-Dimens. Design. Technical courses in metal shaving, stonecutting & polishing, anodization, titanium, inlay, casting, etc. Elective courses. *Dept. of Ceramics*—Yr. 1—basics of all courses in dept. Yr. 2—divided into units of concentrated studies in different subjs. Courses in Basic Design; Ceramics; Ceramic Finishes and Surfaces; Descript. Geom. & Drawing; Morphology, Archaeol. & Hist. of Ceramics; Painting, Drawing, Color, Graphics Techniq.; Photogr.; Presenta. of Exhibits; Product Design; Sculpture, Technol., Unconventional Techniq.; Studio Mgmt.; Wkshps. on Non-Ceramic Subjects.

LINKAGES: Pratt Institute (U.S.).

THE COLLEGE OF ADMINISTRATION, 93 Arlozorov St., Tel-Aviv 62097.

DESCRIPTION: College of Administration has approval through first two stages of the Council for Higher Education's accreditation process (detailed earlier in this chapter). College has been granted a permit to operate and temporary recognition but does not yet have approval from the Council to award degrees. Specializes in afternoon and evening courses in business administration. Programs have been extended from 3 years to 4 years and currently lead to a diploma *(teudat)*. Several centers operating under the College are in Beer Sheva, Haifa, Jerusalem and Tel-Aviv. Only center in Tel-Aviv is being considered for accreditation.

JERUSALEM COLLEGE OF TECHNOLOGY, 21 Havaad Haleumi St., P.O. Box 16031, Givat Mordechai, Jerusalem 16031. Tel.: (02) 423131.

DESCRIPTION: Estd. 1970; accredited 1974. Small, all-male institution providing advanced Torah and *Talmudic* studies in conjunction with a secular technology curriculum. Located on hillside between Bayit Vegan and Givat Mordechai, campus provides residential facilities for about two-thirds of its students. One-Year Program for overseas students (see Chapter 6). Preparatory Program *(Mechina)* for those who do not meet entrance requirements in Hebrew, religious or technological studies. No regional college affiliation or *ulpan*. *Library:* 10,000 vols., Jew. Stud. Library—2,000 vols. *Enrollment:* about 200 (75% Israeli, 25% foreign).

CALENDAR: September - February, March - June.

LANGUAGE OF INSTRUCTION: Hebrew; most texts in English.
ACADEMIC STAFF: 40 FT, 28 PT.
DEPARTMENTS: Applied Physics/Electro-Optics, Computer Science, Electronic Engineering, Industrial Metallurgy/Materials Technology, Teacher Training.
DEGREES AND DIPLOMAS: BACHELOR'S—*4 yrs.* - of Technol. and Applied Sci. (B.Tech. and App.Sc.) in Applied Physics/Electro-Optics, Comput. Sci., Electronic Engr. (approval pending for Indus. Metallurgy/Mats. Technol.). PRACTICAL ENGINEER *(Handassai)—3 yrs. (all technol. depts.).* TEACHER CERTIFICATION.
ADMISSION REQUIREMENTS: All programs—Matriculation Certificate *(Teudat Bagrut), yeshivah* or religious educ. background, letter of recommendation, interview.
PROGRAM STRUCTURE AND COURSE OFFERINGS: Daily program from 7 a.m.-7 p.m.; religious observance and study in the morning, academic study in the afternoon. *Computer Science*—Courses in Appl. Math, Communica., Comput. Graphics, Data Struct., Microcomp., Opera. Sys., Syst. Analysis. *Applied Physics/Electro-Optics*—Courses in Electro-Optic Instrum., Elem. & Advd. Physics, Geometrical Optics, Physics & Quantum Optics. *Electronic Engr.*—Courses in Digital Computers, Elect. Engr. & Electron., Math, Physics. Stress technol. developments in computer hardware, microcomputers, and telecommunications. *Industrial Metallurgy/Materials Technology*—3 yr. program only offering courses in Chem., Computer Applications, Math, Metallurgy, Physics. Study problems in composite and electron. materials, materials structure and behavior of materials, metal alloys, quality control. *Practical Engineering*—See Chapter 7. *Teacher Training*—Provides courses in Computer-Based Testing, Development of Sci. Lab Modules, Sci. Teach. Meth., Video Monitoring, and Student Teaching.

THE JERUSALEM RUBIN ACADEMY OF MUSIC AND DANCE, Smolenskin 7, Givat Ram Campus, Jerusalem 92101. Tel.: (02) 636232.
DESCRIPTION: Estd. 1947 as Rubin Academy of Music. Authorized to award B.Mus. in 1972. Has three joint programs with The Hebrew University of Jerusalem (Musicology Department, Faculty of Humanities, Faculty of Math and Natural Sciences). Trains professional musicians and dancers and music and dance teachers. Offers one-year Overseas Student Programs and Preparatory Program for those needing additional music preparation to pass entrance exams (see Chapter 6). *Enrollment:* 500 in all programs.
CALENDAR: October - January, February - June.
ACADEMIC STAFF: 160.
DEPARTMENTS: Dance and Movement, Music Education, Performing Arts (Keyboard Section, Orchestral Instruments, Voice), Theory Composition and Conducting.
ADMISSION REQUIREMENTS: BACHELOR'S—Standard reqmts. (see text) plus performance entrance exams (those lacking no more than 2 *Bagrut* exams

for the certificate may be granted nonmatriculated status if they meet all other reqmts.). MASTER'S—Standard reqmts. (see text) plus audition. DIPLOMAS—Standard reqmts. (see text) for Artists' Diploma or B.Mus. or Academy Diploma.

GRADING AND TRANSCRIPTS:

95 - 100 = Excellent	65 - 74 = Fair
85 - 94 = Very Good	55 - 64 = Pass
75 - 84 = Good	0 - 54 = Fail

Transcripts record subjs. on yrly. basis with hrs. per week and numerical grade.

DEGREES AND DIPLOMAS: BACHELOR'S—*4 Yrs.* -Music (BMus); joint programs with The Hebrew University of Jerusalem that leads to BMus plus BA in Music. MASTER'S—*2 Yrs.* - joint program with The Hebrew University (MMus). DIPLOMAS—*6 Yrs.* - Artist's Diploma (4 yrs. undergrad., 2 yr. postbacc.). *5 Yrs.* - Teachers certificate as music teachers in kindergarten, elem., secondary schools. *4 Yrs.* for undergrad. profes. diploma.

LINKAGE: New York University joint program leading to (N.Y.U.) M.A. in Music and Music Education.

RUPPIN INSTITUTE (ALSO KNOWN AS THE RUPPIN INSTITUTE OF AGRICULTURE), P.O. Ruppin Institute, Emek Hefer 60960. Tel.: (053) 95131-7.

DESCRIPTION: Estd. 1949 by Arthur Ruppin, dominant figure in agricultural colonization in pre-state Israel. Initially limited to courses in agriculture, it now is a major comprehensive educational complex, offering various levels of education including nonformal programs, postsecondary and higher education. Authorized to award bachelor's degree in 1975. Supported and affiliated with the United Kibbutz Movement, the National Institute for Technological Training (NITT) and the Council for Higher Education. Residential facilities provided; student residency mandatory. *Enrollment:* 177 ("academic" program only).

DEGREES AND DIPLOMAS: BACHELOR'S—4-yr. Administration of the *Kibbutz* Economy (B.Admin.*Kibbutz*). DIPLOMA—2-yr. FT Practical Engineer (*Handassai*).

ADMISSION REQUIREMENTS: BACHELOR'S—Standard reqmts. (see text). DIPLOMA—12 yrs. of educ. and Final Diploma exams in Engl., Math, Physics.

PROGRAMS: One 4-yr. "academic" program; other postsecondary programs (teacher training) for agri. & nature, practical engr., farm mgmt. program with the Alperin Regional College, 2-yr. social work program.

SHENKAR-COLLEGE OF TEXTILE TECHNOLOGY AND FASHION, 12 Anna Frank St., Ramat Gan, 52 526, Israel. Tel.: (03) 719944.

DESCRIPTION: Founded Oct. 1970 to meet growing demand for highly qualified Israeli textile and apparel industry personnel. Sponsored and supported by textile industry and Israeli government. Serves as scientific and technological center for textile and apparel industry by providing know-how, facilities and assistance in plant organization, workers' training, applied research, industrial surveys, lab testing. Physical facilities, including labs and workshops, measure 60,000 square feet. *Library:* 15,000 vols.; 270 periodicals. *Enrollment (1984):* 117 FT Males, 213 FT Females, broken down into Israeli (312 Jewish, 12 Muslim, 1 Christian) and Foreign (5 non-U.S.).

CALENDAR: Two 14-wk. sems. (Oct. - Feb., Feb. - July).

ACADEMIC STAFF: Ph.D. (12 FT, 1 PT), M.A. (16 FT, 3 PT), Other (9 FT, 2 PT). Faculty:student ratio = 1:7.7.

DEPARTMENTS: Fashion Design, Industrial Management, Textile Chemistry, Textile Design, Textile Technology.

GRADING:

100 = A (Excellent)		70 = C (Fair)
90 = B (Very Good)		60 = D (Pass)
80 = B (Good)		50 - 59 = F (Fail)

CREDIT POINT (CP) SYSTEM: 1 CP = 1 lect. hr. (50 min.) per wk. for 1 sem. (14 wks.). 1 studio hr. = .75 CP. 1 lab hr. = .50 CP.

DEGREE AND DIPLOMA REQUIREMENTS:

Bachelor's (4 yrs. FT)	Degree Requirements
Fash. Design (B.Des.[Fash.])	150 CP + 14 wks. FT prac. train.
Indus. Mgmt. (B.Tech.[Tex.])	165 CP + 14 wks. (2 da./wk.) prac. train.
Tex. Chem. (B.Tech.[Tex.])	165 CP
Tex. Design (B.Des.[Tex.])	150 CP
Tex. Technol. (B.Tech.[Tex.])	165 CP

Associate (2 yrs. FT) Applied Science (A.A.S.)

Diploma (2 yrs. FT) Practical Engineer *(Handassai)*

ADMISSION REQUIREMENTS: *Bagrut*, Psychometric Exams required for Indus. Mgmt., Textile Chem., Textile Technol. and, in addition, indiv. interview and entrance exams for Fash. Design, Textile Design. Applicants for Indus. Mgmt., Textile Chem., Textile Technol. with inadequate matric. grades in math and physics required to satisfactorily complete 2-month prep. (pre-acad.) course in summer.

אוניברסיטת חיפה
UNIVERSITY OF HAIFA
جامعة حيفا

Haifa, 15/4/1985

RECORD OF STUDIES

We hereby certify that Mr/Ms ______________

Id. No.______________was a student at the University of Haifa,

in the Pre-academic Unit Preparatory courses, in the New Immigrants class,

in the academic year 1977/78 ______.

The above participated in the following courses:

Subject	Weekly hours	Grade
Hebrew Language	18	74
History of the Jewish People	4	80
Geography of Israel	2	80
Civic Studies	2	90
Judaism for English - Speakers	2	Passed

The above is permitted to enroll at the University of Haifa for the academic

year ______________

STUDENT ADMINISTRATION

8.1b. *Mechina* from the Preparatory Program, the University of Haifa

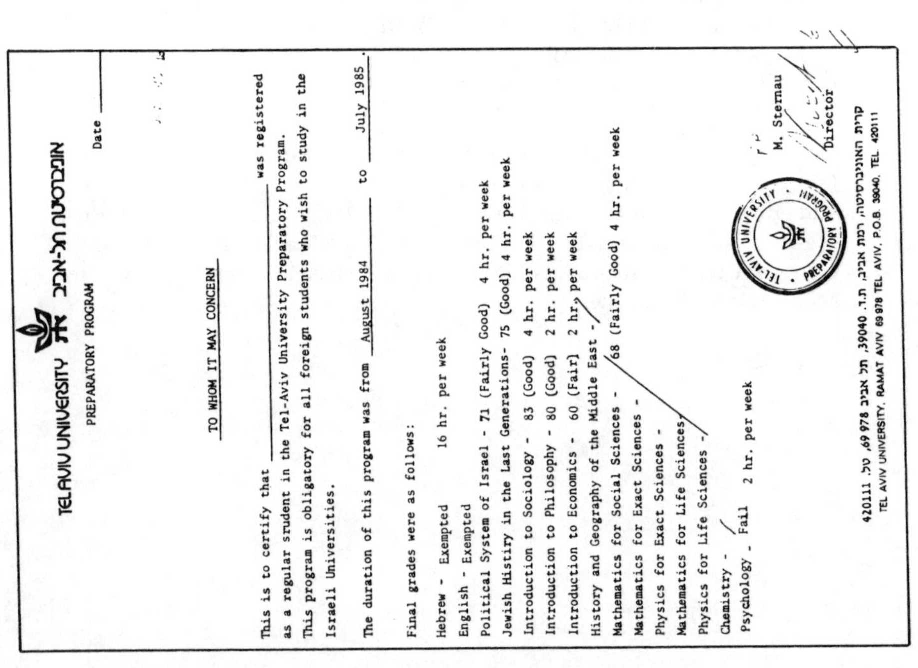

TEL AVIV UNIVERSITY אוניברסיטת תל-אביב

PREPARATORY PROGRAM

Date ______

TO WHOM IT MAY CONCERN

This is to certify that ______________ was registered as a regular srudent in the Tel-Aviv University Preparatory Program. This program is obligatory for all foreign students who wish to study in the Israeli Universities.

The duration of this program was from August 1984 to July 1985.

Final grades were as follows:

Hebrew - Exempted 16 hr. per week
English - Exempted
Political System of Israel - 71 (Fairly Good) 4 hr. per week
Jewish Histiry in the Last Generations- 75 (Good) 4 hr. per week
Introduction to Sociology - 83 (Good) 4 hr. per week
Introduction to Philosophy - 80 (Good) 2 hr. per week
Introduction to Economics - 60 (Fair) 2 hr. per week
History and Geography of the Middle East -
Mathematics for Social Sciences - 68 (Fairly Good) 4 hr. per week
Mathematics for Exact Sciences -
Physics for Exact Sciences -
Mathematics for Life Sciences -
Physics for Life Sciences -
Chemistry -
Psychology - Fail 2 hr. per week

TEL-AVIV UNIVERSITY • PREPARATORY PROGRAM •

M. Sternau
Director

קרית האוניברסיטה, רמת אביב, ת.ד. 39040, תל אביב 69 978, טל. 420111
TEL AVIV UNIVERSITY, RAMAT AVIV 69 978 TEL AVIV, P.O.B. 39040, TEL. 420111

8.1a. *Mechina* from the Preparatory Program, Tel-Aviv University

Section II. The Occupied Territories

Chapter 9

Introduction

Basic Facts: Profiles of the Occupied Territories

The educational systems of the Occupied Territories are the areas under discussion in Section II, Chapters 9-14. The Occupied Territories are those areas which fell under Israeli occupation as a result of the June 1967 War and have remained in that status until today. These areas include the West Bank and East Jerusalem which were incorporated by Jordan in 1949; the Gaza Strip, which was placed under Egyptian administration in 1949, but was not incorporated; and the Golan Heights which was a part of Syria. East Jerusalem and the Golan Heights have subsequently been annexed by Israel, in effect extending Israeli sovereignty and the application of Israeli law to these areas under nonnegotiable conditions. Annexation of these areas is not recognized by the United States or the international community; consequently, East Jerusalem and the Golan Heights are considered occupied in this text. For historical events which preceded and followed the 1967 War, see the "Historical Chronology" located in the front of this volume.

THE LAND—DESCRIPTIVE AREA AND LOCATION

The West Bank. The West Bank is located in the mideastern part of historic Palestine on the western bank of the River Jordan which divides Palestine from Jordan. Since the 1950 Jordanian parliamentary decision on annexation, this area has been referred to as the West Bank, while Jordan itself is referred to as the East Bank. Israel identifies the West Bank (excluding East Jerusalem) as "Judea and Samaria." Officially, reference to "Palestine" is prohibited by both Israel and Jordan.

The West Bank encompasses about 2,270 square miles extending from the plains of central Galilee in the north, down the eastern border made by the Jordan River as far as half the length of the Dead Sea, to the Naqab (Negev) desert in the south. Israel surrounds the area to the south, west, and north, while Jordan lies to the East. The area represents 22% of pre-1948 Palestine. Since Israeli occupation in 1967, 52% of the land of the West Bank has been expropriated or confiscated and given over to Israeli use, whether official, private, or for settlement.

East Jerusalem. Jerusalem is on the edge of a desert in the Judean Hills, 38 miles east of the Mediterranean, 18 miles northwest of the Dead Sea. From 1949-67, the city was divided by the so-called "Green Line" into East and West Jerusalem. West Jerusalem, covering an area of 15 square miles, was claimed by Israel and inhabited by Israeli Jews; East Jerusalem, spanning an area of approximately 27 square miles and including the Old City, was claimed by Jordan along with the adjoining West Bank and inhabited by Palestinians carrying Jordanian citizenship. As a result of the June 1967 War, East Jerusalem was occupied and then annexed by Israel. Today, there are Palestinians living in East Jerusalem and Israelis living in both East and West Jerusalem.

The occupation and annexation of East Jerusalem present certain technical and legal ramifications which tend to complicate and distort the reporting of population and educational statistics. In effect, the land but not the people was annexed. After a period of controversial imposition of the Israeli educational system on the Arab schools, the system reverted back to the Jordanian system for the Palestinian population. As a result, there are two Arab educational systems in operation in Israel: the Jordanian system for Palestinians in East Jerusalem under Israel as a result of the June 1967 War; and the Israeli Arab educational system (subdivided into one for Muslims and Christians and one for Druzes) for 1948 Palestinians living in the rest of Israel and discussed in Section I. Educational statistics for 1967 Palestinian Arabs living in East Jerusalem are sometimes included in statistics for "non-Jews in Judea and Samaria" and/or with statistics for the district of Bethlehem in the West Bank; at other times, no clarification or distinction is provided. (Druze statistics would also include Syrian Druze in the Golan Heights since annexation in 1981.) Due to these complications as well as other reporting inconsistencies, data for the Arab population, schools, and enrollment in East Jerusalem is affected, and, as a direct result, so are statistics reported for Jerusalem, Israel, and the West Bank. (See also "Jerusalem" in Chapter 1 and "Educational Overview " in this chapter.)

The Gaza Strip. Gaza territory is located on the eastern coast of the Mediterranean Sea in the mid-southwest corner of historic Palestine, touching on the Sinai desert and otherwise surrounded by Israel. Gaza encompasses an area of 258 square kilometers, or approximately 150 square miles, extending some 27 miles long and five miles wide. About one-twentieth the size of the West Bank, Gaza, home to two-thirds the populace of the West Bank, is one of the most densely populated areas in the world with 1,300-1,400 people per square kilometer (0.38 of a square mile). Since the Israeli occupation in 1967, over 50% of the land has been expropriated or confiscated and given over to Israeli use, whether official, private, or for settlement.

The Golan Heights. The Golan Heights is a strategic plateau overlooking Israel to the west southwest, bordering Lebanon on the north, Jordan on the south, and Syria to the east. That part of the Golan which was occupied and then annexed by Israel comprises 556 square miles.

POPULATION AND POPULATION CENTERS. Neither Israel nor Jordan has conducted a census in the Occupied Territories since 1967. Consequently, the population figures below are based upon approximations compiled from several sources published between 1984-86.

The total Palestinian population living today within the borders of historic Palestine approximates 2,046,700 distributed by area as follows: East Jerusalem—130,000; Gaza Strip—510,000; the West Bank—786,700; and Israel proper

(Israeli Arabs)—620,000. In addition, the Golan Heights has a population of approximately 15,000 Syrian Druze. Since the annexation of East Jerusalem and the Golan Heights, Israel reports the combined population figures of Arabs in East Jerusalem, the Golan Heights, and Israel proper as the "non-Jews" of their population. (For the Israeli Jewish population, see below and "Settlements," in this chapter.)

In the West Bank outside East Jerusalem, the Palestinian population is concentrated in 25 cities and towns, 324 villages, and 20 refugee camps. Over a quarter million (266,473) Palestinians, or 34% of the West Bank population, live inside refugee camps. An estimated 52,000 Jewish settlers live in 115 settlements in the West Bank, excluding East Jerusalem, which is a major settlement area. The major cities/towns (with Arab population figures) are:

Nablus	(75,000)	Jenin	(40,000)	Ramallah	(25,000)
Hebron	(70,000)	Tulkarm	(30,000)	Bethlehem	(15,000)
Jerico	(55,000)	Al Bireh	(25,000)		

In Gaza, the population is dispersed over 17 municipalities and villages and eight large and overcrowded refugee camps. Over two-thirds of the Gaza population (354,450) live in these eight camps. Since the 1978 Camp David Accords, the Israeli settler population has increased to 2,150 and the number of settlements has tripled from six to 18. The major population centers are:

Gaza (town)	(120,000)	Khan Younis	(75,223)	Rafah	(74,803)

The Golan Heights population is concentrated in the villages of Majdal Shams, Masa'ada, and Beqa'ata. *(The Arabs* 39, 107; *Statistical Abstract of Israel; Al-Fajr Palestinian Publications* 9, 23; *The Gaza Strip, a Demographic, Economic, Social and Legal Survey)*

SETTLEMENTS. Over 133 Jewish settlements in the Occupied Territories (excluding East Jerusalem) introduce some 54,150 Israeli citizens supported by their legal, political, social, and financial institutions into an otherwise Arab society. The Palestinian Human Rights Campaign and American-Arab Anti-Discrimination Committee (ADC), however, report the settler population in the West Bank and East Jerusalem alone as 140,000 in 1985. According to the World Zionist Organization census of July 1985, 46% of the settlers are native-born Israelis, 23% are European or American-born, and 14% are Asian or African-born. (See also "Population and Population Centers" above.)

Settlements are classified as either urban/suburban, rural/semi-urban, or paramilitary outposts (Benvenisti 49). An extensive network of roads, water lines and utilities serve these self-contained communities ranging in size from small enclaves of less than 20 families to nine major settlements of 280 or more families located in and around Jerusalem and Tel-Aviv. The smaller, rural/semi-urban settlements are linked administratively and physically to urban/suburban or community centers where basic health, education, and commercial services are provided. The Israeli educational system, as described in Section I, is followed in settlement schools up through the secondary level.

ETHNICITY, NATIONALITIES, AND RELIGIOUS CONSTITUENCIES. Arabs living in the West Bank, East Jerusalem, the Gaza Strip, and within the 1948 borders of Israel refer to themselves as Palestinians; their ethnicity and culture is Arab. Palestinians generally define a Palestinian as a person who was living or born in Palestine prior to May 14, 1948, his children and his children's children. Palestinians and their descendents who, since 1948 up until today, live within the boundaries of Israel established in 1948-49 constitute the Palestinian Arab population discussed in Section I, "Israel"; 1948 Palestinians are also referred to as Israeli Arabs. Arabs in the Golan Heights are Syrian, not Palestinian.

There is a strong sense of Palestinian nationalism and identity among Palestinians even though their legal nationality and citizenship status reflect the consequences of *al-Nakbah* ("the disaster"). Palestinians not physically present in the West Bank or Gaza Strip at the end of the June 1967 War are considered "foreigners" by Israel; the same is true for those not in residence in 1948 (see the effect on education in "Education Under Occupation" later in this chapter). Thus, many Palestinians are stateless using a *Laissez Passer* as a travel and identification document, while others may be citizens carrying a passport of the country in which they have established residence, where permitted. Palestinians in the West Bank, including East Jerusalem, have Jordanian citizenship and carry Jordanian passports. Palestinians in the Gaza Strip, however, had a different legal arrangement with Egypt than West Bankers had with Jordan, and remain stateless. Although Palestinians do reside in Syria, residents of the Golan Heights are Syrian nationals. Arab residents of the Golan Heights (since annexation) and Israel proper are considered Israeli citizens by Israel. The degree of acceptance of this status, while technically nonnegotiable, varies; the more recent annexation of the Golan finds Golanese the most outwardly resistant, while the Israeli Arab Druze are generally the most accepting.

The Arab population living in the Occupied Territories is represented by three religious groups: Muslims, Christians, and Druze. The West Bank, East Jerusalem, and Gaza Strip are primarily Sunni Muslim (97%) and Christian (3%); the Golan is 100% Druze. See also "The Impact of Cultural Origin, Political Persuasion, and Religious Belief" (Israeli Arabs, Christians and Druze) in Chapter 1. For the Israeli Jewish population in the Occupied Territories, see "Population" and "Settlements" in this chapter.

OFFICIAL LANGUAGE. Arabic is the official language in the Occupied Territories.

THE ISLAMIC CALENDAR. The Islamic calendar is based upon a 354-day lunar cycle; dates based upon this calendar appear on all official documents, including educational records. The Islamic New Year 1408 begins August 8, 1987. Approximate conversions from the Islamic calendar to the Gregorian calendar can be made by adding or subtracting year for year, or by determining the numeric difference between the two systems (1987—1408 = 579 years) and adjusting accordingly. For example, the Islamic year 1400 is eight years before the point of reference year 1408 as well as eight years before the corresponding year 1987; therefore, the Islamic year 1400 corresponds to 1979 (1987—8 = 1979); or, 1400 + 579 = 1979.

HOLIDAYS. The Islamic sabbath is celebrated on Fridays; Christians celebrate on Sundays. The major Islamic holiday is *Ramadan* and involves daily fasting and prayer for one month. In 1987, *Ramadan* began April 28. *Id al-Fitr* is a three-day holiday celebrating the end of *Ramadan* (May 26-29, 1987). Other holidays include *Id al-Adah* or Feast of the Sacrifice, a four-day celebration (Aug. 5-9 in 1987), and *Mawlid al-Nabawi*, a one-day celebration of the birth of the prophet Mohammed. Since religious observances are set by the 354-day lunar calendar their incidence on the solar calendar moves forward 11 or 12 days each year. Christian holidays coincide with those celebrated in the United States and follow either Western or Orthodox calendars. There are also Palestinian national days which commemorate significant events in Palestinian history.

ARABIC NUMERALS. Table 9.1 is provided to assist in the recognition and verification of numeric references on Arabic documents. It is advisable to compare numbers on the original document with their translations to determine whether the translation is complete and accurate. Numbers read from left to right while text reads from right to left.

GOVERNMENT. The system of government or administration in the Occupied Territories varies according to whether or not the territory has been annexed by Israel. Those areas annexed in 1967 and 1981, East Jerusalem and the Golan Heights, have been unilaterally incorporated by Israel and are under the Israeli governmental system (see Section I, Chapter 1). Because of this, the Israeli educational system operates in the Golan Heights, but, in spite of this, the Jordanian educational system is followed in East Jerusalem. Those areas that have not been annexed, the West Bank and Gaza Strip, are administered by the Israeli Defense Forces (IDF), also referred to as the civil administration or military government, and hereafter referred to as the Israeli military authorities.

Since June 7, 1967, and the issuance of Proclamation No. 2, Sec. 3 Concerning the Assumption of Government by the Israeli Defense Forces, every governmental, legislative, appointive, and administrative power has been vested in the military commander, or persons appointed on his behalf. (West Bank Military Government, Collection of Proclamations and Orders, Proclamation No. 2, Sec. 3 [7 June 1967]) The military authorities have assumed full legislative, executive, and judicial powers, functioning through complex adaptations of the then-operational British, Jordanian, or Egyptian systems.

The legislative system exists in terms of the implementation of over 1,300 military orders usually amending or replacing previous laws and encompassing all aspects of life, including education (see "Education Under Occupation" later in this chapter). Such changes are in conflict with international law, specifically the Fourth Geneva Convention, to which Israel is a party. Israel dismisses the applicability of the provisions of the Convention since they consider the area "administered" rather than "occupied."

Table 9.1. Arabic Numerals

0 = ٠	5 = ٥	10 = ١٠	15 = ١٥	20 = ٢٠ or ٢٠
1 = ١	6 = ٦	11 = ١١	16 = ١٦	50 = ٥٠
2 = ٢ or ٢	7 = ٧	12 = ١٢ or ١٢	17 = ١٧	100 = ١٠٠
3 = ٣ or ٣	8 = ٨	13 = ١٣ or ١٣	18 = ١٨	1000 = ١٠٠٠
4 = ٤	9 = ٩	14 = ١٤	19 = ١٩	

With the negation of Jordanian and Egyptian executive functions in 1967, municipal government (mayors and councils) represents the highest level of political participation. In the 1972 and 1976 West Bank local elections, nationalist candidates running on platforms supporting the Palestine Liberation Organization (PLO) won by a distinct majority. As a result, the terms of elected councils and elections were indefinitely postponed. Mayors of most major cities have since been dismissed or deported and replaced by Israeli appointees or Israelis. The basis for municipal government in Gaza, unlike that in the West Bank, follows British law applied in Palestine before 1948. The last municipal elections in Gaza were held in 1946. Gaza (town), run by an Israeli military officer, represents the only municipal government; other towns in Gaza—Khan Younis, Deir Al Balah and Rafah—have Israeli-appointed councils. The Israeli military governor, however, has supreme authority and may prohibit the enactment of local legislation and determine municipal budgets.

The judicial system is based upon various military orders issued since 1967 which transfer to the military commander the authority once vested in the courts and legal system. The rules of evidence and procedure for both civil and criminal cases are established by military personnel and may or may not be in the public domain.

GOVERNMENT IN EXILE. Palestinian nationalism, political expression, or political affiliation are prohibited according to Israeli military orders. Despite this, the majority of residents in the West Bank and Gaza are supporters of the Palestine National Movement (i.e., the Palestine Liberation Organization with all its factions and extensive organizational structure).

The Palestine Liberation Organization (PLO) was established in 1964 at the convening of a Palestinian Congress of 422 participants in Jerusalem. During the Arab Summit Conference in Rabat (1974), the PLO was recognized as the sole representative of the Palestinian people. The PLO has permanent observer-status within the UN and its agencies and maintains diplomatic-informational missions in over 100 countries. These factors along with a multiplicity of other nation-state institutions have resulted in the PLO functioning as the embodiment of a state and government without its territory.

The PLO functions through several major institutional bodies. The Palestine National Council (PNC) is the highest policy-making institution within the PLO and functions as the legislative body and Palestinian parliament. The 394 member PNC is drawn from three groups representing all sectors of Palestinian society: social and cultural organizations, resistance organizations, and independents. The Executive Committee of the PNC is the executive branch, corresponding to a cabinet in a multi-party parliamentary system. Its chairman serves as President and implements PNC decisions. Members of the Executive Committee head major administrative departments corresponding to ministries, e.g., foreign affairs, information, education and culture, etc. The Palestine National Fund serves as the Ministry of Finance, collects all revenues, and supervises the expenditures of the PLO and its organs.

The Department of Mass Organizations and the Department of Social Affairs are the two major departments within the PLO representing the coalition of all sectors of Palestinian society. The former consists of nine general unions—the General Union of Palestinian Workers, Women, Students, Teachers, Engineers, Writers and Journalists, Doctors, Lawyers, and Painters and Artists. The major services of the Department of Social Affairs are provided by the Palestine Red Crescent Society (PRCS) and Samed, the Palestine Martyrs' Works Society. The PRCS provides health and medical services, hospital and laboratory facilities, a training school for nurses and paramedical personnel, and day-care centers for children of PRCS employees. Samed evolved in 1970 to provide vocational training and economic self-sufficiency to Palestinian orphans. Today, it represents the economic infrastructure of the Palestinian community, operates industrial and agricultural factories, and publishes a leading economic journal.

Central to the Palestine National Movement is a commitment to universal quality education and the value of education to all Palestinians for their personal well-being as well as for the survival and viability of Palestinian nationalism. Consequently, an extensive support system is seen operating throughout Palestinian society: day-care centers for children of working mothers, construction and maintenance of kindergartens, vocational training programs, summer courses for teachers, literacy programs, and varying degrees of financial support for qualified students at all levels of education. The Educational Division of the PLO Planning Center has evolved a Palestinian philosophy of education and special educational materials for Palestinian children, who, regardless of where they are educated, are subject to official curriculums void of Palestinian history and culture.

The PLO is involved in other intellectual and cultural endeavors. The Arts and National Culture Section of the Department of Information and Culture has several divisions for the promotion of Palestinian theatre, popular arts, plastic arts, graphic arts, and cinema. The PLO Research Center, established in 1965 and relocated from Beirut to Tunis after 1982, has published over 400 books on the Palestinian problem, issues an Arabic intellectual monthly journal, *Palestine Affairs (Shu'un Filastiniya),* and maintains a library of 25,000 volumes in addition to microfilms, manuscripts, and archives. The PLO has established a Palestinian news agency (WAFA), a radio station, and was in the midst of inaugurating the first Palestinian public university when curtailed by the 1982 invasion of Lebanon.

The United Nations Relief and Works Agency for Palestine Refugees in the Near East (UNRWA)

Since 1950, the United Nations Relief and Works Agency for Palestine Refugees in the Near East (UNRWA), with technical assistance from the United Nations Educational, Scientific and Cultural Organization (UNESCO), has operated a unique and highly successful educational system for Palestinian refugees in Jordan, Lebanon, Syria, the West Bank, and Gaza Strip. More than 900,000 Palestinian children have been educated in UNRWA schools as of 1986 in a system primarily aimed at insuring nine years of education to registered refugees and their families. While UNRWA is not involved in secondary education, it does provide postpreparatory vocational training and, to a limited extent, postsecondary education and teacher training. For more information on UNRWA, see Chapter 12.

Education Under Occupation

The impact of Israeli military occupation on education is registered regularly in the schools and academic community in the West Bank and Gaza Strip. The international community, most notably academics, Amnesty International, The International Commission of Jurists, and Law in the Service of Man have reported and documented innumerable incidents beyond the scope and confines of this book. It is impossible, however, to approach any discussion of education in the Occupied Territories without mention of the ramifications of military occupation, particularly as it affects higher education and academic freedom.

SEIZURE OF IDENTIFICATION CARDS. It is illegal for Palestinian residents of the Occupied Territories to travel locally without a valid Israeli-issued identity card. Confiscation of ID's from students by the military during raids in homes, schools, dormitories, and at check points, etc. prevents students from attending school until the cards are retrieved or reissued (sometimes taking months). The regular occurrence of military road blocks and check points near the universities often prompts students (particularly girls) en route to the campus to return home to prevent seizure of their ID, harrassment, arrest, or being photographed.

ADMINISTRATIVE DETENTION. Administrative detention was reinstituted in 1985 and is the imprisonment of individuals without charge or trial for a period of up to six months, subject to renewal. The proportion of students among administrative detainees since then has been about 50%.

HOUSE AND TOWN ARREST. House and town arrest involves the restriction of individuals to their home or town of residence. Since students and faculty usually have to commute outside their immediate locale, those under arrest are consequently restricted from attending school, class, or work. Orders may also specify restriction from entering the campus of a given university.

RESTRICTIONS ON TRAVEL. Travel outside the Occupied Territories in order to attend conferences, seminars, or other professional activities requires permission from the military authorities. Academics and other professionals are frequently denied travel permits without a reason being given.

WORK PERMITS. Hiring teachers and school administrators in government schools is normally restricted to local residents, subject to approval by the military authorites and the Shen Bet (domestic intelligence agency). At the discretion of the authorities, teachers may be dismissed or transferred to logistically problematic posts. As a result, hiring and continued employment have become a function of political considerations rather than academic or teaching qualifications.

Hiring faculty and administrators from outside the Territories is frequently necessary or desirable in order to staff the quickly evolving university system. Since the majority hired are Palestinians living in the diaspora, a complicated approval procedure is involved. Those not physically present in 1948 and 1967 when Israeli ID cards were issued are considered "foreigners" by Israel. As such, they are required to obtain an entry visa as well as a work permit in order to be hired. Requests for visas and work permits are subject to approval by the military authorities; when granted, they are usually issued on a quarterly basis, subject to renewal and revocation. Renewal requires that the person apply from outside the area and involves regular departure without assurance of when or if it will be granted.

CAMPUS RAIDS AND INTERVENTION. Classes, cultural events, student gatherings, and demonstrations may be disrupted at any time by military intervention. Confrontations between the military and students, faculty and administrators in schools or the universities are occurring with increasing frequency and distressing results—incidents of harrassment, arrests, deportation, detention, injuries and fatalities.

RESTRICTIONS ON PROGRAM OFFERINGS. Any curriculum or program offering must be approved by the military authorities. Once approved, there is little direct intervention in the setting of course curricula, aside from censorship as discussed below. At the university level, where such matters are considered an infringement on academic freedom, examples of restrictions include denial of a request to train tour guides at the Bethlehem University, School of Hotel Management; denial of requests for departments or faculties of agriculture by An-Najah and Bethlehem universities and the Hebron Polytechnic; denial of community service programs at Birzeit University; denial of student teaching as part of teacher education; as well as denial of requests for programs and research in fields considered a security or economic risk by Israel.

CENSORSHIP AND RESTRICTIONS ON BOOKS AND PERIODICALS. Censorship of books and periodicals is implemented through Military Orders Nos. 50, 101, and Article 88 of the Defense (Emergency) Regulations of 1945, among others. There is no comprehensive or public list of prohibited publications. One institution may be permitted to purchase a publication that has been prohibited to another. Publications banned in the Occupied Territories are frequently available for purchase, reading or photocopying in Israeli libraries or book stores. Nevertheless, distribution or possession of prohibited material, knowingly or unknowingly, is subject to reprisal.

Official sources have indicated that some 648 books are banned while other sources indicate from 1,600-5,000 publications are banned or censored. Arabic language and literature are frequently censored in part or in total; "all works," according to Meron Benvenisti, "which express, instill or foster Palestinian-Arab national feelings and national heritage" are censored. (Benvenisti 117) Benvenisti elaborates: "Subjects which include in the title Nasserism, Zionism, and Palestine are automatically censored; . . . every subject which deals with Arab partisan perceptions of controversial issues (are banned) even if the work is a serious study in geography, history (including Arab history), Judaism . . . Poetry and fiction connected even directly and symbolically with

Palestine is banned . . . all areas that constitute national awareness, intellectual, emotional and factual, are perceived as seditious and therefore banned." (Benvenisti 127-8)

School textbooks used in conjunction with the Jordanian and Egyptian governments' curriculums are first subject to censorship. To the extent approved, books are then reproduced and distributed to the schools by Israel (see also Chapter 12, "UNRWA").

CUSTOMS AND TAXATION ON BOOKS AND EQUIPMENT. If a request for purchase of equipment, computers, books, or periodicals is approved, a nonrefundable tax or duty must be paid. Palestinian universities are not granted the same tax exempt status that is applied to Israeli universities. Even those items classified as gifts or donations are taxed. The tax may represent an average of 50% of the value of the goods or may far exceed the actual cost. Further administrative encumbrances exist due to restrictions on the transfer and release of funds for payment.

RESTRICTIONS ON BUILDING AND DEVELOPMENT. A permit for building or expanding educational facilities must be approved before construction begins. This requirement also applies to expansion vertically on structures which were built with a permit. A permit is required even when the property is owned by individual Palestinians, private educational institutions, or the Waqf (Department of Religious Endowments). Requests for permits are frequently delayed (years), denied, or lost and have resulted in restrictions on educational development, increases in the cost of projects, and overcrowded conditions.

UNIVERSITY AND CAMPUS CLOSURES. The military authorities frequently close universities or campuses for periods extending from days to months. Unofficial closures due to military road blocks and check points are common. An official closure not only puts the university off-limits to all students and personnel, but devastates research and laboratory projects which require attention to equipment and experiments. The incidence of closures has increased dramatically since 1985 and now encompasses schools as well as universities in the West Bank and Gaza. Invariably, academic calendars must be extended to make up for closures; graduation ceremonies are seldom on schedule. Supervised study and class meetings, however, do continue under university emergency measures but, for security reasons, are not publicized.

MILITARY ORDER 854 AND THE "LOYALTY OATH." In July 1980, Military Order (MO) 854 was issued, in effect, extending to institutions (offering four or more years of higher education) limitations which were intended, under Jordanian Law 16, only for schools and community colleges. MO 854 gives the military authority over virtually all university operations including the admission of students, supervision of curriculums and textbooks, requirement of annual operating licenses, appointment of faculty and staff, etc. Due to international uproar in response to this action, the Israeli Gavison/Yaari report issued by Israeli academics investigating the cause and justification for such an order, and the general lack of cooperation from the West Bank university community, implementation of MO 854 was suspended—although never rescinded—two years later. In August 1982, the military authorities began demanding that all "foreign" faculty (who were mainly Palestinian) sign a pledge specifically repudiating support of the PLO before a work permit would be issued. Refusal to sign this oath has resulted in many deportations and denials of work permits. Again, international and Israeli academic criticism ensued in response. While the pledge has been somewhat modified and implementation arbitrarily applied, the threat to university stability and individual security still exists.

Educational Overview

Schools in Palestine were first established in the last quarter of the nineteenth century during the period of Turkish rule. The four-year elementary schools established by the Turks held little attraction for the Arabs: the language of instruction was Turkish and irrelevant to the Palestinian population; tradition held that schools were all male, automatically alienating half of the population; the schools were headed by Turkish principals who implemented suppression of Arab nationalism; and there was no continuity in the system, the nearest school for further education being located in Istanbul. As a result, two private school systems developed, Muslim and Christian, and grew out of competition with the Turkish system and with each other. Their tremendous success was considered the direct result of their relevance to the Arab population. The most significant consequences of education during this period were a developed awareness of modern formal education, the association of education with nationalism, and the maintained association of religion with education.

The British presence began as a result of World War I and became official in 1922 when the League of Nations gave Britain mandate over Palestine. During the three decades of British influence, education was free but not compulsory. The number of government schools increased from 100 in 1917 to 550 in 1947 while, during the same period, the percentage of school-age children enrolled in schools increased from 8% to 33%. (Mar'i 14) In the private sector, the number of Muslim schools decreased because most had been semi-nationalized by the Turks towards the end of their rule and as a result became mostly governmental. Private Christian schools, on the other hand, increased in number and were also attended by Muslims. The attraction was their modern and well-equipped facilities, particularly for the teaching of English, the language of potential employers.

In 1948, the British Mandate ended and Israel was proclaimed a state. Armistice agreements in 1949 resulted in the annexation of the Palestinian state on the West Bank of the Jordan River by the Hashemite Kingdom of Jordan and the assigned administration of the Palestinian Gaza Strip to the Egyptian Arab Republic. With the West Bank and Gaza Strip now under the jurisdiction of Jordan and Egypt, respectively, the educational system of each "parent" country was adopted. Tables 9.2 and 9.3 show the educational structure in the West Bank and Gaza Strip, respectively.

Under Jordan, the participation of West Bank Palestinians in education continued to grow and was further institutionalized by the passage of the Jordanian General Law of Education (1955) and the Educational Act of 1964. The General Law of Education stated that all schools (government, private,

Table 9.2. Structure of the Education System of the West Bank

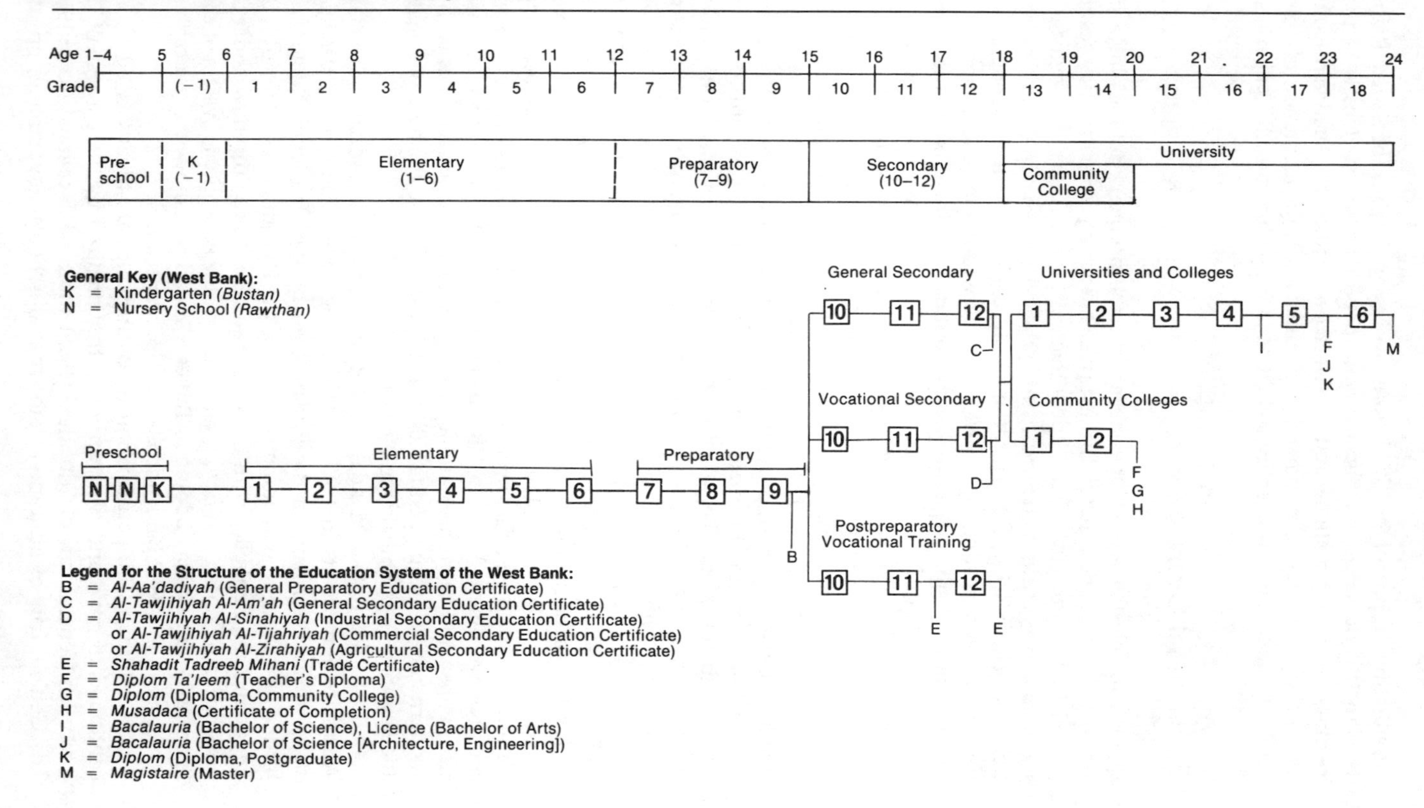

General Key (West Bank):
K = Kindergarten *(Bustan)*
N = Nursery School *(Rawthan)*

Legend for the Structure of the Education System of the West Bank:
B = *Al-Aa'dadiyah* (General Preparatory Education Certificate)
C = *Al-Tawjihiyah Al-Am'ah* (General Secondary Education Certificate)
D = *Al-Tawjihiyah Al-Sinahiyah* (Industrial Secondary Education Certificate)
or *Al-Tawjihiyah Al-Tijahriyah* (Commercial Secondary Education Certificate)
or *Al-Tawjihiyah Al-Zirahiyah* (Agricultural Secondary Education Certificate)
E = *Shahadit Tadreeb Mihani* (Trade Certificate)
F = *Diplom Ta'leem* (Teacher's Diploma)
G = *Diplom* (Diploma, Community College)
H = *Musadaca* (Certificate of Completion)
I = *Bacalauria* (Bachelor of Science), Licence (Bachelor of Arts)
J = *Bacalauria* (Bachelor of Science [Architecture, Engineering])
K = *Diplom* (Diploma, Postgraduate)
M = *Magistaire* (Master)

Table 9.3. Structure of the Education System of the Gaza Strip

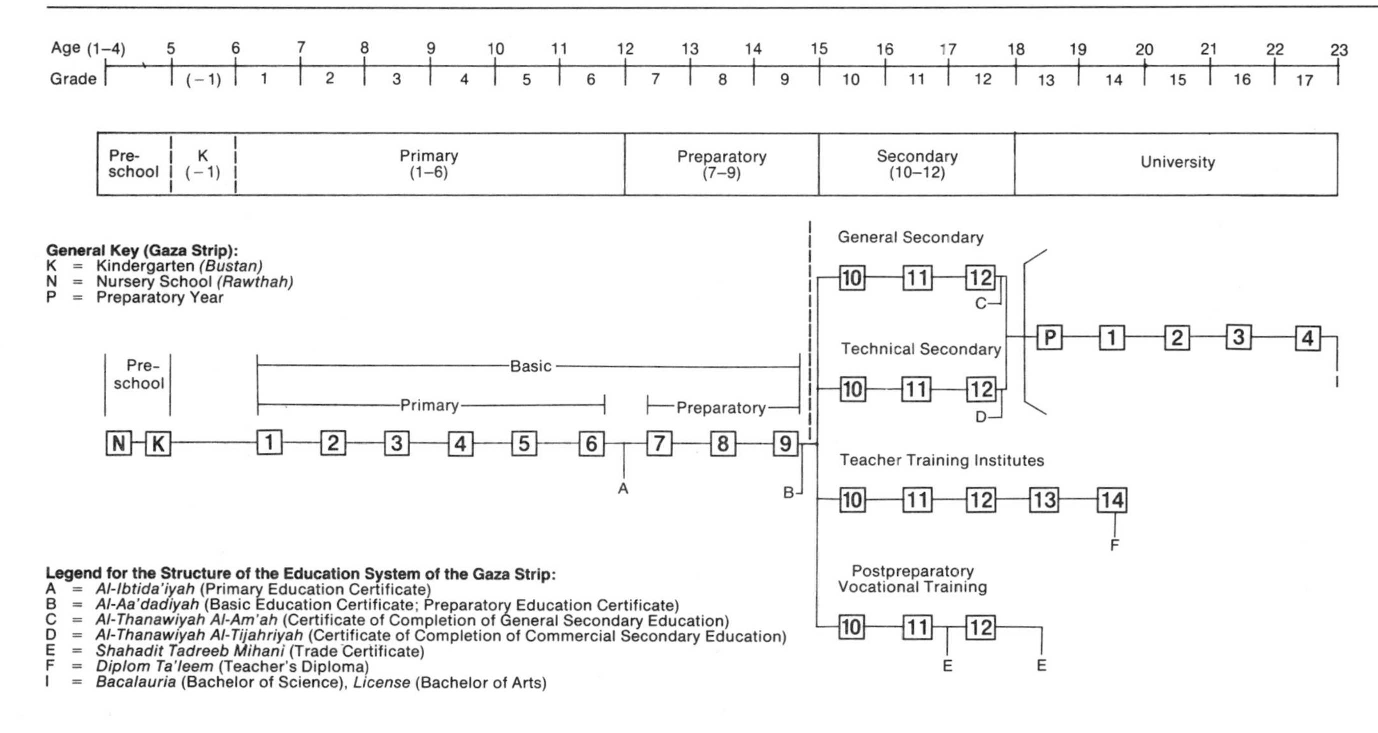

and UNRWA) were to follow the same curriculums, administer the same cyclical examinations, and maintain uniform standards. The 1964 legislation, among other things, established compulsory education through the first nine years of education, and defined these nine years as the elementary cycle (grades 1-6) and the preparatory cycle (grades 7-9).

In the Gaza Strip, education was under the Egyptian Ministry of Education, but Egypt was less directly involved in the administration of education in Gaza than was Jordan in the West Bank. Instead, the large proportion of refugees in Gaza resulted in UNRWA operating over half the schools in the area. Nevertheless, the curriculums, textbooks, and cyclical examinations of Egypt were implemented in all schools—government, UNRWA, and private.

The June 1967 War and subsequent Israeli occupation has further modified education in all the territories under discussion. The initial immediate impact was to place the people and their institutions under the authority of the Israeli military. The results of this in the West Bank, Gaza Strip and Golan Heights (until 1982) are described below. Annexation, which affected East Jerusalem and the Golan Heights (after December 1981), introduced Israeli—rather than military—law and governance. The result of annexation on education theoretically placed education under the official Israeli education system (described in Section I). Such is the case in the Golan Heights; however, in Arab East Jerusalem, the school system is an anomaly.

Arab schools in East Jerusalem have gone almost full circuit. Much resistance was encountered when the Israelis initially demanded that all Jordanian government schools change their curriculum to the Israeli Arab system (described in Section I). The major reasons for Palestinian objection centered on a Jewish/Israeli curriculum emphasizing their language, literature, history and culture. Furthermore, the Israeli Matriculation Certificate *(Teudat Bagrut)* was not and is not recognized in the Arab world. As a result, there was an immediate exodus from government schools and an increase in enrollment in private schools. The number and size of schools under the Waqf (Department of Religious Endowments, Islamic) also increased due, in part, to financial support from Jordan. These responses, in addition to boycotts and demonstrations by Palestinian teachers and parents, resulted in Israeli reconsideration and the reinstitution of the Jordanian system for preparatory and secondary schools, with some modification. In 1979, the primary cycle was also converted back to the Jordanian curriculum. East Jerusalem Arab education today is basically Jordanian, modified by censorship and other factors including the Israeli requirement that Hebrew and Israeli civilization be taught.

Education in the West Bank and the Gaza Strip is under the Israeli military authorities and is administered through a functional unit entitled the Office of Educational Affairs within the Civil Administration for Judea and Samaria. This unit is located in a military complex in Bet El just outside Ramallah and employs 10 Israelis and 858 local employees, i.e., teachers and staff. The responsibilities of this office are described as the day-to-day operation of the government educational system; supervision of educational institutions; training manpower; holding examinations; and planning and building schools, classrooms, and other educational facilities.

In actuality, the administration and implementation of education involves a complex combination of authorities including the Jordanian Ministry of Education/Department for West Bank Education, the Egyptian Ministry of Education, the Israeli Office of Education described above (operating under the Ministry of Defense rather than the Ministry of Education and Culture), District Offices of Education staffed by Palestinians, and UNRWA/UNESCO with their quasi-governmental infrastructure, none of which function without the approval of the Israeli military authorities. Financing of education comes from almost as many sources—Israel, through taxation of local residents, for education classified as government; Jordan, for employees of government institutions on the payroll in 1967; UNRWA/UNESCO for their operations through international contributions; the Joint Jordanian/Palestinian Fund for private higher education; and through private charitable organizations and donations from other nations—none of which is accessible without the approval of the military authorities. Meanwhile, the basic system of education remains Jordanian in the West Bank, including East Jerusalem, and Egyptian in the Gaza Strip, modified to the extent described above and in "Education Under Occupation."

Arab schools at all levels in the West Bank, East Jerusalem, and Gaza are categorized according to supervising authority: government, UNRWA, and private. The extent of involvement of one sector or the other varies considerably from one level of education to another as well as between the three areas. See Table 10.3 for enrollment by supervising authority and level.

The basic structure of education followed in the West Bank, including East Jerusalem, and the Gaza Strip, is essentially the same (see Table 9.2 and Table 9.3). Elementary education in both areas is six years in length. In the West Bank there is no governmental examination marking the end of this cycle; promotion to the preparatory cycle is automatic. In Gaza, however, completion of elementary education and continuation to the preparatory cycle requires success in the governmental Primary School Certificate Examination *(Al-Ibtida'iyah)*. The preparatory cycle in the West Bank and Gaza includes grades 7-9 (Prep. I, II, and III) and is concluded by the General Preparatory Certificate Examination *(Al-Aa'dadiyah)* at the end of grade 9. The results of this examination determine eligibility to continue to the secondary cycle and the stream of education to be followed.

Secondary education in the West Bank, East Jerusalem, and the Gaza Strip is a three-year cycle represented by grades 10-12 (Sec. I, II, and III) which ends in the General Secondary Education Certificate Examination. In the West Bank, this certificate is formally referred to as *Al-Tawjihiyah* and in the Gaza Strip as *Al-Thanawiyah*; in both areas, it is popularly known as *Al-Tawjihi*. Secondary education is designated according to stream as either academic (literary or scientific) or vocational (agricultural, commercial, or industrial). Secondary academic education has been the choice of the vast majority (97% in the West Bank and a similar figure in Gaza). However, the government of Jordan has recently interceded in an attempt to realign the proportion of students in academic and vocational education in the West Bank (as well as the East Bank) in accordance with economic and other related factors. Table

9.4 gives primary through secondary enrollment statistics from 1967-1984.

Higher education in the Occupied Territories has developed dramatically in the past decade, despite considerable political and financial impediments, and is almost exclusively the result of Palestinian determination and private-sector initiative. Essentially the one institution of society allowed to function and develop under the direction of Palestinians, higher education in the private sector is represented by an enrollment of some 17,000 students in 17 institutions including the community colleges, four-year colleges and universities. In the fading public sector, three government community colleges have a total enrollment of 630 students. In addition, there are three UNRWA community colleges accommodating approximately 1,100 students. All of these institutions, with the exception of one university in the Gaza Strip, are located in the West Bank.

The Academic Calendar

The academic year extends from September to June, encompassing 210 days for schools on a six-day week (Muslim) and 185 days for those on a five-day week (Christian). Days lost due to school closures extend the year as needed. Class periods in primary through secondary schools are each 40 minutes, designated weekly by level as follows: elementary, 28-35 periods; preparatory, 35-37 periods; and secondary, 37 periods. Slight deviations from stream to stream occur at the secondary level. The daily schedule is from 8 a.m. to 2 p.m. under ideal conditions. Due to the shortage of schools and classrooms, double- and triple-shifting frequently takes place.

Institutions of higher education establish their own calendars, except for the community colleges which function according to Jordanian government regulations. Four-year institutions operate on a two-semester, 30-32 week year, usually beginning in October and ending in June. Community colleges operate on a 16- to 19-week semester system.

Table 9.4. Primary and Secondary School Enrollments in the West Bank and Gaza Strip

Year	Grade: K	1–6	7–9	10–12	Total
1967–68	3,850	162,051	40,177	15,910	221,988
1969–70	7,636	191,908	55,523	26,345	281,412
1974–75	10,568	231,150	63,842	34,373	339,933
1976–77	11,086	235,830	78,273	39,435	364,624
1978–79	11,164	248,678	84,919	48,579	393,340
1980–81	12,092	259,316	83,248	53,069	407,725
1981–82	13,988	265,112	86,244	53,911	419,255
1982–83	14,665	267,848	86,631	52,172	421,316
1983–84	17,071	272,150	90,430	51,068	430,719

SOURCE: Office of the Vice-President for Planning and Development, Birzeit University 1967–1984; *Statistical Abstract of Israel*, No. 35, 1984.

Chapter 10

Preschool Through Preparatory Education

Preschool and Kindergarten Education

Preschool education in the West Bank and Gaza Strip for Palestinian children, aged 1-6, is outside the formal, free, and compulsory educational system. The availability of nursery schools and kindergartens, consequently, is the result of local initiative, volunteer organizations, and private institutions which usually charge modest fees. Women's organizations have become quite involved in promoting and establishing preschool programs, particularly in the West Bank.

The total West Bank and Gaza Strip kindergarten enrollment in 1983-84 was reported to be 17,071 children—11,630 in the West Bank and 5,441 in Gaza, including an UNRWA enrollment of 1,705. (*Statistical Abstract of Israel*, No. 35, 1984) Other sources indicate that in the West Bank (1977-78) approximately 120 kindergartens with a capacity of 213 classrooms provided preschool programs for approximately 8% of the children in this age group. During the same time period in Gaza, 33 kindergartens with 98 classes served approximately 5% of the age-specific population. More recent information on Gaza indicates there were 48 private kindergartens with 168 classrooms enrolling 4,783 children in 1981-82. (Ministry of Defense 1983, 25)

In 1985, UNRWA reported seven preschool centers for children, aged 3-6, in the West Bank, financed and operated by the Holy Land Christian Mission. They also reported 16 UNRWA-operated preschool centers for 1,705 children, aged 3-6, in the Gaza Strip, including one in the Egyptian sector of Rafah, where activities are directed by trained teachers and funding is provided by the American Friends Service Committee (AFSC), a Quaker Society.

The future status of UNRWA kindergartens in the Gaza is uncertain. (*Al-Fajr*, Vol. VII, No. 306, p. 2) UNRWA has not traditionally been involved with preschool services in the Occupied Territories. In 1980, however, UNRWA was asked to take over the AFSC operation of kindergartens as a result of an attempt by the Israeli authorities to register AFSC kindergartens with the Israeli Ministry of Labor and Social Welfare or face closure. Registration was perceived by Palestinians as an unwanted interference in preschool affairs and a threat to the future job-security of teachers and staff. UNRWA headquarters is again reviewing its involvement in the administration of kindergartens in Gaza refugee camps, despite the fact that operations are funded by the AFSC, and concerns expressed previously by the Palestinian community have re-emerged.

West Bank—Elementary and Preparatory Education

Elementary Education

Elementary education in the West Bank follows the Jordanian system of education with a compulsory six-year cycle for Palestinian children, aged 6-12, and is free for those attending government and UNRWA schools. AMIDEAST (America-Mideast Education and Training Services, Inc. Jerusalem office) estimates that 80% of the children complete this level of education. Schools are administered through one of three supervisory sectors: government, private or UNRWA. All schools, however, follow the curriculums and textbooks prescribed by the Jordanian Ministry of Education within the censorship framework described in Chapter 9.

The curriculum in elementary schools emphasizes basic literacy skills and prepares students for the next stage of education. Students study Arabic and Calligraphy, Arithmetic, English, French (in the private sector), Sciences, Social Studies and other nonacademic subjects for 30–37 (45-minute) class periods each six-day week.

Students are automatically promoted from grade 1 through grade 3. During grades 4 through 6, students who fail the year (i.e., fail more than three subjects) are permitted to repeat the grade twice. Children may be held back only twice during this cycle, after which they are automatically promoted. There is no national examination at the end of the elementary cycle, nor is there a certificate of completion. Promotion to the preparatory cycle is automatic.

The grading system is based upon a scale of 0-100 with a 50% minimum passing grade: 90-100 (Excellent), 80-89 (Very Good), 70-79 (Good), 60-69 (Acceptable), 50-59 (Poor), and 0-49 (Fail).

Preparatory Education

Following the Jordanian system of education, the preparatory cycle is a compulsory three-year program (grades 7-9 or Preparatory Years I through III) for Palestinian students, aged 12-15, and is free for those attending government and UNRWA schools. AMIDEAST estimates that 60% of the children complete the preparatory cycle. As in the elementary cycle, schools are administered through one of three supervising sectors—government, private, or UNRWA—each following Jordanian regulations with regard to prescribed curriculums, textbooks, and examinations within the restrictions of censorship described in Chapter 9.

The preparatory curriculum provides general (academic) education throughout the cycle. Each year of the three-year preparatory cycle, students study the following subjects in 45-minute class periods during the six-day week: Arabic (7 hours/week), Art Education (2), English Language (6), Mathematics (5 hours in Prep. I and II, 6 hours in Prep. III), Physical Education (2), Religion (Islamic Education for Muslims, Christian Education for Christians) (3), Sciences (4), Social Studies (3 hours in Prep. I and II, 4 hours in Prep. III), and Practical Education (Home Economics for girls; Agricultural, Technical, Commercial Education for boys) (3), for a total of 35 hours in Prep. I and II, and 37 hours in Prep. III.

In 1984-85, the Jordanian Ministry of Education reinstituted the General Preparatory Certificate (*Al-Aa'dadiyah*) Examination on the East and West Bank, after having discontinued it in 1976. *Al-Aa'dadiyah,* referred to locally as the secondary entrance examination, determines who will enter the academic or vocational tracks in the secondary cycle. The decision to reinstate the examination was made amidst considerable controversy. At issue were the limited access to academic secondary and university education that implementation would impose; the needs of the society for more vocationally-technically trained people; and a high unemployment rate among college graduates. Despite the controversy, the Jordanian government reinstated the examination and specified that no more than 60% of successful males and 70% of successful females would be allowed to enroll in government general (academic) secondary schools, effective Fall 1985. Others would be encouraged to enroll in technical-vocational education. Prior to this time, admission to the secondary cycle was based on academic performance throughout the preparatory cycle and space availability in the type of school and district desired.

The examination is organized and administered through the Jordanian Ministry of Education to students in Jordan and the West Bank who have completed the third preparatory year (grade 9). The examination is prepared, marked, and supervised by the West Bank Examinations Board through the West Bank District Office of Education in Nablus. Results of the examination are sent to the Ministry of Education in Jordan for verification, computerization, and consolidation of East and West Bank data. The 1985 examination results for the West Bank are given in Table 10.1. Comparative results for 1970-75 and 1984-86, by sector, are given in Table 10.2.

The *Al-Aa'dadiyah* examination comprises individual subject examinations in Arabic, Islamic Education (Muslims only), Mathematics, Sciences, and

Table 10.1. *Al-Aa'dadiyah* Examination Results in the West Bank, 1985

	# Examinees			# Succeeded			Success Rate (%)		
Authority	M	F	T	M	F	T	M	F	T
Government	6,691	4,766	11,457	5,888	4,515	10,403	88.0	94.7	90.8
UNRWA	1,362	1,385	2,747	1,148	1,342	2,490	84.6	96.9	90.6
Private	1,256	973	2,229	1,103	926	2,029	87.8	95.2	91.0
External Examinees	6	5	11	3	3	6	50.0	60.0	54.5
Total	9,315	7,129	16,444	8,142	6,786	14,928	87.4	95.2	90.8

SOURCE: Ministry of Education, Jordan, *Computer Directorate*, 1985. (computer data)
Note: M = Male, F = Female, T = Total.

Table 10.2. *Al-Aa'dadiyah* Examination Results: Pass Rate by Sector in the West Bank, 1970–75 and 1984–86

Year	Government Schools	UNRWA Schools	Private Schools
1970–71	73.17	58.93	65.95
1971–72	78.45	75.33	73.99
1972–73	84.36	85.07	69.00
1973–74	84.63	88.11	74.40
1974–75	84.55	89.22	78.60
*	–	–	–
1984–85	90.80	90.60	91.00
1985–86	86.60	89.90	93.00

SOURCE: *Al Fajr Jerusalem Palestinian Weekly*, Vol. VII, No. 340, p. 9.
**Al-Aa'dadiyah* was discontinued from 1975 to 1984.

Social Studies; Christians are not required to substitute another subject for Islamic Education. The passing mark in each subject is 40%, except in Arabic which requires 50%. Those who do not pass the exam are given the opportunity to repeat the third preparatory year (grade 9) and the examination as many as two times, up to the age of 16; alternatively, students may continue in a private school and retake the examination the following year. In any case, a student cannot sit for the General Secondary Education Certificate Examination (*Al-Tawjihiyah*) without having passed *Al-Aa'dadiyah*.

The Gaza Strip—Primary and Preparatory Education

Primary Education

In 1981-82, Basic Education was introduced with the extension of compulsory education from six to nine years. Basic education includes the primary and preparatory stages. In 1983-84, primary education in Gaza served some 100,000 Palestinian children, aged 6-12, in a six-year cycle which follows the Egyptian system of education. While free to those in government and UNRWA schools, schools are extremely overcrowded, a condition that has resulted in double (sometimes triple) shifting. Ninety percent of UNRWA primary schools operated on double shifts of 46 pupils per class in 1983-84 (*Al Fajr*, Vol. VII, No. 340, p. 8) and similar conditions existed in the government sector. Primary schools in Gaza are administered through one of three supervising authorities—government, UNRWA, or private—with UNRWA educating the majority and the private sector serving from 1% to 3% (see Table 10.3). All schools, however, follow the curriculums and textbooks prescribed by the Egyptian government, within the censorship restrictions described in Chapter 9.

The curriculum in primary schools provides education for basic literacy skills and preparation for the next stage of education. Students study Arabic and Calligraphy, Arithmetic, Sciences, Social Studies and other nonacademic subjects for 26–32 (45 minute) class periods each six-day week.

Government examinations are administered every second year and end with the Primary Education Certificate (*Al-Ibtida'iyah*) Examination upon completion of grade 6. Final exams for grades 1, 3, and 5 are developed and administered by the schools. As in the West Bank, the grading system is based upon a scale of 0-100 with a minimum 50% passing grade.

The Primary Education Certificate Examination represents the satisfactory completion of grade 6 and comprises four separate subject exams: Arabic Language, Arithmetic, Science, and Social Science. Students who do not pass the examination by the age of 14 are no longer eligible to continue their education. The *Al-Ibtida'iyah,* awarded upon passing the examination with a minimum of 50% (150/300), was required for promotion to the preparatory cycle until 1983, the last year the certificate was issued. The methodology used in interpreting the results is described within the section "The Preparatory Education Certificate Examination." The Certificate is issued by the Israeli military authorities.

Results from the 1986 Primary Education Certificate Examination indicate that 22 of the 102 UNRWA primary schools had a 100% pass rate. The UNRWA Field Office in Gaza reported a 91.1% average pass rate for all 102 schools, compared with 79.8% reported for government schools.

Preparatory Education

Following the Egyptian system, the preparatory cycle is the second stage of Basic Education in the Gaza Strip. Preparatory education is a three-year cycle (grades 7-9) for Palestinian students, aged 12-15, and is compulsory since 1981 and free for those attending government and UNRWA schools. Admission to the preparatory cycle required presentation of the Primary Education Certificate (*Al-Ibtida'iyah*) up until 1983 when the certificate was discontinued. As in the primary cycle, schools are administered through one of three supervising sectors: government, private or UNRWA. All schools follow Egyptian regulations with regard to prescribed curriculums, textbooks, and examinations, subject to censorship as previously noted. Education is general (academic) throughout the cycle.

The preparatory curriculum provides general (academic) education in preparation for continued education in one of several secondary streams. Each year of the three year preparatory period, students study the following subjects in 45-minute class periods each six-day week: Arabic (6 hours/week), Arithmetic and Mathematics (4), English or French (5 or 6, respectively), Handicrafts and Arts (2), Music Education (2), Physical Education (2), Practical Education (Agriculture for boys, Home Economics for girls) (2), Religion (2), Science and Hygiene (4), Social Studies (1 hour each in Arab Society, Geography, History) for a total of 31 or 32 hours per week each year.

The Preparatory Education Certificate (*Al-Aa'dadiyah*) Examination in the Gaza Strip is given at the end of the third preparatory year (grade 9). It comprises individual subject examinations in Algebra, Arabic Language, Drawing, English Language, Geography, Geometry, History, National Education, Physical Education and Health, and Religion. The passing mark in each subject is 40%, except for Drawing which is 20%, Arabic which is 50%, and Religion and National Education which are not included in the total results. The total passing mark for the examination is 50%.

Al-Aa'dadiyah examination results are reported in terms of marks achieved in relation to an assigned maximum and minimum number of marks. For each subject, the percent received is calculated by dividing the number of marks achieved by the maximum marks assigned. The same methodology is used to determine the total examination results: divide the total marks achieved by the total maximum marks. Success on the examination is determined by a minimum 50% marks achieved.

Summary Comments and Combined Statistics

Without a central authority for education in the West Bank and Gaza Strip, statistics encompassing the three operating sectors—government, UNRWA, and private—are difficult, if not impossible, to obtain. Those that are available, with the exception of UNRWA, are viewed with skepticism. Further complications exist because East Jerusalem data is rarely provided yet mention of inclusion or exclusion is seldom made. Consequently, figures provided in Table 10.3 are taken from several sources and represent the most recent data available, considering all the variables. To update this, a projected 1986-87 estimated total enrollment of 432,541 has been calculated based upon a 2% annual growth rate. This rate is based on AMIDEAST's estimated primary school growth rate of less than 2% and a combined primary-through-secondary rate of approximately 2.5% (AMIDEAST unpublished report, 1985); 2% is, therefore, a conservative estimate.

Total enrollment figures in Table 10.3 indicate that government schools provide 60% of all primary/preparatory education in East Jerusalem, the West

Table 10.3. Elementary and Preparatory Enrollment in East Jerusalem, the West Bank, and Gaza Strip According to Supervising Authority, 1981–82

Authority	EJ	WB	GS	Total Primary	Total Prep.	Total Combined
Government						
Primary	8,812	132,764	37,616	179,192	—	—
(Schools)		(381)*	(39)			
Preparatory	2,551	43,554	9,615	—	55,720	—
(Schools)		(222)*	(20)			
Combined	11,363	176,318	47,231	—	—	234,912
(Schools)		(603)*	(59)			
% Govt. by Area	27%	78%	37.8%	59.6%	61%	60%

continued

UNRWA						
Primary	17,824	28,568	58,007	104,399	—	—
(Schools)			(102)			
Preparatory	†	10,846	19,349	—	30,195	—
(Schools)			(39)			
Combined	17,824	39,414	77,356	—	—	134,594
(Schools)		(98)	(141)			
% UNRWA by Area	43%	18%	61.9%	34.8%	33%	34%
Private						
Primary	9,012	7,453	237†	16,702	—	—
(Schools)			(1)			
Preparatory	3,379	2,180	†	—	5,559	—
Combined	12,391	9,633	237	—	—	22,261
(Schools)		(70)*				
% Private by Area	30%	4%	0.2%	5.6%	6%	6%
Grand Totals	41,578	225,365	124,824	300,293	91,474	391,767

SOURCES: Leslie C. Schmida and Deborah G. Keenum (eds.), *Education in the Middle East*, AMIDEAST, 1983; State of Israel, Ministry of Defense, "Judea-Samaria and the Gaza District, a Sixteen-Year Survey (1967–83)," November 1983; The Civil Administration of Judea and Samaria, *The Civil Administration of Judea and Samaria Annual Report*, 1984–85. (typewritten)
Note: EJ = East Jerusalem, WB = West Bank, GS = Gaza Strip.
*1985 data.
†Incomplete or no data available.

Bank, and Gaza Strip, while UNRWA contributes 34% and private schools 6%. These figures vary considerably, however, when each area is viewed separately. The private sector calculated contribution of 6% is deceptively low due to little or no data from Gaza. UNRWA, on the other hand, plays a dominant role in education in East Jerusalem and Gaza, providing 43% and 62%, respectively, of all primary/preparatory education.

Chapter 11

Secondary Education

Secondary Education in the West Bank

Secondary education in the West Bank is a three-year cycle designated as first secondary, second secondary, and third secondary (grades 10, 11, and 12) for Palestinian students, 15-18 years of age, and follows the Jordanian system of education. This level of education is free in government schools, but not compulsory. Secondary schools on the West Bank, whether government or private, implement the curriculums, textbooks, and examinations prescribed by the Jordanian Ministry of Education within the censorship restrictions described in Chapter 9.

Secondary education is provided by either government or private schools. The United Nations Relief and Works Agency for Palestine Refugees in the Near East (UNRWA) does not operate secondary schools but does provide, under certain conditions, assistance to enable its preparatory school graduates to attend government or private secondary schools. Within the government and private sectors, further distinction of schools is made according to the type of educational program offered: general or academic (literary or scientific), or vocational (agricultural, commercial or industrial).

In 1985-86, the government operated 212 secondary schools enrolling 30,373 students. According to 1981-82 enrollment figures, government schools provided secondary education to 85% of the student population, leaving the private sector to educate the remaining 15%. In sharp contrast, 70% of East Jerusalem Arab students are enrolled in private secondary schools—9 Christian, 20 private or religious, and 17 owned by the Waqf (Ministry of Islamic Religious Endowments). (See "East Jerusalem" in Chapter 9.)

Admission to the Secondary Cycle

Since Fall 1985, admission to the various types of secondary schools in the West Bank has been determined by the student's results on the General Preparatory Certificate Examination, also referred to as the Secondary Entrance Examination or *Al-Aa'dadiyah*. The Jordanian Ministry of Education has indicated that it will restrict enrollment in government general (academic) schools to no more than 60% of successful males and 70% of successful females, as determined by those who pass *Al-Aa'dadiyah*. Those who fall outside this criteria will be encouraged to enroll in vocational secondary schools. (See "The General Preparatory Certificate Examination" in Chapter 10 and Tables 10.1 and 10.2.)

Prior to 1985, admission to the secondary cycle was based upon overall scholastic achievement during the preparatory cycle and the availability of space in the type of school and district desired.

Types of Secondary Education

Several types of secondary education are available on the West Bank. The two basic classifications of secondary education are general (academic) and vocational. General secondary education becomes further specialized into the Literary Stream and Scientific Stream after the first year secondary (grade 10). Vocational secondary education is designated and differentiated at the onset according to stream as either Agricultural, Commercial, or Industrial. All programs lead to the final examination of the secondary cycle: the Secondary Education Certificate *(Al-Tawjihiyah)* Examination, administered by the General Examinations Board for the West Bank, Examinations Division, in Nablus on behalf of the Jordanian Ministry of Education.

By far the largest proportion of secondary students enroll in general (academic) education. In 1984-85, approximately 96.5% of all third year secondary students in the West Bank were studying in the Literary and Scientific Streams, while the remaining 3.5% were engaged in vocational secondary education. The number and proportion of third year secondary students in each stream who applied for *Al-Tawjihiyah* examination in 1984-85 are as follows: 8,866 (70.0%) in the Literary Stream; 3,348 (26.5%) in the Scientific Stream; 372 (2.9%) in the Industrial-Vocational Stream; 53 (0.4%) in the Commercial-Vocational Stream; and 19 (0.2%) in the Agricultural-Vocational Stream for a total of 12,658 applicants. (See *Al-Tawjihiyah* statistics in Tables 11.2 and 11.8.)

The uneven distribution of students studying in the academic and vocational streams may, within the next several years, show signs of redistribution. The re-introduction of the General Preparatory Certificate Examination in 1985 and restrictions placed on eligibility to academic secondary education in government schools were meant to directly address this imbalance.

General Secondary Programs

General (academic) education seeks to prepare students for higher education. All students of the first year secondary cycle follow a common curriculum. Streaming into the Literary or Scientific sections occurs in the second year secondary (grade 11) and is determined primarily by the student's performance in mathematics and science. Admission to the Scientific Stream is more competitive and prestigious than to the Literary Stream; just over one-quarter of all academic secondary students are enrolled in the Scientific Stream.

Table 11.1 illustrates the prescribed secondary curriculums for the Scientific and Literary Streams with the number of 45-minute class periods each week allocated to each subject. While yearly transcripts from individual schools may reflect an enhancement in some area, such as foreign language, all will contain at least the subjects listed in Table 11.1, which are prescribed by the Jordanian Ministry of Education.

Table 11.1. West Bank General Secondary Curriculums by Stream and Distribution of Class Periods Each Week by Subject

Subjects	Grade 10 Sec. I		Grade 11 Sec. II		Grade 12 Sec. III		*Al-Tawjihiyah* Exam	
	Sci.	Lit.	Sci.	Lit.	Sci.	Lit.	Sci.	Lit.
Arabic	5	5	5	7	5	7	x	x
Arab Society	—	—	—	—	1	1	x	x
Art Education	1	1	1	1	1	1	—	—
Biology	2	2	3	—	3	—	x	—
Chemistry	—	—	3	—	3	—	x	—
English	5	5	5	7	5	7	x	x
General Science	—	—	—	2	—	2	—	x
Geography	2	2	—	2	—	2	—	x
History	2	2	—	3	—	3	—	x
Islamic Education	3	3	3	3	3	3	x	x
Mathematics	5	5	5	2	6	2	x	x
Palestine Problem	—	—	—	—	1	1	x	x
Physical Sciences	5	5	—	—	—	—	—	—
Physics	—	—	5	—	4	—	x	—
Physical Education	2	2	2	2	2	2	—	—
Voc. Educ. (boys) or Home Sci. (girls)	2	2	2	2	2	2	—	—
Totals	34	34	34	31	36	33	—	—

Vocational Secondary Programs

Vocational secondary education is designated as either Agricultural, Commercial, or Industrial and offers curriculums emphasizing general education as well as vocational training. While originally intended to supply skilled manpower to the work force, the aim of vocational education has been influenced by several factors: technological advances have required a more sophisticated and better-educated work force; educational opportunities in postsecondary technical professions have become more available through the network of community colleges and the Polytechnic; and unemployment of university graduates increases annually. Although vocational enrollment is currently low, the (Jordanian) government's recent restriction on admission to academic secondary programs is expected to increase vocational secondary enrollment, upgrade the perceived status of vocational education, and have an impact on postsecondary education in the technical-vocational professions.

Vocational secondary education in the West Bank consists of one agricultural government school in the district of Hebron, one private commercial school in the Bethlehem district, and six industrial schools in the districts of Bethlehem, Nablus, Ramallah, Tulkarm, and the municipality of Jerusalem, both private and government. The names and locations of these schools are as follows:

1. Al-Arrub Agricultural Secondary School, outside Hebron (government).
2. Lutheran Vocational Training Center, Beit Hanina (private).
3. Jerusalem Industrial Secondary School for Arab Orphans Committee, Beit Hanina (from 1965, private).
4. Salisian Industrial Secondary School, Bethlehem (private).
5. Abdullah Bin Hussain Industrial School, Sheikh Jarrah, Jerusalem (municipality of Jerusalem, government).
6. Nablus Industrial School, Nablus (government).
7. Tulkarm Industrial School, Tulkarm (government).
8. Deir Dibwan Industrial Secondary School, Ramallah (government).

VOCATIONAL TRAINING CENTERS. There is a distinction made between vocational secondary schools, which provide three-year programs culminating in *Al-Tawjihiyah*, and Vocational Training Centers which provide two- to three-year "postpreparatory" programs resulting in a trade certificate (*Shahadat Tadreeb Mihani*) rather than *Al-Tawjihiyah*. ("Training Centers" also has a special definition when associated with UNRWA schools where *both* postpreparatory and postsecondary programs are provided. See UNRWA, Chapter 12.) The vocational secondary schools listed above should not be confused with the following postpreparatory vocational training centers:

1. The Lutheran Vocational Training Center.
2. Kalandia Vocational Training Center (UNRWA).
3. The Industrial Islamic Orphans School.
4. Ramallah Women's Training Center (UNRWA).

In addition, there are numerous nonformal vocational training programs in trades such as auto repair, construction, general mechanics, and needlework which lead to unofficial certificates used for employment purposes only.

VOCATIONAL CURRICULUMS. The curriculums for all vocational secondary programs are regulated by the Jordanian Ministry of Education and are implemented in both government and private schools. The agricultural, commercial, and industrial schools which are included under the general classification of vocational secondary education lead to the Agricultural, Commercial and Industrial *Tawjihiyah*, respectively. The curriculums combine general (academic) coursework with vocational studies.

The agricultural curriculum consists of general (academic) education, science, technical, and practical education in the ratios 15%, 15%, 28% and 42%, respectively. Of the 19 agricultural applicants for the Agricultural Secondary Education Certificate Examination *(Al-Tawjihiyah Al-Zirahiyah)* in 1985, 14 students passed and received the Certificate.

The commercial curriculum consists of general (academic) education courses which constitute 40% of the program. The remaining 60% of the program consists of commercial courses which include Accountancy and Bookkeeping; Arabic and English Typing, Commerce and Economics, Commercial Correspondence, Commercial Mathematics, Secretarial and Office Practice, and Statistics. Of the 53 commercial applicants for the Commercial Secondary Education Certificate Examination *(Al-Tawjihiyah Al-Tijahriyah)* in 1985, 34 (or 64.2%) passed and received the Certificate.

The industrial curriculum includes 44 scheduled hours weekly with 22 hours devoted to general (academic) and theoretical study in addition to 22 hours of technical and industrial training in one of many trade specializations. The first year consists of general (academic) coursework, technical-industrial basic training, and general vocational orientation. At the end of the first year the student chooses a trade speciality according to a priority ranking based upon past academic performance. This trade speciality is then studied for the remaining two years, along with the following general (academic) subjects: Arabic, Chemistry, English, Health and Industrial Safety, Homeland and Geography (Cultural Studies), Mathematics, Physical Education, Physics/Mechanics, Religious Education, Technical Drawing, Technology, and Workshop Management. The trade specializations include Air Conditioning and Refrigeration, Auto Mechanics, Building Construction, Carpentry, Electrical Generation, Electrical Transmission and Distribution, Electrical Utilization, Forging and Welding, Plumbing and Central Heating, Radio and Television, Shuttering and Reinforcing, Turning and Fitting, and Upholstery. In 1985, of the 372 industrial applicants for the Industrial Secondary Education Certificate Examination *(Al-Tawjihiyah Al-Sinahiyah)*, 240 (or 65%) passed and received the Certificate.

Grading and Transcripts

Official English translations of Arabic transcripts are available for all streams of general and vocational education. Separate documents for each year are designated First Secondary, Second Secondary, and Third Secondary (or Sec. I, Sec. II and Sec. III), corresponding to grades 10, 11 and 12. (See sample document 11.3 for a grade 12 transcript.)

The transcripts list the minimum passing grade, maximum grade, and grade received in each subject. Grades are reported in absolute percentages and are not equated to a letter grade on the transcript. The passing mark is 50%. The grading system used in the West Bank throughout the primary and secondary cycles (all streams) follows.

90–100 =	Excellent	60–69 =	Acceptable
80– 89 =	Very good	50–59 =	Poor
70– 79 =	Good	0–49 =	Fail

The Secondary Education Certificate Examination *(Al-Tawjihiyah)*

The final external examination of the secondary cycle is called *al-Tawjihiyah*, popularly known as *Al-Tawjihi*. This terminology is used with respect to both the certificate and the examination. The certificate and examination are specifically designated according to type of education as follows:

General Secondary Education Certificate/*Al-Tawjihiyah Al-Am'ah*
Agricultural Secondary Education Certificate/*Al-Tawjihiyah Al-Zirahiyah*
Commercial Secondary Education Certificate/*Al-Tawjihiyah Al-Tijahriyah*
Industrial Secondary Education Certificate/*Al-Tawjihiyah Al-Sinahiyah*

Al-Tawjihiyah is organized and administered through the Jordanian Ministry of Education. As a result of the occupation of the West Bank, *Al-Tawjihiyah* is prepared, marked, and supervised through the district office of education in Nablus by the General Examination Board for the West Bank, Examinations Division. The examination is given in two parts with half the material of each subject being covered in January and the other half in June. Results of the examination are sent to the Ministry of Education in Jordan for verification, computerization, and consolidation of East and West Bank data; publication of the results is made approximately one month after the June examination. The Certificate is issued by both the Ministry of Education, Jordan, and the General Examinations Board for the West Bank, Examinations Division, signed by the Chairman of the Examinations Board, Muta O. Abu Hijleh.

The "transcript of grades" for the Secondary Education Certificate examination is a separate document from the Certificate. The transcript of grades clearly identifies one of the five streams and indicates "Syllabus of 3rd Secondary Class." This latter reference does not refer to the transcript of school grades for the Third Year Secondary which is a separate document. In summary, there are three documents available upon satisfactory completion of *Al-Tawjihiyah* examination: the Certificate (issued by either the Ministry of Education in Jordan or the General Examinations Board for the West Bank), the transcript of the Certificate examination results, and a transcript of the school grades for the Third Secondary class (grade 12). (See sample documents 11.1, 11.2, and 11.3, respectively.)

The regulations for award of the Certificate stipulate that at least 60% must be achieved. In the Science Stream, the grand total from which a passing result is determined is calculated on the sum of grades of six subjects: Arabic, English, Mathematics, and the highest grades of any other three subjects. Arabic and English each carry a maximum score of 200, Mathematics a maximum of 300, and the three optional subjects a maximum score of 100. Since more than six subject scores will be reported, it should be noted that the "Grand Total" reflects the total of six subject examinations only, and not the actual total marks achieved. The method used in calculating the grand total on certificates from other streams is noted at the bottom of the document.

Theoretically, *Al-Tawjihiyah* gives the holder access to higher education. Most local colleges and universities, however, perceive 70% as the minimum acceptable standard for admission and give consideration only to those graduating from the Literary and Scientific Streams. Thus, competition for limited space, especially in sciences and engineering, results in some programs only accepting students with a much higher average. Actually, there is a self-imposed selectivity inherent to the system: in 1985, those passing the examination in the Science and Literary Streams numbered 77% and 59%, respectively, of those sitting for the examination; and the number of students who reach this level of education represent approximately 30% of their age-specific group. While those who achieve less than 70% may be excluded from the program or institution of their choice, opportunity for further education exists in community colleges and in less competitive programs. Comprehensive *Tawjihiyah* statistics for 1985 are presented in Tables 11.2. and 11.3.

Table 11.2. West Bank *Al-Tawjihiyah* Examination Results by Stream, 1985

Stream	# Sat	# Passed	% Passed
Literary	8,770	5,171	58.9%
Science	3,324	2,562	77.1%
Industrial	371	240	64.6%
Commercial	53	34	64.2%
Agricultural	19	14	73.7%
Totals	12,537	8,021	64.0%

SOURCE: Ministry of Education, Jordan, 1985. (in Arabic)

Secondary Education in the Gaza Strip

Secondary education in the Gaza Strip is a three-year cycle represented by grades 10, 11, and 12 for students 15-18 years of age, and follows the Egyptian system of education. Secondary schools in the Gaza Strip implement the curriculums, textbooks, and examinations prescribed by the Egyptian Ministry of Education within the censorship restrictions described in Chapter 9.

Secondary students in the Gaza Strip are almost exclusively enrolled in government schools; one private secondary school exists. As elsewhere, UNRWA does not administer secondary education in the Gaza Strip. Various sources indicate that enrollment in private schools represents from 1%-3% of all secondary enrollment.

The amount of public information and data on secondary education in the Gaza Strip is quite limited. The *Statistical Abstract of Israel* (No. 35, 1984) reports that there were 17,992 students enrolled in "postprimary" schools (grades 10, 11, and 12) during the 1983-84 academic year. Other sources report that during the same year 7,345 students sat for the Certificate of Completion of Secondary Education *(Al-Thanawiyah)* Examination.

Admission to the Secondary Cycle

Admission to each type of secondary education is based upon the results of the Preparatory (Basic) Education Certificate Examination *(Al-Aa'dadiyah)*. Only those who pass the examination and receive the Certificate are eligible to continue their education at the secondary level. Admission is competitive due to the limited number of schools and classrooms. This, along with economic, social, and political factors, results in approximately 30% of the age-specific group completing grade 12. (See "Preparatory Education in the Gaza Strip" in Chapter 10.)

Table 11.3. The West Bank *Al-Tawjihiyah* Examination Results, Combined Streams by District and Sector, 1985

District		Government Schools			Private Schools			External Examinees			Total			Totals: M & F		
		SAT	PASS	%	SAT	PASS	%	SAT	PASS	%	SAT	PASS	%	SAT	PASS	%
Bethlehem	(M)	341	202	59	722	514	71	204	72	35	1,267	788	62	2,397	1,533	64
	(F)	232	151	65	740	528	71	158	66	42	1,130	745	66			
Hebron	(M)	1,080	549	51	202	149	74	305	136	45	1,587	834	53	2,375	1,270	54
	(F)	629	350	56	44	32	73	115	54	47	788	436	55			
Jenin	(M)	733	474	65	170	109	64	228	101	44	1,131	684	61	1,695	1,085	64
	(F)	465	345	74	16	10	63	83	46	55	564	401	71			
Nablus	(M)	776	512	66	356	230	65	301	128	43	1,433	870	61	2,357	1,584	67
	(F)	718	604	84	41	22	54	165	88	53	924	714	77			
Ramallah	(M)	578	387	67	242	189	78	174	73	42	994	649	65	1,583	1,051	66
	(F)	375	267	71	106	87	82	108	48	44	589	402	68			
Tulkarm	(M)	954	718	75	58	27	47	179	81	45	1,191	826	69	1,882	1,356	72
	(F)	588	485	82	11	8	73	92	37	40	691	530	77			
Exam Dept.	(M)	–	–	–	–	–	–	191	100	52	191	100	52	206	105	51
	(F)	–	–	–	–	–	–	15	5	33	15	5	33			
Totals		7,469	5,044	68	2,708	1,905	70	2,318	1,035	45	12,495	7,984	64	12,495	7,984	64

SOURCE: Adaptation from the Ministry of Education, Examinations Division, Jordan. (in Arabic)
Note: M = Male; F = Female.

Types of Secondary Education

Egyptian secondary education provides three types of programs—general (academic), technical (agricultural, commercial, and industrial), and teacher training (for primary schools). Secondary education in Gaza, however, is primarily general (academic). Of the 25 Gaza secondary schools (see Table 11.4), all provide general education except two teacher training institutes, one technical-commercial school, and one technical-agricultural school which was closed at the end of the 1984-85 academic year. Consequently, there is no agricultural or industrial education in the Gaza Strip.

General and technical secondary education leads to the Certificate of Completion of Secondary Studies *(Al-Thanawiyah),* designated according to programs as either general *(Al-Am'ah)* or commercial *(Al-Tijahriyah).* Secondary schools institutes for teacher training do not lead to *Al-Thanawiyah. Al-Thanawiyah* is administered under the direction of the Egyptian Ministry of Education since there is no local examinations board in Gaza as there is in the West Bank. Note: *Al-Thanawiyah* was in the past referred to as *Al-Tawjihiyah,* or, more popularly, *Al-Tawjihi.* These words are interchangeable and carry essentially the same meaning. The change in terminology also accounts for the difference in translations of certificates. The "Certificate of Completion of General Secondary Education" *(Al-Thanawiyah Al-Am'ah)* is the same as the "General Secondary Education Certificate" *(Al-Tawjihiyah Al-Am'ah).*

General Secondary Programs

General (academic) education is a three-year program in preparation for higher education. In the first year, the curriculum is common for all students. Streaming into either the literary or scientific sections occurs in the second year. The Scientific Stream is further specialized in the third year into science (biology)

Table 11.4. Secondary Schools in the Gaza Strip by Locale

Gaza (Town) and Jabaliya	
Agricultural Secondary School (M)	Al-Rafedein Secondary School (M)
Ahmad Shawqi Secondary School (F)	Al-Zahra Secondary School (F)
Basheer Al-Rayes Secondary School (F)	Palestine Secondary School (M)
Al-Falouja Secondary School (M)	Yaffa Secondary School (M)
Al-Falouja Secondary School (F)	School of Female Teachers (I)
Al-Karmel Secondary School (M)	School of Male Teachers (I)
Deir El-Balah and Khan Younis	
El-Khanssa Secondary School (F)	Khaled Secondary School (M)
Al-Manfalouti Secondary School (M)	Khaled Secondary School (F)
Al-Mutanabbi Secondary School (M)	Khan Younis Secondary School (M)
Hatem El-Taa'i Secondary School (M)	Khan Younis Secondary School (F)
Ibn Khaldoun Commercial Sec. School (F)	Sukayna Bent Al-Husein Sec. School (F)
Rafah Area	
Bir Al-Sabba' Secondary School (M)	Rafah Secondary School (F)
Bir Al-Sabba' Secondary School (F)	

Note: M = Male, F = Female, I = Institute

and mathematics sections. Third-year students in any stream may choose to study Arabic, English or French at an advanced level. This option requires an additional class session per week but can increase the total points in *al-Thanawiyah Al-Am'ah* exams. General secondary education curiculums are provided in Table 11.5.

First- and second-year final grades are based 50% on performance throughout the year and 50% on a final written exam. Grades are reported on the basis of a 0-100 point scale with 50 as the lowest passing mark. Upon completion of the third year (grade 12), students sit for the Certificate of Completion of General Secondary Education *(Al-Thanawiyah Al-Am'ah)* Examination. (See sample document 11.4.) The exam is given according to the syllabus of the Egyptian Ministry of Education over a two-week period in June. Subject examinations are given one per day and differ according to stream—literary, science or mathematics. The minimum and maximum passing marks vary by subject and are indicated on the certificate. The minimum total passing mark is 50%. Interpretive methodology is described in "The Preparatory Education Certificate Examination" in Chapter 10. *Al-Thanawiyah Al-Am'ah* statistics for the Gaza Strip from 1979-85 are presented in Table 11.6.

Technical Education Programs

The only technical secondary program currently available in the Gaza Strip is in commercial studies. The three-year curriculum in commercial studies includes general (academic) studies, commercial courses, and practice (see Table 11.7).

Table 11.5. The Gaza Strip General Secondary Curriculums by Stream: Class Periods Each Week by Subject

	Grade 10	Grade 11		Grade 12		
Subject		Arts	Sci.	Arts	Sci.	Math
Arabic	6	7	5	6	5	5
Art	1	1	—	—	—	—
Biology	2	—	3	—	4	—
Chemistry	2	—	3	—	3	3
Civics	1	1	1	1	1	1
Economics	—	1	—	—	—	—
Foreign Lang. 1	6	7	5	6	5	5
Foreign Lang. 2	3	5	3	5	3	3
Geography	2	3	—	3	—	—
History	2	3	—	3	—	—
Mathematics	4	—	6–7	—	4–5	8–9
Philos. & Logic	—	—	—	3	—	—
Phys. Educ.	2	2	2	2	2	2
Physics	2	—	3	—	3	3
Religion	2	2	2	2	2	2
Sociology	—	1	—	—	—	—
Practical Studies	1	2	1	2	1	1
Totals	36	35	35–36	35	35–36	35–36

Table 11.6. The Gaza Strip *Al-Thanawiyah* Examination Results by Stream, 1979–85

	Literary		Science	
Year	# Sat	# Passed (%)	# Sat	# Passed (%)
1979–80	3,101	2,049 (66.1%)	2,316	1,665 (72.8%)
1980–81	3,647	2,691 (73.8%)	2,357	1,846 (78.3%)
1981–82	3,716	3,161 (85.1%)	2,254	1,945 (86.3%)
1982–83	3,992	2,384 (59.7%)	2,256	1,671 (74.1%)
1983–84	4,742	3,465 (73.1%)	2,403	1,862 (69.9%)
1984–85*	7,734	3,465 (66.6%) +1,682 (5,147)	7,734	1,682 (66.6%) +3,465 (5,147)

	Commercial		Agricultural	
Year	# Sat	# Passed (%)	# Sat	# Passed (%)
1979–80	176	157 (89.2%)	29	25 (86.2%)
1980–81	175	148 (90.3%)	41	32 (78.1%)
1981–82	177	169 (95.5%)	20	14 (70.0%)
1982–83	219	203 (92.5%)	27	27 (100.0%)
1983–84	185	176 (95.1%)	—	— —
1984–85*	—	— —	—	— —

*Statistics in 1984–85 provide the # Passed by stream but a combined literary/science figure for the # Sat.

First- and second-year final grades are based 40% on performance throughout the year and 60% on end-of-year examination. Promotion is based upon achieving 50% of the maximum marks in each subject. Upon completion of the third year (grade 12), students sit for the Certificate of Completion of Commercial Secondary Education *(Al-Thanawiyah Al-Tijahriyah)* Examination. Exams are given according to the syllabus of the Egyptian Ministry of Education over each subject taught in the third year and include a practical and oral test. Again, 50% of the maximum marks constitutes a pass and eligibility for the Certificate.

Agricultural education was offered in Gaza in one school until its closure in June 1985. The curriculum included general (academic) courses and professional agricultural courses. Academic subjects and weekly class periods each year include Arabic (3,3,3), Biology (3,-,-), Foreign Language (3,3,3), General Science (2,-,-), Math (3,-,-), and National Education, Physical Education and Religion. Agricultural subjects are taught during 20, 28, and 31 class periods over three years. The three-year agricultural program resulted in the Certificate of Completion of Agricultural Secondary Education *(Al-Thanawiyah Al-Zirahiyah).*

Teacher Training Programs

The third type of secondary education is teacher training for primary schools, a five-year program representing grades 10 through 14. This program does not lead to *Al-Thanawiyah,* as do all other secondary programs, but instead results in a Teacher's Diploma after the final year. See Chapter 13, "Teacher Training" and Table 13.1 for details.

Table 11.7. The Gaza Strip Commercial Secondary Curriculum: Class Periods Each Week by Subject

Subjects	Year 1	Year 2	Year 3
General Subjects	(25)	(18)	(15)
Arabic	7	6	5
Foreign Language	7	6	5
General Science	2	—	—
Mathematics	3	—	—
National Education	3	3	2
Physical Education	1	1	1
Religious Education	2	2	2
Professional Subjects	(6)	(14)	(18)
Accounting	3	4	3
Arabic, Secretarial	3	3	2
Basics of Commerce	2	—	—
Basics of Economics	—	2	2
Commercial Math	—	3	3
Foreign Language, Secretarial	—	2	2
Government Accounting	—	—	2
Insurance Law	—	—	2
Statistics	—	—	2
Practical Subjects	(4)	(5)	(4)
Typewriter Maintenance	1	—	—
Typing, Arabic	3	3	2
Typing, Foreign Language	—	2	2

Certificate No. : ______

GENERAL EXAMINATIONS BOARD
FOR THE WEST BANK

GENERAL SECONDARY EDUCATION CERTIFICATE
THE GENERAL EXAMINATIONS BOARD FOR THE WEST BANK

CERTIFIES THAT ______

BORN IN Jerusalem IN THE YEAR 1967

HAS SUCCESSFULLY PASSED

THE GENERAL SECONDARY EDUCATION EXAMINATION,

Literary STREAM IN THE YEAR 1985

ACCORDINGLY he IS AWARDED THIS CERTIFICATE.

ISSUED AT NABLUS ON THE second DAY OF August

IN THE YEAR ONE THOUSAND NINE HUNDRED AND Eighty four.

General Examinations Board For the West Bank Examinations Division

CHAIRMAN OF THE BOARD

11.1. General Secondary Education Certificate (*Al-Tawjihiyah Al-Am'ah*), West Bank

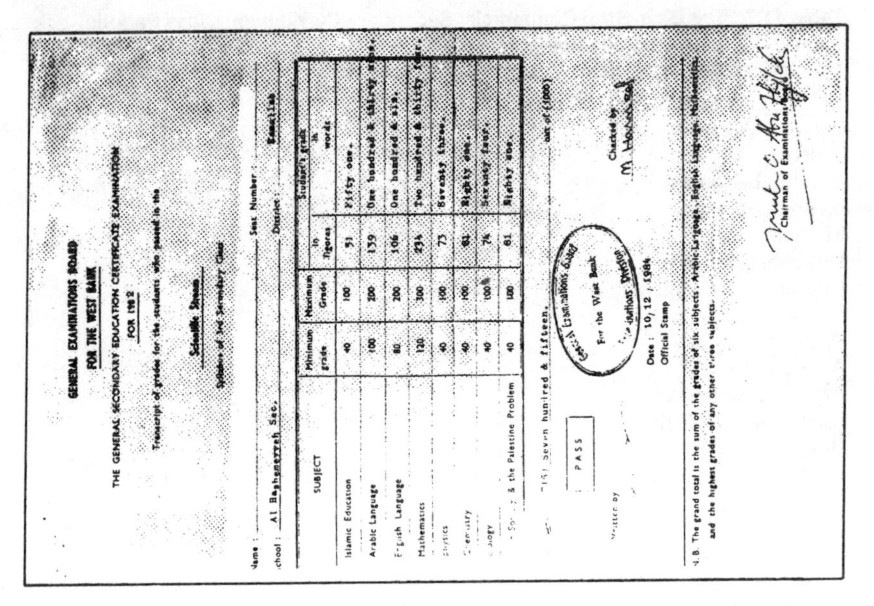

GENERAL EXAMINATIONS BOARD
FOR THE WEST BANK

THE GENERAL SECONDARY EDUCATION CERTIFICATE EXAMINATION
FOR 1982

Transcript of grades for the students who passed in the

Scientific Stream

Syllabus of 3rd Secondary Class

Name : ______ Seat Number : ______

School : Al Bashemeyyeh Sec. District : Ramallah

SUBJECT	Minimum grade	Maximum Grade	Student's grade In figures	Student's grade In words
Islamic Education	40	100	51	Fifty one.
Arabic Language	100	200	139	One hundred & thirty nine.
English Language	80	200	106	One hundred & six.
Mathematics	120	300	234	Two hundred & thirty four.
Physics	40	100	73	Seventy three.
Chemistry	40	100	81	Eighty one.
Biology	40	100	74	Seventy four.
Arab Society & the Palestine Problem	40	100	81	Eighty one.

715 Seven hundred & fifteen. out of (1000)

PASS

Written by

General Examinations Board For the West Bank Examinations Division

Checked by M. Hammad

Date : 10, 12 , 1984
Official Stamp

N.B. The grand total is the sum of the grades of six subjects, Arabic Language, English Language, Mathematics, and the highest grades of any other three subjects.

Chairman of Examinations Board

11.2. General Secondary Education Cerificate (*Al-Tawjihiyah Al-Am'ah*), Examination Results, West Bank

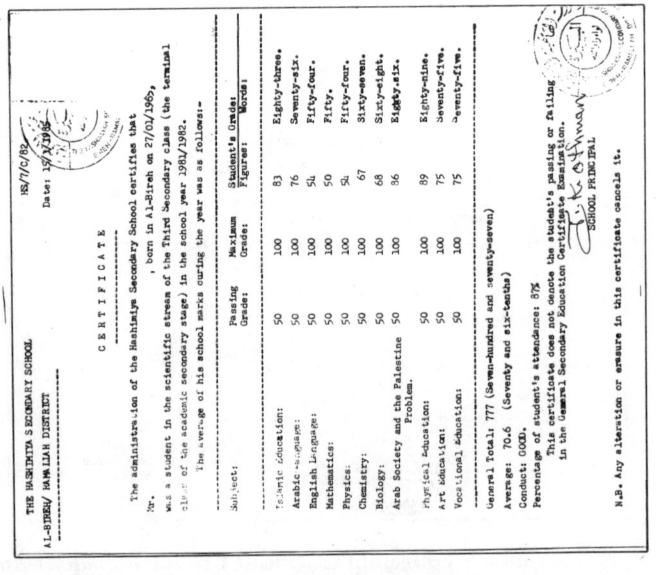

THE HASHIMIYA SECONDARY SCHOOL HS/7/C/82
AL-BIREH/ RAMALLAH DISTRICT Date: 15/3/1982

CERTIFICATE

The administration of the Hashimiya Secondary School certifies that
Mr. , born in Al-Bireh on 27/01/1965,
was a student in the scientific stream of the Third Secondary class (the terminal class of the academic secondary stage) in the school year 1981/1982.
The average of his school marks during the year was as follows:-

Subject:	Passing Grade:	Maximum Grade:	Student's Grade: Figures:	Student's Grade: Words:
Islamic Education:	50	100	83	Eighty-three.
Arabic Language:	50	100	76	Seventy-six.
English Language:	50	100	54	Fifty-four.
Mathematics:	50	100	50	Fifty.
Physics:	50	100	54	Fifty-four.
Chemistry:	50	100	67	Sixty-seven.
Biology:	50	100	68	Sixty-eight.
Arab Society and the Palestine Problem.	50	100	86	Eighty-six.
Physical Education:	50	100	89	Eighty-nine.
Art Education:	50	100	75	Seventy-five.
Vocational Education:	50	100	75	Seventy-five.

General Total: 777 (Seven-hundred and seventy-seven)
Average: 70.6 (Seventy and six-tenths)
Conduct: GOOD.
Percentage of student's attendance: 87%
This certificate does not denote the student's passing or failing in the General Secondary Education Certificate Examination.

SCHOOL PRINCIPAL

N.B. Any alteration or erasure in this certificate cancels it.

11.3. Transcript, Third Year Secondary, West Bank

DEPARTMENT OF EDUCATION & CULTURE
GAZA STRIP

Date: 30 / 8 /1983

BENCH NUMBER

GENERAL SECONDARY EDUCATION CERTIFICATE EXAMINATION 1983
SCIENTIFIC SECTION

"TO WHOM IT MAY CONCERN"

This is to certify that/
has passed successfully the Examination of the General Secondary Certificate Scientific Section which was held in 1983 , according to the E.A.R. Ministry of Education Syllabus and attained the following marks:-

S U B J E C T	MAXIMUM	MINIMUM	MARKS
ARABIC LANGUAGE	50	25	41.5
ENGLISH LANGUAGE	40	16	37
ALGEBRA & GEMETRY	35		30
DIFFERENTIATION & INTEGRATION	20		19
TRIGONOMETRY	30		27.5
MECHANICS	35		31.5
TOTAL	120	48	108
PHYSICS	50	15	41.5
CHEMISTRY	40	12	38
NATURAL HISTORY	40	12	38.5
TOTAL	130	52	118
TOTAL MARKS	340	170	304.5

TOTAL MARKS IN LETTERS:- Three hundred four and a half marks,

OFFICER OF EDUCATION , DIRECTOR OF EDUCATION

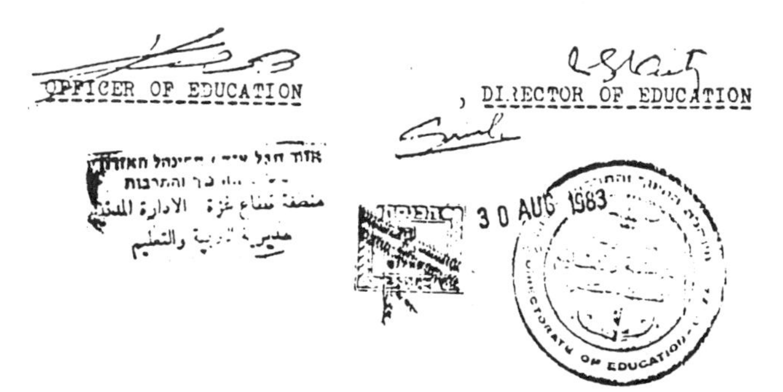

11.4. General Secondary Education Certificate (*Al-Thanawiyah Al-Am'ah*), Gaza Strip

Chapter 12

The United Nations Relief and Works Agency for Palestine Refugees in the Near East

The United Nations Relief and Works Agency for Palestine Refugees in the Near East (UNRWA) provides essential services in the areas of education and training, health (including medical and paramedical education), relief, and welfare. Nonformal education programs are organized by the Departments of Health and Relief Services and include preschool education, youth activities, and adult training in carpentry and crafts. These departments also promote formal education in health-related fields through the Agency Training Centers. UNRWA is operational in Jordan, Lebanon, the Syrian Arab Republic, and the occupied territories of the West Bank and Gaza Strip. In 1984-85, UNRWA educated 351,570 pupils with 10,625 teachers in 648 UNRWA institutions at the primary, preparatory, postpreparatory and postsecondary levels, making it the largest international educational agency in the world. For further statistics on UNRWA schools and training centers, see Table 12.1. Functioning as a quasi-governmental agency, UNRWA has a substantial impact on education in the West Bank and Gaza Strip. Along with the government and private sectors, it is one of three educational sectors in operation in the West Bank, including East Jerusalem, and the Gaza Strip.

Background

In 1948, an estimated three-quarters of a million Palestinians became refugees during disturbances before and after the creation of the State of Israel in the former British-mandated territory of Palestine. Emergency assistance was initially provided by contributions channeled through the United Nations Relief for Palestine Refugees (UNRPR) to refugees located in areas contiguous to Israel: the area of eastern Palestine now known as the West Bank, Jordan, Lebanon, the Syrian Arab Republic, and the Gaza Strip. In 1949, the United Nations General Assembly passed a resolution establishing UNRWA as a temporary organization to provide education, relief, and health services to qualified Palestinian refugees. The June 1967 War resulted in the Israeli occupation of the Jordanian West Bank, including East Jerusalem, and the Egyptian-administered Gaza Strip and further displaced more than half a million Palestinians (including 220,000 UNRWA-registered refugees being dislocated a second time). Today, over 2 million Palestinians are registered with UNRWA (761,000 in the West Bank, East Jerusalem, and Gaza Strip). Since 1967, UNRWA has continued to operate in the occupied territories with the permission of the Israeli authorities.

Not all Palestinian refugees are eligible for UNRWA services. According to the Agency, an eligible registered Palestinian refugee is a person (and his descendants) whose residence was Palestine for at least two years prior to the 1948 conflict, who consequently lost both his home and means of livelihood, and who registered with UNRWA in 1950. Excluded are Palestinian refugees from subsequent wars or hostilities; those who did not register during the 1950 registration period; economic refugees (who lost either their homes or means of livelihood, but not both); and those who re-established their residence outside the Agency's areas of operation. Therefore, use of the UNRWA-qualified definition of a Palestinian refugee normally limits UNRWA educational and relief services to a specific refugee population within the total Palestinian refugee population living in the West Bank, Gaza Strip, and throughout the world.

UNRWA Organizational Structure and UNESCO

The Commissioner-General, based at UNRWA Headquarters, Vienna, is the chief executive officer of the Agency, and reports to the General Assembly of the United Nations. UNRWA activities are independently operated from five field offices in Jordan, Lebanon, the Syrian Arab Republic, the West Bank, and Gaza Strip under the direction of the Commissioner-General. The field offices in the West Bank and Gaza Strip are independent of one another and are each headed by the Field Office Director who is responsible to the Commissioner-General. Education and training are under the Field Education Officer who reports directly to the Field Office Director. Principals of schools, training centers, and community colleges report directly to the Field Education Officer. The Public Information Officer is the official spokesperson for all field office operations and is the public extension of the Field Office Director. Questions are best addressed to the Field Education Officer or Public Information Officer in the field under which the institution operates.

The United Nations Educational, Scientific, and Cultural Organization (UNESCO) is affiliated with UNRWA in an advisory capacity. Under an agreement between UNRWA and UNESCO, UNESCO provides technical and professional advice to the Commissioner-General on aspects of UNRWA educational programs. Education programs, however, are implemented by UNRWA according to the educational system of the parent or host country, i.e., Jordanian in the West Bank and Egyptian in the Gaza Strip.

UNRWA Nomenclature

UNRWA uses nomenclature in literature, reports, and statistics which is different from that used by the parent (Jordanian or Egyptian) system and which may be misunderstood if interpreted literally in a U.S. context. The following defines or explains UNRWA's definition of terminology.

- Agency. The name used interchangeably with UNRWA, the United Nations Relief and Works Agency for Palestine Refugees in the Near East.
- Community College. See "Training Center vs. Community College."
- Postpreparatory Education. Vocational/trade education with a grade 10 entry level; distinct from traditional, official secondary education (see "Vocational Education").
- Vocational Education. UNRWA frequently uses the words "vocational" and "technical" education interchangeably, while teacher training is always categorized separately. Includes vocational/trade education and vocational/technical education as defined below.
- Vocational/Trade Education. Postpreparatory (not secondary or postsecondary) education requiring completion of 3rd Preparatory (grade 9). Not the same as vocational/technical education defined below. Trade programs offered in the West Bank and Gaza include building trades, clothing production, dressmaking, hairdressing, and metal trades. Generally programs are two to three years in length, resulting in an UNRWA institutional diploma and trade certificate, and lead to employment opportunities. (See "UNRWA Postpreparatory Education" and sample document 12.1.)
- Vocational/Technical Education. Postsecondary education requiring presentation of the General Secondary Education Certificate *(Al-Tawjihiyah* [West Bank]; *Al-Thanawiyah* [Gaza Strip]). Not the same as vocational/trade education. Includes programs designated as commercial, engineering, paramedical, social, or technical "professions." Programs are two years in length, follow a Jordanian community college curriculum, and lead to a Jordanian Diploma (in the West Bank).
- Training Center vs. Community College. UNRWA programs in trade vocations, technical "professions," and teacher training are housed in "training centers." There are three training centers in the West Bank and one in the Gaza Strip. With the Jordanian implementation of the two-year postsecondary community college system in 1981, the official names of the training centers in the West Bank were changed accordingly. While UNRWA and the community still refer to these institutions as training centers, the three institutions in the West Bank are classified according to the Jordanian educational system as community colleges, and have technically been renamed. The Gaza Vocational Training Center was not affected.

UNRWA Reference	Jordanian Reference
Kalandia Vocational Training Center	Kalandia Vocational Training Center and Community College
Ramallah Men's Teacher Training Center	Ramallah Community College for Teachers
Ramallah Women's Training Center	Women's Community College in Ramallah

- Vocational Training Center (VTC). A term used interchangeably with Training Center.
- Education Development Centres. Programs for in-service teacher training follow the UNRWA/UNESCO Institute of Education (Jordan) concept and are implemented in the West Bank in education development centres. These

centres provide professional education to teachers to promote professionalism, upgrade qualifications, and update or enrich curriculums and methodology. Courses are available to UNRWA teachers with a two-year community college Diploma in teacher training or to Baccalaureate holders without teacher certification, and lead to a one or two-year Diploma (see Chapter 13, "Teacher Training, UNRWA").

- Pre-Service vs. In-Service Teacher Training. *Pre-service* teacher training refers to the two-year fulltime Diploma program offered by the training centres (community colleges) in the West Bank for secondary school graduates who have no teaching experience. *In-service* teacher training includes 1) part-time professional education programs for teachers employed in UNRWA schools who hold a two-year Diploma or a bachelor's degree, but have no professional education training and 2) in-service courses in areas of further professional development designed for qualified teachers (see Chapter 13, "Teacher Training, UNRWA").
- Schools. Primary and preparatory general (academic) institutions.

UNRWA Preschool Education

Children from ages 3 to 6 are provided supervised play periods under the direction of trained teachers. These services are limited to the availability of financial contributions and include 16 UNRWA-operated centers in the Gaza Strip funded by the American Friends Service Committee including one in the Egyptian sector of Rafah, and seven centers in the West Bank financed and operated by the Holy Land Christian Mission. UNRWA does not traditionally or officially provide preschool education (see Chapter 10).

UNRWA Primary and Preparatory Education

Primary education under UNRWA in the West Bank and Gaza Strip is a free and compulsory six-year cycle for registered, eligible Palestinian refugee children, aged 6 through 12. In the Gaza Strip (since 1981), it is considered the first stage of Basic Education. UNRWA curriculums, examinations, and textbooks follow the Jordanian system in the West Bank and the Egyptian system in Gaza. Promotion from the primary to the preparatory cycle in the West Bank is automatic, assuming the child has successfully completed grade 6. The Gaza Strip permits promotion to the preparatory cycle only to those who pass the Primary Education Certificate Examination *(Al-Ibtida'iyah).*

The three-year preparatory cycle under UNRWA continues to follow the Jordanian or Egyptian systems and encompasses grades 7-9 for students 12-15 years of age. Preparatory education in the West Bank has been compulsory and free since 1964. The Preparatory Education Leaving Certificate Examination *(Al-Aa'dadiyah),* awarded upon completion of grade 9, is administered in the West Bank by UNRWA under the supervision of the local education office which acts on behalf of the Jordanian government. Since 1981, preparatory education in the Gaza Strip has been referred to as the second stage of Basic

Education and is free and compulsory for those who are awarded the Primary Education Certificate *(Al-Ibtida'iyah)*. Prior to 1981, preparatory education was free, but not compulsory. The Preparatory (or "Basic") Education Certificate Examination *(Al-Aa'dadiyah)*, awarded upon completion of grade 9, is also administered by UNRWA on behalf of the Egyptian government (see Chapter 10 for detailed information on primary and preparatory education).

The curriculums and textbooks used by UNRWA follow the Jordanian or Egyptian prescribed program for general education in the primary and preparatory cycles, subject to approval by the Israeli military authorities. Textbooks are subject to a three-layer approval process whereby the Jordanian or Egyptian government prescribes certain texts, UNESCO reviews and approves their use, and the Israeli authorities permit or disallow them from the list submitted by UNESCO. In 1984, the 143 textbooks prescribed by the Jordanian government for use in the East Bank (Jordan) were also the prescribed textbooks for the West Bank. Of the 106 approved by UNESCO, the Israeli authorities refused import permits for nine. In that same year, the total number of books prescribed by the Egyptian Ministry of Education was 124; of these, UNESCO approved 76 from which the Israeli authorities approved the import of 65 and disallowed the import of 11. *(UNRWA Commissioner's Report to the General Assembly*, 1985). See also "Education Under Occupation" in Chapter 9.

West Bank enrollment in UNRWA primary and preparatory schools in 1985-86 totalled 40,221 students (31,173 at the primary level; 9,048 at the preparatory level). The 40,221 students were taught by 1,280 teachers and head teachers in 98 UNRWA schools with an average class size of 50 students. Due to limited funding and facilities, double shifting affected 20.7% of the students, primarily at the preparatory level.

In the Gaza Strip, enrollment in UNRWA primary and preparatory schools in 1985-86 totalled 86,923 students (62,844 at the primary level; 24,079 at the preparatory level). Included are at least 12,566 unregistered refugee children (because UNRWA in Gaza has always in practice deemed these children eligible for educational services) and 1,232 in the now-Egyptian Village of Rafah who were stranded when borders were re-established in 1982 after the Israeli withdrawal from the Sinai. These 86,923 students, taught by 2,360 teachers and headteachers in 145 UNRWA schools, represent a 3.4% increase in enrollment over the preceding year. On the basis of 1984-85 statistics, double shifting took place in 93 of 145 schools involving 1,167 class sections and affecting 64% or 53,750 students. To avoid triple shifting, 24 classrooms were built (1984-85).

UNRWA Postpreparatory (Vocational/Trade) Education

UNRWA provides vocational/trade education requiring the preparatory certificate *(Al- Aa'dadiyah)* and classifies this level of education as postpreparatory. Vocational/trade programs are two to three years in length and are provided in UNRWA training centers, (see Table 12.2), also referred to as vocational training centers (VTC's). These programs lead to a trade certificate and an UNRWA institutional diploma designating the trade specialization.

UNRWA's general criteria for selection is based on academic merit according to priorities for registered vs. non-registered children as well as family economic status and the previous education of other family members. Preference is given to students who pass examinations at the end of the school year in which the course for which they are applying will begin. Applicants passing examinations in the preceding year have second priority. Other applicants require special approval.

In addition, applicants for postpreparatory programs must be less than 19 years of age, have successfully completed the 3rd Preparatory Year, and hold the Preparatory or Basic Education Certificate *(Al-Aa'dadiyah)*. There is a high degree of competition for the limited number of openings in UNRWA postpreparatory programs. Consequently, some programs accept only those with *Al-Tawjihiyah* or *Al-Thanawiyah* rather than *Al-Aa'dadiyah*—the stated minimum requirement.

In the West Bank, UNRWA provides vocational/trade education at the Kalandia VTC for 328 students (1985-86) in 10 trade programs: Auto Body Repair, Auto Mechanic, Blacksmith Welder, Builder/Shutterer, Carpenter and Wood Machinist, General Electrician, Machinist Welder, Plumber, Radio and Television Technician, and Refrigeration and Air Conditioning Technician. Vocational/trade programs are also provided at the Ramallah Women's Training Center for 120 students (1985-86) in Clothing (Mass Production and Dressmaking), and Hairdressing and Beauty Culture. (See sample document 12.2.)

In the Gaza Strip, vocational/trade education is provided by UNRWA at the Gaza VTC to 604 male students in 13 different vocational/trade courses.

UNRWA Secondary Education

UNRWA does not maintain secondary schools or provide secondary-level education. Under certain conditions, however, UNRWA does provide assistance to enable graduates of its preparatory schools to attend government or private secondary schools.

UNRWA Higher (Postsecondary) Education

UNRWA postsecondary education consists of two-year diploma programs at the community college level broadly grouped as either teacher training programs or programs for all other vocational/technical "professions." These programs are carried out through three UNRWA training centers in the West Bank and one in the Gaza Strip (see Table 12.2) and lead to an UNRWA diploma, the Certificate of Completion *(Musadaca*, see sample document 12.1); and/or a Jordanian Diploma (in the West Bank).

In addition to the general criteria for selection described under "Postpreparatory Education" above, applicants for UNRWA postsecondary programs must be less than 22 years of age and hold the Jordanian or Egyptian General

Table 12.1. UNRWA School and Training Centre Statistics, 1984–85

Area	# UNRWA Schools	# UNRWA Teachers	Elem. Enroll.	Prep. Enroll.	Postprep. Enroll. (Voc./Trade) in Training Centers	Postsec. Enroll. (Voc./Tech. and Tchr. Trng.) in Training Centers
West Bank	98	1,297	13,108 (M) 15,223 (F)	5,557 (M) 6,051 (F)	328 (KVTC) (M) 120 (RWTC) (F)	542 (KVTC, RMTTC) (M) 558 (RWTC) (F)
Subtotal			28,331	11,608	448	1,100
Gaza Strip	145	2,280	32,762 (M) 29,541 (F)	11,236 (M) 10,438 (F)	604 (GVTC) (M) —	— —
Subtotal			62,303	21,674	604	—
Total	243	3,577	15,870 (M) 44,764 (F)	16,793 (M) 16,489 (F)	932 (M) 120 (F)	542 (M) 558 (F)
Grand Total			90,634	34,282	1,052	1,100

SOURCE: Adaptation from *Report of the Commissioner-General of the United Nations Relief and Works Agency for Palestine Refugees in the Near East*, 1985, pp. 41, 43. Note: GVTC = Gaza Vocational Training Centre; KVTC = Kalandia Vocational Training Centre; RMTTC = Ramallah Men's Teacher Training Centre; RWTC = Remallah Women's Training Centre; M = Male; F = Female.

Table 12.2. Postpreparatory and Postsecondary Training Places in UNRWA Training Centres, 1984–85

	KVTC		RWTC		RMTTC		GVTC		Total		Combined Grand Total
	M	F	M	F	M	F	M	F	M	F	
Postpreparatory Voc./Trade*	328	—	—	120	—	—	604	—	932	120	1,052
Postsecondary Voc./Technical†	192	—	—	168	—	—	NG	—	192	168	360
Pre-service Teacher Training	—	—	—	390	350	—	—	—	390	350	740
Grand Total	520	—	—	678	350	—	604	—	1,514	638	2,152

SOURCE: Adaptation from *Report of the Commissioner-General of the United Nations Relief and Works Agency for Palestine Refugees in the Near East*, 1985, p. 43. Note: GVTC = Gaza Vocational Training Centre, KVTC = Kalandia Vocational Training Centre, RWTC = Ramallah Women's Training Centre, RMTTC = Ramallah Men's Teacher Training Centre; M = Male, F = Female, NG = Not Given.

*Programs in building, electrical, and metal trades. †Programs in commercial, paramedical, social, and technical "professions."

Secondary Education Certificate *(Al-Tawjihiyah* or *Al-Thanawiyah*, respectively). Certain programs specify the stream required (Scientific or Literary) or emphasize grades in certain subjects, e.g., Laboratory Technicians—Scientific Stream; Secretarial and Office Management—high marks in English; Nutrition and Home Management in Institutions—Scientific Stream. In postsecondary diploma programs, the applicant to acceptance ratio is approximately four to one. Total admission reflects a 60-40 West Bank-Gaza Strip UNRWA quota for postsecondary programs.

The Ramallah Community College for Teachers (Ramallah Men's Teacher Training Center) offers two-year diploma programs in teacher training to 350 young men. The Women's Community College in Ramallah (Ramallah Women's Training Center [RWTC]) offers two-year diploma programs in teacher training, auxiliary medical, commercial, and social services "professions" to 486 young women. The Kalandia VTC and Community College offers two-year diploma programs in business and technical "professions" to 192 young men. The Gaza Vocational Training Centre offers one postsecondary two-year diploma program in Radio and Television Technology. See also the individual institutional profiles under Community Colleges/UNRWA in Chapter 14 and Training Center vs. Community College in "UNRWA Nomenclature" above.

The diploma programs followed in UNRWA community colleges in the West Bank are two years in length, divided into four 19-week semesters. All students are fulltime. A credit hour system is used; most courses carry two credit hours while actual classroom hours frequently are double the number of credit hours. Each specialization follows a standardized Jordanian curriculum. Curriculum requirements include college requirements (16 credits), program requirements (18 credits), and specialization requirements (32 credits). See Table 12.3.

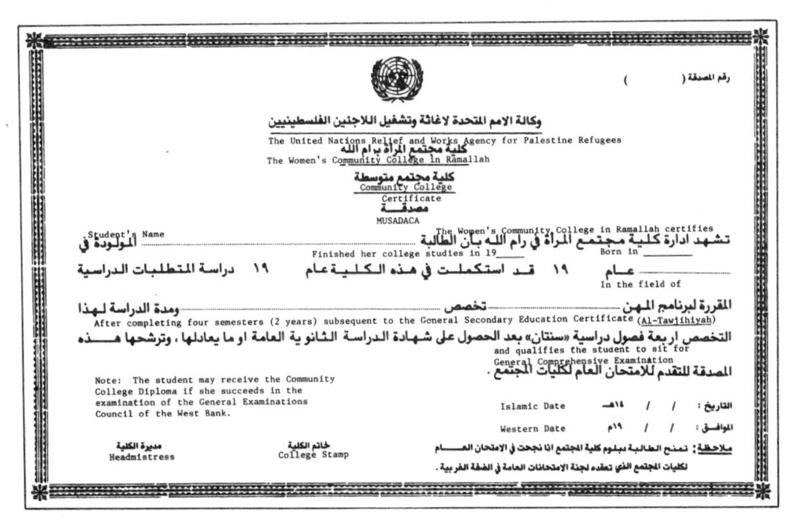

رقم المصدقة (   )

وكالة الامم المتحدة لاغاثة وتشغيل اللاجئين الفلسطينيين

The United Nations Relief and Works Agency for Palestine Refugees

كلية مجتمع المرأة برام الله

The Women's Community College in Ramallah

كلية مجتمع متوسطة

Community College

Certificate

مصدقة

MUSADACA

The Women's Community College in Ramallah certifies

تشهد ادارة كلية مجتمع المرأة في رام الله بأن الطالبة .... المولودة في

Student's Name

Born in ________ Finished her college studies in 19____

.... عام ١٩ قد استكملت في هذه الكلية عام ١٩ دراسة المتطلبات الدراسية

In the field of

المقررة لبرنامج المهن .... تخصص .... ومدة الدراسة لهذا

After completing four semesters (2 years) subsequent to the General Secondary Education Certificate (Al-Tawjihiyah)

التخصص اربعة فصول دراسية «سنتان» بعد الحصول على شهادة الدراسة الثانوية العامة او ما يعادلها، وترشحها هذه

and qualifies the student to sit for General Comprehensive Examination

المصدقة للتقدم للامتحان العام لكليات المجتمع .

Note: The student may receive the Community College Diploma if she succeeds in the examination of the General Examinations Council of the West Bank.

التاريخ : / / ١٤هـ Islamic Date

الموافق : / / ١٩م Western Date

ملاحظة: تمنح الطالبة دبلوم كلية المجتمع اذا نجحت في الامتحان العام لكليات المجتمع الذي تعقده لجنة الامتحانات العامة في الضفة الغربية .

مديرة الكلية
Headmistress

خاتم الكلية
College Stamp

12.1. ***Musadaca*** **from UNRWA/Women's Community College in Ramallah**

Since 1983-84, the Jordanian Ministry of Education has required West Bank students who have completed a two-year community college program to sit for and pass the Jordanian General Comprehensive Examination (also referred to as the General Community College Comprehensive Examination) in order to receive a Jordanian Diploma. This requirement is in effect for all government, private, and UNRWA graduates in the West Bank. Graduates of the program who either did not sit for or pass the examination are provided by the institution with a *Musadaca* or Certificate which designates completion of the prescribed program and eligibility to sit for the General Comprehensive Examination. (See sample documents 12.3 and "General Comprehensive Examination" in Chapter 14.)

Table 12.3. Sample Diploma Program Through an UNRWA Institution: Paramedical Profession, Medical Laboratory Technician

	Class Periods/Term			
Subject	1	2	3	4
College Requirements				
Arabic	–	4	–	–
Art	–	–	–	4
English I	3	3	–	–
English II	–	–	3	3
Islamic Educ.	–	–	4	–
Physical Educ.	4	–	–	–
Profes. Ethics	–	–	–	2
Research	–	–	3	–
Subtotal	7	7	10	9
Program Requirements				
Analy. Chem. I	–	5	–	–
Anatomy & Physiology I	4	–	–	–
Biology	3	–	–	–
Chemistry	4	–	–	–
First Aid I	2	–	–	–
Infec. Diseases	2	–	–	–
Math & Stats.	–	–	–	4
Microbiology	4	–	–	–
Public Health I	–	2	–	–
Typing	3	–	–	–
Subtotal	22	7	–	4

	Class Periods/Term			
Subject	1	2	3	4
Specialization Requirements				
Analy. Chem. II	–	–	5	–
Anatomy & Physiology II	–	4	–	–
Bacteriology & Serology I	5	5	–	–
Bacteriology & Serology II	–	–	5	5
Biochemistry I	–	7	–	–
Biochemistry II	–	–	7	–
Biochemistry III	–	–	–	5
Blood Bank I	–	–	6	–
Blood Bank II	–	–	–	6
First Aid II	–	–	2	–
Hematology I	3	4	–	–
Hematology II	–	–	6	–
Hematology III	–	–	–	6
Histology	–	–	–	3
Parasitology I	–	4	–	–
Parasitology II	–	–	–	2
Public Health II	–	2	–	–
Subtotal	8	26	31	27
Grand Total	37	40	41	40

SOURCE: Ramallah Women's Training Center.

Note: Although the number of class periods/term varies, each course is 2 credit hours. Total number of credit hours = 66.

Chapter 13

Teacher Education

Introduction

Teacher education in the West Bank and Gaza Strip is conducted in postsecondary institutions at community colleges (in the government, private, and UNRWA sectors), at the UNRWA Education Development Centre, in Institutes in Gaza, and in the universities. In the **West Bank,** *government* colleges include the Al-Arrub College, the College of Tulkarm, and the College of Ramallah for Women. *Private* colleges include the Al-Ibrahimiyah College, An-Najah National Community College, College of the Nation (Al-Oumah College), and The Modern Community College. UNRWA colleges include the Ramallah Community College for Teachers (RMTTC), and the Women's Community College in Ramallah (RWTC). In the **Gaza Strip** *government* colleges include the School of Female Teachers (Institute), and the School of Male Teachers (Institute). See Table 14.1 and specific institutional profiles in Chapter 14 for enrollment figures and also Chapter 12.

Qualified teachers employed in elementary and preparatory schools (grades 1-9) hold a two-year Teacher's Diploma (*Diplom Ta'leem*). Qualified teachers employed in secondary schools (grades 10-12) hold a bachelor's degree and a Teacher's Diploma.

Teacher qualifications can be earned through pre-service or in-service teacher training programs. Pre-service teacher training is conducted at the community colleges for teachers of grades K-9 and at the universities for teachers of grades K-12. In-service teacher training programs for teachers of grades K-12 provide professional teacher education programs for uncertified teachers; they also serve to upgrade and enhance the professional credentials of qualified teachers. In-service programs are offered at the UNRWA Education Training Centre and through the universities.

The Jordanian Educational Law No. 16 of 1964 specifies the minimum qualifications of teachers according to level and is applicable for all schools throughout the West Bank. For kindergarten through compulsory stages (grades K-9), the General Secondary Education Certificate (*Al-Tawjihiyah*) plus two years of study including general education, special education, and teacher training (or any equivalent thereof) is required. In case of necessity, the General Secondary Education Certificate will suffice. For the secondary stage (grades 10-12), a university degree (or its equivalent) in addition to one year of study of education methods, or the equivalent thereof in special courses in education, is required.

Teacher Training Programs

Preschool, Elementary, and Preparatory Teacher Training

In the Gaza Strip, teacher training for preschool through primary school is conducted in Teacher Training Institutes. Teacher education at this level is structured to straddle secondary/postsecondary education in five-year programs beginning in grade 10. Only two such institutes operate in Gaza—one for men, one for women. Teaching at the preparatory level requires a university degree.

In the West Bank, the training of teachers for the preschool through preparatory cycles (grades K-9) was originally conducted through postsecondary teacher training institutes. In time, some of these institutes broadened their programs to include other postsecondary fields of study. All institutes were eventually incorporated into the community college system which came into effect in the West Bank in 1981-82 following the adoption of the community college system in Jordan.

Today, West Bank pre-service teacher training for preschool through the preparatory cycle is conducted primarily through government, private, and UNRWA community colleges which may or may not offer teacher education exclusively. These two-year, fulltime programs lead to a Teacher's Diploma awarded by the Jordanian Ministry of Education. Teacher training at the elementary and preparatory level is also conducted through university baccalaureate programs as well as through post-baccalaureate diploma programs serving to qualify those without professional teacher training.

Teacher Training Institute Programs (the Gaza Strip)

Gaza Teacher Training Institutes offer a five-year continuous program which begins in the secondary cycle (grade 10) and is completed after grade 14. No examination marks the break between the secondary and postsecondary levels. At the end of the fifth year, the Egyptian Ministry of Education conducts the Teacher Education Institutes' Diploma Examination for those who have passed all subjects, completed practice teaching, and have attended at least 85% of their classes. The curriculum for this program is given in Table 13.1.

Community College Teacher Training Programs (the West Bank)

Community colleges offer two-year diploma programs in teacher education for kindergarten, elementary and preparatory teachers. These programs designated a specialization in one of the following fields: Agriculture, Arabic Language, Art Education, Elementary Education, English Language, Home Economics, Islamic Education, Kindergarten Education, Library Science and Documentation, Lower Elementary Education, Mathematics, Physical Education, Science, and Social Sciences (Geography and History).

Table 13.1. The Gaza Strip Teacher Training Institute Five-Year Curriculum: Weekly Class Periods Each Year by Subject (Grades 10–14)

	Class Periods		Class Periods
Secondary Subjects Each Year for Years 1–3			
Arabic	7	National Education	1
Crafts	2	Physical Education	3
Foreign Language	2	Practical Education	3*
History and Geography	4	Religious Education	3
Mathematics	5	Sciences	5
Music	3		
		Total	38–39

Postsecondary Subjects	**Arabic/Social Science Years 4 and 5**	**Math/Science Years 4 and 5**
Arabic	7	4
Education	4	4
English	2	2
Hygiene	2	2
Mathematics	–	4
Psychology	4	4
Religious Education	3	2
Science & Health	–	4
Social Studies	4	–
Teaching Practice	4	4
Electives—Major	7	7
—Minor	2	2
Total	39	39

SOURCE: Ministry of Education, Egypt.
*In Secondary, Year 3, Practical Education = 4 class periods per week.

The curriculums for each of these programs are prescribed by the Jordanian Ministry of Education (see sample documents 13.1 to 13.3). The programs usually consist of a total of 66 credits and 92-104 class periods. All programs consist of coursework designated as college requirements, program requirements, or specialization requirements. *College requirements* include coursework in Arabic, Contemporary Problems, English, Islamic Education, Problems of the Arab World, Research Methods or, alternatively, Art, General Science, and Physical Education. Each course carries a value of two credits. College requirements constitute 16 total credits and approximately 29 class periods. *Program requirements* (which in this instance refer to Teacher Education) include Administration and Supervision, Curriculum and Methods, Developmental Psychology, Educational Psychology, Evaluation and Measurement, Introduction to Education, Technology of Education, Practice Teaching (Theory), and Practice Teaching (Practical). Each course carries a value of two credits.

Program requirements constitute 18 total credits and approximately 21 class periods. The *specialization* constitutes 32 credits with class periods ranging from 41-54 (Lower Elementary Education to Science Education).

UNRWA Teacher Training Programs (the West Bank)

UNRWA schools in the West Bank and Gaza Strip are almost exclusively taught by teachers trained through one of UNRWA's two pre-service teacher training institutions: the Women's Community College in Ramallah (RWTC) and Ramallah Community College for Teachers (RMTTC) for men. In addition, UNRWA provides professional development programs through in-service teacher training offered by the Agency's Education Development Centres. As a result of these efforts, more than 94% of teachers in UNRWA schools are professionally qualified. (See Chapter 12.)

Pre-service teacher training is a two-year, fulltime program leading to a Diploma awarded by the Jordanian government. Those who hold this Diploma qualify to teach at the elementary level (grades 1-6) in Agency administered schools. In order to become a special subject teacher at the preparatory level in an Agency school, UNRWA requires a two-year diploma holder to complete in-service teacher training at the Agency's Education Development Centre. While other preparatory schools require only the two-year Diploma, UNRWA teachers at the preparatory level are required to have four years of education, a two-year in-service program beyond the two-year Diploma, a bachelor's degree (without a Teacher's Diploma), or a bachelor's degree plus a one-year in-service program. It should be noted that while UNRWA makes this qualification for their preparatory teachers, UNRWA diploma graduates are qualified to teach in government and private schools at both the elementary and preparatory levels.

UNRWA does not train teachers for the secondary cycle in as much as secondary school teachers are required to hold a bachelor's degree. The Agency does not offer programs leading to a bachelor's degree since it does not administer general secondary school education nor train teaching staff at this level.

UNRWA Education Development Centres provide in-service training for teachers employed in UNRWA kindergarten, elementary, and preparatory schools. In-service programs and courses are organized by the UNRWA/UNESCO (United Nations Educational, Scientific, and Cultural Organization) Institute of Education in Amman, Jordan. The Institute works through the Educational Development Centres located in Field Offices in the West Bank (from 1981, Jerusalem) and the Gaza Strip. These Education Development Centres provide training programs consisting of correspondence courses, weekly seminars, and summer courses in programs that vary in length from one to three years. In addition to upgrading unqualified teachers, the Institute aims to improve the quality of education by providing refresher courses for qualified teachers; courses in educational administration for headteachers; and special seminars and research to address changes, enhance curricula, promote professionalism, and introduce new teaching aids and methodology.

University Teacher Training Programs

Eight of the nine four-year institutions in the West Bank and Gaza Strip offer teacher education through faculties or departments of education that lead to a bachelor's degree or teaching diploma. The bachelor's program in elementary education is standardized with few exceptions, throughout the university system. The four-year program in elementary education at Bethelehem University requires 122 credits, broken down as follows: *university requirements* (31 credits), *faculty requirements* (12), *major* (elementary education) *requirements* (45), *minor requirements* (19), and *electives* (15). *Major courses* include Arabic (9) or English (9 credits), Instructional Materials (2), Mathematics (4), Nursing (2), Physics (4), Teaching Art (2) or Teaching Music (2), Teaching Language Arts (3), Teaching Health and Physical Education (2), Teaching Math and Science (3), Teaching Social Sciences (2), Teaching Special Education Needs (3), and a Senior Seminar in Elementary Education (1). *Minor courses* include Child Development (3 credits), Educational Psychology (3), Foundations in Education (3), General Principles/Methods in Elementary Education (3), Tests and Measurements (3), Practicum I in Elementary Education (2), and Practicum II in Elementary Education (2). One credit represents one hour each week for one semester.

The university diploma program in elementary education is a part-time, 34-credit program designed to qualify in-service teachers. The program extends over two calendar years and consists of two components: 1) basic notions in general education with an emphasis on elementary teaching and 2) specialization coursework in Arabic, English, Mathematics, Science, or Social Studies. See Table 13.2 for a sample program.

Secondary Education Teacher Training

Qualified teachers in the secondary cycle (grades 10-12) are required to hold a bachelor's degree and a post-baccalaurate Teacher's Diploma or a bachelor's degree that incorporates a minor in secondary education.

The bachelor's program in secondary education is also standardized, with few exceptions, throughout the university system. The program includes a major in an academic field plus a minor in education. Sample document 13.4 from the College of Arts for Women (Al-Quds University) illustrates a bachelor's program in English with a minor in secondary education.

A minor in education consists of 24 credits in psychology and education coursework with theory and practice (student teaching). Coursework in the psychology and education component of the program includes the following: Child Development or Developmental Psychology (3 credits), Curriculum and General Methods (3), Educational Psychology (3), Foundations of Education (3), Introduction to Psychology (3), Tests and Measurements (3), Practicum I in Secondary Education (3), and Practicum II in Secondary Education (3).

The university diploma program in secondary education is a 30-credit, post-baccalaureate program designed to qualify degree holders for the teaching profession. This program is identical to the minor in secondary education described above (24 credits) but requires an additional six elective credits.

Table 13.2. Sample Program for the Diploma in Elementary Education with a Specialization in English, Science, or Social Studies—Bethlehem University

Year I	Credits	Year II	Credits
Summer I		Summer II	
Arabic Lang. and Literature	3	Tests & Measurements	3
Engl. Comp./Read. Comprehension	4	Education 321	2
Intro. to Psychology	3		
Fall I		Fall II	
Arabic Composition *or*	3	Engl.: Adv. Oral Comunica. *or*	3
Engl./Intermed. Composition,		The Palestinian Problem *or*	3
Reading Comprehension	4	Physics	4
Child Development	3	Principles & Methods of Teach.	3
Spring I		Spring II	
Engl.: Adv. Communica. Skills *or*	3	Teaching Language Arts *or*	3
History of the Middle East *or*	3	Teaching Math & Sciences *or*	3
Mathematics	4	Teaching Social Sciences	4
Educational Psychology	3	In-Serv. Elem. Class Supervis.	2

SOURCE: Bethlehem University, *Faculty of Education Handbook,* 1985.

		1st Sem.		2nd Sem.		3rd Sem.		4th Sem.		Total	
		CH	P.	CH.	P.	CH	P.	CH	P.	CH	P.
COLLEGE REQUIREMENT	ARABIC							2	4	2	4
	ENGLISH				2		2	2	2	2	6
	ISLAMIC EDUCATION					2	4			2	4
	RESEARCH METHODS			2	3					2	3
	PROBLEMS OF THE ARAB WORLD					2	2			2	2
	CONTEMPORARY PROBLEMS							2	2	2	2
	PHYSICAL EDUCATION	2	4							2	4
	ART	2	4							2	4
	SUB-TOTAL	4	8	2	5	4	8	6	8	16	29
PROGRAMME REQUIREMENT	INTRODUCTION TO ED.	2	2							2	2
	DEVELOPMENTAL PSYCHO.			2	2					2	2
	TECHNOLOGY OF ED.			2	3					2	3
	CURRICULUM & METHODS			2	3					2	3
	ED. PSYCHOLOGY					2	3			2	3
	PRACTICE TEACHING (Th)	2	4							2	4
	EVALUATION & MEASURE.							2	2	2	2
	ADMIN. & SUPERVISION					2	2			2	2
	PRACTICE TEACHING (PRACT.)				2ws		2ws 3wH	2	3ws	2	10wks
	SUB-TOTAL	4	6	6	8	4	5	4	2	18	21
SPECIALIZATION REQUIREMENT	تاريخ الحضارات القديمة — Hist. of Ancient Civ.	2	3							2	3
	تاريخ الدولة العربية الاسلامية ١ — Hist. of Arab. Islamic Nation I	2	2							2	2
	تاريخ الدولة العربية الاسلامية ٢ — Hist. of Arab. Islamic Nation II			2	2					2	2
	تاريخ العرب والمسلمين الحديث — Mod. Hist. of Arabs & Muslims							2	3	2	3
	تاريخ اوربا في العصور الوسطى — Europ. Hist. in the Middle Ages			2	3					2	3
	تاريخ اوربا الحديث (١) — Mod. Europ. Hist. I					2	2			2	2
	تاريخ اوربا الحديث (٢) — Mod. Europ. Hist. II							2	2	2	2
	Islamic Laws — النظم الاسلامية			s		2	3			2	3
	Gen. Geog. — الجغرافية العامة	2	3							2	3
	Region. Geog. — جغرافية اقليمية			2	3					2	3
	جغرافية الوطن العربي — Geog. of Arab Nations							2	3	2	3
	Human Geog. — الجغرافية البشرية					2	2			2	2
	Islamic Religion — العقيدة الاسلامية	2	3							2	3
	الفقه وأصوله — Islamic Jurispru. & Its Fndns.							2	3	2	3
	علوم الحديث — Hadith-Narrat. Relating Deeds & Utterances of the Prophet Mohammed					2	3			2	3
	أساليب تدريس التربية الاسلامية والمواد الاجتماعية — Meth. of Tchng. Islamic Educ. & Soc. Studies			2	1R 3S.St					2	4
	SUB-TOTAL	8	11	8	12	8	10	8	11	32	44
	GRAND TOTAL	16	25	16	25	16	23	18	21	66	94

13.1 Two-Year Community College Diploma Program in Professional Education/Teacher Training Programs (Social Science)

		1st Sem.		2nd Sem.		3rd Sem.		4th Sem.		Total	
		CH	P.	CH	P.	CH	P.	CH	P.	CH	P.
COLLEGE REQUIREMENT	ARABIC			2	4					2	4
	ENGLISH		2				2	2	2	2	6
	ISLAMIC EDUCATION					2	4			2	4
	RESEARCH METHODS	2	3							2	3
	PROBLEMS OF THE ARAB WORLD					2	2			2	2
	CONTEMPORARY PROBLEMS							2	2	2	2
	PHYSICAL EDUCATION							2	4	2	4
	ART							2	4	2	4
	SUB-TOTAL	2	5	2	4	4	8	8	12	16	29
PROGRAMME REQUIREMENT	INTRODUCTION TO ED.	2	2							2	2
	DEVELOPMENTAL PSYCHOLOGY			2	2					2	2
	TECHNOLOGY OF ED.			2	3					2	3
	CURRICULUM & METHODS			2	3					2	3
	ED. PSYCHOLOGY					2	3			2	3
	PRACTICE TEACHING (Th)	2	4							2	4
	EVALUATION & MEASURE.							2	2	2	2
	ADMIN. & SUPERVISION					2	2			2	2
	PRACTICE TEACHING (PRACT.)				2ws		2ws 3wH	2	3ws	2	10wks
	SUB-TOTAL	4	6	6	8	4	5	4	2	18	21
SPECIALIZATION REQUIREMENT	Calc. I—(١) التفاضل والتكامل	2	4							2	4
	Calc. II—(٢) التفاضل والتكامل			2	4					2	4
	Calc. III(٣) التفاضل والتكامل					2	4			2	4
	Numerical Analysis—بنيـة الاعـداد			2	3					2	3
	اساليب تدريس الرياضيات (١)	Meth. of Tchng. Math I				2	3			2	3
	اساليب تدريس الرياضيات (٢) والعلوم			2	2M 2Sc.	Meth. of Tchng. Math II & Sci.				2	4
	مبادئ الاحصاء والاحتمالات	Prin. of Stats. & Probabil.				2	3			2	3
	Analy. Stats.—الاحصاء التحليلي							2	3	2	3
	Engr.—الهندسة اللااقليدية							2	3	2	3
	مبادئ الجبر المجرد (١)	2	3	Fndns. of Abstract Algebra I						2	3
	مبادئ الجبر الخطي (٢)			2	3	Linear Algebra II				2	3
	الهندسة من وجهة نظر حديثة	Engr. from a Mod. Perspective						2	3	2	3
	General Chem.—الكيمياء العامة					2	3			2	3
	Physics—الفيزياء	2	4							2	4
	General Biol.—بيولوجيا عامة							2	3	2	3
	Fndns. of Math—أسس الرياضيات	2	3							2	3
	SUB-TOTAL	8	14	8	14	8	13	8	12	32	53
	GRAND TOTAL	14	25	16	26	16	26	20	26	66	103

13.2. Two-Year Community College Diploma Program in Professional Education/Teacher Training Programs (Mathematics)

		1st Sem.		2nd Sem.		3rd Sem.		4th Sem.		Total	
		CH	P.	CH	P.	CH	P.	CH	P.	CH	P.
COLLEGE REQUIREMENT	ARABIC			2	4					2	4
	ENGLISH		2				2	2	2	2	6
	ISLAMIC EDUCATION					2	4			2	4
	RESEARCH METHODS	2	3							2	3
	PROBLEMS OF THE ARAB WORLD					2	2			2	2
	CONTEMPORARY PROBLEMS							2	2	2	2
	PHYSICAL EDUCATION							2	4	2	4
	ART							2	4	2	4
	SUB - TOTAL	2	5	2	4	4	8	8	12	16	29
PROGRAMME REQUIREMENT	INTRODUCTION TO ED.	2	2							2	2
	DEVELOPMENTAL PSYCH.			2	2					2	2
	TECHNOLOGY OF ED.			2	3					2	3
	CURRICULUM & METHODS			2	3					2	3
	ED. PSYCHOLOGY					2	3			2	3
	PRACTICE TEACHING (Th)	2	4							2	4
	EVALUATION & MEASURE.							2	2	2	2
	ADMIN. & SUPERVISION					2	2			2	2
	PRACTICE TEACHING (PRACT.)				2ws		2ws 3wH	2	3ws	2	10wks
	SUB-TOTAL	4	6	6	8	4	5	4	2	18	21
SPECIALIZATION REQUIREMENT	فيزياء عامة ١	2	4	Gen. Physics I						2	4
	Calc. I—تفاضل وتكامل ١	2	4							2	4
	فيزياء عامة ٢			2	3	Gen. Physics II				2	3
	Calc. II—تفاضل وتكامل ٢			2	4					2	4
	Gen. Chem. I—كيمياء عامة	2	3							2	3
	أساليب تدريس علوم ورياضيات	Meth. of Tchng. Math & Sci.			2M 2Sc.	2	2Sc.			2	6
	كهرباء ومغناطيس	Elect. & Magnetism				2	3			2	3
	Gen. Biol. I—بيولوجيا عامة	2	3							2	3
	كيمياء عامة ٢	Gen. Chem. II		2	3					2	3
	وراثة/بيولوجيا الانسان	Human Biol. & Genetics						2	3	2	3
	Fndns. of Math—أسس الرياضيات					2	3			2	3
	كيمياء عضوية	Organ. Chem.				2	3			2	3
	بيولوجيا عامة ٢	Gen. Biol. II				2	3			2	3
	فلك وارصاد	Astron. & Meteorol.						2	3	2	3
	ديناميكا حرارية	Thermal Dynamics						2	3	2	3
	مصادر الطاقة/جيولوجيا	Sources of Energy/Geol.						2	3	2	3
	SUB-TOTAL	8	14	6	14	10	14	8	12	32	54
	GRAND TOTAL	14	25	14	26	18	27	20	26	66	104

13.3. Two-Year Community College Diploma Program in Professional Education/Teacher Training Programs (Science)

COLLEGE OF ARTS FOR WOMEN
IN JERUSALEM

MAJOR: ENGLISH
MINOR: EDUCATION

YEAR	FIRST SEMESTER: SUBJECT	COURSE NO.	COURSE TITLE	CR. HRS.	SECOND SEMESTER: SUBJECT	COURSE NO.	COURSE TITLE	CR. HRS.
FIRST	ARABIC	131	TEXT APPRECIATION AND THE ART OF WRITING-I	3	ARABIC	132	TEXT APPRECIATION AND THE ART OF WRITING-II	3
	ENGLISH	001	INTRODUCTORY COLLEGE ENGLISH - A	0-(4)	ENGLISH	132	COLLEGE ENGLISH - I	3-(4)
	ENGLISH	002	INTRODUCTORY COLLEGE ENGLISH - B	0-(4)	ENGLISH	134	COLLEGE ENGLISH - II	3-(4)
	HISTORY	131	HISTORY OF THE ISLAMIC CIVILIZATION	3	HISTORY	136	CONTEMPORARY HISTORY OF PALESTINE	3
	SOCIAL SCI	131	INTRODUCTION TO SOCIAL SCIENCE	3	ECONOMICS	132	GENERAL ECONOMICS	3
	PSYCHOLOGY	132	GENERAL PSYCHOLOGY	3	EDUCATION	132	INTRODUCTION TO EDUCATION	3
	SHARI'A	121	ISLAMIC LAW	2	P. E.	112	PHYSICAL EDUCATION	1
	P. E.	111	PHYSICAL EDUCATION	1				
SUMMER	ENGLISH	231-A	COLLEGE ENGLISH FOR MAJORS - A	3	ENGLISH	135	ADVANCED COLLEGE ENGLISH -	3
	ENGLISH	231-B	COLLEGE ENGLISH FOR MAJORS - B	3				
	ENGLISH	231-C	COLLEGE ENGLISH FOR MAJORS - C	3	ENGLISH	136	ADVANCED COLLEGE ENGLISH - I	3
SECOND	ENGLISH	233	COLLEGE ENGLISH - III	3	ENGLISH	234	PRACTICAL ENGLISH	3
	ENGLISH	235	INTRODUCTION TO LINGUISTICS - I	3	ENGLISH	236	INTRODUCTION TO LINGUISTICS - II	3
	ENGLISH	237	SURVEY OF LITERATURE - I	3	ENGLISH	238	SURVEY OF LITERATURE - II	3
	PSYCHOLOGY	231	DEVELOPMENTAL PSYCHOLOGY	3	EDUCATION	232	EDUCATIONAL PSYCHOLOGY	3
THIRD	ENGLISH	331	RHETORIC - I	3	ENGLISH	334	THE ENGLISH SOUND SYSTEM	3
	ENGLISH	333	ENGLISH GRAMMAR	3	ENGLISH	336	MYTHOLOGY	3
	ENGLISH	337	AMERICAN LITERATURE - I	3	ENGLISH	338	AMERICAN LITERATURE - II	3
	EDUCATION	331	MEASUREMENT & EVALUATION IN EDUCATION	3	EDUCATION	332	CURRICULUM & GENERAL METHODS OF INSTRUCTION	3
	C.S.	331	ISLAMIC THOUGHT IN THE MIDDLE AGES	3	C.S.	332	WESTERN CIVILIZATION (FROM RENAISSANCE TO FRENCE REVOLUTION).	3
FOURTH	ENGLISH	431	RHETORIC - II	3	ENGLISH	434	APPLIED LIGUISTICS	3
	ENGLISH	433	TRANSFORMATIONAL - GENERATIVE GRAMMAR	3	ENGLISH	436	INTRODUCTION TO COMPARATIVE LITERATURE	3
	ENGLISH	437	ENGLSIH LITERATURE - I	3	ENGLISH	438	ENGLISH LITERATURE - II	3
	EDUCATION	435	THEORY & METHODS OF TEACHING ENGLISH AS A FOREIGN LANGUAGE	3	EDUCATION	436	METHODS OF TEACHING ENGLISH - PRACTICUM	3
	C.S.	431	WORLD CIVILIZATION IN THE 19th & 20th CENTURIES	3	C.S.	432	MODERN ARABIC THOUGHT	3

COORDINATOR OF THE PROGRAM
SAID M. JAMJUM

13.4. Four-Year Bachelor's Degree with a Major in English, College of Arts for Women in Jerusalem

Chapter 14

Higher Education

Higher education in universities, colleges, and community colleges has developed dramatically since 1967, especially during the past ten years. Seven of the 14 community colleges in the West Bank were established prior to the June 1967 War, excluding one which has since become a university. The nine universities and colleges, however, were established as postsecondary institutions after 1967, some as a result of restructuring or upgrading of existing institutions and all as a result of local Palestinian initiative. The universities and colleges and their dates of establishment at that level are as follows: Birzeit University (1972), Bethlehem University (1973), An-Najah National University (1977), the Islamic University of Gaza (1978), Hebron University (1980), and the four colleges within Al Quds (Jerusalem) University system (1978-82). In 1981-82, all two-year colleges in the West Bank became part of the "community college" system implemented by Jordan throughout the East and West Bank. In total, 23 institutions of higher education in the West Bank, East Jerusalem, and the Gaza Strip (see Table 14.1) enroll approximately 20,000 fulltime students of which over 70% are studying in four-year colleges or universities in programs which are primarily academic and theoretical. These academic endeavors take place almost exclusively in the West Bank and East Jerusalem while the Gaza Strip maintains one university, albeit the largest. There are no institutions of higher education in the Golan Heights. Therefore, the following discussion of higher education primarily reflects the educational environment in the West Bank and East Jerusalem, unless otherwise noted. While now only Birzeit offers an overseas student program, linkages between the universities and institutions throughout the world are detailed in the institutional profiles.

Higher education in the Occupied Territories is frequently characterized as following the educational system which was in place prior to occupation in 1967 (i.e., Jordanian in the West Bank and Egyptian in the Gaza Strip). This characterization may aptly describe the community colleges in the West Bank and East Jerusalem, at least since 1981-82 when Jordan implemented the community college system in the West Bank and standardized their programs. However, prior to that, the occupation essentially prevented Jordan from outward manifestations of involvement and, in terms of the private four-year institutions, the occupation continues to have that effect.

The universities and four-year colleges, however, were established after occupation, are a direct result of Palestinian initiative, and have experienced little to no direct involvement with the Jordanian government. As enrollment figures indicate, higher education in the Occupied Territories is predominantly private (92%) and takes place in institutions that are independent and autonomous. Nevertheless, all institutions in the West Bank initially received authorization to operate from the Ministry of Education in Amman which assumed and continues to assume a certain degree of approval by Jordan and, to some degree, consistency with their standards and practices. While there are out-

Table 14.1 Institutions of Higher Education in the Occupied Territories, 1985–86

Institution	Estab. Date*	Locale	Enrollment†
		Universities	
Bethlehem University	1973	Bethlehem	1,491
Birzeit University	1972	Birzeit	2,424
Hebron University	1980	Hebron (Al-Khalil)	1,750
The Islamic University of Gaza	1978	Gaza (town)	4,102‡
An-Najah National University	1977	Nablus	3,400
Al Quds University (System)	1981	Jerusalem	
College of Al-Da'wa and Ussul Al-Din	1978	Beit Hanina, Jerusalem	325‡
College of Arts for Women	1982	Jerusalem	320
Arab Colleges of Medical Professions	1979	Al-Bireh, Jerusalem	155‡
College of Science and Technology	1979	Abu Deis, Jerusalem	607
Subtotal			14,574
		Community Colleges	
Private Community Colleges			
An-Najah National Community College	1965	Nablus	374‡
College of the Nation (Al-Oumah College)	1983	Jerusalem	295‡
Al-Rawdah Community College for the Professional Sciences	1970	Nablus	661‡
College of Islamic Sciences	1975	Abu Deis, Jerusalem	49‡
College of Islamic Studies	1978	Kalkilia	188‡
Al-Ibrahimiyah College	1983	Jerusalem	648‡
Al-Khalil (Hebron) Technical Engineering College-Hebron Polytechnic	1978	Hebron (Al-Khalil)	706‡
The Modern Community College	1983	Al-Bireh	1,024‡
Subtotal			3,945
Government Community Colleges			
Al-Arrub (Urub) College	1958	Hebron (Al-Khalil)	79
College of Ramallah for Women	1952	Ramallah	236
College of Tulkarm	1965	Tulkarm	315
Subtotal			630
UNRWA Community Colleges			
Women's Community College in Ramallah (or RWTC)	1962	Ramallah	486
Kalandia VTC and Community College	1953	Kalandia	192
Ramallah Community College for Teachers	1960	Ramallah	312
Subtotal			990
Subtotal—Community Colleges			5,565
Grand Total—Higher Education			20,139

*Establishment dates reflect dates of establishment as postsecondary institutions.
†Postsecondary enrollment only; excludes UNRWA postpreparatory enrollment.
‡1984–85 enrollment data.

ward appearances of similarities between the institutions in the East and West Bank (e.g., grading and degree titles), there are certain characteristics which make West Bank institutions distinctly Palestinian as opposed to Jordanian. These characteristics, which may be attributed to the Islamic University in Gaza in relation to Egypt as well, are described as follows:

1. Jordanian institutions are government or state institutions while West Bank institutions are private and independent;
2. The state of occupation under which West Bank institutions function creates an entirely different operational environment;
3. West Bank universities (i.e., their faculty, staff, and student body) identify with Palestinian nationalism, not with the Jordanian government and thereby operate under a different set of ideals and aspirations;
4. Curriculums and programs are created and developed by Palestinians to meet the particular needs of West Bank Palestinians and their society;
5. The faculty and administration in West Bank institutions were educated throughout the world and have lived in different cultural and economic environments, bringing back to their institutions a global perspective, sophistication, and energy which has had an impact on innovation in education;
6. Institutions in the West Bank represent the first results Palestinian higher education developed by and for Palestinians after centuries of foreign rule/ and foreign educational systems.

Institutions of Higher Education

The term "accreditation" is not used in the West Bank and the Gaza Strip. What exists instead is a system of external legal procedures and requirements which serve to assure that no institution operates without the consent of the Jordanian or Egyptian government and the Israeli military authorities. The term "recognition" is a suitable substitute for "accreditation."

There are two levels of authorization in the recognition process. The first level involves the institution's application for a permit or license to operate as a recognized academic institution of higher education from the Jordanian or Egyptian government. The second level concerns a multitude of ongoing approvals, permits, and legalities which involve submission of requests to the Israeli military authorities. Permission to operate, acquisition of land, use of privately owned (Arab) property, construction and building permits (including permits for additions to existing approved facilities), essentially anything and everything of any consequence with regard to the normal functioning of an academic institution require approval from the authorities. Frequently, applications are indefinitely delayed, subject to non-academic considerations, or denied. (See "Education under Occupation," Chapter 9.)

The private universities, four-year colleges, and community colleges are each governed by a Board of Trustees. In the case of Islamic institutions under the Ministry of Waqf (Islamic Trusts), the Ministry authorizes a Board of Trustees to act on its behalf. Most actions of any consequence are subject to approval by the Israeli military authorities.

Institutional structure within the universities and colleges is traditional in character. The Chief Executive and highest ranking official is the President or Chancellor who normally presides over the faculty and administration. Next are Vice-Presidents, some designated for special areas such as Planning and Development, Academic Affairs, Research; Deans; and Departmental Chairmen. Institutions are made up of academic units (such as Faculties or Colleges, Schools, Departments, Programs, special-purpose Institutes, Research Institutes) and administrative units (Offices of the Registrar and Registration, Admissions, Student Affairs, Planning and Development, and Public Relations).

Government community colleges are under the supervision of the local district office of education which acts on behalf of the Jordanian Ministry of Education and functions at the discretion of the Israeli military authorities.

UNRWA community colleges are supervised by UNRWA/UNESCO (United Nations Educational, Scientific, and Cultural Organization) according to the internal organizational structure described in Chapter 12. They are at the same time subject to educational laws and regulations of their "host" country (Jordan) as well as the restrictions and controls imposed by the Israeli military authorities. The community colleges within the government and UNRWA sectors are headed by a Principal, Headmaster, or Headmistress.

The Palestine Council of Higher Education was established in 1977 and is located in the Professional Associations Building in Beit Hanina. The responsibilities of the Council are 1) to support institutions of higher education in the West Bank and Gaza Strip; 2) to coordinate and approve academic programs in order to avoid duplication of efforts and to encourage consolidation and conservation of resources; 3) to assist each institution in faculty and program development; 4) to distribute the bulk of financial resources which are channeled through The Joint Jordanian-Palestinian Committee; and 5) to solicit funding primarily through The Arab League and Arab universities and governments in the Middle East.

Comprised of a 12-member Executive Committee and a 53-member General Assembly, the Council includes all university and college presidents, the President of the Polytechnic, representatives from all professional associations, the head of the Education Department of UNRWA, elected mayors, and post-1975 national leaders. Both the Executive Committee and the President of the General Assembly are elected for two-year terms.

Funding for higher education comes from a multitude of international charitable and religious organizations, international governmental and intergovernmental organizations, The Joint Jordanian-Palestinian Committee channeled through the Palestine Council of Higher Education, the Ministry of Waqf (Islamic Trusts), individual contributions, and modest student fees.

Funding of government institutions comes from Jordan and the Israeli authorities. Israel does not finance higher education but does contribute to the three government community colleges because of their involvement in teacher training programs. Jordan pays teachers hired before 1967 who are still teaching. Israel pays these same teachers, as well as any hired since 1967, in sheckels, at approximately half the rate that is paid to teachers in Israel.

The source of these funds as well as other funding required to maintain the military authorities is said to come from taxes levied on residents of the West Bank.

Institutions of higher education are classified according to supervising authority as private, UNRWA (United Nations Relief and Works Agency for Palestine Refugees in the Near East), or government. The universities, four-year colleges, and the two-year Polytechnic are all private, independent, and autonomous. Seven of the community colleges are also private, while the remaining six are evenly divided between government and UNRWA supervision. The private sector enrolls 18,194 students (91.8%); UNRWA enrolls 990 students (5%); and the government schools enroll 630 (3.2%).

UNRWA's limited involvement at this level of education is primarily a reflection of severe financial constraints. It should be noted that UNRWA was originally established as a "temporary" training and relief service; its assumed responsibility in the area of providing education at higher levels has evolved out of the needs of the refugee population as it has grown older. A primary justification for UNRWA involvement in higher education is to train and employ teachers for its primary and preparatory schools. For this reason, teacher training is the dominant program of studies in UNRWA schools where intake is calculated and limited and competition for admission is high. Further information on UNRWA education and programs is provided in Chapter 12 and in the UNRWA institutional profiles at the end of this chapter.

Government institutions are those postsecondary institutions established and financed by the Jordanian government between 1948 and 1967 and existing today within the framework of the Jordanian community college system. Ironically, Jordan has less access to and influence on these institutions than the others, causing the military presence to be all the more apparent. These institutions and their establishment dates include 1) the Women's Teacher Training Institute in Ramallah (1952), now named the College of Ramallah for Women; 2) the Men's Teacher Training Institute in Al-Arrub (1958), now named Al-Arrub College; and 3) the Khedouri Agricultural School in Tulkarm (1958) now named the College of Tulkarm. Since 1967, these institutions have been and continue to be closely scrutinized and supervised by the military authorities, are the least accessible to local or foreign observation, and have witnessed declining enrollment (noted above as currently 3% of the total).

Admission to Institutions of Higher Education

Admission to all higher education is based upon the Jordanian or Egyptian General Secondary Education Certificate (*Al-Tawjihiyah* or *Al-Thanawiyah*, respectively). The field of study dictates whether preparation through the Literary or Scientific stream is required; there is no crossing over. Since about 96% of *Al-Tawjihiyah* holders come from these two academic streams, universities do not consider applicants from the vocational streams. In addition, competition is so keen, particularly in engineering and science, that the 70% commonly accepted minimum *Al-Tawjihiyah* result is frequently bypassed for averages in the 80's and upwards. Institutions or departments may also require additional university entrance examinations as a screening mechanism. It cannot be said categorically, however, that a certain cutoff point exists. Admissions committees, together with departmental and faculty committees, carefully calculate an individual's average taking into account various factors such as selected subjects relevant to the intended field of study, secondary school grades, and statements of purpose. All applicants are then ranked in relation to one another. Community colleges tend to use a lower standard for admission than do the universities. They may accept students with *Al-Tawjihiyah* results from 50%-70%, but again there appears to be competition for admission in all institutions. See also institutional profiles for specific admission requirements.

Academic Calendar

Universities and four-year colleges operate on a 15-16 week semester system beginning in September or October and ending in June; some offer summer sessions of 6-8 weeks' duration. Community colleges operate on a 19-week semester system beginning in September or October and ending in June; some offer 8-week summer sessions.

The Community College System

The Community College system was first introduced and implemented in Jordan (the East Bank) in 1980-81. The system was implemented in the West Bank one year later in 1981-82. The introduction of this system involved 1) renaming and reclassifying two-year institutions to community colleges; 2) establishing a set curriculum for all programs (listed later in this chapter) by the Ministry of Education (Amman) for implementation by all community colleges (government, UNRWA, and private); 3) instituting the Ministry of Education General Comprehensive Examination to be given upon completion of the two-year program; and 4) instituting the requirement of passing the General Comprehensive Examination as a condition of receiving a government Diploma.

The community college system in the West Bank involves a total of 14 institutions: eight private (including one polytechnic), three UNRWA, and three government. The Polytechnic is the only two-year institution represented in the Council of Higher Education. All these institutions are described within the institutional profiles section of this chapter.

The community college programs are all structured according to the following common format.

1. College Requirements—Constituting 25% of the program and consisting of eight 2-credit general education courses, four of which are required, and four of which are optional or elected;

2. Program Requirements—Constituting 25% of the program and consisting of eight to nine 2-credit courses fundamental to the field of study of the chosen specialization;
3. Specialization Requirements—Constituting 50% of the program and consisting of at least sixteen 2-credit courses.

A minimum of 66 credits is required for the two-year programs where 1 credit normally represents 2 hours of instruction.

The General Comprehensive Examination is a government examination which is written, administered, and graded by government representatives. It is also referred to as the Community College General Examination and the General Comprehensive Examination for Community Colleges. In the West Bank, the Board of Examiners in the district office of education in Nablus carries out these responsibilities on behalf of the Ministry of Education in Amman. The results of the examination are sent to the Ministry of Education for computerization and consolidation of East and West Bank data.

The General Comprehensive Examination was first given in Jordan in 1982 and in the West Bank in 1983. However, while the examination was offered in 1983, all community college students in the West Bank refused to sit for the examination. In 1984, the examination was offered again, with some students participating. Since, after completion of the program, a two-year time limit existed in which to be eligible to take the examination, the 1985 examination included "graduates" from 1983, 1984, and 1985 with a total of 607 participants. Any student not sitting for the examination within two years of completion of the course is not eligible to sit for the examination without first returning to school and completing another major. Anyone not sitting for examinations is not eligible for the Jordanian Diploma and officially is not graduated. In such cases, a student would be able to present yearly transcripts and a Certificate of Completion *(Musadaca)* rather than a Diploma.

The General Examination is a combination of multiple choice and essay questions and usually consists of 4 "papers". The structure of the examination follows the structure of the program described above: Paper 1 examines material covered within College Requirements; Paper 2 examines material from the Program Requirements; Papers 3 and 4 cover the Specialization. The examinations take place over a period of four days, each paper representing a three-hour examination.

Programs and specializations offered by the community colleges each have a prescribed curriculum developed through the Jordanian Ministry of Education. These programs and specializations are described below.

1. Agricultural Professions with specializations in Agronomy, Animal Husbandry.
2. Business/Commercial Professions with specializations in Accounting; Banking and Finance; Business Administration; Commerce and Office Management; Management of Supply and Storage; Secretarial and Office Management; Tax, Custom, and Finance.
3. Computer Profession with specialization in Computer Programming and Systems Analysis.

4. Engineering Professions with specializations in Architecture/Decoration and Interior Design, Architecture/Drawing, Architecture/General, Civil Engineering/Building and Construction, Civil Engineering/General, Civil Engineering/Quantity Accounting, Civil Engineering/Roads, Civil Engineering/Surveying, Electrical Engineering/Ceramics and Glass, Electrical Engineering/General, Electrical Engineering/Power Transmission and Distribution, Mechanical Engineering/Air Conditioning and Refrigeration, Mechanical Engineering/Automotors and Engines, Mechanical Engineering/General, Mechanical Engineering/Production and Machinery.
5. Paramedical Professions with specializations in Assistant Pharmacist, Dental Laboratory Technician, Health Supervisors/Sanitary Inspectors, Medical Laboratory Technician, Physical Therapist, Safety Law Technician. See Table 12.3 for a sample program description.
6. Professional Education/Teacher Training Programs with specializations in Arabic Language, Art, Elementary Education, English Language, Home Economics, Islamic Education, Mathematics, Nursery and Kindergarten Education, Physical Education, Science, Social Studies (Arab Society, Geography, History). See Chapter 13 for a discussion of these programs and sample documents.
7. Social Professions with specializations in Hotel Management, Journalism and Information, Library Science and Documentation, Nutrition and Institutional Management, Paralegal Studies, Prayer Leading and Sermonizing, Social Work, Translation.

Universities and Colleges

Program Structure and Degree Requirements

Bachelor's degree programs offered by the universities and colleges represent a minimum of four years of study. Exceptions to this are degree programs in engineering and architecture which require five years, and all degrees from the Islamic University of Gaza which involve a preparatory year in addition to four years for a total of five years. Almost all undergraduates are fulltime day students who have continued directly from secondary school without a disruption in their education.

Degree requirements are expressed in terms of credit hours in which 1 credit hour represents 1 hour of lecture each week for a 15-16 week semester or 3 weekly hours of laboratory each semester. The bachelor's degree requires approximately 120 to 130 credit hours unless the program is one of the five-year programs mentioned above, in which case the credit requirements approximate 160.

Bachelor's degree programs follow a common format that resembles traditional degree programs in the United States except perhaps for including fewer elective options. The common format includes approximately 18 credits of university requirements, approximately 18 credits of faculty core requirements, and approximately 60 departmental (major and minor) requirements, and the balance consists of university and faculty electives. The program structure of each university is provided within the institutional profiles section of this chapter. Specific degree requirements are available upon request from the universities.

Several graduate programs leading to the Master's degree are available. Graduate programs are two years in length, usually divided into a first and second postgraduate Diploma, the final result being the Master's degree.

Transcripts and Grading

Official transcripts are provided in English by each institution and are usually self-explanatory and familiar in format. Sample documents are located at the end of this chapter.

A commonly used grading scale based upon a 60% passing mark is as follows.

90-100	=	Excellent	60-69	=	Pass, Weak
80-89	=	Very Good	0-59	=	Fail
70-79	=	Good, Fair			

Institutions of Higher Education Profiles

I. Universities in the Occupied Territories

Profiles of the nine universities and colleges include a brief description of the institution; a breakdown of its enrollment and faculty qualifications; library facilities; academic calendar; language of instruction and examination; fulltime (FT) and part-time (PT) degree, diploma and certificate programs offered, and credentials awarded. Grading scales, program structure and requirements as well as institutional linkages are also noted. For more information applicable to all institutions of higher education in the Occupied Territories (e.g., funding), the reader is referred back to the chapter.

AL QUDS (JERUSALEM) UNIVERSITY. See individual constituent colleges for addresses and profiles.

DESCRIPTION: Estd. 1981 as result of decision of Palestine Council of Higher Education to unify and coordinate educational resources, programs and research of West Bank higher institutions. Under guidance of 9-member Central Council of Al Quds (Jerusalem) University; composed of the Chairman and Secretary of each institutional Board of Trustees plus a chairman. Comprises 4 autonomous constituent colleges—Arab Colleges of Medical Professions, College of Al-Da'wa and Ussul Al-Din, College of Arts for Women, College of Science and Technology.

Arab Colleges of Medical Professions, P.O. Box 523, Al-Bireh, West Bank via Israel. Tel.: (02) 951610.

DESCRIPTION: Estd. September 1979 with the College of Nursing specializing in health-related professions. Founded in response to need first expressed by Red Crescent Society of Jerusalem to Ministry of Health (Jordan) who in turn recommended its establishment. One of 4 autonomous constituent colleges of Al Quds (Jerusalem) University. College of Medical Technology opened 1980. College of Radiotechnology to open Feb. or Sept. 1986. In 1982, acquired present name. Located approx. 10 miles to north of Jerusalem, slightly southeast of Ramallah. Private institution governed by Board of Trustees. Recognized by Association of Arab Universities. *Library (1982):* 1,500 vols.

Hospital affiliations for College of Nursing include Caritas Bethlehem Hospital, Military Hospital (Bethlehem), Makased Hospital, Augustav Victoria Hospital, St. Joseph's Hospital, Red Crescent Maternity Hospital. College of Medical Technology maintains same hospital affiliations (except St. Joseph's and the Red Crescent Maternity Hospital) in addition to Ramallah and Beit Jalah Hospitals.

ENROLLMENT: 155 (1985–86). *College of Nursing*—9 M (9%), 93 F (91%). *Medical Technology*—28 M (53%), 25 F (47%).

CALENDAR: Two 16-wk. sems. and one 8-wk. summer session; 5 days/week (Sat.-Wed.), 8 a.m.-4 p.m.

LANGUAGE OF INSTRUCTION AND EXAMINATION: English.

ACADEMIC STAFF: 29 *College of Nursing* (1 M.D., 11 M.Sc., 6 B.Sc.). *Medical Technology* (2 M.D., 1 Ph.D., 6 M.Sc., 2 B.Sc.).

DEGREES: 4-yr. Bachelor's—Sci. (B.Sc.), Nurs., Med. Technol.

ADMISSION REQUIREMENTS: Students accepted from the West Bank and Gaza Strip on competitive basis with min. reqmt. of 75% (Literary Stream) and 65% (Science Stream) on Gen. Secondary Educ. Cert. *(Al-Tawjihiyah)* exam. Applicants required to pass Engl. exam (or complete intensive Engl. course the summer prior to start of classes), medical exam, interview. Transfer reqmts. include 1) meeting freshman admission reqmts., 2) completion of no less than 1 sem. and no more than 3 yrs. prior to sem. of admission, 3) grade ave. of 15% above pass mark of other institution (e.g., if passing grade is 60%, 75% is required), 4) no failure in any subjs.

Special admission program for Registered Nurses (R.N.). Applicants must have Gen. Secondary Educ. Cert. *(Al-Tawjihiyah),* and R.N. Cert. Acceptance on competitive basis limited by quota restrictions. Those accepted take challenge exams for transfer of credit and normally complete program in 5 sems. of PT study.

GRADES AND TRANSCRIPTS:

A = 90 - 100 (Excellent)
B = 80 - 89 (Very Good)
C = 70 - 79 (Good)
D = 60 - 69 (Acceptable/Pass)
F = 0 - 59 (Fail)

General grade written in parentheses after degree awarded is descriptive grade corresponding to cumulative ave. Min. passing grade for course in major is 65 which changes "D" range for major subjs. to 65 - 69.

Award of degree is posted on transcript. B.Sc. diploma will contain signatures of Chairman of Board of Trustees, Chancellor, and Registrar and also one College stamp.

PROGRAM STRUCTURE AND CREDITS: Nurs. curriculum patterned after B.Nurs. programs in State of California, with adaptation for local needs. Programs require 4 yrs. FT study (including summers) with min. 130 credits required in Med. Technol., 143 credits in Nurs. (1 credit = 1 wkly. classroom hr., 2-3 hrs. lab or 3 hrs. practical train.). Min./max. credit load is 12/18 credits per sem., respectively, and 6/9 credits (min./max.) during summer session. All students except R.N.'s must be FT.

LINKAGES: California State University-Long Beach (U.S.), Indiana University (U.S.).

College of Al-Da'Wa and Ussul Al-Din, Beit Hanina, West Bank via Israel.

DESCRIPTION: One of 4 constituent colleges of Al Quds (Jerusalem) University. Estd. 1978 as the *Teacher's Training Center (in Beit Hanina),* granting degrees in Preaching (Al-Da'wa) and Principles of Religion (Islam) (Ussul Al-Din) as well as Arabic Language and Literature. Located slightly northeast of Jerusalem. Private co-ed. institution governed by Board of Trustees. Recognized by Association of Arab Universities. *Enrollment:* 325. *Language of Instruction:* Arabic.

College of Arts for Women, Dar El Tifl, Sheikh Jarrah Quarter, Jerusalem. Tel.: (02) 273477.

DESCRIPTION: Estd. 1948 as school and home for refugee children of annihilated village of Dar Yasseen by Hind Al-Housseini. Known as Dar El Tifl (House of the Arab Child) from 1948-82. College estd. in 1982 as arts institution for women and became 1 of 4 affiliated colleges of Al Quds (Jerusalem) University. Located outside walls of the Old City in predominantly Arab sector of East Jerusalem called Sheikh Jarrah. Owned by Institution of House of the Arab Child which receives contributions from Kuwait, Saudi Arabia, Gulf States, W. Germany, Sweden, The Joint Jordanian-Palestinian Committee, student fees. Recognized by Association of Arab Universities. *Enrollment (1985-86):* 320 Females.

CALENDAR: Two 16-wk. sems. (Oct.-Feb. 1; Feb. 15-June 12), excluding exams. Summer session.

LANGUAGE OF INSTRUCTION: Arabic except English in Dept. of English Language and Literature.

ACADEMIC STAFF: Ph.D. (6 FT, 13 PT), M.A./M.Sc. (11 FT), B.A./B.Sc. (4 FT).

FACULTIES AND DEPARTMENTS: FAC. OF EDUCATION—Depts. (Arab. Lang. & Lit., Educ., Engl. Lang. & Lit., Soc. Welfare).

DEGREE AND DIPLOMA: 4-year Bachelor of Arts, Teacher's Diploma.

GRADING:

A = 90 - 100	D = 60 - 69
B = 80 - 89	F = 0 - 59
C = 70 - 79	

Ave. of 60% is passing for all courses; 70% ave. in major courses required for graduation.

ADMISSION REQUIREMENTS: Min. reqmt. is Gen. Secondary Educ. Cert. *(Al-Tawjihiyah).* Ninety students accepted per year against current college capacity of 360 students. In 1985-86, 350 applicants for 90 places.

PROGRAM STRUCTURE AND CREDIT SYSTEM: Most courses carry 3 credits. Program consists of liberal arts reqmts., Arabic, English, a major and minor, and Phys. Educ. Those selecting Educ. as minor complete 6 credits in Psych., 18 credits in traditional educ. subjs. and earn Teacher's Diploma in addition to bach.'s degree. Bach.'s degree in Arab. Lang. & Lit. requires 127 credits; in Engl. Lang. & Lit., 124, in Soc. Welfare, 134.

College of Science and Technology, P.O. Box 10001, Abu Deis, East Jerusalem. Tel.: (02) 271753.

DESCRIPTION: Located 5 km. southeast of Jerusalem on 190,000 square meters of College property. Construction of campus building initiated 1965 but was disrupted by 1967 War. Temporary site of Arab Jordanian Institute, a primary/secondary school serving mainly Palestinian orphans. College estd. September 1979 as College of Science; closed by military directive until reopening in September 1981 under current name. Co-ed. Funded by Central Board of Trustees (Kuwait) plus funding sources described in text. One of 4 autonomous constituent colleges of Al Quds (Jerusalem) University. Offers arts and science education with emphasis on science, technology and research. Recognized by Association of Arab University, Association of Islamic Universities. *Library:* 25,000 vols. (50% English); 100 periodicals; 15,000 journals. *Enrollment (1985):* 402 Males, 205 Females.

CALENDAR: Two 16-wk. sems. (late Sept. - June); one 8-wk. summer session (July - Sept.).

LANGUAGE OF INSTRUCTION: Arabic and English.

ACADEMIC STAFF: Ph.D. (26 FT, 2 PT, 1 Sabbatic Leave), M.Sc. (26 FT), B.Sc. (28 FT).

FACULTIES AND DEPARTMENTS: FAC. OF SCIENCE—Depts. (Biol., Chem., Computer Sci., Math, Physics). FAC. OF TECHNOLOGY—Depts. (Chem. & Industrial Technol.).

DEGREES AND DIPLOMAS:

Degrees/Diploma	Field of Study	Credits	Years
Bach. of Science (B.Sc.)	Biol., Chem., Computer Science, Math, Physics	135	4
Bach. of Technol. (B. Tech.)	Chem. Technol., Electronics, Med. Technol.	154	4.5
B.Sc. and Tech.	Full B.Sc. major + B. Tech. minor	135	4

Degrees/Diploma	Field of Study	Credits	Years
M.Sc.	Science and Educ.	52	2
Dip. in Science Teach. Technol.	Science Educ.	26	1

GRADING AND TRANSCRIPTS:

1981 - 1982

College or Nonmajor Course Grading		Major Course Grading	
90 - 100	= Excellent	90 - 100	= Excellent
80 - 89	= Very Good	80 - 89	= Very Good
70 - 79	= Good	70 - 79	= Good
60 - 69	= Satisfactory	Below 70	= Fail
50 - 59	= Pass		
Below 50	= Fail		

1982 to Present

A (90 - 100)	= Excellent	A (90 - 100)	= Excellent
B (80 - 89)	= Very Good	B (80 - 89)	= Very Good
C (70 - 79)	= Good	C (70 - 79)	= Good
D (60 - 69)	= Pass	F (Below 70)	= Fail
F (Below 60)	= Fail		

Honors awarded with cumulative ave. of 85% and above, or 80% and above in each course during 1 sem.

Transcripts computerized. Min cumulative ave. for graduation is 65%; in major, 70%. Sem., cumulative and major averages presented numerically at end of each sem. Completion of degree reqmts. and eligibility for degree stated on transcript; award of degree verified by presentation of diploma.

ADMISSION REQUIREMENTS: FRESHMAN—Admission competitive with stated min. of 70% on Gen. Secondary Educ. Cert. *(Al-Tawjihiyah)* exam (Scientific Stream), Engl. Lang. Placement Test, and interview. Min. admission ave. implemented in 1985-86 was 74%. TRANSFER—Same as freshman. Only univ. transfer applicants with cumulative ave. of 70% or better are considered. DIPLOMA—B.Sc. in Sci. or Technology. MASTER'S OF SCIENCE—B.Sc. in Sci. with Distinction.

PROGRAM STRUCTURE AND CREDITS: Degree reqmts. include min. 135 total credits including 33 credits of College required and elective courses, credits required according to full major or major/minor program choice, crswrk. in Engl., and passing College comprehensive Engl. exam. Min. sem. credit load is 17 credits. Course exams and grades given on sem. basis. All students are fulltime.

LINKAGES: Kuwait University, Salford University (U.K.), University of Jordan (Amman), Wentworth Institute of Technology (U.S.), Yarmouk University (Jordan).

AN-NAJAH NATIONAL UNIVERSITY (ALSO KNOWN AS AL-NAJAH NATIONAL UNIVERSITY), P.O. Box 7, Nablus, West Bank via Israel. Tel.: (053) 70042.

DESCRIPTION: Opened 1918 as *An-Najah Nablusi (Secondary) School;* existed as such until 1945 when it became *An-Najah College,* postsecondary institution awarding intermediate commerce degrees. Moved to present location in 1963 on western slope of Nablus. Became *An-Najah Teachers Training Institute* (postsecondary level) in 1965. In 1977, became *An-Najah National University;* accepted as member of Association of Arab Universities. Recognized by International Association of Universities (1981). Located on 8-acre main campus; 30-acre Engineering /Science campus awaiting construction permit from Israeli authorities since 1980. *Library:* 73,000 vols. (33,000 Arabic; 40,000 English), 420 periodicals (Arabic, English).

CALENDAR: Two 16-wk. sems.; one 8-wk. summer session (Oct. - June).

ENROLLMENT BY FACULTY: (1984-85) 3,031 total—*Arts*–434 M (45%), 532 F (55%). *Econ./Bus. Admin.*–457 M (73%), 172 F (27%). *Educ.*–295 M (44%), 376 F (56%). *Engr.*–143 M (67%), 71 F (33%). *Sci.*–322 M (58%), 229 F (42%). Enrollment (1985-86): 3,400.

ACADEMIC STAFF (1984-85): Ph.D. (76), M.A./M.Sc. (83), B.A./B.S. (96), 2-yr. Dip. (1).

LANGUAGE OF INSTRUCTION: Arabic except in Facs. of Engineering, and Science where English is lang. of texts, instruction, exam.

FACULTIES AND DEPARTMENTS: FAC. OF ARTS—Depts. (Arab. Lang. & Lit., Engl. Lang. & Lit., Fine Arts, Geog., History & Archeology, Islamic Studies, Sociol.). FAC. OF ECONOMICS AND BUSINESS ADMINISTRATION—Depts. (Acct., Bus. Admin., Econ., Poli. Sci., Journalism). FAC. OF EDUCATION—Depts. (Educ. & Psych., Phys. Educ., An-Najah National Community College [Institute]). FAC. OF ENGINEERING—Depts. (Arch., Civil Engr.). FAC. OF SCIENCE—Depts. (Agri., Biol., Bio-Med. Technol., Chem., Math, Physics). ATTACHED RESEARCH INSTITUTES—Rural Research Centre (1981, concerned with research in rural develop. needs and potential); Research Documentation Centre (1982, dedicated to preserving Palestinian heritage).

DEGREES AND DIPLOMAS: BACHELOR'S—*4-yrs.* - Arts (B.A.), Sci. (B.Sc.). —*5-yrs.* - Sci. (B.Sc.) (in Arch., and Engr.). MASTER'S—Arts (M.A.) (Educ., Islamic Studies), Sci. (M.Sc.) (Chem.). DIPLOMA—*2-yrs.* - Educ.

ADMISSION REQUIREMENTS: Students accepted from the West Bank and Gaza Strip on competitive basis with min. required score of 70% on Gen. Secondary Educ. Cert. *(Al-Tawjihiyah)* exam. Other min. *Al-Tawjihiyah* results by Fac.: Arts (76%), Econ./Bus. Admin. (78%), Engr. (89%).

PROGRAM STRUCTURE AND CREDIT SYSTEM: Facs. of Arts, Econ./Bus. Admin., Educ., and Sci. offer 4-yr. bach.'s degree requiring min. 120 sem. credit hrs. All programs structured to include univ. reqmts. (18 credit hrs.), fac. reqmts. (30), deptl. reqmts. and electives (66), free electives (6). Fac. of Engr. offers 5-yr. bach.'s in Civil Engr. and in Arch. requiring 165 sem. credit hrs. structured as follows: univ. reqmts. (18 credit hrs.), fac. reqmts. (22), deptl. reqmts. and electives (125 engr., 130 arch.), free electives (6 engr., 10 arch.).

LINKAGES: United States—The American University, Arizona State University, Portland State University, San Francisco State University, Southern Illinois University, University of California-Davis. U.S.S.R.—Moscow University. Sweden—Umea University. United Kingdom—University of Bradford, University of Essex.

BETHLEHEM UNIVERSITY, Frère St., P.O. Box 9, Bethlehem, West Bank via Israel. Tel.: (02) 741241.

DESCRIPTION: Co-ed. nondenominational institution estd. Oct. 1973 under sponsorship of the Vatican with administrative cooperation of De La Salle Brothers (Bros. of the Christian Schools), world's largest professional teaching congregation. Located 8 km. south of Jerusalem on 17,000 square meter campus leased from De La Salle Brothers. Funded by standard contributions and the Vatican. Private institution governed by a Board of Trustees. Recognized by Association of Arab Universities 1981. *Library:* 25,000 vols.; microfiche and microfilm collection on Middle East. *Enrollment (1985-86):* 1,491 total (35% Christian, 65% Muslim; 45% Female, 55% Male).

CALENDAR: Two 15-wk. sems. (Sept.-Jan., Feb.-June). Six-wk. summer session.

LANGUAGE OF INSTRUCTION AND EXAMINATION: Arabic and English.

ACADEMIC STAFF: Ph.D. (35 FT, 3 PT); A.B.D. (5 FT); Master's (39 FT, 6 PT); Dip. (4 FT, 6 PT); Bach.'s (20 FT, 12 PT).

FACULTIES, DEPARTMENTS, AND PROGRAMS: FAC. OF ARTS—Depts. (Arabic [Arab., Hebrew], Engl., Humanities [Cultural Studies, Europ. Langs., Fine Arts, Philos., Relig. Studies]), Soc. Sci. [Anthro., History, Poli. Sci., Psych., Sociol., Soc. Work]). FAC. OF BUSINESS ADMINISTRATION—Depts. (Acct., Bus. Admin., Bus. Math, Econ., Public Admin.). FAC. OF EDUCATION—Depts. (Educ., Library Sci., Phys. Educ.). FAC. OF NURSING. FAC. OF SCIENCE—Depts. (Chem., Life Sci., Math & Computer Sci., Physics). INSTITUTE OF HOTEL MANAGEMENT. COMMUNITY DEVELOPMENT CENTER.

DEGREES AND DIPLOMAS: 4 YEAR BACHELOR'S—Arts (B.A.), Bus. Admin. (B.B.A.), Sci. (B.S.), Sci. in Nurs. (B.S.N.). 2 YEAR ASSOCIATE—Bus. Admin. (A.B.A.). DIPLOMAS—4 YEAR Diploma in Hotel Mgmt., Village Health Worker (60 credits). —Postbach.'s Teachers Dip. in Secondary Educ.; Teachers Dip. concurrent with FT B.A./B.S. program (see Teacher College Programs under "PROGRAM STRUCTURE AND CREDITS" below and Chapter 13).

GRADING: Two grading scales have been used since 1973.

Grade	%	Grade Pts.	Verbal	Grade	%	Grade Pts.	Verbal
A	90-100	4.0	Excellent	D+	66-69	1.5	Below Ave.
B+	86-89	3.5	Very Good	D	60-65	1.0	Inferior, but Passing
B	80-85	3.0	Good				
C+	76-79	2.5	—	F	Below 60	0.0	Failure
C	70-75	2.0	Average	P	Grade of A, B, C, or D		
				I	Incomplete, F after 7th wk. next sem.		

Grade	%	Grade Pts.	Verbal	Grade	%	Grade Pts.	Verbal
A	95-100	4.0	Excellent	D+	65-69	1.5	Below Ave.
A−	90-94	4.0	—	D	60-64	1.0	Inferior, but Passing
B+	85-89	3.5	Very Good				
B	80-84	3.0	Good	F	Below 60	0.0	Failure
C+	75-79	2.5	—	P	Grade of A, B, C, or D		
C	70-74	2.0	Average	I	Incomplete, F after 7th wk. next sem.		

Course Numbering: 001-099 = Voc. courses (not transferable to degree program); 100-199 = Lower division; 200-499 = Upper division.

Honors: *Highest Honors*—student in each fac. with highest sem. G.P.A. above 3.5. *Dean's List*—students with sem. G.P.A. of 3.5-4.0. *Honors*—students with sem. G.P.A. of 3.0-3.49. *Graduation Honors Classification*—Same terminology as above, same G.P.A. range rqmts. but based upon cumulative G.P.A.

ADMISSION REQUIREMENTS: *Freshman*—Gen. Secondary Educ. Cert. *(al-Tawjihiyah Al-Am'ah)* score of 80% or better gives automatic acceptance; 70% gives acceptance subj. to space limitations. Applicants with 65%-69% considered in exceptional circumstances. Six subj. passes on Gen. Cert. of Educ. (GCE) with sci. and Arab. lang. reqd. and at least 1 subj. (other than Arabic) at advanced level; satisfactory results on Bethlehem Univ. Entrance Exams (Arabic, Engl., Aptitude, Math); interview. *Transfer*—Min. cumulative transfer ave. of "C" with no less than 30 transferable credits from accredited college or univ.; if less than 30, freshman admission standards apply. Max. of 60 credits transferable.

PROGRAM STRUCTURE AND CREDITS: Degree reqmts. include gen. univ. reqmts. in arts and humanities and fac./deptl., major/minor reqmts.; 121-136 total credits required. Normal FT credit load = 15 credits/sem. (1 credit = 15 hrs. lect. or min. 30 hrs. of lab or field work). Course exams and grades given each sem.

Fac. of Educ. offers 5 PT Teacher College Programs and 2 FT Baccalaureate Degree Programs. *Teachers College Programs*—PT in-service programs for teachers pursuing degree or dip. Students subject to same program regulations and degree/dip. reqmts. as FT students. PT programs include 1) B.A. in Elem. Educ. (122 credits); 2) Minor in Secondary Educ. for PT B.A. students in Engl. or Arab. and PT B.S. students in Math (19 credit minor); 3) Teachers Dip. in Secondary Educ. for those with bach.'s degree (30 credits); 4) Teachers Dip. in Elem. Educ. (34 credits completed in 2 yrs. + 2 summers); 5) Teachers Dip. in Preschool Educ. (28 credits completed in 2 yrs. + 1 summer). *Baccalaureate FT Programs with Teachers Dip.*—6) B.A. in Elem. Educ. (122 credits); 7) Minor in Secondary Educ. for those pursuing B.A. in Engl. or Arabic (19 credit minor) or B.Sc. in Math & Sci. (major or minor).

Institute of Hotel Mgmt. has been part of Bethlehem Univ. since 1973. Offers academic crswk. and professional train. program (4 yrs. including 2 sems. noncredit practical train.) for hotel and tourism industry. Admission reqmts. include *Al-Thanawiyah Al-Am'ah,* spoken and written Engl., gen. knowl. test and interview. FT and regular attendance mandatory; 1 summer practical train. experience required.

Community Development Center originally estd. to provide educ. opportunities to PT students who did not seek a degree. Dip. of Village Health Worker (60 credits) now offered. In the past, dip. programs in Elem. Teacher Train., Preschool Teacher Train., Village Health Workers offered on 5-sem. basis to those with Gen. Secondary Educ. Cert. *(Al-Tawjihiyah).* Programs in Teacher Train. have been transferred to Fac. of Educ. (see above).

LINKAGES: University College (Dublin, Ireland); VL-VU Institute (Amsterdam, Netherlands).

BIRZEIT UNIVERSITY, P.O. Box 14, Birzeit, West Bank via Israel. Tel.: (02) 954381. Liaison Office: P.O. Box 9942, Amman, Jordan. Tel.: 38572.

DESCRIPTION: Estd. as school in 1924 by Nabiha Nasir. Became full secondary school 1930. Named Birzeit College 1942. Postsecondary classes in Arts and Science introduced Oct. 1953. Estd. as junior college awarding Associate in Arts and in Science by 1962. Articulation program for completion of degree with the American University of Beirut (AUB) in Lebanon. Graduates of 2-year program accepted in Arab universities and elsewhere with advanced standing. Secondary-level education discontinued 1966-67. Junior year added in 1974, senior year in 1975. Name then changed officially to Birzeit University. Recognized by and became member of Association of Arab Universities and International Association of Universities in 1976 and 1977, respectively. Graduate program leading to M.A. in Education offered in 1977. Faculty of Commerce and Economics, and of Engineering estd. 1978 and 1979, respectively. Located 15 miles north of Jerusalem with Old Campus and 50-acre New Campus, since 1980. Six-week Summer Overseas Student Program (see below). On and off campus dormitories. Private institution with autonomous Board of Trustees. *Yusef Ahmed Alghaniim Library:* 85,828 vols. (62,487 Engl.; 23,341 Arabic); 593 periodicals (445 Engl., 54 Arabic); 8,000 reference vols.

ENROLLMENT BY FACULTY: Total 2,430. *Arts*—605 Male (61%), 384 Female (39%). *Commerce/Econ.*—325 M (69%), 146 F (31%). *Engineering*—359 M (81%), 83 F (19%). *Science*—363 M (69%), 165 F (31%).

CALENDAR: Two 16-wk. sems. (Oct. - Feb.; Feb. - June). 8-wk. summer session (July - Aug.).

LANGUAGE OF INSTRUCTION: Arabic and English.

ACADEMIC STAFF BY FACULTY: Total 212 (270 in 1986). *Arts* (42 Ph.D., 44 Master's, 11 Bach.'s). *Commerce/Econ.* (7 Ph.D., 9 Master's, 2 Bach.'s). *Engineering* (13 Ph.D., 20 Master's, 11 Bach.'s). *Science* (31 Ph.D., 12 Master's, 10 Bach.'s).

FACULTIES, DEPARTMENTS, AND PROGRAMS: FAC. OF ARTS—Depts. (Arab. Lang. & Lit., Archaeology, Educ. & Psych., Engl. Lang. & Lit., Middle East. Studies [History, Poli. Sci.], Sociol. & Anthro.). *Programs*—Cultural Studies, Phys. Educ. & Sport, Music, Philos., Press. FAC. OF COMMERCE/ECONOMICS—Depts. (Acct., Admin. Sci., Econ.). FAC. OF

ENGINEERING—Depts. (Civil Engr., Electrical Engr., Mech. Engr.). FAC. OF SCIENCE—Depts. (Biol. & Biochem., Chem., Math, Physics). SPECIAL PROGRAMS AND FACILITIES—Literacy & Adult Educ. (estd. 1976), Community Health Project, Community Work Program, Center for Environ. & Occupa. Health Sciences (estd. 1982), Research & Documentation Center, Computer Center, University Lang. Center.

DEGREES, DIPLOMAS, AND CERTIFICATES: BACHELOR DEGREE (degree names changed as of 1984)—4 yrs. FT from Fac. of Arts (formerly B.A. degree [1976-83]); from Fac. of Commerce/Econ. (formerly B.Com. degree [1976-83]; from Fac. of Sci. (formerly B.Sc. degree [1976-83]). —5 yrs. FT from Fac. of Engr. MASTER OF ARTS—Education (Educational Supervision). No students admitted to program after 1980. ASSOCIATE (as of 1962)—2 yrs. FT in Arts (1962 to 1978), Public Admin. (1962-63), Science (1962-78). TEACHING CERTIFICATE—Offered as of 1978 (formerly Teaching Dip. offered as of 1976). TRANSLATION DIPLOMA—Offered as of 1986.

ADMISSION: Competitive with min. Gen. Secondary Educ. Cert. *(Al-Tawjihiyah Al-Am'ah)* and Engl. Placement exam. Eligibility calculated on basis of percentile ranking on *Al-Tawjihiyah* correlated with number of students each fac. can admit. Competitively-speaking, facs. are ranked as follows: Engr., Sci., Commerce/Econ., Arts. Eligible applicants gen. in top 25%-50% with highest reflecting *Al-Tawjihiyah* ave. result of 80 or above.

GRADING AND TRANSCRIPTS:

90 - 100	=	A (Excellent)	60 - 69	=	D (Weak)
80 - 89	=	B (Good)	0 - 59	=	F (Fail)
70 - 79	=	C (Fair)			

Transcripts: Recently computerized. Provide explanatory information for document interpretation—credits attempted and completed, numerical grades, sem. numerical ave. and cumulative ave. Course numbering system uses 3-digit code: first number indicates course level (1st yr., 4th yr., etc.); grad. courses indicated by numbers 5 and 6; fifth year of engr. program presented by number 5.

PROGRAM STRUCTURE AND CREDITS: BACHELOR'S—Requires min. 120 credit hrs. in Arts; 128 in Commerce/Econ.; 128 in Sci.; 170 in Engr. Credits represent 1 hr. of lecture (3 hrs. of lab) each week for 1 sem.

Program structured according to degree reqmts. as follows: 1) univ. reqmts. (approx. 25%)—courses in Arab., Engl., Library Sci., Phys. Educ., and sequence of 4 courses in Cultural Studies; 2) fac. reqmts. (20%-30%)—intro. courses in basic disciplines; 3) deptl. reqmts. (approx. 35%-55%)—intro. and advanced courses in specialization; 4) electives; 5) community work reqmt.—noncredit, min. 120 hrs. of voluntary community service.

MASTER'S—in Educ. requires min. 30 credit hours. Engl. Dept. offers special Translation Diploma (1986). Educ. Dept. awards Teaching Cert. which qualifies holder to teach at secondary level (grades 10-12).

OVERSEAS STUDENT PROGRAM—6-wk. summer program for native Engl. speakers at least at sophomore level from an accredited college or university. Three credit courses in Arabic, Poli. Sci., and Sociol.

LINKAGES: Academic relations with universities abroad for joint research, fac. and student exchanges, guest lectures, special programs. Bremen University (FRG), Cornell University (U.S.), Essex University (U.K.), Georgetown University (U.S.), Indiana University (U.S.), Oxford University (U.K.), Tübingen University (FRG), Umea University (Sweden), University of Amsterdam (Netherlands), University of Durham (U.K.), University of Paris VII (France), University of Pittsburgh (U.S.), University of Mississippi (U.S.).

HEBRON UNIVERSITY (ALSO KNOWN AS AL-KHALIL UNIVERSITY, ARAB UNIVERSITY OF HEBRON), P.O. Box 40, Hebron, West Bank via Israel. Tel.: (02) 976034.

DESCRIPTION: Founded 1971 by Sheikh Mohammed Al-Jabari as Center for Islamic Studies (College of Shari'a), a theological institute. In 1980, after opening of College of Arts and in conjunction with College of Shari'a, Hebron University was estd. as co-ed., private institution governed by a Board of Trustees. Officially recognized by Association of Arab Universities in 1984. Hebron is 40 km. south of Jerusalem with a population of approx. 120,000 (including surrounding villages). Campus is 2 km. north of center of Hebron in area referred to as Beir Al-Mahjar and occupies 56 dunams (56,000 square meters) of land. *Library:* 25,000 vols. *Enrollment (1985-86):* 1,750 (60% Female).

CALENDAR: Two 15-wk. sems. (Oct.-June) plus 1 wk. for exams, one 8-wk. summer session including exam period.

LANGUAGE OF INSTRUCTION AND EXAMINATION: Arabic in all depts. except English for Dept. of English Language & Literature.

COLLEGES, DEPARTMENTS AND INSTITUTES: COLLEGE OF AGRICULTURE (verbal approval by military authorities, permit approval pending). COLLEGE OF ARTS—Depts. (Arab. Lang. & Lit., Educ. & Psych., Engl. Lang. & Lit., History). COLLEGE OF ISLAMIC LAW (SHARI'A). COLLEGE OF SCIENCE (status pending as with College of Agriculture)—Depts. (Biol., Chem., Math, Physics & Computer Sci.). ATTACHED INSTITUTES—Research Institute, K-12 Experimental School under Dept. of Educ. & Psych. (to open 1986).

DEGREES, DIPLOMAS AND CERTIFICATES: BACHELOR'S—Agriculture (B.Ag.), Arts (B.A.), Islamic Law, Sci. (B.Sc.). DIPLOMA—Agriculture (2 yrs.; pending, see College entry above), Educ. (24 credit supplementary undergrad. program for secondary school teachers).

ADMISSION REQUIREMENTS: Students accepted from West Bank and Gaza Strip on competitive basis with min. reqmts. of 60% on Gen. Secondary Educ. Cert. *(Al-Tawjihiyah Al-Am'ah)* and pass in Admission Committee's Exam.

GRADING AND TRANSCRIPTS: Grades calculated and recorded at end of each sem. Failing grades recorded and added into cumulative ave.; credits for failed course not recorded or added to completed credits. Final course grade based on final exam (60%) and sem. grades from 2 written exams, and oral tests, reports, term papers or research papers (40%). Arabic 100, Engl. 100, Islamic Culture 100, Foreign Lang. 101 are Pass/Fail intro. courses excluded from any average.

Individual Course Grades	Cumulative Grades/Semester Evaluation
90 - 100 = Excellent	90 - 100 = Very Good (First Class Honors)
80 - 89 = Very Good	80 - 89 = Very Good (Second Class Honors)
70 - 79 = Good	70 - 79 = Good
60 - 69 = Acceptable	65 - 69 = Acceptable
50 - 59 = Poor	0 - 64 = Failing
0 - 49 = Failing	

PROGRAM STRUCTURE AND CREDITS: Similar to U.S. institutions in terms of sems., courses, evaluation. "Credit" terminology is used; most courses carry 3 credits. Bach.'s degree normally 4 yrs. Min. credits/sem. is 12; max. is 18. Summer session load may not exceed 9 credit hrs. Students classified as 1st yr., 2nd yr., 3rd yr. or 4th yr. students.

Sample program (129 credits) offered by Dept. of Engl. Lang. & Lit., College of Arts, is as follows: Univ. reqmts. (18 credits), college reqmts. (18), deptl. compulsory reqmts. (60), deptl. electives (21), univ. and college electives (6 credits each).

THE ISLAMIC UNIVERSITY OF GAZA (ALSO KNOWN AS GAZA ISLAMIC UNIVERSITY), P.O. Box 108, Gaza, Gaza Strip via Israel. Tel.: (051) 63554.

DESCRIPTION: Estd. 1978 as first (and remains only) university or postsecondary-level institution in Gaza Strip. Idea of establishing university grew out of "Al-Azhar"—Palestine Institute of Religion, located in Gaza. University is "National, Palestinian Arabic Islamic institution for higher education which aims to serve the Arabic, Islamic society, especially the Palestinian society in the cultural and educational fields." University suffers under political and economic duress as result of impositions of military occupation in Gaza. Opened with 3 faculties—Art, Principles of Religion (Islam) (Ussul Al-Din), and Islamic Law (Shari'a). In 1980-81, 3 additional faculties opened: Economics and Administrative Science, Education, and Science. Permission to open Faculty of Nursing denied by Israeli authorities despite faculty hirings, student enrollment, dire need for trained nurses in the Gaza Strip. Located on 1050 dunams (262.5 acres) in mostly temporary facilities due to inability to access funds and permits. Private institution governed by a Board of Trustees. Recognized by Association of Arab Universities. *Library:* 25,000 vols. (Arabic, English), periodicals, other publications.

ENROLLMENT BY FACULTY (1984-85): Total 3,464. *Arts*—333 Male (59.0%), 231 Female (41%). *Econ./Admin. Sci.*—526 M (82.5%), 112 F (17.5%). *Educ.*—594 M (56.7%), 454 F (43.3%). *Islamic Law*—277 M (76.5%), 85 F (23.5%). *Nursing*—28 M (68.3%), 13 F (31.7%). *Principles of Islam*—228 M (54.2%), 193 F (45.8%). *Science*—284 M (72.8%), 106 F (27.2%).

ACADEMIC STAFF BY FACULTY: Total 162. *Arts* (5 Ph.D., 14 Master's, 11 Bach.'s). *Econ./Admin. Sci.* (5 Ph.D., 5 Master's, 13 Bach.'s). *Educ.* (3 Ph.D., 7 Master's, 2 Bach.'s). *Islamic Law* (5 Ph.D., 5 Master's, 14 Bach.'s). *Nursing* (3 Master's, 1 Bach.'s). *Principles of Islam* (2 Master's, 13 Bach.'s). *Science* (15 Ph.D., 11 Master's, 28 Bach.'s).

FACULTIES AND DEPARTMENTS: FAC. OF ARTS—Depts. (Arab. Lang. & Lit.). FAC. OF FOUNDATION PRINCIPLES OF RELIGION (ISLAM) (USSUL AL-DIN). FAC. OF ISLAMIC LAW (SHARI'A). FAC. OF EDUCATION—Depts. (Arab., Sociol., Sci.). FAC. OF ECONOMICS & ADMINISTRATIVE SCIENCES—Depts. (Acct., Bus. Admin., Econ.). FAC. OF SCIENCES—Depts. (Biol., Chem., Geol., Math, Physics).

DEGREES: All faculties award a 5-year bachelor's degree.

ADMISSION REQUIREMENT: Egyptian Certificate of Completion of Gen. Secondary Educ. Cert. *(Al-Thanawiyah).*

PROGRAM STRUCTURE AND CREDITS: Univ. programs initially structured on yearly, 8-month basis, culminating in annual exams. In 1981-82, system changed to credit hr., sem. system including implementation of sem. exams and grades. All bach.'s programs require 144 credits, are 5 yrs. long and include 1-yr. prep. course of 36 liberal arts credits, structured as follows: Preparatory Year—Arabic (6 credits), Engl. (6), Hebrew (6), Principles of Religion (Islam) (12), Soc. Sci. (6).

LINKAGES: Al-Azhar University (Egypt), King Abdul Aziz University (Saudi Arabia), University of Jordan (Amman).

II. Polytechnic and Community Colleges

The 14 West Bank community colleges (including the one polytechnic) are two-year institutions of higher education, offering diploma programs that are prescribed by the Ministry of Education, Jordan. The three UNRWA schools also offer trade courses which are postpreparatory (see Chapter 11). Six of the community colleges and the polytechnic are classified as private institutions; three as government; three as UNRWA. Admission to the diploma programs offered by the polytechnic and community colleges requires the General Secondary Education Certificate *(Al-Tawjihiyah);* any variations are noted in the specific profile. The language of instruction at all institutions is Arabic. For more information on these institutions, see "The Community College System" earlier in this chapter, Chapter 12, Chapter 13, and the profiles below.

Government, Public Community Colleges

AL-ARRUB COLLEGE, Hebron (Al-Khalil), West Bank via Israel.

DESCRIPTION: Estd. 1958 as Al-Arrub Agricultural Institute. Became secondary agricultural school in 1964; added teacher training school in 1969. Became community college in 1982 and was renamed Al-Arrub College (Note: Arrub also spelled Arroub and Urub). Supervising authority is the Ministry of Education and Teacher Training, Jordan. *Enrollment (1984-85):* 79.

2 YEAR DIPLOMA PROGRAMS: *Prof. Educ./Teacher Training*—Arab. Lang., Engl. Lang., Islamic Educ., Soc. Studies.

ADMISSION REQUIREMENTS: Gen. Secondary Educ. Cert. *(Al-Tawjihiyah Al-Am'ah),* Literary Stream.

COLLEGE OF RAMALLAH FOR WOMEN: Ramallah, West Bank via Israel. NOTE: Not the same as Women's Community College in Ramallah/RWTC.

DESCRIPTION: Estd. 1952 as Women's Teacher Training School ("Dar Al-Mu'allimat") in Ramallah; operated as such until 1967 when it was renamed Women's Teacher Training Institute in Ramallah. Became community college and acquired present name in 1983. Supervising authority is the Ministry of Education and Teacher Training, Jordan. *Enrollment (1984-85):* 236.

2 YEAR DIPLOMA PROGRAMS: *Profes. Educ./Teacher Training*—Arab. Lang., Engl. Lang., Home Econ., Islamic Educ., Math, Phys. Educ., Sci., Soc. Studies.

COLLEGE OF TULKARM, Tulkarm, West Bank via Israel.

DESCRIPTION: Estd. 1931 as El Houssain's Agricultural Institute. Teaching began as secondary agricultural school under the name of Kheddouri Agricultural School in 1934, also known as Kaduri Agricultural Institute. Operated under name Houssain College for Agriculture between 1961-65. In 1965, became Teacher Training Institute for teaching of science and agriculture. Curriculum adapted in 1967 to include teaching of arts and name was changed to The Agricultural Institute (Al-Ma'had Al-Zirai). Existed as such until 1983 when institute became community college under current name. Supervising authority is the Ministry of Education and Teacher Training, Jordan. *Enrollment (1984-85)* 315 (288 in profes. educ./teacher training, 27 in agricultural professions).

2 YEAR DIPLOMA PROGRAMS: *Prof. Educ./Teacher Training*—Arab. Lang., Engl. Lang., Islamic Educ., Soc. Studies. *Agricultural Professions*—Agronomy and Animal Husbandry.

ADMISSION REQUIREMENT: Gen. Secondary Educ. Cert. *(Al-Tawjihiyah Al-Am'ah),* Literary Stream.

United Nations Relief and Works Agency for Palestine Refugees in the Near East (UNRWA) Community Colleges

KALANDIA VOCATIONAL TRAINING CENTER AND COMMUNITY COLLEGE, UNRWA, Kalandia, East Jerusalem, West Bank via Israel.

DESCRIPTION: Estd. 1953 as The Kalandia Vocational Training Center for young men and boys. Became community college in 1981; acquired present name in 1982. Funded by UNRWA Headquarters, Vienna, through contributions by government and intergovernmental organizations. Supervising authority is UNRWA. *Enrollment (1984-85):* 520. Diploma programs enrolled 192; trade courses, 328. In 1985-86, total enrollment was 528.

CALENDAR: *Community College*—Two 19-wk. sems. (mid-Oct.-mid-Aug.). *Training Center*—Two 21-wk. sems.

2 YEAR DIPLOMA PROGRAMS AND TRADE COURSES: DIPLOMAS. *Business/Commercial Professions*—Commerce & Office Mgmt. *Engineering Professions*—Architecture/Gen. (Arch. Drawing), Civil Engr. (Bldg. & Construction Surveying, Quantity Surveying). TRADE COURSES—Auto Mechanic,

Auto Body Repair, Blacksmith/Welder, Builder/Shutterer, Carpenter & Wood Machinist, Gen. Electrician, Machinist Welder, Plumber, Radio & T.V. Technician, Air Conditioning & Refrigeration.

GRADING: 90 - 100 = A, 80 - 89 = B, 65 - 79 = C, 50 - 64 = D, 0 - 49 = E.

ADMISSION REQUIREMENTS: *Diplomas*—Gen. Secondary Educ. Cert. *(Al-Tawjihiyah Al-Am'ah)* with min. score of 60%. *Postpreparatory Trade Courses*—Completion of 3rd Prep. (grade 9).

RAMALLAH COMMUNITY COLLEGE FOR TEACHERS, UNRWA, Ramallah, West Bank via Israel.

DESCRIPTION: Estd. 1960 as The Training Center for Teachers in Ramallah. Official name used by UNRWA - Ramallah Men's Teacher Training Center, UNRWA/UNESCO. Became community college in 1981; and acquired present name. Offers only diploma programs. Supervising authority is UNRWA. Funded by UNRWA Headquarters, Vienna, through contributions by governments and intergovernmental organizations. *Enrollment (1985-86):* 312.

CALENDAR: Two 19-wk. sems. (Sep. 23 - Jan. 31; Feb. 15 - June 30).

ACADEMIC STAFF: Master's (3), Bach.'s (14).

2 YEAR DIPLOMA PROGRAMS: *Profes. Educ./Teacher Training*—Arab. Lang., Elem. Educ., Engl. Lang., Math, Sci.

WOMEN'S COMMUNITY COLLEGE IN RAMALLAH (RAMALLAH WOMEN'S TRAINING CENTER/RWTC), RWTC - UNRWA, P.O. Box 214, Ramallah, West Bank via Israel. Tel.: 952 533/4.

DESCRIPTION: Estd. 1962 as The Training Center for Girls and Women Teachers in Al-Tireh, a combined teacher training and vocational training center for women, with capacity of 712 students. Acquired present name in 1980. Located on 28-acre residential site donated by the Municipality of Ramallah, 10 miles north of Jerusalem. Prior to 1967 War, refugee girls were accepted from Gaza Strip, Jordan, Lebanon, Syria. Since that time, student body is 60/40 West Bank/Gaza Strip, respectively, except for Home Economics program which takes 80% from the West Bank. Funded by UNRWA Headquarters, Vienna, through government and intergovernmental organizations. Supervising authority is UNRWA. *Library:* 13,000 vols. (8,589 Arabic; 4,611 English); 35 periodicals (Arabic, English). *Enrollment (1985-86):* 588. Diploma programs enrolled 486 (331 in profes. educ./teacher training, 39 in paramedical professions, 84 in business/commercial professions, 32 in social professions); postpreparatory trade courses, 102 (73 in clothing, 29 in hairdressing and beauty culture).

CALENDAR: Sept. 23 - Jan. 31; Feb. 15 - June 30.

ACADEMIC STAFF: Master's (10), Bach.'s with Teach. Dip. (22), Bach.'s (12), 2-yr. Dip. (4).

2 YEAR DIPLOMA PROGRAMS AND TRADE COURSES: DIPLOMAS. *Profes. Educ./Teacher Training*—Arab. Lang., Art, Elem. Educ., Engl. Lang., Kindergarten Educ., Math, Phys. Educ., Science. *Paramedical Professions*—Asst. Pharmacist, Medical Lab Technician. *Business/Commercial Professions*—Secre-

tar. & Office Mgmt. *Social Professions*—Nutrition & Institutional Mgmt. TRADE COURSES—CLOTHING (Dressmaking, Mass Production), Hairdressing & Beauty Culture. INTENSIVE ENGLISH COURSE for students accepted to commercial program.

ADMISSION REQUIREMENTS: *Diplomas*—Gen. Secondary Educ. Cert. *(Al-Tawjihiyah Al-Am'ah)* with min. score of 60%. *Trade Courses*—Theoretically, completion of 3rd Prep. (grade 9). In practice, completion of 3rd Secondary (grade 12) for past 7 yrs.

GRADING: *Current:* 90 - 100 = A, 80 - 89 = B, 70 - 79 = C, 60 - 69 = D, 0 - 59 = E. *Before 1980:* 4 = A, 3 = B, 2 = C, 1 = D, 0 = F.

Private Community Colleges

AL-IBRAHIMIYAH COLLEGE, Jerusalem.

DESCRIPTION: Estd. 1931 as secondary school in Jerusalem. Became community college in 1983. Co-ed. Supervising authority is Board of Trustees. *Enrollment (1984-85):* 648 (214 in profes. educ./teacher training, 401 in business/commercial professions, 33 in social professions).

2 YEAR DIPLOMA PROGRAMS: *Profes. Educ./Teacher Training*—Arab. Lang., Engl. Lang., Islamic Educ., Nursery & Kindergarten Educ., Sci., Soc. Studies. *Business/Commercial Professions*—Acct., Banking, Bus. Admin., Secretar. & Office Mgmt. *Computer Professions*—Computer Program. & Systems Analysis. *Social Professions*—Journalism & Information.

AL-KHALIL (HEBRON) TECHNICAL ENGINEERING COLLEGE, P.O. Box 198, Hebron, West Bank via Israel.

DESCRIPTION: Estd. 1978 under the name Hebron Polytechnic (also referred to as Polytechnic Institute in Hebron) by the University Graduates Union. Became Hebron Technical Engineering College in 1983. The only two-year institutional member of the Palestine Council of Higher Education. Located 40 km. south of Jerusalem. Supervising authority is the University Graduates Union (Hebron) under permission from the Ministry of Education, Jordan, to operate as community college. *Enrollment (1984-85):* 706.

CALENDAR: Two 16-19 wk. sems., 9-wk. summer session, including 1-wk. exam period.

DEPARTMENTS AND MAJORS: ARCHITECTURE DEPT.—Majors (Arch. Drawing, Decoration & Interior Design). CIVIL ENGINEERING DEPT.—Majors (Bldg. & Construc., Roads, Surveying). COMPUTER DEPT.—Major (Computer Program. & Systems Analysis). ELECTRICAL ENGINEERING DEPT.—Majors (General/Electrical Wiring, Electrical Power Transmission & Distribution, Radio/T.V., Engr. Construc. for Technicians). GLASS & CERAMICS DEPT.—Major (Art of Glass & Ceramics). MECHANICAL ENGINEERING DEPT.—Majors (Automotors & Engines, Gen. Engr. of Agricultural Machinery, Production & Machinery, Air Conditioning & Refrigeration).

ADMISSION REQUIREMENTS: Gen. Secondary Educ. Cert. *(Al-Tawjihiyah Al-Am'ah),* Scientific Stream, for all depts. or Industrial Stream corresponding to specialization.

2 YEAR DIPLOMA PROGRAM STRUCTURE: College compulsory courses (10 credits), college elective courses (6 credits), deptl. reqmts. (20 credits), major reqmts. (38 credits).

AL-RAWDAH COMMUNITY COLLEGE FOR THE PROFESSIONAL SCIENCES, Nablus, West Bank via Israel.

DESCRIPTION: Estd. 1961 as secondary school under name of Al-Rawdah National College. Name changed to Al-Rawdah Secondary School, then to Al-Rawdah High School in 1970. In same year, Al-Rawdah National Institute for Teachers was estd. and continued operation until 1977. In 1974, Rawdah Medical Institute was estd. and continued operation until 1977. In 1983, Institute was reauthorized (licensed) under name Al-Rawdah College for the Professional Sciences. Supervising authority is Board of Trustees. Co-ed. *Enrollment (1984-85):* 661.

2 YEAR DIPLOMA PROGRAMS: *Business/Commercial Professions*—Acct., Bus. Admin., Banking & Finance, Secretar. & Office Mgmt. *Paramedical Professions*—Asst. Pharmacist, Medical Lab Technician. *Social Professions*—Translation.

AN-NAJAH NATIONAL COMMUNITY COLLEGE, Nablus, West Bank via Israel.

DESCRIPTION: Estd. 1965 under name of Al- (An-) Najah National Institute (also referred to as An-Najah Teachers Training Institute) in Nablus. Became community college in 1983; acquired present name. Co-ed. Affiliated with and located on campus of An-Najah National University. Began as Teacher Training College; now equal emphasis on business/commercial professions. Supervising authority is Board of Trustees. *Enrollment (1984-85):* 374 (164 in prof. educ./teacher training, 172 in business/commercial professions, 38 in social professions).

2 YEAR DIPLOMA PROGRAMS: *Prof. Educ./Teacher Training*—Arab. Lang., Elem. Educ., Engl. Lang. *Business/Commercial Professions*—Acct., Banking & Finance, Secretar. & Office Mgmt. *Social Professions*—Library Sci. & Documentation.

COLLEGE OF ISLAMIC SCIENCES, Abu Deis, Jerusalem.

DESCRIPTION: Estd. 1975 under name of the Shari'a (Islamic Law) Institute located in Jerusalem. Relocated to town of Beit Hanina in 1978 and to Abu Deis in 1980. Became community college in 1983 under current name. Supervising authority is Waqf Department represented by Board of Trustees. *Enrollment (1984-85):* 49.

2 YEAR DIPLOMA PROGRAM: *Social Professions*—*Imamah & Wa'dh* (Prayer Leadership & Sermonizing).

COLLEGE OF ISLAMIC STUDIES, Kalkilya, West Bank via Israel.

DESCRIPTION: Estd. 1978 as Shari'a Institute in Kalkilya. In 1983, began implementing teaching methodology and curriculum of community colleges to field of Islamic Studies. In 1984, renamed College of Islamic Science. Acquired current name 1985. Co-ed. Supervising authority is Waqf Department represented by Board of Trustees. *Enrollment (1984-85):* 188.

2 YEAR DIPLOMA PROGRAM: *Profes. Educ./Teacher Training*—Islamic Educ. *Social Professions—Imamah & Wa'dh* (Prayer Leadership & Sermonizing).

COLLEGE OF THE NATION (AL-OUMAH COLLEGE), Jerusalem.

DESCRIPTION: Estd. 1939 as co-ed. secondary school in Jerusalem. Moved to Bethlehem in 1949 and to Al-Bareed (Postal Plaza) outside Jerusalem in 1959. Designated under jurisdiction of general Waqf Department (Ministry of Religious Endowments) in 1972. Estd. co-ed. community college in addition to secondary program in 1983. Now jointly supervised by Waqf Department and Ministry of Education and Teacher Training, Jordan. *Enrollment (1984-85):* 295 (172 in profes. educ./teacher training, 123 in business/commercial professions).

2 YEAR DIPLOMA PROGRAMS: *Profes. Educ./Teacher Training*—Arab. Lang., Elem. Educ., Engl. Lang. *Business/Commercial Professions*—Acct., Secretar. & Office Mgmt. *Computer Professions*—Computer Program. & Systems Analysis.

THE MODERN COMMUNITY COLLEGE, Al-Bireh, West Bank via Israel.

DESCRIPTION: Co-ed. institution estd. 1983. *Enrollment (1984-85):* 1,024 (375 in prof. educ./teacher training, 266 in business/commercial professions, 79 in engineering professions, 159 in paramedical professions, 8 in agricultural professions).

2 YEAR DIPLOMA PROGRAMS: *Prof. Educ./Teacher Training*—Art, Elem. Educ., Engl. Lang., Math, Sci., Library Sci. & Documentation. *Agricultural Professions*—Animal Husbandry. *Business/Commercial Professions*—Acct.; Banking & Finance; Bus. Admin.; Mgmt. of Supply & Storage; Secretar. & Office Mgmt.; Tax, Customs & Finance. *Computer Professions*—Computer Program. & Systems Analysis. *Engineering Professions*—Architecture (Arch. Drawing, Decoration & Interior Design), Civil Engr. (Bldg. & Construction, Surveying), Mechanical Engr. (Automotors & Engines). *Paramedical Professions*—Asst. Pharmacist, Dental Lab Technician, Health Supervisors/Sanitary Inspectors, Medical Lab Technician. *Social Professions*—Hotel Management, Journalism & Information, Library Sci. & Documentation, Paralegal Studies, Social Work, Translation.

Arab Colleges Of Medical Professions
EL-Bireh

الكليات العربيه للمهن الطبيه
البـــيره

Name of Student :
Student Number :
Date of Birth :
Student Address :
Major :
Classification at Admission : Freshman Student

Summer Semester:

Intensive English*	E	100	Pass	9 cr.

FIRST YEAR 1979/80
Fall Semester :

Sociology	SS	120	82	3 cr.
English	E	101	83	4 cr.
Biology	BS	110	73	4 cr.
Biostatistics	BS	111	87	3 cr.
Introduction to Nursing I	N	130	86	2 cr.
	Average		81	

Spring Semester :

Anatomy and Physiology I	BS	113	78	4 cr.
Chemistry/Biochemistry	BS	112	69	4 cr.
Psychology	SS	121	73	3 cr.
English	E	102	76	4 cr.
Introduction to Nursing II	N	131	100	2 cr.
Introduction to P. Health	BS	100	88	1 cr.
	Average		78	

Summer Semester :

Intensive English#	E	108	Pass	–

SECOND YEAR 1980/81
Fall Semester :

Fundementals of Nursing I	N	232	87	6 cr.
Microbiology	BS	215	65	4 cr.
English	E	103	80	1 cr.
Physics	BS	216A	62	2 cr.
Nutrition and Dietetics I	BS	217	76	2 cr.
Anatomy and Physiology	BS	214	84	4 cr.
	Average		77	

Spring Semester :

Pharmacology	BS	220	57	3 cr.
English	E	104	82	1 cr.
Fundementals of Nursing II	N	233	72	6 cr.
Nutrition and Dietetics II	BS	219	66	2 cr.
Physics	BS	216B	62	2 cr.
Intro. to P. Health & Epid.	BS	218	78	4 cr.
	Average		70	

Summer Semester :

Nursing Practicum	N	235	74	5 cr.

Grading System : Excellent (90-100) Very Good (80-90)
Good (70-79) Pass (60-69) Fail (Below 60)
Passing grade for Nursing Course is (65)
I : Incomplete
W : Withdraw
* : Pre-admission requirement
# : Non Credit Requirement

.... Date .... Registrar

Valid only when signed and stamped.

Arab Colleges Of Medical Professions
EL-Bireh

الكليات العربية للمهن الطبيه
البـــيره

Name of Student

Summer Semester :

Pharmacology	BS	220	67 R	3 cr.
	Average		71	

THIRD YEAR 1981/82
Fall Semester :

Mental Health Hygiene	SS	324	92	3 cr.
Educational Pshycology	SS	323	90	3 cr.
Pediatric Nursing	N	347	73	6 cr.
Psychiatric Nursing	N	349	82	6 cr.
	Average		82	

Spring Semester :

Medical Surgical	N	347	73	12cr.
Nursing Research	N	345	89	3 cr.
	Average		76	

Summer Semester :

Methods of Teaching	Ed	331	87	3 cr.
Nursing Practicum	N	351	79	5 cr.
	Average		82	

FOURTH YEAR : 1982/83
Fall Semester :

Maternity Nursing	N	456	A	69	6 cr.
Community Health Nursing	N	453		80	6 cr.
Nursing Ethics	N	234		87	2 cr.
	Average			76	

Spring Semester :

Nursing Service Administ.	N	456	B	85	6 cr.
Nursing Seminar	N	454		89	3 cr.
Management & Economics	Ed	461		72	3 cr.
	Average			83	

منحت شهادة البكالوريوس في التمريض بتاريخ ١٩٨٣/٧/٣٠
بتقدير جيد .

Cumulative Credits 152
Cumulative Average 78
Cumulative Average in Major 79
Awarded Bachelor of Science in Nursing,(Good),July 30 , 1983

14.1. Transcript of Bachelor of Science in Nursing Degree from Arab Colleges of Medical Professions

COLLEGE OF SCIENCE & TECHNOLOGY

DEPT. OF ADMISSION & REGISTRATION

ABU-DEIS/JERUSALEM P.O.B.20002/TEL.271753

NAME :
REG.NO. :
SEX : FEMALE
MAJOR: MATHEMATICS
MINOR: COMPUTER SC.

DATE & PLACE OF BIRTH : 23/02/60 JERUSALEM
RESIDENCE : JERUSALEM
LAST SCHOOL ATTENDED : IBRAHEEMYEH SEC.
ADMISSION CREDENTIALS:(TAWJIHI/SCIENTIFIC STREAM)

DATE OF ADMISSION : SPRING 1981
CLASS. ADMISS. : (FRESH/REGULAR)
SCH. AVE.:827

CRS-NO.	COURSE-TITLE	CR	GR
	FALL 1981		
CU101	ARABIC LANG. I	3	T
CU102	ARABIC LANG. II	3	T
LA101	ENGLISH LANGUAGE I	3	T
LA102	ENGLISH LANGUAGE II	3	T
CH101	GENERAL CHEMISTRY I	4	T
CH102	GENERAL CHEMISTRY II	4	T
CU171	CULTURAL STUDIES	3	T

S.AV.= 0 C.AV.= 0 MJ.AV.=
CR.ATT.=23 EARN=23 CU.CR.= 23

CRS-NO.	COURSE-TITLE	CR	GR
	SPRING 1982		
MA102	CALCULUS II	3	75
PH101	GENERAL PHYSICS I	4	86
BI101	GENERAL BIOLOGY I	4*	85

S.AV.= 82.6 C.AV.= 81.3 MJ.AV.=
CR.ATT.=11 EARN=11 CU.CR.= 34

CRS-NO.	COURSE-TITLE	CR	GR
	FALL 1982		
MA201	CALCULUS III	3	80
CS211	PROG. IN BASIC	3	88
MA281	LINEAR ALGEBRA	3R	60
PH102	GENERAL PHYSICS II	4	40
LA103	FRENCH LANGUAGE I	3	P
CU211	HUMANITIES I	3	73

S.AV.= 66.4 C.AV.= 71 MJ.AV.= 70
CR.ATT.=19 EARN=15 CU.CR.= 46

CRS-NO.	COURSE-TITLE	CR	GR
	SPRING 1983		
MA203	DIFF. EQUATIONS I	3	81
MA251	SET THEORY	3	80
MA271	APPLIED MATHEMATICS	3	69
CS214	PROG. IN FORTRAN	3	60
CS101	COMPUTER SCIENCE	3	75
PH102	GENERAL PHYSICS II	4	50
LA104	FRENCH LANG. II	3	F

S.AV.= 68.2 C.AV.= 69.7 MJ.AV.= 74

CR.ATT.=22 EARN=15 CU.CR.= 61

CRS-NO.	COURSE-TITLE	CR	GR
	FALL 1983		
MA101	CALCULUS I	3	76
MA301	PARTIAL DIFF. EQUATIONS	3	84
MA311	REAL ANALYSIS I	3	69
MA312	COMPLEX ANALYSIS I	3	75
MA382	ABSTRACT ALGEBRA	3	80
CS216	PROG. IN COBOL	3*	67
LA201	ENGLISH LANGUAGE III	3	70

S.AV.= 74.4 C.AV.= 71.5 MJ.AV.= 75.3
CR.ATT.=21 EARN=21 CU.CR.= 82

CRS-NO.	COURSE-TITLE	CR	GR
	SPRING 1984		
MA321	NUMARICAL ANALYSIS I	3	83
MA332	PROBABILITY THEORY I	3	90
MA383	THEORY OF NUMBERS	3	77
MA482	ABSTRACT ALGEBRA II	3	67
CS332	LINEAR PROG.	3	71
CU186	CURRENT AFFAIRS	3	95
PH102	GENERAL PHYSICS II	4	78

S.AV.= 80 C.AV.= 73.8 MJ.AV.= 76.5
CR.ATT.=22 EARN=22 CU.CR.=104

CRS-NO.	COURSE-TITLE	CR	GR
	SUMMER 1984		
MA351	HISTORY OF MATHEMATICS	3	90
CS215	PROG. IN OTHER LANGUAGES	3	79

S.AV.= 84.5 C.AV.= 74.5 MJ.AV.= 77.5
CR.ATT.= 6 EARN= 6 CU.CR.=110

CRS-NO.	COURSE-TITLE	CR	GR
	FALL 1984		
CS341	DATA STRUCURES	3	74
LA104	FRENCH LANG. II	3	P
MA281	LINEAR ALGEBRA	3	82
MA304	VECTOR ANALYSIS	3	91
MA331	PRINC. OF STATISTICS	3	91
MA381	ADV. LINEAR ALGEBRA	3	83
MA462	TOPOLOGY	3	85

S.AV.= 84.3 C.AV.= 76.2 MJ.AV.= 79.8
CR.ATT.=21 EARN=21 CU.CR.=131

CRS-NO.	COURSE-TITLE	CR	GR
	SPRING 1985		
CS214	PROG. IN FORTRAN	3R	80
CS312	COMPUTER ORG.&.ASSEMB. LANG	3	87
MA411	REAL ANALYSIS II	3	90
MA461	DIFF. GEOMETRY	3	82
MA492	SPECIAL TOPICS	3	90

S.AV.= 85.8 C.AV.= 77.4 MJ.AV.= 80.9
CR.ATT.=15 EARN=15 CU.CR.=143
DEAN'S HONOR LIST

REMARKS:(1)EXCELLENT:90-100(2)VERYGOOD:80-89(3)GOOD:70-79(4)PASS:60-69(5)FAIL:BELOW 60 IN MINOR & ELECTIVE COURSES , BELOW 70 IN MAJOR COURSES(6)WP:WITHDRAWAL WITH PERMISSION(7)WF:WITHDRAWAL WITHOUT PERMISSION(8)F:FAILED(9)P:PASSED(10)I:INCOMPLETE(11)T:TRANSFER COURSE (12)*:FREE COURSE(CREDIT ONLY NO GRADE VALUE)(13)R:REPEATED COURSE(NO CREDIT) GRADUATION REQUIREMENT: A) ACCUMULATIVE AVERAGE 65% & ABOVE (B) MAJOR ACCUMULATIVE AVERAGE 70% & ABOVE (C) MINIMUM ACCEPTABLE CREDIT HOURS 135 CR

<<<<<<<<<<< VALID ONLY WHEN SIGNED & STAMPED <<<<< DATE:-.................. REGISTRAR:-..........

14.2. Bachelor's Degree (Mathematics) from the College of Science and Technology

Chapter 15

Placement Recommendations

The Role of the National Council on the Evaluation of Foreign Educational Credentials

The placement recommendations that follow have been approved by the National Council on the Evaluation of Foreign Educational Credentials. In order that these recommendations may be of maximum use to admissions officers, the following information on the development of the terminology used in stating the recommendations, along with instructions for their use, is offered by the Council and the World Education Series Committee.

The recommendations deal with all levels of formal education in roughly chronological order up through the highest degree conferred. Recommendations, as developed through discussion and consensus in the Council, are not directives. Rather, they are general guidelines to help admissions officers determine the admissibility and appropriate level of placement of students from the country under study.

The recommendations should be applied flexibly rather than literally. Before applying the recommendations, admissions officers should read the supporting pages in the text and take into account their own institutional policies and practices. For example, a recommendation may be stated as follows: ". . . may be considered for up to 30 semester hours of transfer credit. . ." The implication is that the U.S. institution may consider giving less than or as much as one year of transfer credit, the decision to be based on various factors—the currentness of the applicant's transfer study, applicability of the study to the U.S. curriculum, quality of grades, and the receiving institution's own policies regarding transfer credit. Similarly, the recommendation ". . . may be considered for freshman admission" indicates possible eligibility only; it is not a recommendation that the candidate be admitted. Although consideration for admission at the same level may be recommended for holders of two different kinds of diplomas, use of identical phrasing in the recommendations does not mean that the two diplomas are identical in nature, quality, or in the quantity of education they represent.

In most cases, the Council will not have attempted to make judgments about the quality of individual schools or types of educational programs within the system under study. Quality clues are provided by the author and must be inferred from a careful reading of the text.

Certain phrases used repeatedly in the recommendations have acquired, within Council usage, specific meanings. For example, "through a course-by-course analysis" means that in dealing with transfer credit, each course taken at the foreign institution is to be judged on an individual basis for its transferability to the receiving institution. Another phrase "where technical training is considered appropriate preparation" suggests that the curriculum followed by the candidate is specialized, and this wording is often a hint that within the foreign system the candidate's educational placement options are limited to certain curriculums. However, while the Council is aware of the educational policies of the country under study, the Council's policies are not necessarily set in conformity with that country's policies. Rather, the recommendations reflect U.S. philosophy and structure of education.

In voting on individual recommendations, Council decisions are made by simple majority. Although consistency among volumes is sought, some differences in philosophy and practice may occur from volume to volume.

Placement Recommendations

Credential	Entrance Requirement	Length of Study	Gives Access in Country to	Placement Recommendations
I. Israel				
A. Primary Credentials				
1. Primary Grade Reports for grades 1–8 (Pre-Reform) (pp. 11–12, 14, 17–21)	–	1–8 years	Further education	May be placed on a year-for-year basis.
2. Primary Grade Reports for grades 1–6 (Reform) (pp. 11–12, 14, 17–21)	–	1–6 years	Further education	May be placed on a year-for-year basis.
B. Intermediate Credentials				
3. Intermediate Grade Reports for grades 7–9 (Reform) (pp. 11–12, 14, 17–21)	Completion of grade 6	1–3 years	Further education	May be placed on a year-for-year basis.
C. Secondary Credentials				
4. Secondary School Final Diploma/*Teudat Gemer Tichonit* (Certificate of Completion of Secondary School/*Teudat Hagamar Hatichonit*) (Pre-Reform or Reform) (pp. 11–12, 14, 31–32)	Completion of grade 8 (Pre-Reform) or 9 (Reform)	4 years (Pre-Reform) or 3 years (Reform)	Normally terminal	May be considered for freshman admission upon careful review of the program.
5a. Final Diploma/*Teudat Gemer*, MASMAR or MASMAM (Regular Technical/Vocational Track—MASMAR or Practical Technical/ Vocational Track—MASMAM) (pp. 14, 82–	Completion of grade 8 (Pre-Reform) or 9 (Reform)	4 years (MASMAR), 3–4 years (MASMAM) (Pre-Reform); 3 years (MASMAR), 2–3 years (MASMAM)(Reform)	Employment	Represents secondary vocational training; admission and placement should be based on other credentials.

b. Final Diploma/*Teudat Gemer*, MASMAT (Secondary Technical/ Vocational Track—MASMAT) (pp. 14, 82–88)	Completion of grade 8 (Pre-Reform) or 9 (Reform)	4 years (Pre-Reform) or 3 years (Reform)	Further postsecondary technological study; employment	May be considered for freshman admission where technical/vocational education is appropriate preparation.
6. Matriculation Certificate/ *Teudat Bagrut* (pp. 14, 32–41)	Completion of grade 8 (Pre-Reform) or 9 (Reform)	4 years (Pre-Reform) or 3 years (Reform)	Postsecondary or higher education	May be considered for freshman admission.
D. Teacher Training Certificates				
7. Teacher's Certificate (pp. 48–50)				
a. Qualified Teacher/*Teudat Horahah*	Matriculation Certificate/*Teudat Bagrut*	2 years	Employment	May be considered for undergraduate admission with 0–30 semester hours of transfer credit determined through a course-by-course analysis.
b. Senior Qualified Teacher/ *Teudat Horahah Bachir*	Matriculation Certificate/*Teudat Bagrut*	3 years	Employment or further teacher education	May be considered for undergraduate admission with 0–60 semester hours of transfer credit determined through a course-by-course analysis.
8. Teacher's Certificate (pp. 48–51)	Completion of second year of Bachelor's degree *or* Bachelor's degree	2 years fulltime *or* 1 year fulltime; 2 years part-time	Employment	May be considered for 0–30 semester hours of under-graduate transfer credit determined through a course-by-course analysis.
E. Nursing and Health Credentials				
9. Practical Nurse (Hospital Nurse School from 1947–1980) (pp. 56–57)	Completion of grade 10 (grade 8 prior to 1981)	18 months (12–15 months prior to 1981)	Employment and further nursing education	Represents specialized training; may be considered for admission and placement based on other credentials.

continued

Credential	Entrance Requirement	Length of Study	Gives Access in Country to	Placement Recommendations
10. Practical Nurse (secondary school program from 1973) and Secondary School Final Diploma/*Teudat Gemer Tichonit* or *Teudat Bagrut* (pp. 56–57)	Completion of grade 9	3 years + 6 months' practical training	Further nursing education and employment	May be considered for freshman admission where a specialized program is considered appropriate preparation.
11. Registered Nurse (Qualified Professional Nurse) (p. 57)	Completion of grade 12 or Matriculation Certificate/*Teudat Bagrut or* Practical Nurse (transition)	3 years *or* 18 months	Employment, further nursing education, and B.Nurs.Sc. programs	May be considered for undergraduate admission with transfer credit awarded on the same basis as for graduates of U.S. hospital schools of nursing.
12. Post-Basic Certificates, Diplomas and Licenses (e.g., License in Midwifery, Certificate in Public Health Nursing, Certificate in Mental Health Nursing) (pp. 57–59)	Registered Nurse (except Operating Theatre, RN or PN)	7–12 months	Professional advancement	May yield undergraduate transfer credit determined through a course-by-course analysis; undergraduate admission and placement should be based on other credentials.
13. Diploma in Physiotherapy (pp. 60–62)	Matriculation Certificate/*Teudat Bagrut*	3 years	Employment; further education	May be considered for undergraduate admission with 0–90 semester hours of transfer credit determined through a course-by-course analysis.
F. Postsecondary (Technical) Credentials				
14. Technician/*Technai* (pp. 90–94, 97)	Secondary Track Final Diploma/*Teudat Gemer*, MASMAT or Matriculation Certificate/*Teudat*	1 year fulltime or 1 ½ years part-time	Further technical/ vocational education; employment	May be considered for undergraduate admission with 0–30 semester hours of transfer credit determined through a course-by-course analysis.

15. Practical Engineer/ *Handassai* (pp. 90–94, 96)				
a. –	Secondary Track Final Diploma/*Teudat Gemer*, MASMAT or Matriculation Certificate/*Teudat Bagrut*	2 years	Employment; further education	May be considered for undergraduate admission with 0–60 semester hours of transfer credit determined through a course-by-course analysis.
b. –	*Technai*/Technician)	1 year	Employment	May be considered for undergraduate admission with 0–30 semester hours of transfer credit determined through a course-by-course analysis.
G. University and Institutions of Higher Education				
16. *Mechina*/Preparatory Program (pp. 115–117)	Variable	7 months to 2 years	Further education	Admission and placement should be based on other credentials; does not yield transfer credit.
17. TAKA *(Tochnik Klita Academic)* Advanced Preparatory Program/ Academic Absorption (p. 117)	Conditional acceptance of foreign students into Israeli degree programs	5 months	Further education	Admission and placement should be based on other credentials; does not yield transfer credit.
18. One-Year Program for Overseas Students (academic)(pp. 63–64)	Variable	1–2 semesters	–	May be considered for undergraduate transfer credit determined through a course-by-course analysis.
19. 3-Year Bachelor's degree (pp. 119–129, 132)	Matriculation Certificate/*Teudat Bagrut*	3 years	Further education	May be considered for up to 90 semester hours of undergraduate transfer credit; in some cases, may be comparable to a U.S. bachelor's degree.

continued

Credential	Entrance Requirement	Length of Study	Gives Access in Country to	Placement Recommendations
20. Bachelor of Arts/Bachelor of Science program for Overseas Students (Four-Year Program) (p. 65)	Variable	1 + 3 years	Further education	May be considered for up to 90 semester hours of undergraduate transfer credit; in some cases, may be comparable to a U.S. bachelor's degree.
21. 4-Year Bachelor's degree (pp. 119–122, 125–128, 129–132)	Matriculation Certificate/*Teudat Bagrut*	4 years	Further education	May be considered for graduate admission.
22. 4-Year Bachelor of Education (pp. 48, 50, 119–122)	Matriculation Certificate/*Teudat Bagrut*	4 years	Further education	May be considered for graduate admission.
23. Bachelor of Laws (LL.B.) (pp. 120, 137, 139)	Matriculation Certificate/*Teudat Bagrut*	4 years	Further education	May be considered for graduate admission.
24. 5-Year Bachelor's degree (pp. 120, 137, 139)	Matriculation Certificate/*Teudat Bagrut*	5 years	Further education	May be considered for graduate admission.
25. Diplomas and Certificates (e.g., Archivists, Librarians, etc.) (p. 137; *see also* institutional profiles)	Variable	1–2 years	Further education	Admission and placement should be based on other credentials. The amount of undergraduate or graduate transfer credit should be determined through a course-by-course analysis.
26. Master's degree (pp. 51–52, 60, 120–121, 133–135, 138, 139, 140, 142–143)	Bachelor's degree	1 ½–2 years	Further education	May be considered for graduate admission with transfer credit determined through a course-by-course analysis.

27. Doctor of Philosophy (Ph.D.); other doctoral degrees: Juris Doctorate (Dr. Jur.), Science Technology (D.Sc. Tech.) (pp. 121, 133, 134, 135–137, 142)	Master's degree (Track A)	Minimum 2 years	–	May be considered comparable to an earned doctoral degree in the United States.
28. Doctor of Dental Medicine (D.M.D.), Doctor of Medicine (M.D.) (pp. 121, 137–138, 139–140)	Matriculation Certificate/*Teudat Bagrut*	6 years + 1 year internship	–	May be considered to have a first professional degree in the field; may be considered for graduate admission.
29. Doctor of Veterinary Medicine (D.V.M.) (pp. 121, 143)	Completion of 2 years of Bachelor of Science program	4 years	–	May be considered to have a first professional degree in the field; may be considered for graduate admission.
II. Occupied Territories: the West Bank and Gaza Strip				
A. Primary and Secondary Credentials				
30. Grade Reports for grades 1–6 (pp. 184, 190, 192–193)	–	1–6 years	Further education	May be placed on a year-for-year basis.
31. Primary Education Certificate/*Al-Ibtida'iyah* (Gaza Strip only) (pp. 185, 192–193)	Completion of grade 6	6 years	Further education	May be placed in grade 7.
32. Grade Reports for grades 7–9 (pp. 190–194)	Primary Education Certificate/*Al-Ibtida'iyah* (Gaza Strip); completion of grade 6 (West Bank)	7–9 years	Further education	May be placed on a year-for-year basis.
33. Preparatory Education Certificate, (from 1981) Basic Education Certificate/	Primary Education Certificate/*Al-Ibtida'iyah* (Gaza Strip);	3 years	Further education	May be placed in grade 10.

continued

Credential	Entrance Requirement	Length of Study	Gives Access in Country to	Placement Recommendations
Al-Aa'dadiyah (Gaza Strip); General Preparatory Certificate, Secondary Entrance Exam and *Al-Aa'dadiya* (West Bank) (pp. 184–185, 190–194, 213–214)	completion of grade 6 (West Bank)			
34. Trade Certificate/*Shahadit Tadreeb Mihani* or UNRWA/UNESCO Diploma from Vocational/Trade Training Centers (pp. 184–185, 199, 212, 214–215)	Preparatory Education Certificate (Gaza Strip); General Preparatory Certificate (West Bank)	2–3 years	Employment	Represents postpreparatory vocational training; admission and placement should be based on other credentials.
35. General Secondary Education Certificate/*Al-Tawjihiyah* or Certificate of Completion of Secondary Education/*Al-Thanawiyah*				
a. (Scientific or Literary Stream) (*Al-Tawjihiyah Al-Am'ah*, West Bank) (*Al-Thanawiyah Al-Am'ah*, Gaza Strip) (pp. 184–185, 196–198, 200–205)	*Al-Aa'dadiyah* Preparatory Education Certificate, (from 1981) Basic Education Certificate (Gaza Strip) or General Preparatory Certificate (West Bank)	3 years	Further education	May be considered for freshman admission.
b. (Industrial/*Al-Tawjihiyah* or *Al-Thanawiyah Al-Zirahiyah*, Commercial/*Al-Tawjihiyah* or *Al-Thanawiyah Al-Tijahriyah*, Agricultural/*Al-Tawjihiyah* or *Al-Thanawiyah Al-Sinahiyah* (pp. 185, 204–206)	Preparatory (Basic) Education Certificate (Gaza Strip); General Preparatory Certificate (West Bank)	3 years	Further education	May be considered for freshman admission where vocational education is appropriate preparation.

Credential	Entrance Requirement	Program Length	Gives Access in Country to	Placement Recommendation
B. Tertiary Credentials				
36. Associate in Arts or Science (1962–78, only Birzeit), Associate in Public Administration (1962–63, only Birzeit) (p. 244), Associate in Business Administration (current, only Bethlehem) (p. 241)	General Secondary Education Certificate/*Al-Tawjihiyah* (West Bank); Certificate of Completion of Secondary Education/*Al-Thanawiyah* (Gaza Strip)	2 years	Further education; employment	May be considered for undergraduate admission with 0–60 semester hours of transfer credit determined through a course-by-course analysis.
37. Diploma/*Diplom* or Certificate of Completion/*Musadaca* (pp. 184–185, 219–222, 225, 232–234)	General Secondary Education Certificate/*Al-Tawjihiyah* (West Bank); Certificate of Completion of Secondary Education/*Al-Thanawiyah* (Gaza Strip)	2 years	Employment	May be considered for undergraduate admission with 0–60 semester hours of transfer credit determined through a course-by-course analysis.
38. Teacher's Diploma/*Diplom Ta'leem* (pp. 184–185, 212–213, 215–217, 219–222, 225, 232–234)	General Secondary Education Certificate/*Al-Tawjihiyah* (West Bank)	2 years	Employment	May be considered for undergraduate admission with 0–60 semester hours of transfer credit determined through a course-by-course analysis.
39. Diploma in Education/*Diplom Ta'leem* (university program) (pp. 184, 219, 223–224)	Bachelor's degree	1 year fulltime or 2 years part-time	Employment	May yield 0–30 semester hours of undergraduate transfer credit determined through a course-by-course analysis.
40. Bachelor of Arts/*Licence*, Science/*Bacalauria* (pp. 184–185, 226, 234–235)	General Secondary Education Certificate/*Al-Tawjihiya Al-Am'ah* (West Bank) or *Al-Thanawiyah Al-Am'ah* (Gaza Strip)	4–5 years	Further education	May be considered for graduate admission.

continued

Credential	Entrance Requirement	Length of Study	Gives Access in Country to	Placement Recommendations
41. Postgraduate Diploma in Science Teaching Technology from the College of Science and Technology (pp. 184, 235, 239)	Bachelor's degree	1 year	Further education	May yield graduate transfer credit determined through a course-by-course analysis.
42. Master's/*Magistaire* degree (pp. 184, 235)	Bachelor's degree or Postgraduate Diploma in Science Teaching Technology for Master of Science in Teaching Technology	2 year or 1 year beyond Postgraduate Diploma	–	May be considered comparable to a master's degree in the United States.

Appendix A

NITT Postsecondary Technological/Vocational Schools

The following postsecondary technological/vocational schools fall under the jurisdiction of the Ministry of Labor and Social Welfare, the National Institute of Technological Training/NITT (commonly known by its Israeli acronym, MAHAT). This list does not include postsecondary technological/vocational schools which are exclusively under the Ministry of Education and Culture, Department of Technological Education. Some schools (e.g., Tel-Aviv University Technical College) cross over both jurisdictions.

Some of these NITT schools are profiled in Chapter 7 with information on the programs and diplomas offered. Any discrepancies in the name of schools listed in this appendix and in Chapter 7 may be attributed to differences in translation. The schools are listed alphabetically according to the following categories: Independent, ORT, AMAL, and IDF. Where schools are known by more than one name, alternate names are listed in parentheses.

Independent Schools

1. Achavah Regional College near Sderoth
2. Bezek, Israel Telephone Company
3. College of Photography, Kiriyat Ono near Tel-Aviv
4. Etgar (Challenge) School, Tel-Aviv
5. Hadassah Community College, Jerusalem
6. Israel Aircraft Industry School at Ben-Gurion Airport
7. Jerusalem College of Technology (Jerusalem Higher School of Technology, Jerusalem Institute of Technology)
8. Labor Productivity Institute (Israeli Institute of Productivity), Tel-Aviv
9. Mania Shohat Agricultural School, Nahalel
10. Michlalah-Jerusalem College for Women
11. MMG (Nuclear Institute) between Beer-Sheva and Eilat
12. Neri Bloomfield Institute for Advanced Studies, Haifa (Neri Bloomfield Haifa Institute)
13. P. Shapir Regional College of the Negev (Sha'ar Hanegev Regional College)
14. Practical Engineering College of Beer-Sheva (Beer-Sheva Technical College)
15. RAFA-EL, Haifa (Israeli Agency for Warfare Technology Development)
16. School for Industry and Management (IDF, Division of Maintenance and Ammunition)
17. School for Practical Engineers, Ruppin Institute of Agriculture, Emek Hefer, School for Farming Managers, Ruppin Institute of Agriculture, Emek Hefer
18. School for Technical Landscape, Petah Tikvah (School for Gardening and Landscape)
19. Shenkar - College of Textile Technology and Fashion
20. Technical College, Nazareth
21. Tel-Aviv University Technical College (College of Practical Engineering, Tel-Aviv; Technical College at Tel-Aviv University)

22. Tel-Aviv College, Giboray Israel 30, Tel-Aviv
23. Tel Hai Rodman Regional College
24. The Municipal College of Eilat
25. The National School for Handassaim, Technion City, Haifa (Technion Junior Technical College)
26. Vinick Institute, Mikve Israel
27. Western Galilee College in Yad Natan

ORT Schools

28. Max A. Braude ORT International School, Carmel
29. ORT Afula
30. ORT Aranne Comprehensive High School, Beit Sha'an
31. ORT Givatayim Technical Junior College
32. ORT HaNaviim (ORT Technical School, Jerusalem)
33. ORT Lane Technical High School (ORT Laine School)
34. ORT Levinson (Technical School, Kiryat Bialik)
35. ORT Lod
36. ORT Lvovitch Junior Technical College (ORT Technical College, Netanya)
37. ORT School of Engineering, Givat Ram, Jerusalem (ORT School of Engineering at The Hebrew University)
38. ORT Shapiro Junior Technical College, Kfar Saba (The Practical Engineering School for Ecology)
39. ORT Technical College Abdullah Hussein
40. Tel-Aviv ORT Junior College for Technicians, Tel-Aviv (Technical School, Tel-Aviv)
41. ORT Yad Singalowski Junior Technical College, Tel-Aviv

AMAL Schools

42. College for Training Adult Practical Engineers
43. College for Training Adult Practical Engineers AMAL, Hadera
44. College for Training Adult Practical Engineers in the Western Galilee, Yad Natan

IDF Schools

45. Air Force School for Control and Equipment
46. Air Force Technicians School
47. Electronics and Communication School (IDF Section)
48. M.M.R.M. (IDF Computer Center)

Glossary

NOTE: I = Israel, OT = Occupied Territories

absorption centers. Areas or communities for new immigrant groups (I)
academia. Academy; exclusive word to be used only by institutions of higher education (I)
Aggadah. Name given those sections of *Talmud* and *Midrash* containing homiletic expositions of the Bible, stories, maxims, legends, or folklore (I)
Aleph. "A"; one of six proficiency levels (Lower Beginners) in academic *ulpanim* (I)
Al Quds. Arabic for "Jerusalem" (OT)

Bagrut. Matriculation (I)
Bamidbar. Book of Numbers (I)
Beit. House (I)
Beit Sefer. School (I)
Beit Sefer Gavoach. High school, i.e., school above secondary school; an exclusive word to be used only by institutions of higher education (I)
Beit Sefer Tichon. Secondary or postprimary school (I)
Beit-Midrash. Any "house" or place of study, or focal point of the *yeshivah* (I)
Beit-Ya'akov (Jacob). Girls' teacher training institutes under Agudat Israel and Independent school system (I)
Beth. "B"; one of six proficiency levels (Upper Beginners) in academic *ulpanim* (I)
B'nai Akiva. Largest religious pioneering movement affiliated with HaKibbutz Ha-Dati and the National Religious Party; Overseas Student Program (I)
B'reishit. Book of Genesis (I)

Certificate of Completion of Secondary Studies. *Teudat Gemer Techonit* (I)
Chassidut. Hassidic movement (I)
Chativat Beinayim. Intermediate or junior high schools offering grades 7-9 under the Reform system (I)
Chativat Elyona. Secondary or postprimary schools (I)
Chevruta. Method of learning in pairs, learning partners (I)
Chumash. The five Books of Moses, the Torah in book form (I)

Daleth. "D"; one of six proficiency levels (Upper Intermediate) in academic *ulpanim* (I)
Diaspora. Dispersion of a people from their homeland (I, OT)
Druze. A religious sect represented by an Arab community following a secret religion originating in, but since the eleventh century, separated from Islam (I, OT)
D'Varim. Book of Deuteronomy (I)

East Bank. Jordan; land east of the River Jordan (OT)
Eretz Israel. Land of Israel; Greater Israel; Palestine (I)

Fiqh. Islamic jurisprudence (OT)

Gadna. Israeli government youth movement for training 13-18 year-olds in defense and national service; a school program (I)
Gemara. One of two primary sections of the *Talmud* providing discussion and elaboration of the Mishna (I)
gemer. Final or completion (I)
Gimmel. "C"; one of six proficiency levels (Lower Intermediate) in academic *ulpanim* (I)

Hadassah. Women's Zionist Organization of America (I)
Hadith. Sayings of the Prophet Mohammed (OT)
Halacha. Jewish law
Handassai (Handassaim, plur.). Qualified Practical Engineer (I)
Hashkafah. Ethical and philosophical literature (I)
haskala gevohah. "Higher education"; an exclusive word to be used only with institutions of higher education (I)
hativa. Section; an element of certain bachelor's degree programs, a group of courses from one field taken over a two-year period (I)
Hé. "E"; one of six proficiency levels (Lower Advanced) in academic *ulpanim* (I)
Hebraica. Bible study with textual analysis and commentaries (I)
heder (hadarim, plur.). Unofficial and unrecognized school; ultra-orthodox, traditional religious school for teaching Jewish observance
Hinuch Atzma'i. Independent schools; "nonofficial recognized" schools (I)
hinukh gavoach. "Higher education" (I)
Histadrut. General Federation of Labor in Israel; trades union organization for every profession and trade, the self-employed, and housewives

Imam. In Islam, an informal leader of prayers (OT)
Islam. A religion based on the teachings of the Prophet Mohammed, believing in one God, *Allah,* and having a body of law put forth in the Koran and the Sunna; followers of Islam are Muslims. (I, OT)

Judea and Samaria. Israeli reference for the West Bank
Judaica. Jewish studies including Jewish history, law, and philosophy

Kashrut. Jewish dietary laws
Ketavim. The sacred writings (I)
kibbutz (kibbutzim, plur.). Collective or communal settlement in Eretz Israel based originally on agriculture but also involved in industry
Kiriyat. Community or district (I)
Koran. The sacred text of Islam containing the revelations made by *Allah* to Mohammed
magan. Internal final examination which prepares students for *Bagrut* examination and is similar in content and structure; overall internal assessment (I)

Maimonides. Jewish philosopher
makif. Multi-track or comprehensive secondary schools (I)
masadot le haskala gevohah. "Institutions of higher education" (I)
Matriculation Certificate. *Teudat Bagrut* (I)
mechina (mechinot, plur.). Pre-academic, preparatory program (I)
Mesorati. One of three main trends in Judaism (Traditional/Conservative) advocating observance to *Halacha*
Michlalah. Postsecondary college or "seminar" (I)
Midrash. Expositions or written commentary of the Bible (I)
Miktzoi. Technological/vocational secondary schools (I)
Mishlei. Book of Proverbs (I)
Mishna. Introductory teachings in the *Talmud;* one of two primary sections of the *Talmud* along with *Gemara* (I)
moshav (moshavim, plur.). Cooperative agricultural settlements in Eretz Israel
Musadaca. Diploma or certificate (Certificate of Completion) (OT)
Muslim. A follower of the Islamic religion (I, OT)
Mussar. Jewish ethics, ethical movement, teaching of morals and ethics

Nach. Second and third parts of the Old Testament (I)
Nachmanides. Jewish philosopher, same as Ramban (I)
Niivim. The Prophets (I)

Orthodox. One of three main trends in Judaism maintaining adherence to *Halacha*, embracing both the written and oral law

Palestinian. A person living or born in Palestine prior to May 1948, his children and his children's children (I, OT)
Patour. Exempt schools; ultra-orthodox, unofficial schools not recognized by the MOEC and operating without any government intervention (I)
Progressive (Reform). One of three main trends in Judaism, more flexible adaptation with emphasis on ethical aspects and the individual's right to choose among the precepts of *Halacha*

Ramban. Jewish philosopher, same as Nachmanides

secular. Worldly rather than spiritual; not relating directly to religion (I)
seker. State scholastic test given at completion of grade 8 to determine suitability for postprimary academic education (discontinued in 1972-73) (I)
Semicha. Rabbinic ordination program (I)
Shaharit. Jewish morning prayers
Shari'a. Holy Law of Islam (OT)
Shiurim. Lecture, lesson (I)
Sh'mot. Book of Exodus (I)
Shoftim. Book of Judges (I)
Siddur. Prayer book (I)
Sunni. Main body of Islam commonly regarded as orthodox (I, OT)

Talmud. Jewish Oral Law; compendium of rabbinic legal teaching and discussion
Talmud Torah. Term generally applied to Jewish religious (and ultimately to *Talmudic* studies); ultra-orthodox, traditional religious school (I)
Tanach. Entire Old Testament; acronym formed from Hebrew words meaning the Bible; formed from abbreviations of the three major parts of the Bible: Torah (Books of Moses), Niivim (the Prophets), Ketavim (the sacred writings) (I)
Technai (*Technaim*, plur.). Qualified Technician (I)
Tehillim. Book of Psalms (I)
Teudat. Certificate; diploma (I)
Torah. Bible; first five Books of Moses (I)

universita. University (I)

Va'ad Le'umi. National Council of Jewish Community in Palestine during British mandate (I)
Vav. "F"; one of six proficiency levels (Upper Advanced) in academic *ulpanim* (I)

Waqf. Department of Islamic Religious Endowments; endowment set apart for a charitable or religious purpose (OT)

Yerushalayim. Hebrew for Jerusalem (I)
Yeshivat Hesder. Arrangement of *yeshivah* students whereby induction into the Israeli Defense Forces and military training is combined with Torah studies in a 4- to 5-year program
Yishuv. The Jewish community of Eretz Israel prior to 1948
Yisrael. Hebrew for Israel

Zionism. A plan or movement of the Jewish people to establish a homeland in Palestine

Selected References

The following includes all references cited in the text as well as useful resources for further reading.

A. Publications on Israel:

Bentwich, Joseph S. *Education in Israel*. Philadelphia: The Jewish Publication Society of America, 1965.

Braham, Randolph L. *Israel: A Modern Education System*. Washington, D.C.: U.S. Government Printing Office, 1966.

Council for Higher Education. Planning and Grants Committee. *Higher Education in Israel. Statistical Abstract 1983-84*. Jerusalem: Council for Higher Education, 1985.

Education and Science. Jerusalem: Keter Publishing House, Jerusalem Ltd., 1974.

Facts About Israel. Jerusalem: Ministry of Foreign Affairs, 1979.

Facts About Israel. Jerusalem: Ministry of Foreign Affairs, 1985.

Frey, James S., and Fisher, Stephen H.. *Israel, A Guide to the Academic Placement of Students from Israel in Educational Institutions of the United States*. Washington, D.C.: American Association of Collegiate Registrars and Admissions Officers, 1976.

Halperin, Samuel. *Any Home a Campus: Everyman's University of Israel*. Washington, D.C.: The Institute for Educational Leadership, Inc., and the Jerusalem Center for Public Affairs, Inc., 1984.

Higher Education in Israel; A Guide for Overseas Students. Jerusalem: Department of Information for *Olim*, The Jewish Agency, 1972.

Higher Education in Israel; A Guide for Overseas Students. 3d ed. Jerusalem: Department of Information for *Olim*, The Jewish Agency, 1984.

Higher Education in Israel; A Guide for Overseas Students. 4th ed. Jerusalem: Department of Information for *Olim*, The Jewish Agency, 1987.

Iram, Yaacov, and Balicki, Chaim. "Vocational Education in Switzerland and Israel: A Comparative Analysis." *Canadian and International Education* 9 (1980), 95-104.

Israel Central Bureau of Statistics. *Statistical Abstract of Israel*. No. 35. Jerusalem: Central Bureau of Statistics, 1984.

Mar'i, Sami Khalil. *Arab Education in Israel*. Syracuse: Syracuse University Press, 1978.

Mar'i, Sami Khalil. "The Future of Palestinian Arab Education in Israel." *Journal of Palestine Studies* 14 (Winter 1985): 52-73.

The Council for Higher Education. The Planning and Grants Committee. *Annual Report 10, 1982-83*. Jerusalem: The Council for Higher Education, 1984.

____________. *Annual Report 11, 1983-84*. Jerusalem: The Council for Higher Education, 1985.

____________. *The Higher Education System in Israel: Guidelines on the Development of the System and its Planning for 1988 with a First Glance at 1995*. Jerusalem: The Council for Higher Education, 1984.

The Technological Education in Israel. Jerusalem: The Ministry of Education and Culture, The Department of Technological Education, 1984.

United Nations Educational, Scientific, and Cultural Organization. *World Survey of Education V: Educational Policy, Legislation and Administration*. Paris: UNESCO, 1971.

Yonai, Yosef. "Ministry of Education and Culture: Report for the Years 1979-80–1980-81." Jerusalem, 1981.

B. Publications on the Occupied Territories:

Al-Fajr 1986. Jerusalem, 1985. (Compendium/Diary)

Al-Fajr Jerusalem Palestinian Weekly. July 1985 - June 1987.

Al-Fajr Palestinian Publications 1987. Jerusalem, 1986. (Compendium/Diary)

Benvenisti, Meron. *The West Bank Data Project: A Survey of Israel's Policies*. Washington, D.C.: The American Enterprise Institute for Public Policy Research, 1984.

Dembleby, Jonathan. *The Palestinians*. London: Quarter, 1979.

Gerner, Deborah, and Schrodt, Philip. *Universities Under Occupation: A History and Review of the Denial of Palestinian Academic Freedom Under Israeli Occupation*. Chicago: North American Academics in Solidarity with Palestinian Universities (NAASPU), 1986.

Graham-Brown, Sarah. *Education, Repression and Liberation: Palestinians*. London: World University Service, 1984.

Hallaj, Muhammad. *The Palestinians and the PLO*. Information Paper Series, no. 1. Washington, D.C.: Palestine Research and Educational Center, 1983.

___________ . *Israel's West Bank Gamble*. Information Paper Series, no. 2. Washington, D.C.: General Union of Palestinian Students (GUPS), 1986.

Kimball, John C. *The Arabs 1983*. Washington, D.C.: The American Educational Trust, 1983.

___________ . *The Arabs 1984-85*. Washington, D.C.: The American Educational Trust, 1984.

Nuseibeh, Hazem Zaki. *Palestine and the United Nations*. New York: Quartet Books, 1981.

Roy, Sara M. *The Gaza Strip, a Demographic, Economic, Social and Legal Survey*. Washington, D.C.: West Bank and Gaza Strip Databank, 1986.

Said, Edward W.. *The Question of Palestine*. New York: Times Books, 1979.

Said, Edward W.; Abu-Lughod, I.; Abu-Lughod, J.; Hallaj, M.; and Zureik, E. A Profile of the Palestinian People. Chicago: Palestine Human Rights Campaign, 1983.

Schmida, Leslie C., and Keenum, Deborah G., eds. *Education in the Middle East*. Washington, D.C.: America-Mideast Educational Training Services, Inc., 1983.

Shipler, David. *Arab and Jew: Wounded Spirits in the Promised Land*. New York: Times Books, 1986.

Smith, Pamela Ann. *Palestine and the Palestinians 1876-1983*. New York: St. Martin's Press, Inc., 1984.

State of Israel. Ministry of Defense. *Judea-Samaria and the Gaza District: A Sixteen-Year Survey (1967-1983)*. Jerusalem: Ministry of Defense, 1983.

The Hashemite Kingdom of Jordan. Ministry of Education. *Education in Jordan*. Amman: Ministry of Education, 1978.

United Nations. Committee on the Exercise of the Inalienable Rights of the Palestinian People. *The Legal Status of the West Bank and Gaza*. New York: United Nations, 1982.

United Nations. General Assembly, 38th Session. *Report of the Commissioner-General of the United Nations Relief and Works Agency for Palestine Refugees in the Near East, 1 July 1982 - 30 June 1983*. Supplement No. 13 (A/38/13), 1983.

United Nations. General Assembly, 39th Session. *Report of the Commissioner-General of the United Nations Relief and Works Agency for Palestine Refugees in the Near East, 1 July 1983 - 30 June 1984*. Supplement No. 13 (A/39/13), 1984.

United Nations. General Assembly, 40th Session. *Report of the Commissioner-General of the United Nations Relief and Works Agency for Palestine Refugees in the Near East, 1 July 1984 - 30 June 1985*. Supplement No. 13 (A/40/13), 1985.

Index

NATIONAL COUNCIL ON THE EVALUATION OF FOREIGN EDUCATIONAL CREDENTIALS

The Council is an interassociational group that serves as a forum for developing consensus on the evaluation and recognition of certificates, diplomas, and degrees awarded throughout the world. It also assists in establishing priorities for research and publication of country, regional, or topical studies. One of its main purposes is to review and modify admissions and placement recommendations drafted by World Education Series authors or others who might ask for such review. (The practices followed in fulfilling this purpose are explained on page 255.)